1999

University of St. Francis Library

P9-ASA-870

SOME CHOICE

ALSO BY THE AUTHOR

The Rights of Patients

Judging Medicine

Standard of Care: The Law of American Bioethics

Co-authored

Informed Consent to Human Experimentation:
The Subject's Dilemma
(with Leonard Glantz and Barbara Katz)

The Rights of Doctors, Nurses and Allied Health Professionals
(with Leonard Glantz and Barbara Katz)

Reproductive Genetics and the Law
(with Sherman Elias)

American Health Law
(with Sylvia Law, Rand Rosenblatt, and Ken Wing)

Co-edited

Genetics and the Law
Genetics and the Law II
Genetics and the Law III
(with Aubrey Milunsky)

The Nazi Doctors and the Nuremberg Code:
Human Rights in Human Experimentation
(with Michael Grodin)

Gene Mapping: Using Law and Ethics as Guides
(with Sherman Elias)

Health and Human Rights: A Reader
(with Jonathan Mann, Sofia Gruskin, and Michael Grodin)

SOME CHOICE

LAW, MEDICINE, AND THE MARKET

George J. Annas

LIBRARY
UNIVERSITY OF ST. FRANCIS
JOLIET, ILLINOIS

New York   Oxford
Oxford University Press
1998

Oxford University Press

Oxford   New York
Athens   Auckland   Bangkok   Bogota   Buenos Aires   Calcutta
Cape Town   Chennai   Dar es Salaam   Delhi   Florence   Hong Kong   Istanbul
Karachi   Kuala Lumpur   Madrid   Melbourne   Mexico City   Mumbai
Nairobi   Paris   Saõ Paulo   Singapore   Taipei   Tokyo   Toronto   Warsaw

and associated companies in
Berlin   Ibadan

Copyright © 1998 by George J. Annas

Published by Oxford University Press, Inc.
198 Madison Avenue, New York, New York 10016

Oxford is a registered trademark of Oxford University Press

All rights reserved. No part of this publication may be reproduced,
stored in a retrieval system, or transmitted, in any form or by any means,
electronic, mechanical, photocopying, recording, or otherwise,
without the prior permission of Oxford University Press.

Library of Congress Cataloging-in-Publication Data
Annas, George J.
Some choice : law, medicine, and the market / George J. Annas.
p.   cm.   Includes index.
ISBN 0-19-511832-4
1. Informed consent (Medical law)—United States.
2. Choice (economics)   I. Title.
KF3827.I5A953   1998
344.73'0412—dc21   97-48975

1 3 5 7 9 8 6 4 2

Printed in the United States of America
on acid-free paper

344.73 ^G
A 613 ᴅ

To My Mother,
Margaret Pallansch Annas

ACKNOWLEDGMENTS

As with all of my writing, I owe enormous thanks to the conversations and debates with, and comments and criticisms of, my colleagues in the Health Law Department of Boston University School of Public Health: Leonard H. Glantz, Wendy K. Mariner, and Michael A. Grodin. Many of the chapters might have had a different emphasis without the social conscience of Mary Annas. Most of these chapters also benefited from the comments and questions of audiences of physicians, lawyers, judges, students, and the general public who heard them in their early forms as lectures. I also want to acknowledge the editing skills of Marcia Angell of the *New England Journal of Medicine*, who helped shape all of the chapters that were originally published there, as well as the support of the Journal's editor in chief, Jerome Kassirer for his continuing support of the "Legal Issues in Medicine" feature.

Frances Miller deserves special mention as the coauthor of the original (and much longer) version of chapter 6, as does Michael Grodin (again) as the coauthor of some of the original material found in chapter 22 and the cofounder of Global Lawyers and Physicians. I also want to thank Lori Andrews and Dan Callahan for their comments on Chapter 1, and Emily Friedman for her help with Chapter 2. The exceptional staff of the Health Law Department, Marilyn Ricciardelli and Debbie Darling, made the manuscript preparation almost painless. Finally I am happy to acknowledge the strong support of Dean Robert Meenan of the Boston University School of Public Health for all of my work and that of the Health Law Department.

Initial versions of chapters 2 through 5, 7 through 12, and 15 through 21 appeared in the *New England Journal of Medicine*. Chapter 6 initially appeared in the *American Journal of Law & Medicine* (coauthored by Frances Miller), chapter 14 in the *Journal of Law & Contemporary Health Policy*, chapter 22 in *Health and Human Rights* (coauthored by Michael Grodin) and a part of chapter 13 in *Medicine Unbound* (Robert H. Blank and Andrea L. Bonnicksen, eds.).

CONTENTS

V. CHOICES IN DYING

VI. GLOBAL CHOICES

INTRODUCTION

In a *New Yorker* cartoon by Cheney, a guillotine executioner offers the condemned man a final choice before he is beheaded. Displaying two buckets, he asks, "Paper or plastic?" Not all choices are so meaningless; but in American medical and health care, choice rhetoric is often more ironic than real and routinely serves to camouflage issues that would otherwise demand our serious attention.

Some Choice is meant to be taken both ways: Thanks to the law, Americans do have some choices in medical and health care, but usually these choices range from trivial to illusory. Because of the high value Americans place on liberty and autonomy, and because it supports market values, choice rhetoric has assumed such prominence in public discourse that merely labeling something as a "choice" has a tendency to arrest conversation and prevent more than superficial analysis of the nature of the choice in question. We seem to recognize the shallowness of our choice language, but we do not seem to be able to help ourselves. Choice rules our public policy rhetoric and our lives to the point of distracting us from much more basic issues.

Couple the power of choice with the language of rights, and their combined force is all but irresistible. Choice chants replace policy debates. Over the past 25 years, for example, abortion has become simply the "right to choose." And choice rhetoric runs throughout life to the end. Americans want "choice in dying," and assisted suicide has become just another "personal choice" (although limited to only one method—a physician's prescription of a drug overdose—some choice). Choice talk pervades discussions of virtually every aspect of health care, from the failed Clinton health care plan to commercial health plan advertising, to advertising by major tobacco companies (it's not a cigarette, it's a choice), from recruiting subjects for medical research, to voting for a (healthy) president.

The book's subtitle, "Law, Medicine, and the Market" portrays the subject matter of this book. "Legal Issues in Medicine" is a regular feature on health law that I have written for the *New England Journal of Medicine* since 1991. Most of the chapters in this book are adapted from articles that originally appeared in the *Journal*. It was only in rewriting them and trying to weave them together that I realized how consistently they centered on the issue of choice, and especially the use of the law to enlarge the choices of patients, subjects, soldiers, and others caught in a health care system in which they have virtually no power or influence.

Choice rhetoric has also strongly supported the rise of market medicine in the United States. Not only did the possibility of Americans being denied their "choice" of physicians doom the Clinton health care plan, the precepts of the market have dominated all policy discussions of American health care ever since. The law is no exception. For example, President Clinton announced in his 1998 State of the Union address that he wanted Congress to pass legislation for patient rights saying, "You have the right to know your medical options, not just the cheapest. You have the right to choose the doctor you want for the care you need. You have the right to emergency room care, wherever and whenever you need it. You have the right to keep your medical records confidential," he strangely described this as a "consumer bill of rights." And a month later the president relabeled this same collection of rights a "Patient Bill of Rights."

Language matters. Thus when market language is imposed on the health care system, it seems natural to transform patients into consumers, and patient rights into consumer rights. But patients are not consumers who pick and choose among physicians and treatments on the basis of price and quality. Patients are sick and vulnerable people who are truly not themselves and are incapable of shopping around for the best deal. The law has recognized this by seeking to guarantee patients certain rights, such as the right to complete and accurate information about diagnosis, prognosis and reasonable medical treatment alternatives; the right to emergency care; the right to privacy and confidentiality; the right to refuse any treatment; and the right to sue physicians who injure them through negligence. These are all critical patient rights. Consumer rights, and consumer protection laws, are something altogether different.

Consumer rights tend to focus not on the context of diagnosing and treating patients, but on the purchase and sale of a health care policy. Thus consumer rights will tend to be about full disclosure of the terms of the policy, how decisions about coverage are made, who can authorize specialist and out of network care, and how decisions to deny coverage can be appealed. These are all important, but hardly central to the needs of sick people. Market language, with its emphasis on choice, tends to marginalize the sick and treat the practice of medicine as just another occupation, and medical care itself as just another commodity, like breakfast cereal. Like choice rhetoric, the market model and its language obscures more than it clarifies and lets us avoid facing the myriad modern problems in the way health care is defined, delivered, and denied in the United States.

This book is the third in a series. The first, *Judging Medicine*, consisted of approximately 100 articles on health law that were published as a regular feature in the *Hastings Center Report* from 1976 to 1987. The second, *Standard of Care*, grouped more pieces from the *Hastings Center Report* together with others from the *New England Journal of Medicine* (and other publications as well)—most

written from 1985 to 1991. In *Judging Medicine* the essays were reprinted as originally published. In *Standard of Care*, they were updated with some revision. In
Some Choice, I have combined the two methods, drawing almost exclusively on
works published in a single journal, but updating and rewriting them. I have also
jettisoned articles that did not fit the theme of choice—such as those on DNA
profiling in criminal investigations and scientific evidence in the courtroom—but
few of my *New England Journal of Medicine* health law articles were unrelated
to choice.

I should not have been surprised. In *Judging Medicine* I had written about the
choice faced by the world's first heart transplant recipients, described by Chris-
tiaan Barnard as the "lion and crocodiles choice." Barnard said that a heart transplant recipient should not be considered a brave man, even though in the early
days of heart transplantation the risks were grave. Barnard argued that "for a dying
man it is not a difficult decision. . . . If a lion chases you to the bank of a river
filled with crocodiles you will leap into the water convinced you have a chance to
swim to the other side. But you would never accept such odds if there were no
lion." Similarly, heart surgeon Denton Cooley argued that even accepting an un-
tried temporary artificial heart is an easy choice because "a drowning man can't
be too particular about what he's going to use as a life preserver." And surgeon
William DeVries, asked if he himself would ever accept a permanent artificial
heart, said he would if the choice was life or death, "because life is precious to
me." His patient–subject, Barney Clark, in his only televised interview, reluctantly
agreed. When asked what he would recommend to others, he said: "I would tell
them to take it if the only choice was to go ahead and die." Some choice.

The subtitle of *Standard of Care* is "The Law of American Bioethics," and
the theme of that book is the dominance of law in the development of the field of
bioethics. The law's dominance over philosophy and medicine in bioethics sur-
prises and disturbs many commentators, but in America this dominance is inevitable. It may also be said that American bioethics draws both its strengths and
weaknesses from the fact that it is rooted in and dominated by American law.[1] Its
strengths are derived from the rich tradition of American constitutional law, which
itself is founded on concepts of liberty, equality and justice, and the universal
concept of inalienable rights. Its weaknesses stem from the fact that the multicultural American experience is unique in the world and that its once-famous
melting pot is threatened with cultural fragmentation. This, combined with
America's secular humanist liberalism, helps explain why its free market economic
system, a system based on consumer choice, often seems to provide a more coherent value system for its citizens than any religious creed.

The Declaration of Independence is the foundational document of the American Revolution and the American experience. At its core is the belief that all persons are endowed with "certain unalienable rights" including the rights of "life,
liberty and the pursuit of happiness." The document which established our gov-

ernment, the U.S. Constitution, was almost immediately amended by adding the Bill of Rights to it, the first ten amendments. These specify individual rights, such as freedom of speech and freedom of religion, that the government cannot interfere with (at least not unless it can demonstrate a compelling state interest for such interference). Thus when we discuss Americans we are talking about people with rights, and when we discuss the life and death of Americans, we cannot help but frame the discourse in terms of rights.[2]

The simplistic notion that choice (or liberty) is always good and government interference with individual choice is always bad is, of course, socially destructive and leads to a law of the jungle with those in power feeding off those for whom choice is almost always an illusion. Government must not only protect those who cannot protect themselves (e.g., children, the mentally impaired, the sick): It must also act in ways that help insure that the choices we think we have are made on the basis of accurate and truthful information (e.g., informed consent, truth in advertising, fraud prevention). As Jedediah Perdy has put it, "Boundless individualism, in which law, community, and every activity are radically voluntary, is an adolescent doctrine, a fantasy shopping trip without end."[3]

It has become commonplace for communitarians to argue that liberty or choice has become the only American value and has overwhelmed our sense of community and of obligations to our fellow citizens. There is something to this, but I think (and argue in this book) that the choices that are honored by our contemporary society very often turn out to be "some choice" in both senses of the words: They do provide another option and with it the illusion of control, but the choice is usually not a particularly good one, and is virtually irresistible because of more powerful factors such as poverty, illness (both mental and physical), and social status.

Three examples presented by two thoughtful commentators who have urged us to curb our "culture of autonomy" are illustrative: (1) a mentally ill street person who is in need of medical care, but is left on the street to die because he tells emergency medical technicians that he refuses treatment; (2) the right of a pregnant woman to refuse to be screened for HIV infection, even though the risks to her future child of contracting AIDS could be significantly reduced if she is infected and takes zidovudine during the pregnancy and childbirth; and (3) the demise of a program to pay teenagers a dollar a day to avoid pregnancy on the basis that this is coercive and thus a denial of their autonomy.[4]

All of these choices are, I think, good examples of some choice and of how the use of choice as an incantation prevents us from looking more deeply into the underlying causes of real problems, and therefore from trying to solve them. Each example involves an option, and choosing among options permits the illusion of control—but none of the individuals in any of these cases is in control of anything meaningful in their lives related to health or medical care. The street person does have the right not to be confined to a shelter against his will; but whether or not he was competent to refuse to be taken to an emergency department for evaluation, and what kind of a choice such a refusal would represent, is the real question. Living on the streets is one thing (although that's some choice too); dying on the streets is something much different. Likewise, the pregnant woman who may have HIV infection is likely also poor, homeless, addicted to drugs, and at high risk for physical and sexual abuse. HIV may be the least of her problems. Of course, she should be encouraged to be screened and offered possibly preventive treatment for her fetus/future child; but we would do better as a society to try to deal with the underlying causes of poverty and drug abuse than to focus our efforts only on doing damage control during pregnancy. Her situation is an American tragedy, not a choice. The high school girls whom we would like to see graduate without having children of their own are in a similar—although not as dramatic—situation. The idea that children are exercising their choice to have other children is ludicrous on its face. But that's the point; torpedoing an experimental program to pay children not to have children is not about honoring choice, but about limiting it. Choice and coercion language simply serves to stop discussion of the much deeper problem of teenage pregnancy and sex, instead of providing an opportunity for deeper reflection and social commitment to try to solve it. The truth is that all of the individuals in these examples are out of control, and hollow choices that are likely to make their lives worse are problems, not solutions. That's not to say choice is bad—only that limited, illusory, or coercive choices do not deserve to be honored with liberty rhetoric or taken seriously. General Colin Powell once said, "When I hear surgical strike, I head for the bunker." In America, when we are told of something new that is proposed because it will increase choice and control, we should all head for the bunker—and dig deeper to try to discover what's really at stake.

This book is divided into five sections, each of which explores choice in a different setting. The first section concentrates on market choices in medicine because the market has become the dominant force in contemporary American medicine. The suggestion is that market choice makes little sense in medicine and that the only real choices that matter to real people are those involving treatment decisions, usually made in a doctor–patient relationship. The second section deals with these treatment choices explicitly, tracing the development of the doctrine of informed consent in the United States and abroad, underlining the limits of choice and exploring illegal choices, such as medical marijuana, and future genetic choices.

The third section is the heart of the "some choice" analysis; it looks at choices we tout as central to our way of life but which turn out to be illusory. They include voting for a (healthy) president, women's choice at work, soldiers' choices in battle, and choices made by critically ill patients to undergo experimental interventions. Illusory choices can be seen as illusions and dispatched as such. But some choices are well recognized as toxic, and government action is necessary to prevent harm on a large scale. The fourth section, on such toxic choices, examines government response to epidemics, especially quarantine, but mainly deals with the primary cause of preventable premature death in the world: tobacco. The fifth section is devoted to choices in dying and the remarkable way that suicide became not only a choice (it can be seen as the ultimate choice), but something to be encouraged by physicians to the extent that physician-assisted suicide should be elevated to the status of a fundamental constitutional right. The choice for a severely suffering, terminally ill patient to either take an overdose of drugs and die now or be sedated into unconsciousness and die in a few days really is some choice.

The book concludes by suggesting that rather than continue to bitterly bicker domestically about illusory choices or market medicine, the professions of law and medicine can act much more constructively by working together transnationally to foster the values on which these professions are founded: care and compassion, and justice and equality. A globalization of human rights and medical ethics is proposed; it is suggested that this can help move us in a direction that both honors human rights and enhances human life and health.

PART I

Market Choices

CHAPTER ONE

Choice's Echo

The chant is "cloning, cloning, cloning;" but the echo is "choice, choice, choice." From all the hoopla about human cloning as a human choice it would seem that cloning must be the most important scientific issue of our age. My intent in opening this book on choice with a discussion of cloning is not to join this chorus. Rather my aim is to take advantage of cloning's high visibility to explore the nature of the choice it offers. What is it that makes human cloning at once so appealing to a few and so repulsive to most? The answer, I think, can be found in Roman mythology: The cloning myth recalls Ovid's story of Echo and Narcissus.

Echo was a devastatingly beautiful woodland nymph who had one flaw, a fondness for chatter and an insistence on having the last word. One day Echo detained the goddess Juno with her conversation while Jove, who was cavorting with the nymphs, made his escape. When she discovered Echo's treachery, Juno cursed Echo, saying that she would henceforth only have the last word, but never the power to speak first. When Echo pursued Narcissus, a beautiful youth, she could not speak to him, but could only repeat his last words. He rejects her, and she pines away until her bones change to rock and nothing is left but her reply voice.

Narcissus, who was equally cruel to all, was ultimately cursed himself and fell in love with his own reflection, which he admired greatly. Being unable to attain it, and being shunned by it, he was ultimately consumed by his passion for his reflection and pined away and died without obtaining his objective. In cloning terms, Narcissus can be seen as the clonee, and his reflection as his clone. Echo is the personification of the curse that the clonee passes to its clone: never to speak first, but always to repeat that which has gone before. The lesson from mythology is clear. Duplicating yourself is sterile, self-absorbed, and ultimately destructive.

Moreover, creating a clone in your own image is to curse your child by condemning it to be only an echo.

The myth of Echo and Narcissus helps explain the almost universal horror at the prospect of human cloning that greeted the news in 1997 that embryologist Ian Wilmut had cloned a sheep, creating the genetic twin of an adult animal by reprogramming one of its somatic cells to act as the nucleus of an egg.[1] He called the cloned lamb Dolly. This achievement was trumpeted as a scientific milestone. Debate about its implications for human cloning began immediately. Should this cloning technique be applied to humans? Who should decide and on what basis? Could human cloning be stopped?

The international press featured photographs of Dolly, usually duplicated one or more times, and often accompanied by bad puns (e.g., Could there ever be another ewe?; Cloning is baaad). The most provocative cover appeared in the French edition of *Courrier International*, which ran photos of 21 identical sheep with the headline "*Dessine-Moi un Homme*" ("Draw Me a Man"). These words would immediately bring to the mind of most French readers perhaps the 20th century's most famous fable, *The Little Prince*.[2] The little prince introduces himself to pilot–philosopher Antoine de Saint Exupery, who has just crash-landed in the desert, with the words "Draw me a sheep" (*Dessine-moi un mouton*). Saint Exupery was unable to draw a sheep to the liking of the little prince, and in exasperation drew him a box with holes in it that he says houses a sheep. This unseen sheep completely satisfies the prince. *Dessine-moi un homme* suggests that, like the prince, we will never be satisfied with the results of human cloning because the clone will never live up to our image of what it should be.

We can learn a lot from the almost universal condemnation of human cloning and the international movement to ban it even if we never create a delayed genetic twin of an existing human. The most important things we can learn will likely be about life, not science, about values, not technique—things, like the prince's sheep, that are "invisible to the eye." The reason Ian Wilmut, and leaders around the world, called for a ban on applying cloning to humans is that the genetic replication of a human by cloning could radically alter the very definition of a human being by asexually replicating an existing or deceased human to produce the world's first human with a single genetic parent. The danger is that through human cloning we will lose something vital to our humanity, the uniqueness of every human. Cloning a human is also uniquely disturbing because it is the manufacture of a person made to order, it represents the potential loss of individuality and freedom, and it symbolizes science's unrestrained quest for mastery over nature for the sake of knowledge, power, and profits. Cloning can also be seen as undermining our very concepts of parenthood and parental responsibility, fertility and the status and value of children.

Cloning can also be categorized as just another reproductive choice for infertile couples trying to have a baby, or as just another area of scientific research that scientists should have the choice to pursue. Choice is the overarching subject and theme of this book, and I begin the exploration of the power of choice rhetoric with the debate over human cloning because human cloning itself is not currently possible, and may never be. Human cloning is a hypothetical and remote future choice for others, probably not yet born, that some Americans nonetheless want to preserve. Choice for its own sake.

CLONING AND IMAGINATION

For a brief time, in the early 1970s, human cloning was a centerpiece issue in bioethical debates in the United States. After the birth of Louise Brown, the world's first IVF (in vitro fertilization) baby in 1978, however, it became tangential. The President's Bioethics Commission, for example, devoted only a single footnote to cloning in its 1982 report on genetic manipulation, *Splicing Life*. The footnote concluded: "The technology to clone a human does not—and may never—exist. Moreover, the critical nongenetic influences on development make it difficult to imagine producing a human clone who would act or appear 'identical.'"[3] And although cloning reemerged as a major bioethics issue in the popular press in October 1993, the NIH (National Institutes of Health) Human Embryo Research Panel Report on human embryo research in September 1994 devoted only a single footnote to this type of cloning: "Popular notions of cloning derive from science fiction books and films that have more to do with cultural fantasies than actual scientific experiments."[4]

Scientists themselves have always taken human cloning more seriously. Joshua Lederberg summarized many of the arguments for and against governmental regulation of cloning in his 1966 essay "Experimental Genetics and Human Evolution."[5] And James Watson, the codiscoverer of the structure of DNA, argued in 1971 for a serious discussion of human cloning that might lead to a "blanket declaration of the worldwide illegality of human cloning."[6] Some bioethicists took up the challenge. Paul Ramsey used Lederberg's arguments as a starting point for his own arguments against cloning.[7] Joseph Fletcher, on the other hand, argued not only in favor of cloning ("if the greatest good of the greatest number" could be thus served) but also in favor of biodesigning "parahumans or 'modified men'— as chimeras (part animal) or cyborg-androids (part prostheses)."[8]

Scientific musings and ethical discussions of cloning garnered Congressional interest as well. In 1972, a Congressional subcommittee asked the Library of Congress to study the status of genetic engineering. Among other things, the resulting report dealt specifically with cloning and parthenogenesis applied to humans. Although the report concluded that the cloning of human beings by nuclear substitution "is not now possible," its authors wrote that cloning "might be considered an advanced type of genetic engineering" if combined with the introduction of highly desirable DNA to "achieve some ultimate objective of genetic engineering": cloning, in other words, not as a replicative evolutionary dead end, but to try to make improvements to existing human genotypes. The report called for assessment and detailed knowledge, forethought and evaluation of the course of genetic developments, rather than "acceptance of the haphazard evolution of the techniques of genetic engineering [in the hope that] the issues will resolve themselves."[9]

Six years later, in 1978, a subcommittee of the House Committee on Interstate and Foreign Commerce held hearings on human cloning in response to the publication of David Rorvick's *The Cloning of a Man*.[10] All of the scientists who testified assured the committee that the account of the cloning of a human being was fictional and that the techniques described in the book could not work. One scientist testified that he hoped that by showing that the book was false it would also become apparent that the issue of human cloning itself "is a false one, that the apprehensions people have about cloning of human beings are totally unfounded." The major point the scientists wanted to make, however, was that they didn't want any laws enacted that might affect their research. In the words of one, "There is no need for any form of regulatory legislation, and it could only in the long run have a harmful effect."[11]

Rorvik purported to tell a true story of Max, a wealthy man who wanted help to find a physician who would clone the avowed bachelor, surviving twin, and orphan. A physician with the unlikely code name of Darwin was found, and laboratory facilities were constructed in a remote country. Surrogate mothers were commandeered without knowledge or consent, and eventually a clone was successfully implanted into one of them, named Sparrow. She was secretly flown to California just prior to the birth of Max's clone and heir. Rorvik's tale makes good reading, and it summarizes most of the ethical and scientific arguments about cloning well. Unfortunately, the ensuing public debate on cloning centered not on the ethical issues but on whether or not the book was a hoax. This, of course, missed the point. The book was an elaborate fable and presented a valuable opportunity to discuss the ethical implications of cloning. The failure to see it as a fable was a failure of imagination: we normally do not look to novels for scientific knowledge, but they provide more: insights into life itself.[12] The issues Rorvik unearthed were quickly reburied.

Like ethical debate, Congressional discussion of human cloning was interrupted by the birth of Louise Brown in 1978. The ability to conceive a child outside the human body not only added a new way (in addition to artificial insemination) for humans to reproduce without sex, but also made it possible for the first time for a woman to gestate and give birth to a child to whom she had no genetic relationship. Since 1978 a child can have a least five parents: a genetic and rearing father, and a genetic, gestational, and rearing mother. We pride ourselves as having adapted to this brave new biological world, but in fact we have yet to develop reasonable and enforceable rules for even so elementary a question as, "Who, among these five possible parents, should the law recognize as parents with rights and obligations to the child?" Many other serious problems, including embryo storage and disposition, posthumous use of gametes, and information available to the child regarding genetic and birth parents also remain unresolved.[13]

IVF represents a striking technological approach to infertility; nonetheless the child is still conceived by the union of an egg and sperm from two human beings of the opposite sex. Even though no change in the genetics and biology of embryo creation and growth is at stake in IVF, society continues to wrestle with fundamental issues involving this method of reproduction 20 years after its introduction. For example, now that we can separate genetic from gestational motherhood, we must acknowledge that the resulting child has two mothers and determine which (or both) society should consider "the" mother of the child. Mother identification is also an issue in cloning (which will not only always require both an egg donor and a woman to gestate the clone but could also add yet a third mother—the nucleus donor who will contribute mitochondial DNA to the child). Attorney Nanette Elster has identified 13 different parental configurations in human cloning with 4 to 10 competitors in each for the status of parent.

Twinning by splitting an extracorporeal human embryo in two is the most rudimentary form of human cloning, and the closest to natural twins. The primary justification for embryo splitting has been to improve the efficiency of IVF, and the American Society for Reproductive Medicine (ASRM) has justified research on embryo splitting as a possible way to improve the efficiency of IVF. ASRM's ethics committee cautions, however, that all twinned embryos should be implanted and gestated together to prevent the copy–original "delayed twin" problem that is at the center of the cloning debate.

This is because cloning of existing humans is replication, not reproduction, and represents a difference in kind, not in degree, in the manner in which human beings reproduce. Cloning has nothing inherently to do with either infertile couples or natural twins because women would be able to replicate themselves without male involvement, and without a limit of one clone at a time or per woman. Asexual cloning by nuclear substitution represents such a discontinuity in the way humans reproduce. It is such a challenge to human dignity (by limiting the clone's life choices), and so devalues human life (by comparing the "original" to the "copy" in terms of which is to be more valued) that even the search for an analogy has come up empty handed. This discontinuity means that although the constitutional right not to reproduce would seem to apply with equal force to a right not to replicate, to the extent that there is a constitutional right to reproduce if one is able, no existing liberty doctrine would extend this right to replication by cloning. One could, of course, drastically stretch existing doctrine to encompass replication, but as the law now stands choice is an insufficient justification for human cloning. We must probe deeper—and we can, by siting our discussion on the operating table of science fiction.

CLONING AND SCIENCE FICTION

The witnesses at the 1978 Congressional hearing should have taken Rorvik's fictional account more seriously and used it as an opportunity to explore the public policy issues raised by his scenario, rather than attempting to discredit the book's factual premise. This mistake has been made repeatedly. The President's Bioethics Commission in 1981 and the NIH Embryo Panel in 1994 each failed to use the wide-ranging fiction literature on human cloning to inform their deliberations. And in 1997, when President Clinton asked his National Bioethics Advisory Commission (NBAC) to make recommendations about human cloning, the panel members failed again. Although acknowledging in their report that human cloning has always seemed the stuff of "science fiction" rather than science, the group did not commission even one background paper on how science fiction writing informs the debate. This is a fundamental error that prompts us to treat cloning as just another choice along the American highway of ever-increasing choices.

Fiction has probably done more than anything else to produce society's reaction to cloning—a mixture of fascination and horror—as exemplified by films such as *Blade Runner*, *Sleeper*, *Jurassic Park*, and *Multiplicity*. In *Multiplicity*, for example, a full-grown adult twin can be produced in two hours. This is totally outside even scientific speculation, although a similar technique was employed in an episode of *Star Trek: The New Generation*. In both of these dramas, repeated cloning produces errors and degeneration, much the way repeated Xeroxing of copies does. The Star Trek crew, a group committed to scientific exploration and open to virtually any new experience or culture rejects cloning as fundamentally opposed to basic human values.

Literary treatments of cloning have gone deeper. Cloning was the basis for governing Aldous Huxley's *Brave New World* (1932). The key to social control in Huxley's society was the "Bokanovsky Process," in which a single embryo is stimulated to divide into 96 identical copies. These 96 embryos (or all the survivors, 82 on average) are then artificially gestated together under identical conditions designed to produce five classes of workers: Alphas, Betas, Gammas, Deltas, and Epsilons in descending order. Specific "batches" were conditioned to perform specific tasks and to love performing them.

Other novels have explored nongovernmental uses of cloning. In Ira Levin's *The Boys from Brazil* (1976), Mengele succeeds in creating 94 clones of Adolf Hitler. The idea of 94 Hitlers is a horrible one. Readers of the book, however, quickly realize that a Hitler clone would grow up in a far different world than Hitler did, and that environment and learning would result in a very different person. As the Nazi-hunter Liebermann puts it near the end of the novel, "I say in my talks it takes two things to make it happen again, a new Hitler and social conditions like the thirties. But that's not true. It takes three things: the Hitler, the conditions . . . and the people to follow Hitler." Liebermann decides the real issue is not genetics, but humans values. The children are not Hitler, no matter how identical their genetic makeup; and by killing them the Nazi-hunters would become what they despised: child killers. Liebermann explains to Rabbi Gorin that although Mengele thought he could produce another Hitler through cloning, this was "his project, his ambition": "It could be that none will be what their genes are. Children. How can we kill them? This was Mengele's business, killing children."[14] The lesson is that a clone, even a clone of Hitler, is an individual human being with all the rights to life of any other human person.

In Fay Weldon's *The Cloning of Joanna May* (1989) we witness four clones develop into four very different women. The wealthy Carl May secretly clones his wife after he discovers she has been unfaithful to him. When she later learns of the existence of the four clones of herself she thinks:

> I am horrified, I am terrified, I don't know what to do with myself at all, whatever myself means now. I don't want to meet myself, I'm sure. I would look at myself with critical eyes, confound myself. I would see what I don't want to see, myself when young. I would see not immortality, but the inevitability of age and death. As I am, so they will become. . . . I can't even kill myself—they will go on. Now night will never fall.[15]

Personal identity is at the heart of objections to human cloning. The loss of personal identity is well-recognized by the clone's following the already-lived life of its genetically identical parent–original. This is unlike identical twins born at the same time, neither of which is destined to follow or echo the other. Weldon argues that clones can undermine the lives of their genetic original as well. Joanna, nonetheless, seems to forgive her former husband on his death bed, and agrees to his dying wish: to raise his own clone. The author thus poses, but does not resolve, the issue of whether posthumous cloning is better or worse than cloning during one's lifetime. The knowledge that one's life choices have been limited, if not defined, by the choices of one's parent is a terrible burden. As Kirsten Banks puts it in her evocative *Lives of the Monster Dogs* (1997) (dogs bred for intelligence, and given speech and hands so they can be soldiers), "It is a terrible thing to be a dog [clone] and know it."

What could the various panels have learned about cloning from an examination of these works of science fiction? That there are a wide variety of possible motives for cloning. That cloning is an evolutionary dead end that can only replicate what already exists—not improve it. That cloning is not about infertile couples nor twins born together, but about replicating an indefinite number of genetic duplicates of existing humans. That exact replication of a human is not possible. That governments, corporations, wealthy individuals, and rogue scientists might all want to do cloning experiments, many because they misunderstand what is possible. That clones must be accorded the same human rights as persons as other humans. And they could have understood that personal identity, human dignity, and parental responsibility are at the core of the cloning debate.

Literary treatments of cloning help explain why applying this technology to humans might undermine our concepts of human life, responsibility, and relationships. Dolly's "creator," Ian Wilmut, has consistently argued that his cloning technique should not be applied to humans. He has not used literature to bolster his argument, but he could. The reporter who described Wilmut as "Dolly's laboratory father," for example, probably couldn't have conjured up images of Mary Shelley's *Frankenstein* better if he had tried. Frankenstein was also his creature's father/god; the creature tells him: "I ought to be thy Adam." Like Dolly, the "spark of life" was infused into the creature by electric current. Unlike Dolly, the creature was created fully grown (not a cloning possibility, but what many Americans fantasize and fear), and wanted more than creaturehood: He wanted a mate of his "own kind" with whom to live and reproduce. Frankenstein reluctantly agreed to manufacture such a mate if the creature agreed to leave humankind alone. But in the end, he viciously destroys the female creature–mate, concluding that he has no right to inflict the children of this pair, "a race of devils," upon "everlasting generations." Frankenstein ultimately recognized his responsibilities to humanity, and Shelley's great novel explores virtually all the noncommercial elements of today's cloning debate.

The naming of the world's first cloned mammal also has great significance. The sole survivor of 277 cloned embryos (or "fused couplets"), the clone could have been named after its sequence in this group (e.g., C-137), but this would have only emphasized its character as a produced product. In stark contrast, the name Dolly (provided for the public and not used in the scientific report in *Nature*, where she is identified as 6LL3) suggests a unique individual. Whether Wilmut actually adopted this name because, as he has said, he used a mammary cell for the cloning, and Dolly Parton has famous mammary glands, is unimportant. The name Dolly works at many levels. Even at the manufactured level, a doll evokes joy in our children and is itself harmless. Victor Frankenstein, of course, never named his creature, thereby repudiating any parental responsibility. Naming the world's first mammal-clone Dolly is meant to distance her from the Frankenstein myth both by making her something she is not (a doll) and by accepting parental responsibility for her.[16] The name Dolly thus serves as a semantic intermediary that makes passage from rejection to acceptance possible.

Unlike Shelley's, Aldous Huxley's *Brave New World* future, in which all humans are created by cloning through embryo splitting and conditioned to join a specified worker group, was always unlikely. There are much more efficient ways of creating killers or terrorists (or even soldiers and workers) than through cloning. Physical and psychological conditioning can turn teenagers into terrorists in a matter of months—far easier than waiting some 18 to 20 years for the clones to grow up and be trained themselves. Cloning has no real military or paramilitary uses. As discussed, even Hitler's clone would himself be a quite different person than the Hitler original because he would grow up in a radically altered world environment.

Science fiction helps us to articulate and understand the major social policy issues raised by attempting to clone a human; but it cannot make us apply its lessons. In deciding how to proceed, society has four basic policy models to choose from: the market model, professional standards, government regulation, or an outright ban.

THE MARKET MODEL

Both the genetics and bioethics communities have consistently underestimated the power of market forces and commercialism to shape the demand for and uses of new reproductive technologies. In fact, the debates in the 1960s, 70s, and 80s are virtually silent about the likely role of the market in setting the practice parameters of the new genetics. We must not be so naive. Medicine itself is now widely viewed as a market good, and the once-nightmare scenario has become a reality: Medicine has become a business, and business ethics have eclipsed medical ethics.[17]

The market is a utilitarian's dream. And it is in the market's maximization of utility that its ideology is united with the libertarian belief in the primacy of personal choice as the ruling value in society. In the market all value preferences (choices) are measured in dollars. Private demand, often itself created by advertising, creates incentives to supply the demanded service to a point where marginal cost equals marginal revenue. Advertising to promote IVF services, for example, has catapulted IVF clinics into a billion dollar annual business that continues to grow. In the private market, private interests prevail; those with the money can purchase services from willing sellers. Sellers themselves have the primary motivation of making profits, since the ideology of the marketplace is the ideology of profit maximization.

We have a private market in sperm (donor insemination, or DI), ova (ova "donation"), and IVF but have so far not developed a private market in human embryos. In one horror scenario (which I suggested during the 1993 embryo-splitting cloning debate *could* occur when and if human embryo cloning becomes feasible) an embryo could be split or cloned a number of times—let's say 8 for the sake of argument. One would be implanted and the rest frozen. After the implanted embryo develops, is born, and is a few months old, its picture could be taken, and a complete genetic profile of the child, possibly with some rough intelligence score, produced. The photo and information could then be placed in a catalog, and the other seven embryos could be offered for sale on the basis that they would produce children phenotypically *exactly* like the one pictured. This method of embryo splitting follow by freezing of some embryos has all of the problems of the "delayed-twin" somatic cell cloning since the later-born genetic twins would have to follow in the genetic steps of their first born twin. This is the same type of genetic bondage somatic cell clones must endure. Nonetheless, this might prove commercially attractive, since many people now select sperm donors, surrogate mothers, and ova donors based on their physical characteristics from similar catalogs with no guarantee that the desired characteristics will be inherited, and a genetic tie may be seen as unimportant by some couples.

What would be wrong with this practice? The problem is that the practice would set a price on *all* human characteristics (e.g., tall children would be worth more on the market than short ones, thin worth more than fat, etc.) and thus tend to commodify not only embryos but children themselves. The problem of selling human embryos can be illustrated by applying the sales provisions of the Uniform Commercial Code (UCC), demonstrating that at the least we will need new sales rules if we decide to let the market rule in embryo distribution. The UCC provides, for example, that goods can be rejected, and "if the seller gives no instructions within a reasonable time after notification of rejection, the buyer may store the rejected goods for the seller's account, or reship them to him, or resell them for the seller's account" (sec. 2-604). This could be read as applying more directly to the frozen embryo itself, but its potential application to the child produced as a result of the embryo transfer process simply illustrates the inappropriateness of sales in this area at all, and the ease with which the sale of embryos can quickly become confused with sale of children. A simple way to stop commercialization in embryos before it starts is to regulate or manage the market by prohibiting the purchase and sale of human embryos, much the way we now prohibit the purchase and sale of human organs and fetal tissues: A federal statute prohibiting commerce in human embryos should be enacted.

It is worth noting that the major reason the cost of health care is out of control in the United States is that medical goods are viewed as market goods, and the individuals who deliver them, and the companies that produce them, earn money based both on price and volume. As economist Uwe Reinhardt has put it, "necessity used to be the mother of invention, now [in medicine] invention is the mother of necessity."[18] He seems correct. When something new is "invented" in medicine, be it a drug or a procedure, its inventor immediately seeks to find or manufacture reasons that it is "medically necessary" for as many people as possible. For example, when IVF was first introduced into the United States in 1981, Howard Jones said it would be used only "to solve infertility problems that are otherwise unsolvable" (e.g., blocked fallopian tubes). Now, however, idiopathic infertility is a sufficient indication. Likewise, it was not surprising to see the George Washington University cloners explain in 1993 that their "embryo splitting" procedure could be used to make IVF more efficient. Efficiency, of course, is a market value, not a precept of medical ethics.

Free marketeers and libertarian ethicists have already suggested that there might be good reasons to clone a human. Perhaps most compelling is cloning a dying child if this is what the grieving parents want. But this should not be permitted. Not only does this encourage the parents to produce one child in the image of another, it also encourages all of us to view children as interchangeable commodities. The death of a child thus need no longer be a singular human tragedy, but rather an opportunity to try to duplicate the no longer priceless deceased child. Moreover, cloning children demeans their personhood by denying them a say in their own replication. When a child is cloned, it is not the parents that are being replicated (or are "reproducing") but the child. The fact that all of the child's DNA came from the parents does not diminish the child's personhood or right to make his or her own reproductive choices. No one should have such dominion over a child (even a dead or dying child) as to be permitted to use its genes to create the child's child.

Population geneticist R. C. Lewontin has challenged my position that the first human clone would also be the first human with a single genetic parent by arguing that instead, "A child by cloning has a full set of chromosomes like anyone else, half of which were derived from a mother and half from a father. It happens that these chromosomes were passed through another individual, the cloning donor, on the way to the child. That donor is certainly not the child's 'parent' in any biological sense, but simply an earlier offspring of the original parents."[19] This position takes genetic reductionism to perhaps its logical extreme: People become no more than containers of their parent's genes, and their parents have the "right" to treat them not as individual human beings, but rather like human embryos— entities that they can "split" and "replicated" at their whim without any consideration of the child's choice or welfare. Children (even adult children) under this view have no say in whether they are replicated or not, because it is their parents, not them, who are "reproducing." This radical redefinition of reproduction and the denial to children of the choice to procreate or not turns out to be an even stronger argument against cloning children than its biological novelty.

Humans have a basic right not to reproduce, and human reproduction (even replication) is not like reproducing farm animals, or even pets. Ethical human reproduction properly requires the voluntary participation of the genetic parents, as Joanna May would certainly insist. This is one reason, for example, why fetal eggs cannot be used for human reproduction: Voluntary participation is not possible. Children are not medicine or treatment (even for intense grief) and should not be used solely as means to other people's ends. Related human rights and dignity would also prohibit using cloned children as organ sources for their father/ mother original. Nor is there any "right to be cloned" that an adult might possess that is triggered by marriage to someone with whom the adult cannot reproduce. While it is possible to posit some scenarios in which cloning could be used for infertility treatment, in all of them having children to rear by existing means is possible: The use of cloning simply provides another choice for choice sake, not out of necessity. Moreover, in a fundamental sense cloning cannot be a treatment for infertility. This replication technique changes the very concept of genetic infertility itself—since all humans have somatic cells that could be used for replication.

My colleague John Robertson published the free marketer's guide to new reproductive technologies in 1994, entitled *Children of Choice*. His basic thesis is that "procreative liberty" requires the government to keep out of any private deals between adults and their physicians that might result in the production of a child (assuming, of course, that the adults can pay the price demanded by the physician to exercise this choice). Robertson, and most IVF clinics, use the allure of children to make their quest seem altogether benign and natural. Nonetheless, children have virtually no place in either Robertson's book or in the practice of IVF clinics: The market rules and no one in the entire contracting process speaks for the future child.

In the cloning context Robertson adopts the same rationale to discount our obligations to our children as he does with IVF generally: It is impossible to harm a child of cloning because if cloning were not used, the child would not exist at all. In his words:

> there is no unharmed state, other than nonexistence, that could be used as a comparison. If cloning did not occur, the cloned individual would not exist. If she had been given a different genome, that is, not been cloned, she would not be the same individual. Thus even if the clone suffers inordinately from her replica status, there is no alternative for her if she is to live at all. Unless the life were a wrong (an unlikely scenario), cloning would then—whatever its psycho-social effects—not harm offspring.[20]

This classic argument is actually a tautology. It applies equally to all of us—none of us would exist were it not for the precise and unpredictable time the sperm from our father and egg from our mother met. This fact, however, does not justify a conclusion that our parents had no obligations to us as their future children. There are many ways to harm future children prior to conception, and the fact that we may not permit these harmed children to sue their parents for damages because we are unable to compare their damaged existence with no existence at all (the "choice" for them if their parents had not decided to have children) does not mean that future children can be manufactured in any way parents want. If it did, it would be equally acceptable, from the child's perspective, to be gestated in a great ape, or even a cow; or to be composed of a mixture of ape genes and human genes. It would also be acceptable to make conjoined twins by design. But in these cases real and predictable harm will be done to future children, and this harm can be avoided. The biological fact that these particular children would not exist but for great ape genes or great ape gestation, or as conjoined twins, provides no ethical justification to visit these harms on children by subjecting them to these manipulations. Harm to the child is thus not the right (or at least not the only) question: It takes children out of context by ignoring or marginalizing parental obligations and family ties and posits the morally untenable postulate that it is acceptable to use any method to produce a child as long as that method is likely to produce a child whose existence is preferable to nonexistence. Daniel Callahan has put it another way: "Nowhere has anyone suggested that cloning would advance the cause of children."[21]

PROFESSIONAL GUIDELINES

Because IVF is a medical procedure, it has seemed reasonable to ask the medical profession, through its specialty groups, to set standards not only for IVF but for the entire range of assisted reproduction techniques, and for research on these techniques as well. Control of IVF research was de facto ceded to the medical profession by the U.S. government when the Reagan and Bush administrations refused to provide federal funding for embryo and IVF-related research and abandoned the Ethics Advisory Board. This prompted fertility specialists to "skip" the research phase altogether and move IVF immediately into clinical practice. Research protocols like that used in the George Washington University embryo cloning experiment are often reviewed only by local institutional review boards (IRBs). Such review is unimpressive because local IRBs have no special expertise in embryo research, are composed primarily of other researchers, meet in secret, and generally approve whatever projects their colleagues want to perform. Today Max would not have to secretly hire a physician and have his cloning research done offshore. Max could have funded his cloning experiment at any of a variety of private facilities in the United States. Unless the facility chosen was affiliated with a hospital or medical school, Max's cloning experiment would not have to be reviewed by anyone.

Geneticist–obstetrician Sherman Elias and I have consistently urged medical specialty organizations to set and follow standards of care, and that in regard to reproductive technologies, "primary consideration should always be given to the welfare and best interests of the potential child."[22] Unfortunately, to date the relevant professional associations have not been able to move beyond the market–consumer model. Current practice is to provide consumer–patients whatever they want (and can pay for) rather than attempt to develop a professional model that sets meaningful practice and ethics standards, or that takes the welfare of resulting children seriously.

Professional-organization ethics committees composed primarily of practitioners are simply too narrow to be anything but self-serving in their outlook and actions. A similar observation can be made concerning IRBs and state licensing boards. We cannot expect physician-dominated groups to protect the interests of patients any more than a guard-dominated group would protect the interests of prisoners, a landlord-dominated group would protect the interests of tenants, or a police-dominated group would protect the interests of suspects.

As my colleague Michael Baram put it more than 20 years ago when he was teaching at MIT:

> I do not think scientific peer groups presently have the objectivity or capability to function as coherent and humane social controls. The members of a peer group share the narrow confines of their discipline, and individual success is measured by the degree to which one plunges more deeply into and more narrowly draws the bounds of his research. There are no peer group rewards for activities or perceptions that extend beyond the discipline or relate it to social problems. Members are therefore neither motivated nor trained to relate their peer group activity to broader social problems. Self-enclosed peer groups cannot be entrusted with self-control.[23]

If anything has changed over the past twenty years, it is the emergence of the market as an even stronger force in shaping professional standards than professional self-identity. Professional organizations, of course, exist to foster the interests of their members. Thus it is not surprising that the ethics committees of these organizations exist primarily to give ethical cover to the practices of their members. The 1994 publication of the Ethics Committee of the American Fertility Society (now the American Society for Reproductive Medicine), for example, has 30 separate statements—not one is about children.[24]

I have been a member of that ethics committee for the past four years. In December 1995, when we were reviewing drafts of five position papers (on oocyte donation to postmenopausal women, use of fetal oocytes in reproduction, preimplantation genetic diagnosis and sex selection, informed consent and the use of gametes and embryos for research, and disposition of abandoned embryos), I suggested that the committee's work to date supported the following description of the committee's operating assumptions: (1) The ethical acceptability of new reproductive technologies is assumed, and the burden of proof is on anyone who would question a new technology to show how its use is unethical; (2) A use of a new technology cannot be declared unethical if there is any possible ethical application of that technology, no matter how hypothetical; (3) It is assumed that imagined new technologies will ultimately work and will produce benefit, and that any imagined harms from the technology are speculative or can be controlled unless proven otherwise; (4) The major values to be taken into account in evaluating new reproductive technologies are economic (efficiency, supply, and cost) not ethical.

I rather naively thought that the committee would find these operating assumptions threatening or at least embarrassing. I was wrong. Most of the members simply found this assessment descriptive. As the chairman put it, this is a generally accurate description of how the committee works: If any good can be imagined from a new technology its use should not be declared unethical. Whatever one thinks about this stance as applied to the new reproductive technologies in general, it has been adopted by the proponents of human cloning, who argue that it is just another choice for reproduction and should not be outlawed if any possible ethically acceptable scenario, no matter how speculative, can be imagined. It is thus notable that ASRM's governing board has taken a strong position against somatic cell cloning—the first technique it has ever opposed.

If it is true that market values have been de facto incorporated into professional medical values (and are often indistinguishable), then professional ethics and practice standards provide no public protection—only monopoly protection for the medical profession itself. We must then turn to governmental regulation to "manage" medicine's market competition in research related to the new reproductive technologies, as well as clinical practice itself.

GOVERNMENT REGULATION AND OVERSIGHT

The United States is virtually unique in the developed world in its hands-off attitude toward government regulation of embryo research specifically and the new reproductive technologies in general. Although NIH did form an advisory panel to make recommendations about embryo research in February 1994, prior to this there had been no federal activity in this area since the Ethics Advisory Board was abandoned in 1979. This lack of activity (and thus of oversight) was caused by the antiabortion agenda of the Reagan and Bush administrations, which identified embryo research with abortion and condemned all embryo research on the basis that human life begins at conception. This view has not ultimately prevailed in either Congress or the U.S. Supreme Court, and honest and open discussion and regulation of embryo research and human cloning now seems possible. It is about time.

There are societal issues involved in embryo research and cloning, especially regarding the rights of potential parents and the welfare of their children, that demand governmental oversight.[25] The United States has long recognized the government's interest in protecting subjects of human experimentation, most forcefully in the 1947 Nuremberg Code pronounced by U.S. judges sitting in judgment of the Nazi physicians at Nuremberg. Nor has Congress been silent, establishing a National Commission for the Protection of Human Subjects of Biomedical and Behavioral Research (1974–78), the President's Commission for the Study of Ethical Problems in Medicine and Biomedical and Behavioral Research (1979–83), and the Biomedical Ethics Advisory Committee (1988–89). This last body was unable to function because of its split on abortion, but the other two produced important and useful ethical guidelines. An NIH body, the Ethics Advisory Board (1977–79), also produced a set of useful recommendations regarding IVF-related embryo research, as did an NIH panel in 1994.

President Clinton's National Bioethics Advisory Commission (NBAC), formed in the fall of 1996, continues this tradition. This is laudable, but I believe it is time to move beyond an advisory committee and establish a regulatory commission, a federal Human Experimentation Agency (HEA), with both rule-making and adjudicatory authority in the area of human experimentation. This would mean HEA could both promulgate rules governing human research and have authority to review and approve or disapprove research proposals in specific areas such as xenografts, artificial organs, embryo research (including cloning), genetic engineering, and other similar experiments that local IRBs are simply incapable of meaningfully reviewing. HEA should also recommend legislation to Congress, including, for example, a ban on the sale of human embryos. Finally, HEA could provide the United States with an authoritative voice in the international arena, where cooperation will become increasingly important.

The need for this type of agency goes far beyond cloning, as I will explore later, in chapters 13 and 14. A cloning-related example helps illustrate why such an agency is needed. Cloning is replication and as such holds little attraction or interest for people who want to have children. Most of us want our children to have better lives than we've had, not to repeat them. That's why although it received almost no public press, the experiment that Wilmut and his team published at the end of 1997 was in many ways much more important than Dolly. In that experiment, human genes and gene markers were added to fetal cells, and the resulting combined cells were used as nucleuses in enucleated eggs. As a result 6 transgenic lambs were born: 3 contained the human gene for blood coagulation (factor IX).[26] The potential (but far futuristic) possibility this technique raises (if it works with adult somatic cells as it did with fetal cells) is that an adult might have him or herself cloned, but *add* genes or partial gene sequences to his or her genome to try to enhance or better the clone. The enhanced clone would then not be genetically identical, but "better" in terms of height, immune system, intelligence, or whatever genes could be successfully added to the cell that serves as a nucleus to the enucleated egg. This prospect could hold mass appeal, and deserves much more attention than mere replication does.

Although NBAC could not agree on much, it did conclude that any attempt to clone a human being should be prohibited by basic ethical principles that prohibit putting human subjects at significant risk without their informed consent. Dolly's birth was a 1-in-277-embryo chance (of 277 embryos, 29 developed to the blastocyst stage and were implanted in ewes, resulting in 13 pregnancies and 1 live birth). The experiment has yet to be repeated, and in early 1998 Wilmut himself said he thought it would take more than 1,000 tries before he could clone another lamb from a somatic cell.[27] The birth of a human from cloning might be technologically possible, but we could only discover this by unethically subjecting the planned child to the risk of serious genetic or physical injury, and subjecting a planned child to this type of risk will likely never be justified. Because we will likely never be able to protect the human subject of cloning research from serious harm, the basic ethical rules of human experimentation may always prohibit us from ever using it on humans. On the other hand, safety is the same argument that was used against trying IVF in humans; an argument that Baby Louise's birth falsified. Because danger itself will not prevent scientists and physicians from first-of-their-kind experiments, from a baboon heart in a baby to an artificial heart in an adult, and because the technique may be both safer and more efficient in the future, we must identify a more stronger basis on which to resist human cloning in the long term.

Virtually all those who have studied the matter have concluded that a broad-based *public* panel is needed to oversee human experimentation in the areas of genetic engineering, human reproduction, xenografts, artificial organs, and other boundary-crossing experiments. Any new national regulatory panel must be composed almost exclusively of nonresearchers and nonphysicians so it can reflect public values, not parochial concerns. One of the most important procedural steps a federal Human Experimentation Agency could take would be to put the burden of proof on those who propose to do novel experiments that call deeply held societal values into question, including cloning. I continue to think that this shift in the burden of proof is critical to effective societal influence over science, and is the most important point I tried to make in my testimony before a U.S. Senate committee, at which Ian Wilmut also testified, in March 1997.[28] Without this shift, social control is not possible. This model applies the "precautionary principle" of international environmental law to cloning. The principle requires governments to protect public health and the environment even in the absence of clear evidence of harm. Under it human cloning proponents would have the burden of proving that there is an important societal purpose for such an experiment before it is permitted, rather than the regulators having the burden of proving that there is some compelling reason not to approve it. This regulatory scheme would depend upon at least a de facto if not de jure ban or moratorium on such experiments before their societal approval. Is this possible?[29]

MORATORIA AND BANS ON HUMAN CLONING

It has been almost 30 years since James Watson first suggested the world might want to outlaw human cloning, although no serious thought was given to this prospect until 1997. Is a worldwide ban possible? Reaction to the birth of Dolly almost exclusively centered on such a ban. Countries around the world, including France, China, Argentina, and Iran, almost immediately adopted bans and called upon the world community to enact an international ban. Such a ban was also urged on the world by the G-7 countries, meeting in Denver in June 1997. Only in the United States, leaders of the other countries suggested, would government hesitate to ban use of cloning a technology in humans on the basis of personal liberty or choice.

President Clinton initially said he would wait 90 days for his ethics advisory board to report to him on what to do, but a few days later he issued an executive order outlawing the use of any federal funds to do research designed to produce a human clone, and urged private industry to voluntarily refrain from human cloning research. Ninety days later his advisory commission (NBAC) recommended a time-limited ban of three to five years on the creation of a human "delayed genetic twin" by somatic cell transfer, during which time more discussion and debate could take place.[30] This recommendation was adopted primarily on the basis that attempting human cloning at this time is too dangerous to the physical health of the resulting child. The chair of the board, Harold Shapiro, wrote in *Science*, in explaining the recommendation, that the board had to consider "vitally important social and constitutional issues," listing as the first one, "protecting the widest possible sphere of personal choice."[31]

On the recommendation of NBAC, the White House sent proposed legislation to Congress on June 9, 1997. The proposed "Cloning Prohibition Act of 1997" would outlaw human cloning for the next five years. The operative portion of the proposal is its prohibition: "It shall be unlawful for any person or other legal entity, public or private, to perform or use somatic cell nuclear transfer with the intent of introducing the product of that transfer into a woman's womb or in any other way creating a human being."

"Somatic cell nuclear transfer" is defined as "the transfer of a cell nucleus from a somatic cell into an egg from which the nucleus has been removed." The proposed Act specifically does not prohibit or restrict any other type of research, including "(1) the use of somatic cell nuclear transfer or other cloning technologies to clone molecules, DNA, cells, and tissues; or (2) the use of somatic cell nuclear transfer techniques to create animals." Penalties for violation of the prohibition are a fine of "$250,000 or two times the gross gain or loss from the offense," whichever is greater.

The Clinton proposal joined two others in Congress and almost a dozen in various states. Because it is specific about both what it seeks to outlaw (the replication of an existing or deceased human being by somatic cell transfer) and what it permits (all other cloning techniques), it is the most understandable. The president's laudable goal is to prohibit the cloning of a human while permitting a wide range of other cloning research. His bill, for example, would not prohibit cloning by embryo splitting, although to prevent the creation of a "delayed genetic twin" all such embryos must be implanted at the same time. Virtually all other proposals have definitional problems so severe that they are either too vague to provide guidance or overly broad in their reach. For example, a Senate bill introduced by Christopher Bond (R–Missouri) defines cloning as "the replication of a human individual by the taking of a cell with genetic material and the cultivation of the cell through the egg, embryo, fetal, and newborn stage into a new human individual." This seems to permit research through implantation and fetal development. A House version, introduced by Vern Ehler (R–Michigan), defined cloning as "the use of a human somatic cell for the process of producing a human clone." What exactly this means is unclear.

In early 1998 a Chicago physicist, Richard Seed made national news by announcing that he intended to raise funds to clone a human. Because Seed lacked both the scientific knowledge and laboratory tools to attempt cloning and had no understanding of the ethical controversies involving cloning or research on children, his proposal was greeted with almost universal condemnation.[32] Like the 1978 Rorvik hoax, however, it did provide another opportunity for public discussion of cloning, and President Clinton took the opportunity to renew his call for federal legislation outlawing human cloning. The Seed affair provided the impetus to get the president's proposal introduced into Congress, but only as a reasonable alternative to a much more draconian Senate bill (S. 1601) that would have outlawed not only the attempt to clone a human being, but all cellular cloning based on the creation of human embryos for research. This anti-cell cloning bill was rejected by the U.S. Senate in February 1998.

The Clinton proposal seems to have been modeled on California's draft legislation, which in modified form became the first U.S law outlawing human cloning in October 1997. The California law imposes a five-year moratorium on human cloning and selling gametes, embryos, or fetuses for human cloning. Under the law, cloning "means the practice of creating or attempting to create a human being by transferring the nucleus from a human cell from whatever source into a human egg cell from which the nucleus has been removed for the purpose of, or to implant, the resulting product to initiate a pregnancy that could result in the birth of a human being."[33]

Because it ignored the rich literature on cloning, NBAC was unable to do more than recommend that it be given another five years to study the problem of human cloning. This is reasonable, but much too narrow. Cloning is unique, but the concerns it raises are not. If choice is the only rationale for cloning, for example, there is no sufficient rationale for human cloning. The moratorium deserves to be made permanent in the form of a ban, and we should use it as an opportunity both to develop a national human experimentation agency and to foster international cooperation in the regulation of human research that affects us all.

Treating infertility by using the new reproductive technologies has become a multibillion dollar business that is itself dominated not by the medical ideology of the best interests of patients and their children, but by the market ideology of profit maximization under the guise of reproductive liberty. Government in our constitutional, democratic society has the authority to make reasonable regulations to manage the market in a way that protects the interests of the public, prospective parents, and their future children. The domination of the divisive and narrow abortion debate has meant that the federal government has not played any role for almost two decades in the regulation of embryo research and clinical application of the new reproductive technologies. This inactivity must end as we attempt to replace the ideology of the market with an ideology of human welfare that takes its responsibility to future generations seriously.

In this respect, I can conclude the discussion of choice and cloning on the same note with which I opened this chapter: Juno's curse of Echo. The primary reason for banning human cloning was articulated by philosopher Hans Jonas in the early 1970s. He correctly noted that it does not matter that creating an exact duplicate of an existing person is physically and psychologically impossible. What matters is that a specific person is chosen to be cloned because of some characteristic or characteristics that person possesses (and, it is hoped, would be also possessed by the copy or clone). Jonas argued that cloning is a crime against the clone, the crime of depriving the clone of his or her "existential right to certain subjective terms of being"—most particularly, the "right to ignorance" of facts (about his original) that are likely to be "paralyzing for the spontaneity of becoming himself." This advance knowledge of what another has or has not accomplished with the clone's genome destroys the clone's "condition for authentic growth" in seeking to answer the fundamental question of all our beings, "Who am I?" Jonas continues:

> In brief [the clone] is antecedently robbed of the freedom which only under the protection of ignorance can thrive; and to rob a human-to-be of that freedom deliberately is an inexplicable crime that must not be committed even once. . . . The ethical command here entering the enlarged stage of our powers is: never to violate the right to that ignorance which is a condition of authentic action; or: to respect the right of each human life to find its own way and be a surprise to itself.[34]

Jonas is correct. His argument applies only to a "delayed genetic twin" created from an existing human, not to genetic twins born at the same time. Even if one doesn't agree with Jonas, however, it is hypocritical to argue that a cloning technique that limits the liberty and choices of the resulting child can be justified on the basis that cloning expands the liberty and choices of would-be cloners. There is more at stake here than a hollow chant of choice.

To summarize, there are a series of reasons to ban human cloning. At the individual/family level there is the issue of human experimentation and the danger to the health of the clone. More important is the Echo-Narcissus syndrome: the parent who is so in love with him or herself that only a duplicate can fulfill his or her yearning for perfection (though this yearning can never be fulfilled and will only result in disappointment and death); and the child-clone who is cursed by its parent never to speak first, but only to be an echo of the parent's already-lived life. Cloning is simultaneously self-indulgent and self-destructive, and creates a child with a curse rather than a blessing. At the societal level cloning threatens to change the value of children by seeing them as products made to order, and all humans by undermining the uniqueness of every individual on which human dignity is based. Finally, at the species level, cloning changes the essence of human sexuality by abolishing the necessity of sexual reproduction, and with it our concepts of fertility and infertility.

CATEGORIES AND CLONING

French philosopher Michel Foucault writes that a passage from the great Argentine writer Jorge Luis Borges incited him to write an entire book exploring how science and society categorize or order things (*The Order of Things: An Archeology of the Human Sciences*).[35] The passage quotes "a certain Chinese encyclopaedia" which divides animals into "(a) belonging to the Emperor, (b) embalmed, (c) tame, (d) sucking pigs, (e) sirens, (f) fabulous, (g) stray dogs, (h) included in the present classification, (i) frenzied, (j) innumerable, (k) drawn with a very fine camelhair brush, (l) et cetera, (m) having just broken the water pitcher, (n) that from a long way off look like flies." Borges did not add (but we can) " (o) cloned lambs," to his list. While each separate category is possible, Foucault (who writes that he could hardly stop laughing, albeit uneasily, at this ordering), observes that the "monstrous quality" in this categorization is the fact that "the common ground" on which a "meeting" of all of these animals would be possible "has itself been destroyed." We can thus never find a container to accommodate all of the entries. Put another way, "Absurdity destroys the *and* of the enumeration by making impossible the *in* where the things enumerated would be divided up."

Foucault was concerned with order (and disorder) and how society orders things to make meaning out of them. Foucault was not so much interested in proving the "truth" of life as he was in understanding why we think the way we do, and therefore what things seem normal or natural to us. The question of human cloning can usefully be examined from a categorical ordering perspective. More precisely, where does cloning "fit"? If we put cloning into the category of human reproduction, it will be in a list including such things as in vitro fertilization, embryo transfer, and artificial insemination, and we will judge it through the same lens that we have judged these other methods of "artificial reproduction." We could also put it in an ordered list of embryo manipulations, a list of scientific challenges, or a list of manufactured products. I think the list it fits into is a different list altogether. It is a list of types of asexual reproduction or replication. Other possibilities include a list of science fiction scenarios, a list of unnatural activities, and a list of crimes against humanity. The "list" into which we "fit" human cloning matters—and will likely determine how society both in the United States and the world deals with it.

Cloning does not "fit into" the category of international crimes against humanity: (a) genocide, (b) murder, (c) torture, (d) slavery. Indeed, the international preoccupation with human cloning can be made to seem absurd in the company of these 20th-century horrors. Cloning would, however, fit well in a list of things that should never be done to children, including female genital mutilation, forced labor, unconsented-to reproduction, and sterilization. For children, it is a form of child abuse, asexual child abuse. An international ban on human cloning could be the first entry into a new category of international bioethics crimes: (a) human cloning. The clear implication would be that this category should grow and that effective transnational enforcement mechanisms should be created. On this view, which I think is the proper one, the remote prospect of human cloning provides the world community with a rare, perhaps unique, opportunity to agree that something that can be done scientifically to change the nature of humanity should not be done. This agreement could (and should) serve as a model for much wider international cooperation and regulation in the bioethics and genetics spheres generally.

Later in this book I will explore other possible entries to this now only imagined (and invisible) category, including (b) research on humans without consent, and (c) physician killing (with or without patient consent). Choice seems a mistaken category for cloning, just as children seem an improper entry under the category products. Like the sheep the little prince finally accepted because he could not see it in its enclosed box, all human children should have the right to live an uncharted life, a life filled with choices they must make themselves, not choices made for them by another who is fixated on duplicating or copying parts of an already-lived life. How we view parental (and societal) responsibility to children is at the core of our concept of the family and the treatment of children. Cloning is at the far extreme. In the next chapter I take up the question of how medicine's adoption of market values has affected an everyday event—childbirth and the care of mothers and their newborns.

CHAPTER TWO

Women and Children First

In the lore of the sea there are few events that have so exemplified heroism and self-sacrifice as the acts of the soldiers and sailors of the British ship the *Birkenhead* when it sank in 1852. The soldiers of the 74th Highland Regiment stood at attention on deck (with the band playing) "while the women and children were saved and the captain very properly went down with his ship."[1] More than 450 lives were lost, and the phrase "women and children first" was introduced into the language as part of the "*Birkenhead* drill." As Kipling put it in his poem "Soldier an' Sailor Too": "to stand an' be still to the *Birken'ead* drill is a damn tough bullet to chew."[2]

In the rapidly evolving lore of managed care, the *Birkenhead* drill's rule of women and children first took on a new meaning when so-called drive-through deliveries were required by more and more health plans. These plans often restricted hospitalization benefits to 24 hours after a vaginal delivery and 48 hours after a cesarean section. The primary rationale was not to benefit mother and child, but to enable the health plan to retain more insurance premium dollars. The new drill was that the passengers must sacrifice for the captain and crew; women and their newborns were expected to chew the tough bullet.

CULTURAL CONTEXT

Why were women and children the focus of the first major public debate over market-driven managed care medicine? The answer is that this population is irresistible to both health care entrepreneurs and politicians, whether the issue is balancing the budget, welfare reform, health care reform, or even mandatory HIV screening. Poor women and children, who do not have the political influence or financial resources to resist even draconian actions against their interests, are easy

LIBRARY
UNIVERSITY OF ST. FRANCIS
JOLIET, ILLINOIS

targets. What went wrong with drive-through deliveries is that the affected women are not limited to the poor but also include the insured middle class, who can fight back. Moreover, politicians found middle class women and their children "telegenic and sympathetic" in a way that allowed the drive-through delivery issue to serve as a surrogate for more pervasive and dangerous problems with market-driven medicine.[3]

The rush to embrace the ideology of the marketplace is based on the theory that Americans are motivated primarily by money; therefore changing financial incentives will change behavior. True believers in the market think this applies to every phase of life. Women, for example, will decide not to have more children, at least at the margin, if the government refuses to increase welfare payments; and physicians will discharge women and their newborns from hospitals early if the insurance company refuses to pay the physician and hospital for longer stays. It is difficult to predict how the 24-hour rule (or even a 12- or 6-hour rule) will affect the health of mother and newborns, because there is little more than anecdotal data available to help determine the appropriate length of stay after delivery. In the absence of better data, it is not surprising that many health plans pushed early discharges to minimize their costs and that physicians fought to retain decisionmaking authority over hospital discharges.

IN-HOSPITAL DELIVERIES

Childbirth in the hospital was not widely promoted until the 20th century. The major reasons for the shift from home delivery were greater safety for mother and child, relief from pain, convenience for physicians, efficiency, the rise of scientific medicine, and the need for a regular supply of patients to train medical students. But gains for women were purchased "at the expense of being processed as possibly diseased objects." By the 1950s, in-hospital delivery had become "unpleasant and alienating . . . women were powerless . . . playing a social role of passive dependence and obedience."[4] A consumer movement to regain some control began. Women were behind the shift to natural childbirth, the routine participation of fathers in the delivery room, and drastic cuts in the length of stay in the hospital after delivery.

By the 1990s, as Ellen Goodman put it, "with shorter and shorter hospital stays, the postpartum world isn't just like home, it is home."[5] We are poised to move full circle, with homebirth again becoming the norm. This is not necessarily bad for women at low risk for labor and delivery complications. Hospitals are expensive and long stays are often, perhaps almost always, unnecessary. The central issue, however, is not only cost, but also the quality of care: How can we make the hospital experience of childbirth responsive to the needs and wishes of women, rather than to the wishes of health care entrepreneurs and politicians? The issue can also be restated as one of choice: Who should decide when a mother and her newborn are ready to go home?

The proponents of discharging new mothers and their babies more quickly from the hospital argue that the long hospitalizations of the past were both unnecessary and potentially dangerous (because of the increased risk of nosocomial infections) for both mother and child. They point, quite rightly, to past excesses in terms of length of stay and argue that increases in efficiency can be achieved without adverse affects on mother and child. The average length of hospital stay for childbirth has already fallen steadily from approximately four days in 1970 to two days in 1992 for all vaginal deliveries, and from eight to four days for cesarean deliveries.[6] Since childbirth is the most common reason for inpatient care in the United States, billions of health care dollars could potentially be saved if the average length of stay for mothers and babies were further shortened. Nor was it only the for-profit plans that moved to cut the length of stay. Kaiser Permanente, a nonprofit health plan that has a solid track record of taking care of its patients over the long term, also saw shorter stays after delivery as cost-effective, safe medical care. Its physicians and nurses have reportedly been instructed on how to encourage new mothers to leave the hospital by saying things like "hospital food is not tasty," the mother can have "unlimited visitors at home," and the mother will sleep better in her own bed.[7] This is all true, and almost all women will prefer to leave the hospital as soon as possible, especially if good follow-up care at home is available.

Opponents of early discharge almost immediately turned to the law to change the practice. At both the state and federal levels legislation was introduced to modify or limit drive-through deliveries by requiring health plans to pay hospitals for longer stays under certain conditions. The success of these efforts is worth examining, because it holds lessons that will be applied to a much larger legislative agenda to reform managed care.

STATE LEGISLATION

In May 1995, Maryland became the first state to enact legislation to curtail 24-hour discharge policies. As one of its primary reasons for acting, the legislature noted that "hospital stays of less than 24 hours after childbirth typically result in unsatisfactory PKU specimens [for phenylketonuria testing] as a result of insufficient milk feedings" and that "the state's statutes and regulations direct the screening of newborn infants for hereditary and congenital disorders in the hospital prior to discharge." (Maryland is one of the country's leaders in newborn screening.) The law, entitled the Mothers' and Infants' Health Security Act, specifically requires insurance plans to provide coverage for maternity and newborn care, including inpatient stays, "in accordance with the medical criteria outlined in the most current version of the *Guidelines for Perinatal Care* prepared by the American Academy of Pediatrics [AAP] and the American College of Obstetricians and Gynecologists [ACOG]." Because the AAP and ACOG recommend a 48-hour stay for uncomplicated deliveries, the law had the effect of eliminating provisions for shorter lengths of stays by insurance companies and health plans.

Also in May 1995, ACOG urged a moratorium on further shortening of hospital stays after delivery until their safety is established, saying:

> The routine imposition of a short and arbitrary time limit on hospital stay that does not take maternal and infant need into account could be equivalent to a large, uncontrolled, uninformed experiment that may potentially affect the health of American women and their babies.[8]

The second state to enact legislation was New Jersey. On June 29, 1995, Governor Christine Todd Whitman went to Holy Name Hospital, in Teaneck, to sign a bill that specified minimum lengths of stay that insurance companies must cover. She told the audience at the hospital, "I have two children—one by C-section—and I know that 24 hours is not enough." She added that the new law used "common sense to give women a chance to recover and babies a chance to get a good head start."[9] Unlike the Maryland law, which followed medical standards as formulated by AAP and ACOG, the New Jersey law specifies that insurance plans must cover "a minimum of 48 hours of in-patient care following a vaginal delivery and a minimum of 96 hours of in-patient care following a cesarean section for a mother and her newly born child in a health care facility."[10]

The law further specifies that such coverage is not required unless the care either is "determined to be medically necessary by the attending physician" or "is requested by the mother." The provision that women themselves make the final decision is a legislative determination that their obstetricians and pediatricians cannot exercise appropriate medical judgment when under intense pressure to contain costs. From the physicians' and patients' perspective, however, how the financial incentives are structured and whether any financial benefit accruing to the health plan goes to enrich investors or to improve services will probably be more important.

North Carolina became the third state to enact legislation, in late July 1995, providing simply that "a health benefit plan that provides maternity coverage shall provide coverage for inpatient care for a mother and her newly born child for a minimum of forty-eight hours after vaginal delivery and a minimum of ninety-six hours after delivery by cesarean section."[11] By 1997 more than half of the states had restricted premature discharge by statute or regulation.[12]

Nonetheless, states probably do not have the legal authority to require this type of benefit for employee group plans provided by corporations that are self-insured, because the Employee Retirement Income Security Act (ERISA) precludes the application of state mandated-benefit laws to self-insured employee-benefit plans.

It seems unlikely that courts will consider this a health-and-safety measure (which is within the state's power) rather than a mandated-benefit law.[13] Whatever the final outcome, however, ERISA does not limit the ability of the federal government to require uniform health care benefits across the country. Accordingly, federal legislation was soon identified as the most effective in this area.

FEDERAL LEGISLATION

Shortly after New Jersey adopted its law, Senator Bill Bradley (D–New Jersey), along with Senator Nancy Kassebaum (R–Kansas), introduced a federal bill entitled the "Newborns' and Mothers' Health Protection Act." At the Senate hearing on the bill in September 1995, Bradley argued that uniform federal legislation that covered all American women and children was needed. Horror stories helped drive the bill toward passage. In dramatic testimony, Michelle and Steve Bauman of New Jersey told the committee how their daughter had died from a streptococcus B infection two days after she was born. She and her mother had been discharged 28 hours after the baby's birth. Although there may be no way to know for sure, the Baumans believe that their daughter would have been properly cared for had they spent another 24 hours in the hospital. Mrs. Bauman testified that "her death certificate listed the cause of death as meningitis when it should have read: 'Death by the system.'"[14]

Senator Bradley's bill followed the New Jersey model in that it required all insurance plans that provide benefits for childbirth "to ensure that coverage is provided for a minimum of 48 hours of in-patient care following a vaginal delivery and a minimum of 96 hours of in-patient care following a cesarean section for a mother and her newly born child in a health care facility." The bill also contained the same waiver of the minimum lengths of stay when care is not deemed medically necessary and is not requested by the mother. The managed care industry opposed the bill on the grounds that government should not interfere with the market in this area. Silent on similar legislation, the American Medical Association (AMA) supported the bill as "a good first step" to ensure that women are not discharged until they and their physicians think appropriate.[15] The "Newborns' and Mothers' Health Protection Act of 1996" was signed into law by President Clinton in September 1996. The operative section of the law provides that unless "an attending provider in consultation with the mother" decides otherwise, no group health plan may restrict hospital benefits "for mother or newborn child, following a normal vaginal delivery, to less than 48 hours" or for a cesarean section "to less than 96 hours." This federal law applies only to states that do not have the same provisions in their own laws, require that ACOG and AAP or other professional guidelines be followed, or require that the length of stay be "left to the decision of the attending provider in consultation with the mother."[16]

WHEN LEGAL REGULATION IS NECESSARY

In the most general sense these anti–drive-through-delivery statutes represent classic government regulation of the market and follow in the tradition of child labor laws, laws protecting worker health and safety, and minimum wage laws. Because the market has no inherent morality, whenever the market is used to produce and distribute goods and services, government regulation is required to protect the welfare of both workers and consumers. Specific regulations, like those outlined in these statutes, are inevitable when industries, especially for-profit corporations, go too far in pursuing their own goals at public expense.

These statutes also reflect a concern about power. At least since World War II, physicians have held most of the decisionmaking power in medicine. The informed consent doctrine, which will be explored in chapters 5 and 6, has sought to move decisionmaking toward a model of partnership between the physicians and patients. In situations like childbirth, where the woman is not sick, there have been notable successes, including an increase in natural childbirth. In most managed care settings, insurance companies and health maintenance organizations (HMOs) are attempting to take decisionmaking authority away from physicians and their patients and to put more of it in the hands of managers, who base their decisions on cost–benefit analysis. But cost–benefit analysis in medicine is still rudimentary, and is now being used primarily on a "trial and error" basis—seeing how much can be cut before physicians and their patients begin to bitterly complain.

Neither organized medicine nor the public wants managers to decide how patients will be treated. The Maryland legislation attempts to put decisionmaking back in the hands of physicians by requiring that health plans and insurance companies accept as necessary any care that is so designated by physicians and is consistent with professional medical guidelines. Since both AAP and ACOG also endorse collaborative decisionmaking grounded in informed consent, this approach may be seen as the traditional medical model. The New Jersey law is different. Although it bows to the historical ability of physicians to determine medical necessity, it moves beyond it by directly empowering patients to make their own decisions, based on their own values, regardless of their physician's view of medical necessity. Specifically, even if 48 hours in the hospital after delivery is determined not to be medically necessary by a woman's attending physician (and the child's pediatrician), the woman and her child may still stay 48 hours if this is what the woman wants. This is a powerful endorsement of patient rights. Of course, the hospital is not a prison, and women cannot be required to stay for the entire authorized time period. Doctors and hospitals can continue to use incentives, such as improved prenatal education and home care and child care after delivery, to make leaving the hospital quickly after birth even more attractive. If they do, this could be an example of a change that benefits both patients and the health plan's bottom line.

COST, QUALITY, AND ACCESS

But what about cost containment? Don't laws like these undercut efforts to save money? The answer is that it depends. Specifically, it depends on such things as the contract that the health insurance company has with the hospital, and whether the hospital is owned by the HMO. In terms of actual cost to the hospital for a healthy woman and her baby to spend an additional 24 hours in the hospital, the amounts in question are probably closer to $100 than $1000, at least if the hospital has excess maternity bed capacity. University Medical Center in Stony Brook, New York, for example, quickly adopted a new policy guaranteeing mothers a stay of at least 48 hours if they wish it. If the insurance company refuses to pay for the second day, the hospital agreed to absorb the estimated $300 in added cost.[17] At least one major hospital, Florida's Tampa General, went even further by offering all of its maternity patients an extra 48 hours of postdelivery care after discharge from the hospital at no cost to the patient.[18] The patients who opt for this program are cared for in a hotel-like unit. To the extent that these programs meet the needs of women and children in a reasonable and compassionate way, they are praiseworthy. They are also consistent with the New Jersey model of putting more control in the hands of women and thus forcing managers to deal directly with women when refashioning obstetrical care.

It was not until the summer of 1997, more than two years after Maryland enacted its law, and almost a year after the federal law was signed, that the first large childbirth discharge outcomes studies were published. One appeared to show that early discharge was safe; the other that it was not.[19] Both studies were published in the *Journal of the American Medical Association* (JAMA) and were accompanied by a thoughtful editorial in which four independent experts tried to make sense of the new data. The experts concluded that only a randomized, prospective study would have the statistical power to reveal the optimal length of stay and that such a study could not ethically be done. Nonetheless, they believed the data was sufficient to determine that the major problems that result in readmission to the hospital for newborns are neonatal jaundice, dehydration, and feeding difficulties. Most of these problems show up between days 3 and 4. The 48-hour-stay laws cannot address these problems; only longer hospital stays, or more cost-effective follow-up care in the home, can. In their words, "Good clinical judgment, based on careful consideration of available evidence, suggests that the difference between a postpartum stay of 24 hours and a stay of 48 hours is unlikely to be a critical determination of newborn or maternal health outcomes (although the difference between 1–2 days and 3–4 days may be significant)."[20] Thus, giving women (and their physicians) a choice between 24 and 48 hours of postpartum hospitalization turns out to be irrelevant to health outcomes—some choice.

"Drive-through delivery" legislation is thus a sideshow in the debate over managed care reform that will have little real effect on cost, quality, or access to health care by women and their children. Although the length of stay is important, especially after a cesarean section, it is not an accurate measure of quality of care. It has, nonetheless, taken on a life of its own for the public and politicians because it can be easily understood and is a specific illustration of the general problem of premature hospital discharge. Moreover, and perhaps most importantly, action on this front permits politicians to appear to be doing something positive to protect women and children that costs the government nothing.

BEYOND DRIVE-THROUGHS

We cannot solve either the real or perceived problems with market-driven medicine by passing statutes dealing with single aspects of medical care (such as length of stay) or single reasons for hospitalization (such as childbirth). No one, I take it, would consider it reasonable for Congress to enact legislation on types of treatment and minimum stays for coronary bypass surgery or the treatment of head injuries, although these would probably have a much greater impact on the overall quality of care than longer stays after childbirth. On the other hand, there will be more legislation on so-called "drive-through mastectomies" if health plans don't act more rationally in this area.

Unlike the proposals regarding hospital stays after childbirth, which arbitrarily use the total number of hours in the hospital as a surrogate for quality, Congress was on much firmer ground when it adopted the Emergency Medical Treatment and Active Labor Act, requiring hospitals to admit women in active labor for childbirth whenever there was either "inadequate time to effect safe transfer to another hospital prior to delivery" or when a "transfer may pose a threat [to] the health and safety of the patient or the unborn child."[21] Under this law, judgments about the health and safety of the woman in labor must be made by a physician, and a hospital may not lawfully transfer a woman in active labor (or any other patient requiring emergency care) unless the patient requests the transfer, or the physician, in exercising reasonable medical judgment, determines that the benefits to the patient that could be "reasonably expected" to result from transfer outweigh the increased risks.[22] This legislation puts patient protection first by supporting decisions made within the doctor–patient relationship.

If Congress and the states are serious about protecting the welfare of women and children, there are clear steps that should be taken, the most important of which is the guarantee of basic health care services to all children and their mothers. Moreover, although it makes no sense for Congress to regulate the details of specific medical interventions, it is reasonable for Congress to require that all health plans offer the same minimum benefit package to all subscribers; this requirement could help protect patients both by guaranteeing this minimum and encouraging health plans to compete on the basis of the quality of care and their responsiveness to patients' needs and wishes, rather than on the basis of cost alone. The question of how to make health plans more responsive to patient choice is discussed in the next chapter.

In the Navy it is traditional to fire a shot across the bow of a ship before taking more aggressive action. The legislative initiatives on the length of hospital stays after childbirth are shots across the bow of marketplace medicine and managed care that go too far. The new health industry ignores such a signal at its own peril; politicians will not remain their captives forever. The message is that patients are patients, not customers. Patients need care, not management. And patients must play a central role in deciding how our new health system will operate.

The 74th Highland Regiment went down with the ship to save the women and children aboard. We expect no such heroics from our government leaders. It should not be too much to expect of ourselves, however, that instead of helping to raise symbolic flags like legislation regulating drive-through deliveries and mastectomies we renew our efforts to provide decent health care for all Americans. Since this effort must be made piecemeal, it seems reasonable to pass legislation to guarantee the right to a decent minimum of health care for women and children first.

CHAPTER THREE

Exit, Voice, and Choice

In *Exit, Voice, and Loyalty*, economist Albert O. Hirschman argues that the ability to take one's business elsewhere may not be enough to empower consumers in markets where all providers act similarly.[1] Instead of simply going elsewhere by exiting, consumers must be able to effectively voice their complaints to give producers and service providers an incentive to be responsive to consumers' interests. Marc Rodwin has suggested that the Hirschman analysis may be particularly relevant to members of managed care plans and "individuals with on-going relations with providers such as nursing homes."[2]

Providing patients, who depend on their physicians for expert advice, with an effective voice is a long-standing problem that has been highlighted, but not caused, by managed care. The backlash against managed care, nonetheless, provides an opportunity to develop meaningful voice options for patients.[3] Because of this backlash, the questions of dispute resolution, grievance mechanisms, and appeals procedures have taken on urgency in the courtroom, as well as in legislative reform proposals at the state and federal levels. In this chapter I explore the rights of patients to appeal benefit denials in managed care by examining the decisions of U.S. District Court Judge Alfredo C. Marquez, in *Grijalva v. Shalala*.[4] *Grijalva* is a class action suit on behalf of the Medicare members of a health maintenance organization (HMO), who sought to compel the Department of Health and Human Services (HHS) to adopt more user-friendly rules for patient appeals. The class action suit was brought by the Center for Medicare Advocacy and other public interest groups on behalf of patients like Gregoria Grijalva, an elderly amputee with an indwelling catheter who had been told by her HMO that she was not eligible to receive home health care.

MEDICARE HMOS

All health insurers have daunting dispute resolution mechanisms. Managed care organizations are under special scrutiny because they deny treatment more often, physicians may be restricted in their role as advocates for their patients, and patients may have little opportunity to exit. Federal law requires that HMOs enrolling Medicare patients provide them with the same range of services provided to all other Medicare patients. The law also requires that HMOs provide "meaningful procedures for hearing and resolving grievances." Dissatisfied enrollees have a right to a hearing before an administrative law judge, if the dispute involves $100 or more, and to judicial review if the amount exceeds $1,000. HMOs must have procedures for appealing the denial of payment for emergency treatment, the denial of payment for services rendered by a non-HMO provider, and the refusal to provide services.[5] The essence of the complaint in *Grijalva* was that HMOs were not following these appeal requirements and that HHS was not enforcing them, thus violating both the statutory and constitutional due process rights of Medicare recipients.[6]

Constitutional rights, of course, only protect citizens against government actions. Criteria that courts have used to find private health care entities subject to constitutional due process standards include government payment for services, government regulation of HMO activities as they apply to Medicare recipients, HHS regulations and directives to HMOs, the creation by HHS of a legal framework governing HMO activities, and the right of Medicare beneficiaries in HMOs to appeal directly to the Secretary of HHS if services are denied. Applying these factors, Judge Marquez found sufficient evidence of government action to invoke the protections of the Constitution. The next step was for the judge to determine what due process the Constitution required be afforded to the *Grijalva* plaintiffs.

MANAGED CARE DISPUTES

There are major distinctions between indemnity (fee-for-service) insurance plans and risk-bearing (capitated) managed care plans when it comes to disputes over benefit determinations. With fee-for-service insurance, the medical services have been provided to the patient, and the only issue is payment. Moreover, the physician can be expected to act as the patient's advocate with regard to denial of payment for services the physician has already provided. In managed care plans, however, disputes often occur *before* medical services have been rendered, and the physician often acts as the gatekeeper who decides that a specific medical service sought by the patient is not needed. Physicians in managed care plans may also have a financial incentive not to advocate for the patient.

Most important, taking one's business elsewhere is an almost cost-free option for patients with indemnity insurance, who can usually simply go to another physician for the care they want and have it paid for by their health insurance company. But exit is not a realistic option in most managed care plans, because employers may limit their employees' choice of plans; employees may not be able to afford a more expensive plan or to pay out of pocket, and the opportunity to change plans is usually limited to one brief period each year, which is seldom the time medical care is sought. These generic problems, however, most severely affect people under the age of 65. In Medicare, exit is more freely available (although Medicare patients who exit to obtain treatment for a new illness may find that Medigap insurance is no longer available for their new "preexisting" condition), and many Medicare enrollees leave their HMO when they need expensive treatment and return to indemnity insurance.[7] So the ability to voice complaints is even more important for non-Medicare HMO patients, who may not realistically have the choice of exiting the plan.

HHS argued in court that in 1993 and 1994 the rates of appeals for denials of service by fee-for-service insurers were 30 times higher than those for denials by HMOs. HHS contended that the much lower rates of appeals for HMOs were evidence of the good job they were doing. Judge Marquez, however, concluded that a more likely explanation for this wide discrepancy was the failure of HMOs to provide a meaningful appeals process. The judge noted, for example, that a review of 570 denial notices to HMO members disclosed three problems. First, 52% of the notices were illegible, primarily because most were printed in type that was smaller than 12 points, the recognized minimal print size for readability by elderly persons. Second, 74% of the notices provided vague or ambiguous reasons for denial of services. Third, only 41% of the notices contained an explanation of personal responsibility for paying for care obtained after the denial.

Judge Marquez also found that the notices tended to "hide the ball" by obscuring the eligibility requirements, thus making it very difficult for a claimant to "fathom what additional evidence to present to rebut the denial." He was also concerned about the general lack of any face-to-face setting such as an informal hearing and noted, "Due process requires a meaningful opportunity to present one's case at a meaningful time." The judge also pointedly observed that denial of treatment can result in "unnecessary pain and suffering or death," and thus the ability to appeal an adverse decision quickly is essential to due process in these circumstances.

Exactly what process is due a person under the Constitution depends on a balancing test that includes an examination of "the private interest at stake; the risk of an erroneous deprivation; the probable value of additional procedural safeguards; and the fiscal and administrative burdens" that the additional safeguards would require. The U.S. Supreme Court has ruled, for example, that an evidentiary hearing is required before the welfare benefits are terminated, but not when disability benefits are denied.[8] In the welfare case, *Goldberg v. Kelly*,[9] which Judge Marquez found to be most like the denial of medical treatment, the Court had noted that "termination of aid pending resolution of a controversy over eligibility may deprive an eligible recipient of the very means by which to live while he waits." Similarly, of course, denial of a needed treatment could lead to death or severe suffering.

Goldberg v. Kelly, written by Justice William Brennan in 1970, is perhaps the most important procedural due process case of the century. This is because it recognizes that poor people have a statutory entitlement to welfare benefits, and entitlements carry procedural due process requirements with them. Justice Brennan was especially interested in removing reliance on rational abstraction from government decisionmaking and supplementing it with passion. In *Goldberg* he described the effects on real people of the loss of welfare benefits:

> Angela Velez and her four young children were evicted for nonpayment of rent and all forced to live in one small room of a relative's already crowded apartment. The children had little to eat during the four months it took the Department to correct its [termination] error. Esther Lett and her four children at once began to live on handouts of impoverished neighbors; within two weeks all five required hospital treatment because of the inadequacy of their diet. Soon after, Esther Lett fainted in a welfare center while seeking an emergency food payment of $15 to feed herself and her family for three days.

In such circumstances, *Goldberg* requires the following due process elements be afforded prior to cutting off welfare benefits: timely and adequate notice of reasons for termination; an effective opportunity to appeal the termination by confronting adverse witnesses and presenting evidence orally; legal counsel, if desired; an impartial decisionmaker; a decision based on law and evidence presented at the hearing; and a statement of reasons for the decision.

Goldberg was the first time the Court extended due process protections to the poor by requiring the government to treat them with dignity. But, as Justice Stephen Breyer has pointedly observed, in writing *Goldberg*, Justice Brennan did even more: "he created a symbol, a symbol of the need for equality, dignity, and fairness in the individual's relation to the administrative state."[10] Of course, sick people in Medicare HMOs may be either rich or poor, but only the poor have no choice but to try to obtain their medical care from their health plan. Judge Marquez rightly recognized the applicability of *Goldberg* to Medicare HMO patients, concluding that HHS violated federal law by continuing to contract with an HMO that failed to meet the following constitutional due process notice and hearing requirements:

Notice:
1. Shall always be given for any and all denials of service;
2. Shall be timely;
3. Shall be readable: at least 12 point type;
4. Shall state the reason for denial clearly and in such terms as to enable the enrollee to argue his or her case;

5. Shall inform the enrollee of all appeal rights, including PRO [peer review organization] review;
6. Shall inform the enrollee of the right to a hearing on reconsideration and that additional evidence may be presented, in person, and shall explain the procedure for securing an informal hearing; and
7. Shall provide instruction on how to obtain supporting evidence, including medical records and supporting affidavits from the attending physician. The HMO must abolish any policy or procedure which would impede such advocacy.

Hearing:
1. Shall be informal, in-person communication with the decisionmaker;
2. Shall be available upon request for all service denials; and
3. Shall be timely according to the seriousness of the medical condition implicated by the denied service: Immediate hearing shall be available for acute care service denials, specifically where delivery of the service is prevented by the denial. . . . All other hearings can be within the normal course of the HMO's 60-day time frame for reconsideration.

AFTER *GRIJALVA*

The *Grijalva* criteria apply only to the approximately 5 million Medicare patients in HMOs. But problems with dispute resolution must be addressed throughout the health care industry. Fair procedures for the resolution of disputes are critical, because decisions that are not subject to review by impartial decisionmakers are themselves unlikely to be made fairly, especially when there are financial incentives not to provide treatment. Of course, people often lack the resources or the stamina to use a grievance process even when available, and many people fear that a complaint could result in retaliation. Effective dispute resolution mechanisms must be easier to use and less threatening than existing mechanisms. Facilitating appeals (voice and choice) in the form of fair dispute resolution mechanisms should help improve both access to services and quality of care.

In late 1996, the American Association of Health Plans (AAHP), a trade association which represents managed care plans, pledged to streamline appeals processes and make them more "patient-friendly." The association said that its member plans "recognize that accessible, fair, and timely grievance and appeals procedures must be in place and understood by both enrollees and all providers and health plan personnel."[11] The group repeated its pledge in early 1997, although it was greeted with a great deal of skepticism since it looked like a hollow promise designed primarily to forestall legislative reform.

HHS announced that it would adopt new regulations to bring it into compliance with *Grijala*.[12] Nonetheless, Judge Marquez issued an additional ruling in early 1997 in which he ordered Medicare HMOs to provide written notice of a benefit denial "no more than five working days after written or oral request for a service or referral" or "at least one working day before reduction or termination of a course of treatment." The judge also ordered that the notice be "clear, readable" and "in at least 12-point type" and that it include "an explanation in lay language of the coverage rule" on which the decision is based, an explanation of appeals available, a description of additional evidence that would support the enrollee's position and how it could be submitted, and procedures for securing an informal hearing before the decisionmaker for reconsideration." HHS was required to provide enrollees with an expedited reconsideration, within three working days, including in-person communication with the decisionmaker in cases in which "services are urgently needed," with the review itself completed within an additional 10 working days. Urgency could be established by a physician's written explanation, and plan doctors shall "be free to give supporting documentation without fear of retaliation or reprisal from the HMO."[13]

In April 1997, HHS published its final rules for an expedited review process for Medicare beneficiaries enrolled in HMOs.[14] In an apparent attempt to camouflage its courtroom defeat, the department barely mentioned Judge Marquez's opinion. Instead HHS said it was guided primarily by a model grievance act prepared by the National Association of Insurance Commissioners. The new HHS rules require an expedited review process for any denial of service that could "jeopardize the life or health of the enrollee or the enrollee's ability to regain maximum function." The expedited review process must include acceptance of an oral request for review, regardless of whether the physician is affiliated with the organization. Should the request be denied, the enrollee also has the right to reconsideration of the decision, including an expedited reconsideration under essentially the same procedures and with the same time frame as the initial review. Perhaps the most noteworthy provisions of these new rules are the required notification of the decision within 72 hours (HMO representatives had argued for five working days) and the mandatory expedited review when requested by a physician.

Consumer groups criticized the new rules, noting especially that they give the health plan discretion to determine whether the beneficiary should receive an expedited review (if not requested by a physician), and do not require in-person communication with the patient for first-level reconsiderations. Within days of announcing its new rules, HHS announced it would appeal Judge Marquez's March order. Legislation mandating specific dispute resolution mechanisms and appeals processes is pending before the Congress and in many state legislatures. The issue is complex, but Judge Marquez has provided a very useful set of guidelines on which to base legislation that applies to all patients in all health insurance plans.

FACILITATING CHOICE

The role of the physician in the resolution of disputes over medical care is central. Managed care proponents often declare at national conferences that physicians

can no longer be advocates for patients. The exact meaning of this statement is
unclear, but it implies that the traditional doctor–patient relationship is no longer
financially feasible. Decisions about what is best for the patient are made in the
context of that relationship, through a process of informed consent in which all
reasonable medical alternatives are discussed, with the physician acting as the
patient's advocate to ensure that the patient obtains the agreed upon treatment. Of
course, just such a system, driven by fee-for-service indemnity insurance plans,
led us to overutilization, unnecessary care, and financial ruin. The new model is
said to require physicians to advocate for a group of patients (members of their
managed care organization) and take the allocation of resources within the group
into account when deciding which medical treatment alternatives to present to the
patient. In such a managed care model patients may be left alone to advocate for
themselves if they believe they need a medical treatment that is either not mentioned by the physician or not covered by the plan. As an insurer, the managed
care plan (like all insurers) has a financial incentive to encourage patients need-
ing expensive medical treatments to exit the plan to obtain expensive treatments
and no financial incentive to provide patients with an effective way to voice their
objections to denial of treatment through a user-friendly dispute resolution.

All insurers have a financial incentive to discourage all appeals, since the
appeals process itself costs money, and any decision in favor of the patient will
cost even more. Discouraging appeals may encourage patients to seek desired or
needed care elsewhere and to pay for it themselves. Of course, patients need to
know about alternative treatments in order to seek them and must know about any
financial incentive their physician might have not to recommend alternative treatments or not to refer them to specialists or for diagnostic testing. Recognizing these
problems, another court ruled in *Shea v. Eisenstein* that managed care plans must
disclose physicians' financial incentives to patients so that they can make informed
decision about whether or not to accept their physician's advice.[15] In that case, a
primary care physician allegedly advised Patrick Shea, a 40-year-old man who
was experiencing shortness of breath, muscle tingling and dizziness, and had an
extensive history of heart disease, that referral to a cardiologist was unnecessary
because Shea was too young to have heart disease. The primary care physicians
associated with Shea's HMO, Medica Health Plans, operated by the Minneapolis-
based Allied Health System, "were rewarded for not making covered referrals to
specialists [by bonuses] and were docked a portion of their fees if they made too
many." The patient accepted the advice, and soon thereafter died of a heart attack. His widow filed a wrongful death action against health plan, arguing that
had her husband known about the way his physician was paid by the HMO, he
would have sought a second opinion with a heart specialist and paid for the consultation himself.

Shea and the HHS rules highlight the tension in the doctor–patient relationship created by capitation (a set fee per patient per year) and the limits of even the

best-designed dispute resolution mechanism to address this tension. A user-friendly appeals mechanism that protects the physician from retaliation by the HMO can help the patient obtain a recommended treatment. But if the physician does not recommend a treatment, or even suggest it as a reasonable option, the patient may not have sufficient knowledge to realize that a decision not to offer further treatment has been made. The possibility of appealing the decision may never enter the patient's mind. Of course, the equivalent of a warning label for all doctor–patient conversations, stating that the physician is being paid to minimize referrals and treatments, could be provided, but this would simply serve to erode patients' trust in their physicians. Although user-friendly appeals mechanisms are helpful, even essential, they cannot address the fundamental issue of trust in the doctor–patient relationship. And to the extent that managed care plans are undermining this trust by recasting the doctor–patient relationship, confronting that problem will require much more than simply providing more accessible dispute-resolution mechanisms.

Wall Street Journal health columnist Marilyn Chase advises her well-heeled readers that if you're really convinced you need a specialist and your plan balks, you should go to the specialist anyway, pay out of pocket, and "fight later about who [ultimately] pays."[16] But such responses put all of the burden on patients and none on the managed care plan and its physicians. This is unfair. Managed care plans and their physicians are certainly not incapable of error in making decisions about coverage. As administrative law expert Eleanor Kinney has properly emphasized, "It should never be forgotten that procedures are an important mechanism to confer power and adjust the balance of power among the parties to the process."[17] How should such a system be designed?

DISPUTE-RESOLUTION MECHANISMS

Mechanisms for resolving disputes about medical care should be quick, easy to use, and fair. In the case of prospectively denied services, patients should be able to obtain a second medical opinion within hours, and in the case of a denial of services that is based on contractual language, they should be able to appeal to an internal neutral decisionmaker within two days. It also seems reasonable for states to require that all health insurers in their jurisdiction have dispute resolution procedures that not only meet the *Grijalva* requirements but go even further.

All patients, not just Medicare patients in HMOs, should have legally established grievance and appeal rights. While some variation seems reasonable, the basic provisions, including those governing notification, face-to-face review by a neutral decisionmaker, representation by a qualified advocate, a timely response, and a written explanation of the reasons for the decision, should be uniform. In addition, the state should provide patients who have been turned down by the health plan and their physicians with a neutral and fair appeals process (separate from the judicial system), such as independent arbitration by a knowledgeable panel, which can quickly review and reverse or uphold an adverse decision. The hearing officers for appeals could come from the state health department, the attorney general's office, or the insurance commissioner. Decisions by independent arbitration panels or hearing officers should be binding on the health insurer, but because of the imbalance of power, patients should be able to appeal these decisions. In cases requiring treatment within days or weeks, the internal appeals process should take less than 48 hours, and the external appeals process no more than another 48 hours. Both should be face to face; and the burden of proof should always be on the health plan to demonstrate that the wanted treatment is unnecessary or not covered by the contract. In the case of an HMO's decision to discontinue ongoing treatment, whether inpatient or outpatient, treatment should be continued during the expedited appeals process.

Records of all internal and external appeals should be publicly available (although the names and identifying characteristics of patients should be withheld to protect their privacy) for the purpose of comparison and improvement in the quality of care. All costs of nonjudicial appeals should be borne by the health plan. Patients should always have the option to challenge decisions in court, but once a dispute is taken to court, both parties have already lost in terms of time, money, and efficiency in decisionmaking. The closer to the bedside the dispute can be resolved, in terms of both time and distance, the better.[18] No health care plan that is delivering high-quality medical care has anything to fear from a speedy dispute-resolution process that treats patients fairly.

The primary problems with existing grievance mechanisms are that they are slow and one-sided. A survey of 196 Kaiser Permanente arbitrations in Northern California, for example, found that the final resolution of disputes took an average of more than 28 months.[19] And in the summer of 1997, the California Supreme Court found major problems in the way Kaiser handled arbitration with its dissatisfied members, including large gaps between the way arbitration was described in the contract and how it worked in practice.[20] Early in 1998 Kaiser announced that it would hand over its arbitration system to an independent administrator. This is a step in the right direction, but a small one. Without the choice of either going to court or to arbitration, patients are still at the mercy of a mandatory arbitration system. They don't even have some choice; they have no choice.

If physicians cannot or will not act as patient advocates, some other person will have to assume this role for patients who wish to challenge denials of benefits quickly and effectively. It seems unlikely that a patient would be satisfied with an advocate hired by their health plan, and in any event, it is unlikely that such a person could act independently on the patient's behalf. For any system to succeed in resolving disputes quickly, patients must believe it is fair. Thus, advocates will have to be provided by an independent organization, such as the state consumer protection agency or the state attorney general's office.[21] Of course, private, independent consumer groups could also make advocates available for patients. To be feasible, an advocacy program requires predictable funding. An increase in licensing fees paid by all entities doing business as health-insurance or claims-management companies seems a reasonable source of funding. Such funding should avoid preemption under ERISA, because it does not tax group health insurance benefits or premiums.[22]

Relying solely on the ability of patients to exit one health plan and join another is not sufficient to ensure either the rights of patients in managed care plans or improvement in the plans' quality of care. Improving opportunities for enrollees to voice their objections can both enhance patient rights and highlight areas of potential concern with respect to quality. Most of the managed care backlash has been played out in Congress and the state legislatures. Courts are slower to react, but will intervene, especially in cases involving services to Medicare recipients and alleged violations of due process. Prevention is almost always preferable to cure, and the states and the federal government should act quickly to ensure that all patients have access to dispute-resolution mechanisms that are quick, easy to use, and fair, as well as to advocates who can help them use these mechanisms. Only Congress can give all patients the right to sue their health plans for harm caused by the plans' wrongful acts. To improve quality and hold health plans accountable to patients for their acts, Congress should give all plan members the right to sue their health plans.[23]

Supplementing exit with voice can foster real choice and thereby enhance patient rights. Nonetheless, readers of this rather technical chapter might well conclude that there is something fundamentally flawed in market-based medicine that requires such elaborate consumer protection mechanisms to provide some level of basic fairness to patients. The next chapter suggests replacing the market metaphor for the health care industry with one that could help us take a more constructive and sustainable direction.

CHAPTER FOUR

Metaphors, Medicine,
and the Market

Our post-Clinton health plan medical care system is often described as a train wreck
or a shipwreck, although entrepreneurs have seen the failure of universal health
care entitlement as a market opportunity.[1] The metaphors we adopt to describe
reality have a powerful effect on how we think, and thus on what reactions we see
as reasonable and responsible.[2] Julian Barnes, for example, describes his reaction
to studying Gericault's great painting, "The Raft of Medusa" (which portrays 15
survivors of a shipwreck on their 13th day at sea as they spot a ship), as shifting
us "through currents of hope and despair, elation, panic and resignation."[3] All of
these emotions are appropriate responses to our current health care crisis; but how
one chooses to react is determined in large measure by the metaphors one adopts.
This can be seen by exploring two metaphors that have dominated American
medicine in the recent past: the military and market metaphors. These metaphors
have made some thoughts and actions seem natural, and others seem totally out
of place. Not surprisingly, the metaphor we have at least temporarily adopted is
the only one that places choice on a pedestal.

We live in a country founded on the proposition that we are all endowed by our
creator with certain inalienable rights, especially the rights to life, liberty, and the
pursuit of happiness. Any government-sponsored health care plan must account for
the reality that many Americans assume these rights support entitlement to whatever makes them healthy and happy. Perhaps as importantly, we live in a wasteful,
technologically driven, individualistic, and death-denying culture. Every health plan,
government-sponsored or not, must also take these postmodern American characteristics into account. How is it even possible to think seriously about reforming a
health care system that reflects these primal and pervasive American values and
characteristics? I believe the first necessary step, which will require us to look deeper

44

than money and means, to goals and ends, is to engage a new metaphor to frame our public policy discussion and help us develop a new conception of health care. We have tried the military metaphor and are currently using the market metaphor; both narrow our field of vision and neither can take us where we need to go.

THE MILITARY METAPHOR

The military metaphor has historically had the most pervasive influence over both the practice and financing of medicine in the United States, perhaps because until recently most US physicians had served in the military.[4] Examples are legion. Medicine is a battle against death. Diseases attack the body, uniformed physicians intervene. We are almost constantly engaged in wars on various diseases, such as cancer and AIDS. Physicians, who are mostly specialists backed by allied health professionals, and trained to be aggressive, fight invading diseases with weapons designed to knock them out. Physicians give orders in the trenches and on the front lines and use their armamentaria in search of breakthroughs. Treatments are conventional or heroic, and the brave patients soldier on as gallant fighters who hope to conquer their diseases. We engage in triage in the emergency department, invasive procedures in the operating theater, and even in defensive medicine when a legal enemy is suspected.

The military metaphor leads us to think of medicine in terms that have become dysfunctional. It encourages us to overmobilize and ignore costs, and it leads hospitals and physicians to engage in medical arms races. It tempts us to believe that all problems can be solved with more sophisticated technology. It leads us to accept as inevitable organizations that are hierarchical and male-dominated. It suggests that seeing the patient's body as a battlefield is appropriate, as are short-term, single-minded, tactical goals. Military thinking concentrates on the physical, sees control as central, and willingly expends massive resources to achieve dominance.

As pervasive as the military metaphor is in medicine, the metaphor itself has been so sanitized that it is virtually unrelated not only to the reality of delivering health care, but to the reality of war itself. The military metaphor itself has become mythic.[5] We have not, for example, used it to assert that medicine, like war, should only be financed and controlled by the government. Nor have we applied the concept of war crimes and crimes against humanity to medicine. As historian John Keegan cogently argues, modern warfare has become so horrible that "it is scarcely possible anywhere in the world today to raise a body of reasoned support for the opinion that war is a justifiable activity."[6]

THE MARKET METAPHOR

The market metaphor has already transformed the way we describe and think about fundamental relationships in medical care, but it is just as dysfunctional as the military metaphor. In the language of the market, health plans and hospitals market products to consumers who purchase them based on price. Medical care is a business that necessarily involves marketing through advertising and competition among suppliers who see profit making as their primary motivation. Health care becomes managed care. Mergers and acquisitions become core activities. Chains are developed, vertical integration is pursued, and antitrust concerns proliferate. Consumer choice becomes the central mantra of the market metaphor.[7] In the language of insurance, consumers become "covered lives" (or even "money-generating biological structures"[8]). Economists become health financing gurus. The role of physicians is radically altered as they are instructed by managers that they can no longer be patient advocates (but rather must advocate for the entire group of covered lives in the health plan). The percentage of premiums a health plan spends on the actual delivery of health care to its members is referred to as the medical loss ratio, or simply as the loss ratio. The goal of medicine becomes a healthy bottom line instead of a healthy patient or patient population.

The market metaphor leads us to think about medicine in already-familiar ways: emphasis is placed on efficiency, profit maximization, customer satisfaction, ability to pay, planning, entrepreneurship, and competitive models. The ideology of medicine is displaced by the ideology of the marketplace.[9] Trust is replaced by *caveat emptor*. There is no place for the poor and uninsured in the market model. Business ethics supplants medical ethics as the practice of medicine becomes corporatized. Hospitals become cost centers. Nonprofit medical organizations tend to be corrupted by adopting the values of their for-profit competitors. A management degree becomes as important as a medical degree. Public institutions, by definition, cannot compete in the for-profit arena, and risk demise, second-class status, or privatization.

Like the mythologized military metaphor, the market metaphor is also a myth. Consumer–patients are to make choices, but these are now relegated to employers and other corporate entities. The consumer–patient is not always right. As consumers we do not participate directly in care or insurance creation: We instead only passively express preferences as tastes which we have little commitment to and "can shed easily and routinely."[10] The market metaphor conceals inherent market imperfections, ignores the medical commons, and disregards the inability of the market to distribute goods and services whose supply and demand are unrelated to price. It pretends that there is such a thing as a free market in health insurance plans, and that purchasers can and should be content with their choices when an unexpected injury or illness strikes them or a family member. The reality is that American markets are highly regulated, major industries enjoy large public subsidies, industrial organizations tend to oligopoly, and strong consumer protection laws, including consumer access to the courts to pursue product liability suits, are essential to prevent profits from being too ruthlessly pursued.

Robert McNamara made the mistake of thinking he could run the Department of Defense like the Ford Motor Company. To this day he insists, "Obviously, there are things you cannot quantify: honor and beauty, for example. But things you can count, you ought to count."[11] The problem with this incredibly narrow perspective is that quantification causes numbers to take on a life of their own and to assume an importance they don't have in the real world. Thus McNamara wound up using the "body count" to judge success in Vietnam—a disastrous and deadly management mistake. Columbia/HCA's top for-profit leaders, who were forced to resign in mid-1997 in the midst of financial scandal, offer parallel examples. Second-in-command David Vandewater has said, "Hospital operations are not much different from a ball bearing company. . . . We treat this industry as a business and try to get our inpatient and outpatient capacity totals up."[12] This might be plausible if ball bearings got sick, died, suffered, and had relatives who loved and cared for them. Columbia/HCA CEO and attorney Richard Scott, asked under oath if he understood the concept of fiduciary duty, said "The exact definition, I do not know."[13] Perhaps inevitably, the physician CEO of for-profit Health Systems International actually seems to believe, "The market can and will resolve all outstanding health care issues."[14] It could and would if patients were ball bearings.

THE CLINTONS' MIXED METAPHORS

This summary of American medicine's two dominant metaphors helps explain why Bill and Hillary Clinton were never able to articulate a coherent view of their goals for a reformed health care financing system. The Clinton plan was said by the President and First Lady to rest on six pillars (also termed the guiding six "shining stars"): security, savings, choice, simplicity, responsibility, and quality. These six characteristics mix the military and market metaphors in impossible and inconsistent ways, and add new, unrelated concepts as well. The predominant metaphor of the Clintons seems to have been the military one: security was goal number one ("Health care that will always be there"). But in a post–cold war era, security as a reason to make major change is a tough sell. Even harder was selling the health care alliances that were the centerpiece of the new security arrangement. The military metaphor (undercut by words like savings and choice) simply could not provide a coherent vision of the Clinton plan.

Nor could the market metaphor. The key to the market is, of course, consumer choice, and this was promised. However, the Clinton plan was founded on choice of health care plan, not choice of physician or treatment, and when the latter choices were seen as central (by Harry and Louise, for example, who said of government health care, "They choose, we lose") the plan itself collapsed, and the alliances with it. Choice, quality, and even savings can be generated by a market plan; but such an approach has little room for either responsibility or simplicity—ecology-related goals that have generated little enthusiasm among contemporary Americans. In retrospect, the Clinton vision seems to have been doomed from the day its six inconsistent foundational principles, goals, or guides were articulated.

The Clintons also failed to engage the four deep-seated negative characteristics of American culture that dominate medical care (wasteful, technologically driven, death-denying, and individualistic). Of special note is our denial of death. In perhaps the best response to the successful Harry and Louise campaign against their proposal, the Clintons videotaped a parody for the annual Gridiron Dinner. The centerpiece was the following dialog:

> Hillary: On page 12, 743 . . . no, I got that wrong. It's page 27, 655; it says that eventually we are all going to die.
>
> Bill: Under the Clinton Health Plan? (*Hillary nods gravely*) You mean that after Bill and Hillary put all those new bureaucrats and taxes on us, we're still going to die?
>
> Hillary: Even Leon Panetta.
>
> Bill: Wow, that *is* scary! I've never been so frightened in all my life!
>
> Hillary: Me neither, Harry. (*They face the camera*)
>
> Bill & Hillary: There's *got* to be a better way.[15]

Some commentators, like ABC's Sam Donaldson, reacted by stating that discussing death in political discourse can only hurt your cause. The Clintons apparently agreed, and the White House refused to release copies of the videotape of the spoof even for educational use (and even though it had been played on national TV), adopting another leaf from military metaphor by treating the videotape as a top-secret document.

THE ECOLOGY METAPHOR

It seems reasonable to conclude that if Congress is ever to make meaningful progress on reforming our fast-changing medical care finance and delivery system, a new way must be found to think about health itself. This will require a new metaphorical framework that permits us to re-envision and thus to reconstruct America's medical care system. I suggest that the leading candidate for this metaphorical replacement is the ecology metaphor.

Ecologists use words like integrity, balance, natural, limited (resources), quality (of life), diversity, renewable, sustainable, responsibility (for future generations), stewardship, community, and conservation.[16] The concepts embedded in these words and others common to the ecology movement could, if applied to health care, have a profound impact on the way the debate about it is conducted and on plans for change that are seen as reasonable.

The ecology metaphor could, for example, help us confront and accept limits (both on the expected length of our lives and the amount of resources we think reasonable to spend to increase longevity), to value nature, and to emphasize quality of life. It could lead us to worry about our grandchildren and thus to plan long term, to favor sustainable technologies over ones that we cannot afford to provide to all who could benefit from them, to emphasize prevention and public health measures, to debate the merits of rationing, and to accept the function of responsible gatekeepers to act as stewards of the medical commons.

Using the ecological (sometimes referred to as the environmental) metaphor is not unprecedented in medicine. Two physician writers, for example, used it extensively. Lewis Thomas often invoked it in his essays in the *New England Journal of Medicine*, and his idea that the Earth itself could best be thought of as a "single cell" was the inspiration for the title for his first collection of these essays, *The Lives of a Cell*. Using this metaphor helped him, I think, to develop many of his important insights related to modern medicine, including the concept of a "halfway technology," the notion that death should not be seen as the enemy, and the idea that in viewing humans as part of the environment we could see ourselves in a new perspective, as highly specialized handymen for the Earth: "Who knows, we might even acknowledge the fragility and vulnerability that always accompany high specialization in biology, and movements might start up for the protection of ourselves as a valuable, endangered species. We couldn't lose."[17]

The other leading physician spokesperson for an ecological view of medicine is Van Rensselaer Potter, who in coining the term "bioethics" in 1971 meant it to apply not just to medical ethics (its contemporary meaning) but also to a blend of biological knowledge and human values that take special account of environmental values. In his words, "Today we need biologists who respect the fragile web of life and who can broaden their knowledge to include the nature of man and his relation to the biological and physical worlds."[18]

Drawing on the attempts of the "deep ecologists" to ask more fundamental questions than their "shallow" environmental counterparts (who concentrate on pollution abatement),[19] psychiatrist Willard Gaylin fruitfully suggested that the Clinton approach to health care reform was itself shallow. He correctly, I think, suggested that what was needed was a "wide-open far-ranging public debate about the deeper issues of health care—our attitudes toward life and death, the goals of medicine, the meaning of health, suffering versus survival, who shall live and who shall die (and who shall decide)."[20] Without addressing these deeper questions Gaylin rightly argues, we can never solve our health care crisis.

The ecological metaphor also naturally leads to considerations of population health rather than concentration solely on the health of individuals. It leads away from concentration on individual risk factors, for example, "toward the social structures and processes within which ill-health originates, and which will often be more amenable to modification."[21] Using the ecological metaphor leads us to look "upstream" (reference to another metaphor about villagers who devised even more complex technologies to save people from drowning, rather than looking upstream to see who was pushing them in) to see what is causing the downstream illnesses and injuries.[22] It leads us to put much more emphasis on early prevention and public health interventions, and less on wasteful end-of-life interventions.[23]

An extreme example is useful. Twelve years ago, a city in India was experiencing an outbreak of tetanus in newborns. The babies were extremely sick, and many were dying. A group of experts was called in from Harvard. They visited the hospital, examined the children, and verified that they were suffering from tetanus. Their solution? They recommended that the city build a neonatal intensive care unit to treat these infants. But this solution would have taken more than the health care budget for almost the entire region of India. Another team, this one from Boston University, was called. The second team tried to trace the cause of the epidemic. What they found was that the midwives who were delivering these babies were using unsterile instruments to cut the umbilical cords. Their solution to that problem was simpler technology. The midwives were provided with a clean cloth, a length of string, a small piece of soap, and a razor blade, all tied together. The soap and cloth were for hand washing, the razor blade to cut the cord, and the string to tie it. And that was that. The tetanus epidemic ended at a cost of about four cents a birth, rather than $400,000 for each case of tetanus.

This story, related by John McKinlay, medical sociologist and a member of the team who came up with the low-tech solution, offers an example of two very different approaches to health care: the first, catastrophe-response military medicine, the second, an ecology-based prevention approach.

CONTROL, CONFORMITY, AND COMMUNITY

The dominance of the military and market metaphors in our thinking about medicine has reinforced two quests that seem to define both modern medicine and postmodern politics: quests for control and conformity. Control of nature, of course, remains contemporary medicine's primary goal, and its accomplishments have been astonishing at both borders of life. Medical technology has, as discussed in Chapter 1, eliminated the necessity to engage in sexual intercourse to procreate, and in the process radically altered the meaning of parenthood in ways we have yet to confront socially. At life's other border, we continue our quest to banish death—and if that cannot be done, as will be discussed in chapters 19 to 21, control is asserted in the name of freedom to end life itself through physician-assisted suicide.

The quest for conformity seems an anomaly in a society of individualists who value choice. Nonetheless, cosmetic surgery designed to sculpt bodies to conform to a socially-constructed ideal of "healthy" has become a major industry. Mind-altering drugs promise mental conformity, and new drugs, such as human growth hormone, promise at least a degree of physical conformity. The human genome project (the subject of Chapter 9) promises even more: that we will understand and be able to manipulate our genes in a way that makes our current surgical and chemical manipulations of human characteristics seem primitive. By valuing diversity and rejecting complete control over nature as a reasonable goal, the ecological metaphor may help us reexamine our commitments to the goals of control and conformity in medicine.

Unlike the military and market metaphors, which reinforce our counterproductive American characteristics of wastefulness, technology obsession, fear of death, and individualism, the ecological metaphor could help us to confront them. The ecological metaphor in medicine can encourage an alternative vision of resource conservation, sustainable technologies, stewardship of our resources, acceptance of death as natural and necessary, responsibility for others, and at least some degree of communitarianism.[24] It can also help move us from predominantly law-based practice standards that are an integral part of the market to a greater role for ethics and ethical behavior in the practice of medicine.

The challenge to recreate a health care system that provides affordable high-quality health care for all remains; and we will not face, let alone meet, this challenge if we continue to rely on visions of health care mediated by the military and market metaphors. Language powerfully affects how we think and is infectious: as William S. Burroughs aptly put it, "language is a virus." We need a new vision of health care, and the ecology metaphor provides one that can directly address the major problems of our current culture as well as the "deep" issues in health care—a way to energize the stagnating and depressing health care reform debate and reshape it.[25] We need a new metaphorical construct that can in turn lead society to think and act about health care in a new way.

Adoption of the ecological metaphor could also help us confront what Vaclav Havel has called the end of the modern age, and move us to something new—a state of human affairs that values universal human rights but that also has space for an appreciation of "the miracle of Being, the miracle of the universe, the miracle of nature, the miracle of our own existence."[26]

For at least the short term, however, the market metaphor will be seriously challenged only by what may be termed the "rights metaphor." This metaphor is founded on the notion that patients have rights, and that these rights must be respected by putting patients at the center of the health care system. In the next section of this book I explore the rights metaphor in the context of the law's doctrine designed to afford patients the right to choose: the doctrine of informed consent.

PART II

Treatment Choices

CHAPTER FIVE

Cancer, Prognosis, and Choice

Barbara Tuchman records that during the Black Death epidemic in the early 14th century, "Doctors were admired, lawyers universally hated and mistrusted."[1] The great plagues and wars of the Middle Ages produced a "cult of death" including a vast popular literature that had death as its theme.[2] As the 20th century closes, our emphasis is on the denial of death, and honest discussion of death remains rare both in the popular literature and in conversations between physicians and patients. That is one reason why Shana Alexander shocked a national conference of bioethicists by saying, "I trust my lawyer more than I trust my doctor." She explained that she trusted her lawyer to tell her the truth about her alternatives and to execute faithfully the one she chose; she did not have this confidence in her physician, at least if she was terminally ill.

To the extent Alexander's attitude is shared by Americans, it is an indictment, because nowhere in medicine is trust so necessary as in physician–patient conversations near death. A national survey conducted by Louis Harris for the presidential commission on bioethics in 1982 supports her view. It found that 96% of Americans wanted to be told if they had cancer and 85% wanted a "realistic estimate" of how long they had to live if their type of cancer "usually leads to death in less than a year." On the other hand, fewer than half of the physicians surveyed said they would either give a "straight statistical prognosis" (13%) or "say that you can't tell how long [the patient] might live, but stress that in most cases people live no longer than a year" (28%) if the patient had a "fully confirmed diagnosis of lung cancer in an advanced stage."[3]

The law's way to try to preserve the rights of patients to choose among treatment alternatives, even when the only alternative is no treatment, is the doctrine of informed consent. This doctrine requires physicians not only to obtain the

55

patient's consent prior to treatment, but also to give the patient some specific information before asking for consent to treatment. Although there are times when real treatment options are available, more often the choice itself is illusory (the patient will say, for example, "I really had no choice"), or amounts to a choice between taking it and leaving it. In this chapter, I discuss the most important informed consent case of the 1990s, which involved a treatment decision that the patient's surviving family members believed was uninformed, in which the patient might reasonably have chosen to "leave it" had full information been shared with him by his physicians: *Arato v. Avedon*.[4] *Arato* centers on whether the law should require physicians to disclose a specific piece of information, statistical life-expectancy data, in the case of a terminal illness.

THE CASE OF MIKLOS ARATO

On July 21, 1980, Miklos Arato, a 43-year-old electrical contractor, was operated on to remove a nonfunctioning kidney. During the surgery a tumor was found in the tail of his pancreas. The tumor, along with surrounding tissue and lymph nodes, was also removed. Several days later the surgeon met with Mr. Arato and his wife. The surgeon told them that he thought he had removed all of the tumor and referred them to an oncologist. The surgeon did not tell them that only about 5% of patients with pancreatic cancer survive for five years or give Mr. Arato either a prognosis or an estimate of his life expectancy. The oncologist told the Aratos that there was a substantial chance of a recurrence of the cancer and that a recurrence would mean that the cancer was incurable. The oncologist recommended experimental chemotherapy and radiation treatment, acknowledging that this might produce no benefit. The oncologist was not asked for and did not volunteer a prognosis.

While the chemotherapy and radiation treatment were continuing, in April 1981, a recurrence was detected. Even though the physicians believed Mr. Arato's life expectancy could then be measured in months, they did not tell him this. Mr. Arato died on July 25, 1981, three months later, and approximately one year after his cancer had been first diagnosed. After his death, his wife and two adult children brought suit against the surgeons and oncologists. They alleged that the physicians had an obligation, under California's informed consent doctrine, to tell Mr. Arato, before asking him to consent to experimental chemotherapy, that approximately 95% of people with pancreatic cancer die within five years.

At trial it was proven that at the first meeting with his oncologist, Mr. Arato had filled out an 18-page questionnaire in which he answered "yes" to the question, "If you are seriously ill now or in the future, do you want to be told the truth about it?" The physicians who treated Mr. Arato justified their nondisclosure of statistical prognosis data on a variety of grounds, most based on traditional medical paternalism: The doctor knows best. His surgeon, for example, thought that because Mr. Arato had shown such great anxiety about his cancer, it was "medically inappropriate" to disclose specific mortality rates. His oncologist said he understood that patients like Mr. Arato "wanted to be told, but did not want a cold shower." The oncologist thought that reporting extremely high mortality rates might "deprive a patient of any hope of a cure" and that this was medically inadvisable. The physicians also said that during his 70 visits with them over one year Mr. Arato had never specifically asked about his own life expectancy and that this failure to inquire indicated that he did not want to know the information. In addition, all the physicians testified that the statistical life expectancy of a group of patients had little predictive value when applied to a particular patient. In other words, the fact that 95% of all pancreatic cancer patients would die soon did not mean that Mr. Arato would be one of them.

Mrs. Arato argued that the statistical prognosis should have been disclosed because it indicated that even with successful treatment (the physicians measured success in terms of added months of survival), Mr. Arato would probably live only a short time. If Mr. Arato had known the facts, she believed, he would not have undergone the rigors of the experimental cancer treatment but would instead have chosen to live out his final days at peace with his wife and family, and would have made arrangements for his business affairs. Mr. Arato had failed to put his financial affairs in order before his death, and this resulted in the eventual failure of his contracting business and substantial tax losses after his death.

On the basis of standard California jury instructions on informed consent, the jury returned a verdict in favor of the physicians. The Aratos appealed. A California court of appeals reversed. The appeals court ruled that physicians were under an obligation to disclose statistics concerning life expectancy to patients so that they could take timely action to plan for their deaths, including the financial aspects of their deaths.[5] The physicians appealed to the California Supreme Court.

THE CALIFORNIA SUPREME COURT

The California Supreme Court unanimously reversed the appeals court's decision and reinstated the jury verdict in favor of the physicians. The judges began their analysis by reviewing California's most important informed consent cases—*Cobb v. Grant*,[6] *Truman v. Thomas*,[7] and *Moore v. Regents of University of California*.[8] The court noted, as it had in *Cobbs*, that the doctrine of informed consent is "anchored" in four postulates:

- Patients are generally ignorant of medicine.
- Patients have a right to control their own bodies and thus to decide about medical treatment.
- To be effective, consent to treatment must be informed.
- Patients are dependent upon their physicians for truthful information and must trust them.

The final postulate is the most important to understanding the doctrine of informed consent. Historically, consent was always required before any physician could touch or treat a patient; and an unconsented to, offensive touching (like being hit with a fist) is a battery. But the law of battery always seemed strange in the context of the doctor–patient relationship. The patient who consented to have an operation on his right kidney, for example, was not upset about being touched or treated on his left kidney because the touching itself was offensive. The patient was upset because the wrong kidney had been operated on, usually because of negligence on the part of the surgeon. In battery, only the offensive touching itself matters. In negligence, a physician is obligated to live up to the standard of care of other physicians; the physician has an affirmative duty to the patient to act in a competent, professional manner. *Cobbs* involved a patient with an duodenal ulcer. His surgeon recommended that his duodenum (small intestine) be removed but did not inform him that this operation carried a further, small risk of losing his spleen and of later developing a stomach ulcer. Both of these risks happened after the surgery, and the patient sued, arguing that he never would have consented to the surgery had he been properly informed of the risks. The California Supreme Court ruled that patients had a right to at least the following information prior to being asked to consent to treatment:

- The nature and benefits of the proposed treatment, including the probability of success
- The risks of death and serious bodily harm of the proposed treatment
- Alternative treatments (and their risks and benefits)
- Anticipated problems of recuperation
- Anything else a qualified physician would disclose

These disclosure obligations were justified because of the nature of the doctor–patient relationship, which the court described as a fiduciary or trust relationship. In other words, the California Supreme Court recognized that when a person is sick the person becomes dependent upon experts, especially physicians. These experts are licensed by the state to "practice medicine," and this practice is not just a routine business where deals are made with other business people on a so-called "arms-length basis." Instead, the doctor–patient relationship is intensely personal and imbalanced. The patient literally *must* trust the physician. But trust will be misplaced if at least some basic, truthful information is not shared by the physician with the patient. Defining just what that information should be is what both *Cobbs* and *Arato* are all about.

In *Truman*, a case about the refusal by a patient to have a Pap smear, the court rejected the battery analysis in favor of negligence. The court concluded that information had to be disclosed even if the patient refused treatment (and thus would not be touched or treated by the physician and therefore could not be "battered"). Otherwise, the court said, patients would not have a real choice because they would not be able to "meaningfully exercise their right to make decisions about their own bodies." And in *Moore*, a case about creating a profitable immortal cell line from a diseased patient's spleen that the surgeon had removed, the court held that the physician must disclose "personal interests unrelated to the patient's health, whether research or economic, that may affect the physician's personal judgment." This disclosure was required so that patients could learn if a physician had an ulterior motive, such as a financial incentive, to make a particular treatment recommendation.

Instead of taking the opportunity to resolve what the California Supreme Court described as a "critical standoff" in the development of the doctrine of informed consent between the extremes of absolute patient sovereignty and medical paternalism, the court in *Arato* focused on one very narrow question: whether California's standard instructions to juries should be revised to require the specific disclosure of a patient's life expectancy as predicted by mortality statistics. Framing the question so narrowly made the court's job relatively easy. The court described the physician–patient relationship as "an intimate and irreducibly judgment-laden one" that had to be judged within "the overall medical context." As to statistics on life expectancy, the court (remarkably) found them of little use to individual patients. The court thought, for example, that "statistical morbidity values derived from the experience of population groups are inherently unreliable and offer little assurance regarding the fate of the individual patient."

Perhaps most important, the court described this case as one that was "fairly litigated" and properly put in the hands of "the venerable American jury," which had rendered a reasonable verdict that it was not prepared to second guess. The California Supreme Court concluded:

> Rather than mandate the disclosure of specific information as a matter of law, the better rule is to instruct the jury that a physician is under a legal duty to disclose to the patient *all material information*—that is, *information which would be regarded as significant by a reasonable person in the patient's position* when deciding to accept or reject a recommended medical procedure—needed to make an informed decision regarding a proposed treatment [emphasis added].

The patient's desire to be told the truth, as evidenced by his answer on the questionnaire, was found irrelevant, since the physician has an independent legal duty to tell the "truth." The court also dealt with the issue of expert testimony, noting that in addition to the specific disclosures required by *Cobbs* (the proposed treatment, its risks and benefits, reasonable alternatives, and problems of recuperation), physicians must also disclose any other information that another skilled practitioner would disclose. The court ruled that specific data on life expectancy fell within this latter standard (rather than being the type of information a trusted physician must disclose because of the nature of the doctor–patient relationship itself). Thus, the trial court properly permitted the defendant physicians to call expert medical witnesses to testify that it was *not* standard practice in the medical community in 1980 to disclose specific life-expectancy data to patients, and therefore physicians were not required to make this disclosure as part of their standard of care.

PROGNOSIS AND SUCCESS

If the only issue is whether the law should require physicians always to disclose statistical life-expectancy data to critically ill patients as part of the informed consent process, the conclusion of the court is arguably defensible. But this is much too narrow a basis for the decision. Although by itself the statistical probability of survival for an individual patient may not always be material, it is always material if it indicates whether the patient is likely to survive and the probable quality of life with and without the proposed treatment. In other words, the issue of informed consent in this instance centers on the disclosure of the *success rate* of the proposed treatment in terms of both the prospects for long-term survival and the patient's quality of life. This is what a patient needs to know, and this is the type of material information a patient has a right to—not only because it is the patient's body, but, more important, because it is the patient's life.[9]

It is unfortunate that the plaintiff did not argue *Arato* on the necessity to explain success rates, because the result could have (and should have) been different. In *Cobbs*, which *Arato* affirms, the California Supreme Court had said:

> A medical doctor, being the expert, appreciates the risks inherent in the procedure he is prescribing, the risks of a decision not to undergo the treatment, and *the probability of a successful outcome of the treatment*. . . . The weighing of these risks against the individual subjective fears and hopes of the patient is not an expert skill. Such evaluation and decision is a nonmedical judgment reserved to the patient alone [emphasis added].

This language explicitly requires physicians to explain the probability that a proposed treatment will be successful and implicitly requires the physician to tell the patient what the physician means by "success."[10] The court seems correct in concluding that a statistical life-expectancy profile of all patients with pancreatic cancer, by itself, might not have been needed to properly inform Mr. Arato of his prognosis. But such information is very valuable when coupled with an explanation of why the physician thinks the patient's case is or is not typical. Group data are the basis for predictions in individual cases—including both treatment recommendations and statements about probable risks and benefits. The physicians relied on group data, for example, to tell Mr. Arato that if his cancer recurred it would be "incurable." The court should have made it clearer that *it is always material to a reasonable person to know both the probability of success of a proposed treatment and the meaning of success*. Without this information, it is the physician, not the patient, who is making the treatment decision. Insuring that the patient has the right to make this choice is precisely what the doctrine of informed consent is designed to accomplish.

CULTURE AND DEATH

As I will explore in more detail in the next chapter, a culture's general attitude toward death strongly influences what prognosis information will be provided to terminally ill patients. In the Middle Ages, for example, "when death was to be met any day around the corner, it might have been expected to become banal; instead it exerted a ghoulish fascination." There was an emphasis on "worms and putrefaction and gruesome physical details"; instead of emphasizing a spiritual journey, the culture concentrated on the rotting of the body.[11] In our culture, with its unprecedented life expectancy, we tend to deny death altogether and celebrate new forms of medical technology designed to forestall death. In this context, it is not surprising that physicians often conceal prognostic information from their patients, just as most physicians once refused to use the word cancer. But concealment of prognosis from patients makes them feel abandoned and makes physicians feel estranged.[12] Candor toward the dying is an old problem, which Tolstoy described so well in *The Death of Ivan Ilych*: "What tormented Ivan Ilych most was the deception, the lie . . . that he was not dying but was simply ill, and that he only need keep quiet and undergo treatment and then something very good would result."

Ilych, a former prosecutor, also recognized that his physician's manner, which implied "if only you put yourself in our hands we will arrange everything—we know indubitably how it has to be done, always the same way for everybody alike," was "just the same air towards him as he himself put on towards an accused person." Of course, the doctrine of informed consent is based on the recognition that people are not all the same and that physicians must let patients decide about treatment options so that they do not treat them "always the same way for everybody alike."

After almost three decades of legal and ethical debate, neither the idea nor the ideal of informed consent governs the doctor–patient relationship. Professor Jay Katz has properly noted that for conditions in which "prognosis is dire and fatal outcome a likely prospect . . . physicians should be guided by the strongest presumption in favor of disclosure and consent which can be modified only by clear and carefully documented evidence that patients do not wish to be fully informed."[13]

Four years ago I concluded that "in affirming *Cobbs*, the court's decision in *Arato*, although very narrow, is consistent with Katz's vision and should be understood as an affirmation of information sharing and patient-centered decision making in the context of a physician–patient relationship based on trust."[14] I now think that this conclusion was wishful thinking. If prognosis information is an integral part of what "successful" treatment means—and it must be for anyone concerned about continuing to live—then prognosis information must be disclosed. More-over, prognosis information itself is incomplete and misleading without additional information on the experience and outcomes of the treating physician with the patient's particular diagnosis and prognosis. This information should also be rou-tinely made available to the patient. Even though the jury in this case believed that Mr. Arato got all the information he had a legal right to obtain, and made his own choice based on it, without the prognosis information Mr. Arato's choice was uninformed and illusory. Some choice.

CHAPTER SIX

Culture, Economics, and Choice

In J. G. Ballard's autobiographical *Empire of the Sun*, the U.S., British, and Japanese cultures are contrasted through the eyes of a young British boy incarcerated by the Japanese army in China during World War II.[1] Ballard describes "the emergence of a particularly American world out of the failures of two traditionally dominant forms of social authority." British society was organized according to rigid social class structure, and Japanese society was based on the cult of the emperor, but as the war progressed, Japan and the United Kingdom found their traditional power relationships undermined. The more egalitarian United States attained world dominance through the use of death-producing atomic technology. Young Ballard learned not only that power is arbitrary but also that his survival required "absolute submission to the conditions of power."[2]

Fifty years later, and since the end of the cold war, the United States concentrates more on death-defying than on death-producing technology. The United Kingdom and Japan use death-defying technology much less frequently. In the British and Japanese cultures, death seems both less feared and yet more hidden from public discourse. Obsession with both the manner of death and the use of ever-improving medical technology to postpone it is not apparent. In part as a consequence, health care costs in Britain and Japan are less than half of ours and remain relatively stable while ours continue to escalate.

Death and technology still remain linked in all three cultures, but this link now appears more in medicine than in the military. It may not be surprising that medical power—the authority of physicians and the potency of medicine—still appears arbitrary to many patients. But U.S. patients no longer accept that survival depends on "absolute submission to the conditions of power." And, as discussed in the previous chapter, the law's doctrine of informed consent seeks to tame both death and arbitrary medical control to the will of the individual. Nonetheless, many Americans spend much of their time and many of their health care dollars attempting to prevent death by unproven means.

A country's total health expenditures can be profoundly affected by the type and amount of information that individual patients receive. And a society's general attitude toward death dictates both the content and the style of imparting medical information. Choices can be examined in the context of consent to medical care by exploring the cultural role and the economic impact of telling patients the truth about what doctors actually know—or don't know—about their medical conditions and about therapy alternatives that might help (but could also harm) them. It is useful to concentrate particularly on truth-telling about prognosis related to death when life-threatening illness has been diagnosed, because this dramatic case most clearly reveals systemic values. In this chapter I focus on the United States, and compare our informed consent law to that in Japan and England to explore the cultural determinants of medical practice in each country, and how the law affects physician–patient interaction. What doctors truthfully tell U.S. patients about prognosis and treatment alternatives and about the degree of scientific uncertainty associated with their illnesses will affect the way health service rationing takes place in the future. When U.S. patients are more honestly informed about prognosis and about the negative aspects of aggressive therapy, public perceptions about the definition and desirability of limiting health services—particularly for terminal illness—will change.

Somewhat surprisingly, the definition of good medical care varies enormously from country to country.[3] For example, German and French physicians have for decades routinely prescribed government-financed "spa cures" for their patients, and a mere decade ago Japanese physicians allegedly resorted to leeches in treating Emperor Hirohito's intestinal cancer.[4] Those therapy choices would invite professional scorn (and would not be covered by insurance) if prescribed by U.S. doctors. The international medical community often disagrees significantly about appropriate diagnosis and treatment, and most physicians are relatively ignorant— if not openly skeptical—about scientific findings reported from foreign countries.

At the most fundamental level, medical experts often frankly disagree about what constitutes disease. Many physical states defined and treated as worthy of medical intervention in the United States, such as moderately elevated blood pressure, are considered unremarkable variations of the human condition elsewhere in the world. Low blood pressure is treated as a medical disorder in Germany, while at the same time it is welcomed as a longevity indicator in both the United States and the United Kingdom. American travelers becoming ill in foreign countries are often surprised to learn that 98.6° is not even the gold standard for normal body temperature that they have been led since childhood to believe. Far from being an exact science with commonly acknowledged definitional, diagnostic, and treatment principles, medicine turns out to be permeated with scientific uncertainty.

Although my focus is on choice at the treatment level, choice in medicine occurs at two preliminary stages as well—first, when health plans are selected, and second, when patients pick their personal physicians. Each of these decisions is subject to cultural influences, which may affect the range of choice available. In countries with single-payer systems, the government chooses the basic health plan on behalf of all its citizens. Under the United Kingdom's National Health Service, for example, the patient's primary care physician functions as gatekeeper to medical specialists, who generally will not see patients except on referral.

In insurance-based systems, like those in the United States, Germany, and Japan, citizens can usually go directly to the doctor of their choice, including specialists, although the growth of more restrictive managed care plans may limit this option. Their range of choice may also be limited by the precise nature of their insurance coverage. In all systems, however, decisions about the treatment of particular patients are made within the confines of the physician–patient relationship. The central issue is the amount of information the law of each country requires to be conveyed within this relationship, and the doctrine of informed consent serves as a convenient vehicle for comparing the relationship between culture and choice.

THE UNITED STATES

A British physician has described the United States as "the land of freedom, democracy, self-reliance, and market competition."[5] This description applies equally to the U.S. health care system and is reflected in the modern U.S. version of informed consent, which itself can be traced to the early part of the 20th century. As an Illinois Court put it in 1906:

> Under a free government at least, the free citizen's first and greatest right which underlies all others—the right to the inviolability of his person, in other words his right to be himself, is the subject of universal acquiescence, and this right necessarily forbids a physician . . . to violate without permission the bodily integrity of his patient by a major or capital operation.[6]

As discussed in the previous chapter, initially courts described the requirement of consent to medical treatment as necessary to avoid the intentional tort of battery. By the 1970s, however, courts had begun to reformulate the physician's duty to inform as a negligence concept, required by the fiduciary nature of the doctor–patient relationship. Doctors in fact had been telling patients relatively little, and informed consent became recognized as necessary to promote "shared decision-making." It soon became not only a legal doctrine promoting self-determination, but a core ethical principle as well. As the president's bioethics commission put it in 1982, informed consent requirements implement the fundamental principle that "adults are entitled to accept or reject health care interventions on the basis of their own personal values and in furtherance of their own personal goals."[7]

California courts, especially the California Supreme Court, have been the nation's most influential in shaping the U.S. doctrine of informed consent. Their leading case, decided in the wake of the consumer, civil rights, and women's movements of the 1960s, is the 1972 decision of *Cobbs v. Grant*.[8] In *Cobbs* a patient had sued his physician for failure to disclose the inherent risks of ulcer surgery, two of which—a splenectomy and development of an additional ulcer—later occurred. The court abandoned the battery theory and replaced it with a negligence cause of action, holding that the physician owed the patient an affirmative duty to disclose certain information. This duty could not be derived from practices customarily engaged in by other reasonably prudent physicians, since few surgeons then disclosed this type of risk information to their patients. Rather, the court found the duty inherent in the "fiduciary nature" of the doctor–patient relationship.

Under the *Cobbs* rule, the ultimate choice among alternative treatments rests with the patient–consumer, like all other choices in the marketplace. Just as banks must disclose annual percentage interest rates, just as used car sellers must disclose actual mileage, and just as landlords must disclose latent defects in property, so physicians must disclose risks and alternatives of proposed procedures. After all, the free market presumes that individual decisions will be based on consumer information. Informed consent doctrine assumes that the patient's doctor is the appropriate person to provide this information and requires disclosure so that the patient can be a knowledgeable consumer of the medical product.

As I discussed in the previous chapter, more recently the California Supreme Court refused to expand the required content of informed consent to include prognosis information, underlining the difficulty we still have in dealing with death.[9] Nevertheless, end-of-life care is coming under increasing scrutiny since cost control has become the dominant concern of U.S. medical policy. Approximately 30% of the Medicare budget is spent on treatment during the last year of its beneficiaries' lives, and at least some significant savings could be achieved by decreasing utilization within that period.[10] Congress had both cost containment and autonomy objectives in mind when it passed the Patient Self-Determination Act in 1990. The statute requires health facilities receiving Medicare and Medicaid funding to give patients written information about their rights to refuse treatment under state law. Subjecting people to expensive and unwanted treatment at the end of life makes no economic sense, and it drastically undermines patient sovereignty.

In the United States, informed consent is well entrenched in theory, but in practice patient autonomy continues to be elusive for many reasons. First, patients (particularly seriously ill ones) remain abjectly dependent on their physicians, who still make most choices for them because of the information inequality between doctor and patient. Arnold Relman estimates that in the United States "probably more than 70 percent of all expenditures for personal health care are the result of decisions of physicians."[11] Moreover, the way physicians impart information influences patient choice. For example, patients tend to go along with therapy their physicians recommend when probable outcomes are discussed in terms of survival percentages, but reject it when those very same outcomes are presented in terms of death statistics. Also, although the United States is a capitalistic, market-driven society, and although medicine is still viewed as a private good, public expenditures on health care account for more than 40% of the trillion dollars that Americans spend on health care annually. Finally, financial incentives in our system may simply overwhelm the legal pressure to adequately inform patients.

THE UNITED KINGDOM

In the United Kingdom medical care has, at least since World War II, been viewed as a publicly provided good, and choices are constrained by, among other things, the total budget government commits to medical services. In Britain's leading informed consent case, Amy Doris Sidaway underwent a laminectomy (her second) which had an inherent risk of 1 to 2% paralysis. The surgery left her paralyzed on her right side. The trial court ruled that her physician was under no legal obligation to disclose those inherent surgical risks; the appeals panel affirmed, as did the House of Lords.

The primary question before the five law lords hearing the case was the source of the physician's duty to disclose information. As in the United States, English malpractice law is based on the proposition that a physician "is not guilty of negligence if he has acted in accordance with a practice accepted as proper by a responsible body of medical men skilled in that particular art." This is known as the *Bolam* test. While many U.S. courts have abandoned this physician-oriented rule for informed consent, the House of Lords did not; four of five law lords accepted a physician-centered standard of disclosure, although with differing emphases.

Lord Diplock's speech held that the physician's duty to disclose should be based on that "accepted as proper by a body of responsible and skilled medical opinion." Lord Templeman believed that physicians fulfill their duty of disclosure when they provide patients with sufficient information to make a "balanced judgment." In his view the decision of what precise information to impart was for the doctor, so long as the goal is honoring "the patient's right to information which will enable the patient to make a balanced judgment."

Lord Bridge, joined by Lord Keith, generally agreed that *Bolam* governed disclosure, but would reserve judicial authority to overrule medical custom in certain instances: "I am of the opinion that the judge might in certain circumstances come to the conclusion that disclosure of a particular risk was so obviously necessary to an informed choice on the part of the patient that no reasonably prudent medical man would fail to make it." Lord Scarman alone would have altered the *Bolam* rule in informed consent cases in favor of a patient-centered standard of disclosure, since he considered self-determination a "basic human right."[12]

What *Sidaway* actually stands for is a matter of some dispute. David Meyers has argued that Lord Bridge's speech giving judges the right to second-guess the sufficiency of the information doctors disclose "may well lead to a modified version of the 'informed consent' doctrine the Lords apparently were so anxious, for policy reasons, to avoid."[13] He does, however, offer the trite caution that "Only time will tell." So far, time has not been particularly kind to informed consent doctrine in England. As Meyers and others have noted, a post-*Sidaway* Court of Appeals decision, *Gold v. Haringey Area Health Authority*,[14] wrongly concluded that *Sidaway* stood for the proposition that the *Bolam* test was decisive on informed consent. Other commentators have, properly I think, suggested that *Gold* misinterpreted *Sidaway*:

> [Under *Sidaway*] the Judge was 'free' to form his own view if he regarded the information which was lacking as 'obviously necessary for an informed choice' or a 'balanced judgment.' The problem with the Court of Appeals approach in *Gold* was that their reading of *Sidaway* failed to look beyond the strict limits of Lord Diplock's speech. Had they done so, this backward step, giving conclusive force to medical evidence, could have been avoided.[15]

Consumer advocates in Britain are not persuaded that physicians alone should set disclosure rules. In his book *Breast Cancer: The Facts*, British surgeon Michael Baum says, "Women should trust the medical profession that they are working for the benefit of womankind, once this trust is lost there is no hope at all." Sarah Boston and Jill Louw, advocates for full disclosure when breast cancer has been diagnosed, counter that "trust is a two-way relationship based on mutual respect," and go on to say: "[B]etter-informed patients can no longer be treated in the paternalistic and autocratic manner of the past." As in Japan, cancer is often a loaded word in British medical practice. As Boston and Louw observe: "Our society regards the word cancer as a taboo word and its usage is still evaded, particularly by doctors in talking to their patients. . . . It is often the patient herself who wants and needs the word spelled out clearly to grasp the reality."[16]

Consumer complaints about continuing medical paternalism have had some effect. For example, the National Health Service (NHS) has taken Lord Bridge's *Sidaway* statement seriously: It issued *Patient Consent to Examination or Treatment* and a *Guide to Consent for Examination or Treatment* to all NHS doctors in 1990. These documents are intended to govern NHS practice, and each includes the statement, "where treatment carries substantial risks the patient must be advised of this by the doctor so that consent may be well-informed." Christopher Heneghan, a surgeon at Ealing Hospital, subsequently responded with a textbook example of persisting medical paternalism. He argued that the department's advice is "clearly wrong," and puts patients "at risk by giving them so much information that they refuse *necessary* treatment."[17] It seems likely that British doctors—not their patients—are the ones who really fear that imparting information raises patient anxiety.[18]

JAPAN

As an island nation with a homogeneous population enjoying universal access to reasonably priced medical care, Japan resembles the United Kingdom. Japan has borrowed many aspects of Western culture during this century, while retaining its unique cultural identity. For example, its universal health insurance is patterned on the German model organized around employment, but other aspects of the German system have been rejected. Although it is impossible to encapsulate a culture in one person's works, Japan's great, albeit eccentric, writer, Yukio Mishima, probably speaks of the Japanese culture as articulately as anyone can. In *Temple of Dawn*, he has his main character, the lawyer Honda, contemplate death at the same time he contemplates taking a mistress:

> If Honda had been so inclined, he could have selected the most beautiful of the young geishas and become her patron. It could be a pleasure to buy her anything she requested and enjoy her coquetry, tenuous as a spring cloud . . . those tiny feet so neatly clad in white custom-made *tabi*. She would be a perfectly dressed doll in her kimono. All this could belong to him. But he could at once foresee the conclusion. *Boiling water of passion would overflow and the dancing ashes of death would fly up to blind him.*

Temple of Dawn was the third work of fiction in the author's *The Sea of Fertility* cycle. Mishima committed suicide on the day he finished the fourth and final novel, as he had said he would. The Japanese people may deny death in daily life as much as Americans do but, as this passage reflects, their culture and their literature express its inevitability without romance.

Japan has yet to accept the concept of informed consent, "although ever since Professor Koichi Bai introduced the West German legal concept of informed consent into Japanese academic legal theory in 1970, the number of medical malpractice suits alleging the physician's breach of duty to obtain informed consent has increased steadily."[19] Nevertheless, "the right of the patient to take part in the decisionmaking process to a large extent remains ignored."

Japan's leading informed consent decision, *Makino v. The Red Cross Hospital*, involves a cancer patient.[20] In January 1983 Makino went to a major hospital in Nagoya complaining of stomach pain. Her doctors told her that they suspected a gallbladder condition and asked her to return in a week for more tests. At that time her doctors made a preliminary diagnosis of cholecystic cancer, which they reaffirmed on three additional visits within the month. However, they never communicated their suspicions to the patient. Her physicians wanted a biopsy to make a definitive diagnosis, but they did not tell her the real reason for wanting her to return for surgery. Instead they simply told her she had "a rather bad gallbladder."

Makino had planned a trip to Singapore in March and made an appointment to return to the hospital in April. She later canceled the appointment, and she never returned, because she felt quite well. In June, however, she collapsed and was treated for cancer at another hospital. She died in December. The lawsuit filed by her husband and children alleged that the hospital should have informed her (or her husband) of the preliminary cancer diagnosis in January or February, and that their failure to do so induced the patient to make a mistaken and fatal judgment to postpone treatment.

The district court ruled that physicians have a duty to make a diagnosis and to provide adequate treatment. Physicians must also inform patients or their families about the nature of the illness, the expected course of therapy, and its anticipated effects, "since the patient has a right to self-determination on his own therapy." Thus far the opinion seems consistent with those of most U.S. courts, but the right enunciated was quickly gutted. The decision articulated an extraordinarily broad therapeutic privilege which permits doctors to decide, in their discretion, when, to whom, and in how much detail information shall be conveyed: "How such information should be given is in the discretion of the doctor to the extent that the patient's right of self-determination is not infringed."

The court concluded in *Makino* that since the physicians had never confirmed their diagnosis of cholecystic cancer by biopsy, they had no duty to disclose their suspicions. Moreover, even if such a final diagnosis had been made, "it would be unreasonable" to require physicians to disclose the diagnosis of a virtually incurable disease to a patient. Finally, such a diagnosis is most properly disclosed to the family, not the patient. The *Makino* court found that the physicians' plan to disclose only upon the subsequent admission, which was canceled by the patient, was reasonable. The doctors had no duty to do anything more than they had. Japanese commentator Norio Higuchi found this case very helpful, noting that:

> The decision takes a step forward at the least, even though, I admit, it is only a small step, from the previous rulings by courts. While the prior decisions have held it depends upon the doctor's discretion whether he should inform or not, the court says that the discretion in the doctor is limited to the questions as to whom, when and in how much detail he should inform.[21]

Professor Higuchi also argues that to conclude that the court found a duty to disclose and a right to self-determination only after a definitive diagnosis has been made oversimplifies the opinion. Instead, Higuchi believes that the physician had a duty to inform under the facts of this case, but properly exercised his discretion within the confines of that duty.

A Westerner is struck not so much with the amount of discretion ceded to physicians—essentially the state of U.S. law prior to the 1970s, and of British law today—but by the accepted concept that informing the patient's family is equivalent to (and perhaps superior to) informing the patient herself. The Japanese concept of the group may best explain the failure of informed consent to be adopted. Professor Hihito Kimura explains:

> Autonomy . . . is out of keeping with the Japanese cultural tradition. Our culture, nurtured in Buddhist and Confucian teaching, has developed the idea of suppress-

ing the egoistic self. To be autonomous and independent is sometimes regarded as egocentric. Thus, in Japan, each human being is dependent on others in the family, and the social, economic and political communities.[22]

Stephan Salzberg notes in his study of Japan's mental health laws that in the Japanese worldview, "autonomy, to a lesser or greater extent, yields to the nurturance and security provided by one's group, and especially one's family." He goes on to note that obtaining consent from family members instead of from the patient "is a common practice . . . especially when patients themselves are kept in the dark regarding their own cancerous or other life-threatening conditions."[23] Other Japanese observers concur:

> Even in cases where the patient is competent to give his or her individual consent, substitute consent by the family or close relatives is a common practice in order to avoid disturbing the patient emotionally . . . the Japanese favor being indirect and do not like complete information about a serious condition to be stated explicitly.[24]

Japan's failure to embrace Western notions of informed consent may also be dictated by the economics of its health care system. While the health sector is very strong on universal access and cost control, the general quality of care leaves something to be desired by Western standards. Medical training in Japan is relatively weak and classroom-based only, and little medical specialty certification exists. Physicians spend an average of less than five minutes with each patient they see, and all physicians are paid on the same tightly regulated fee-for-service schedule regardless of experience or training. Doctors increase their incomes by seeing patients repeatedly and by directly selling them an average of five drugs which are prescribed at each clinical encounter. Drug retailing accounts for as much as 40% of the average physician's income. Doctors also tend to hospitalize most of their patients in private solo-practice office-based clinics which they own, where the average patient stay is fifty-two days. Physicians resist sending patients to the relatively few Japanese hospitals offering sophisticated care because patients tend not to return thereafter for the lower-technology services they offer.

These entrepreneurial aspects of medical practice explain, among other things, why the Japanese spend a larger percentage of their health care expenditures on drugs (30%) than does any other country in the world. The comparable U.S. figure, for example, is approximately 7%. Not only do Japanese doctors prescribe and sell many drugs, but many of those drugs appear useless from a scientific perspective. For example, Krestin, an anticancer drug with no proven efficacy anywhere else in the world, has been one of the most popular drugs in Japan. Physicians apparently feel less guilty about failing to inform patients that they have cancer when they prescribe Krestin, because although Krestin is ineffective, it produces no debilitating side effects, either.

In short, the Japanese health care system "works" at a relatively low level of expenditure in large part because patients are rarely informed about diagnoses or about the relatively few available alternative forms of treatment. This suggests that major changes in the Japanese health care system will require doctors to give patients more information. Pressure is mounting to develop more specialty referral hospitals, but patients must be persuaded to utilize them. As the *Makino* case illustrates, more candid disclosures about diagnosis and treatment may also be required to secure patient compliance with the therapy physicians recommend.

Japan has only recently begun to accept brain-death criteria, and heart transplantation has thus been impossible in Japanese hospitals. Some observers contend that difficult interpersonal relationships among families and physicians at the time of death generate this resistance, not general religious or societal views about the innate meaning of death.[25] However, Japanese physicians must give families far more detailed explanations and much fuller disclosure, at a time when such discussions are not currently held, for Japan to implement brain-death criteria. Perhaps as a portent of change, the Japanese Ministry of Health and Welfare began arguing for modifications in traditional physician practices of nondisclosure in the early 1990s. The ministry has concluded that even in the case of terminally ill cancer patients, truthful diagnosis should be revealed.

CULTURE, CHOICE, AND RESOURCE ALLOCATION

Patient knowledge advances personal autonomy; it elevates consent to medical treatment from a flak jacket merely protecting doctors from battery liability to an enhancement of patient sovereignty. But not all cultures place the same value on truth-telling and on an individual's ability to make choices, especially where medical treatment has status as a public good. Informed consent doctrine both shapes and reflects societal value choices, and these vary from country to country and over time within countries.

Total expenditures on health care vary considerably from country to country as well. It is not just coincidence that the United States, which treats health care as a market good, spends far more money on the health sector (per capita, in absolute terms, and in percentage of gross domestic product [GDP]) than does any other country in the world. Moreover, it does so while approximately 14% of its population remains uninsured. Five years ago the United States spent 131% more per capita on health care than did Japan, and almost 200% more than the United Kingdom. For all that expenditure, however, the United States trails behind the United Kingdom, Japan, and many other industrialized nations in such basic health-outcome measurements as infant mortality, perinatal mortality, and male life expectancy.

The United States accords the highest status to informed consent in part because we engage in the fiction that patients actually exercise economic choice when they purchase medical services. Health care markets have traditionally deviated significantly from the competitive ideal, propelled by a variety of forces. Chief among these in all cultures are information problems and purchasing subsidies.

Medical information is often difficult for patients to assimilate and sometimes emotionally painful for them to absorb. Moreover, the financial ramifications of patients' treatment choices are usually obscured by health insurance and tax subsidies for medical and insurance purchases, if not by governmental provision of care. Defensive medicine and the technological imperative further skew health markets toward unnecessary services, particularly in the United States.

Different cultures take differing official approaches to health resource allocation. Some countries rely primarily on governmental price and spending controls, affecting everything from technology acquisition to hospital and physician reimbursement rates. For example, in the circumstances of tightly managed supply that exist in the United Kingdom, primary care physicians assume powerful gatekeeping functions; they must filter patient demand for the limited supply of specialist and high technology care. This entails correspondingly narrower scope for individual choice. When medical choice is constrained by supply limitations, telling patients about potentially beneficial, but economically unattainable, therapy can be criticized as inhumane. But it can also mobilize public opinion to challenge resource allocation inconsistent with societal values.[26]

The General Medical Council (which licenses British doctors) explicitly reinforces the gatekeeping function by warning in its principles of professional conduct: "a specialist should not usually accept a patient without reference from the patient's general practitioner." Violation of this ethical rule could at least theoretically result in licensure sanctions. The British Medical Association contemplates political activism when its ethical principles state, "the doctor may decide to tell the patient that [specialist] treatment is not available because of lack of funds," adding that "patients may complain to politicians."

In countries officially dependent on gatekeeping like the United Kingdom, informed consent doctrine favors professional rather than patient-oriented standards of disclosure, particularly with regard to treatment alternatives. Other cultures prefer to let a more entrepreneurial market set the basic dimensions for health sector investment. U.S. informed consent law generally reflects support for market allocation mechanisms and thus tends to expand the possibilities for patient choice through more thorough-going informed consent requirements.

But how can Japan be explained, where physicians are highly entrepreneurial and most hospitals and all clinics are privately owned, yet the law supports keeping patients in the dark about diagnoses of serious illness? To begin with, Japan does not impose the budgetary controls that cap total health care spending in the United Kingdom, although it regulates physician fees tightly and capped the number of hospital beds in 1985. It is dangerous for outsiders to generalize about any culture. Nonetheless, cultural analysts from both Japan and America agree that in Japan individuality is presumed subservient to group needs and ideals; as a consequence the proper role of the patient is to follow the instructions of the physician.[27]

Regardless of official government policy concerning health sector resource allocation, in practice significant flexibility usually exists within any society. This flexibility is strongly influenced by what patients, health policy experts, and financiers actually know, or think they know, about the availability and efficacy of medical services. In the majority of industrialized nations, where health care is considered a public good in essence guaranteed by government, spending caps, regulated fees, and central planning for capital expenditures are philosophically *de rigeur*.

Perfect health sector efficiency and equity are unattainable goals for any society; neither scientific truth nor the human condition remains static, and economic resources are never infinite. Setting limits on medical expenditures seems related to a society's view of mortality, but it begins with a recognition that limits are necessary. British Minister of Health Enoch Powell aptly described the demand for medical care as potentially infinite:

> There is virtually no limit to the amount of medical care an individual is capable of absorbing . . . not only is the range of treatable conditions huge and rapidly growing; there is also a vast range of quality in the treatment of these conditions. . . . There is hardly a type of condition from the most trivial to the gravest which is not susceptible of alternative treatments under conditions affording a wide range of skill, care, comfort, privacy, efficiency [etc.] . . . there is a multiplier effect of successful medical treatment. Improvement in expectation of survival results in lives that demand further medical care. The poorer (medically speaking) the quality of the lives preserved by advancing medical science, the more intense are the demands they continue to make. In short, the appetite for medical treatment *vient en mangeant* [the more you get the more you want].[28]

Any country's health policy must continuously grapple with economic scarcity and scientific, political, and cultural change. The successes and failures of other systems can be illuminating, but cultural attitudes toward medical information must be unearthed and understood if reform imported from other countries is to succeed in new environments.

CULTURE AND DEATH

How can we account for the continuing formal differences in informed consent doctrine in the United States, Britain, and Japan, notwithstanding burgeoning respect for autonomy in the latter two countries and a new appreciation for setting limits in the United States? One explanation could be that although the governing legal theories are different, reflecting different cultural expectations, physician disclosure practices are actually quite similar. Japanese researcher Naoko Miyaji conducted structured interviews with 32 American East Coast physicians in various specialties. She found that while physicians routinely told patients about their diagnosis, when dealing with prognosis, "many physicians try to give patients very vague information." Half of the physicians would not explicitly tell patients they were dying. Doctors often justify their evasion by explaining that patients usually know this anyway, but as Miyaji observes, there may be "a significant gap between the patient's perception and the physician's." Miyaji notes the information-giving process can be used as much to control the situation as information-withholding, and regarding prognosis information, she concludes: "physicians' focusing on treatment options and leaving out prognosis (the worst part of the information) is the key to understanding the coexistence of information control with patient-centered ethical norms in the context of current American medicine."[29]

These studies and the *Arato* case discussed in the last chapter support the hypothesis that U.S. doctors in fact behave similarly to those Japanese physicians who will not tell patients they have cancer because they believe patients see cancer as a death sentence, and will become depressed if informed of their diagnosis. They also behave like British doctors, who are able to rationalize economic limits on their ability to offer cancer patients every kind of sophisticated therapy as long as they can avoid getting "eyeball to eyeball," where frank conversation might have to ensue. Not surprisingly, the hospice movement, which rejects heroic medical treatment and is frankly designed to ease the natural transition to death, first flowered in England.

A culture's general attitude toward death seems to dictate what prognosis information will be provided to patients. Where cultures are more homogeneous than is the United States, such as those of Japan and England, more cultural agreement on treatment recommendations would be expected, so prognosis disclosure may be less important. Moreover, the closer the physician and patient are in terms of economic class and views of death, the less likely explicit disclosure will be seen as necessary or appropriate. On the other hand, in the United States, where cultural diversity is more pronounced and there is a wider gulf between the economic and spiritual belief systems of physicians and those of their patients, the law is needed to enforce disclosures because patients cannot trust their doctors to act based on shared values. However, even legal sanctions will often be insufficient to make candid disclosure a reality.

Ultimately a culture's view of death, and the role of medicine in preventing or postponing it, is at work when unpleasant or uncertain medical facts are not communicated to patients. In the United States, for example, we seem to accept that prolonging life (at virtually any price) is a reasonable goal for medicine. Thus, procedures are introduced and utilized that offer hope of extending life without regard to cost or even to the quality of the life prolonged. Our seemingly automatic use of technology to protract the dying process has spawned development of a clearly articulated right to refuse treatment. More than 50 state appeals court decisions and 3 opinions of the U.S. Supreme Court have affirmed this patient prerogative. In a country where, still, no right of access to basic health services exists, and where the major problem for approximately 40 million Americans is obtaining any medical care at all, at least outside hospital emergency rooms, this seems remarkable. The rallying cry of U.S. medical ethics remains not the right to health care, but the right to die. We continue to debate physician-assisted suicide and euthanasia far more passionately than we debated the minimum or benchmark benefits package. Americans rightly fear that doctors often ignore their wishes to refuse treatment and for proper medication for pain control near the end of life. Physician surveys consistently indicate that doctors routinely ignore patient wishes to end treatment, undermedicate for pain, and continue to see death as professional failure.

Daniel Callahan seems correct in asserting that the U.S. health care system is ultimately driven by an attempt to cope with our own mortality. Illness is seen not as leading to inevitable death but as a challenge to be overcome. Callahan has compared improvements in medical care with space exploration, noting that, "No matter how far you go, there's always farther you can go." He believes U.S. society will never accept limits on either medical expenditures or personal autonomy until we learn to accept our own mortality. In his words:

> To me, the great question is: How are we going to think about progress in the future? What kind of progress is genuinely of benefit to people? . . . I think the answer has to be something more complex than the fact that people get sick and die. For me, the fundamental reality underlying progress is that *no matter how far we go, people are still going to get sick and they are still going to die.* No matter how much money we throw into progress, that fundamental human reality will remain [emphasis added].[30]

Callahan has also asserted that there are no acceptable causes of death in the United States; we set up national institutes of health designed to "prevent" death from all its leading causes. Ivan Illich argues that in "every society the dominant image of death determines the prevalent concept of health." He continues, "A society's image of death reveals the level of independence of its people, their personal relatedness, self-reliance and aliveness." Illich traces Western civilization's view of death as it has evolved from "God's call," to a natural occurrence, to a force of nature, to an "untimely" event, to "the outcome of a specific disease certified by the doctor." In his view, "The hope of doctors to control the outcome of specific diseases gave rise to the myth that they had power over death." And, one might add, it fueled their patients' hopes that death could be overcome.

In a market-driven economy, where physicians are producers and patients are consumers, Illich argues that society permits people to die only when their bodies "refuse any further input of treatment," after which they "become useless not only as a producer but also as a consumer . . . [and] must finally be written off as a total loss."[31] In this intensive care unit (ICU)–maximal-treatment model, "Death has become the ultimate form of consumer resistance."

In countries like Japan and England which do not spend inordinate amounts of money on health care at the end of life, failure to discuss prognosis seems to be socially acceptable because death is not viewed as professional defeat. It is accepted as both natural and necessary by physicians and patients alike. As Rihito Kamura has explained of Japan, "Death is an integral part of the Japanese cultural tradition. Most Japanese people resist the modern, technological death in which machines can supplant important rituals surrounding death and dying."[32] Because members of these relatively more homogeneous societies share common perceptions about how much medical intervention is appropriate at the end of life, comprehensive discussion of treatment alternatives between doctor and patient seems less necessary.

In the more pluralistic U.S. society, however, there is less social consensus on the role of medicine toward the end of life, and physician biases toward more aggressive treatment often offend the value systems of many Americans. Great lengths are gone to, from executing living wills, to petitioning courts to terminate treatment, to committing suicide, to assert that merely prolonging the dying process is unacceptable. Physicians often tend to treat patients with terminal illness aggressively for a variety of motives, including misplaced fear of civil (or even criminal) litigation if they do not. Their heroic efforts to ward off the inevitable often compromise the quality of their patients' remaining lives in ways that doctors rarely elect for themselves. When physicians impart straightforward information about prognosis, their patients are able to exercise the same degree of informed choice about end-of-life care as physicians can. In such situations, the right to refuse treatment may be more important to patient self-determination than the ability to demand it, or even to choose among options. Accurate information about prognosis thus promotes patient autonomy and can save significant health care expenditures on treatment that many informed patients would decline.

The new emphasis on evidence-based medicine in the United States could result in both better informed patients and savings in medical expenditures.[33] These studies will identify treatments and procedures falling into a variety of efficacy categories. "Never beneficial" or "futile" treatments will (or arguably should be) simply eliminated from the medical care system, at least insofar as they are financed by government insurance. But most treatments will be at least marginally beneficial for some patients.

Jack Wennberg has suggested, correctly I believe, that patients should make final treatment choices based in large measure on their own evaluation of outcomes data, as applied to their own lives. An early Wennberg study, for example, demonstrated that the prostate surgery which many physicians recommended was done primarily to relieve symptoms. When the patients themselves were queried, however, their attitudes toward their symptoms varied; some were not bothered much at all by them. Patients also differed from doctors in their views of treatment risks, "particularly surgery-induced impotence and operative mortality." The key to "reducing variations," in Wennberg's words, thus depends not on learning more from laboratory findings or clinical exams, but "on learning what patients want, and this can only be ascertained by asking patients . . . [who should be informed] that they indeed have a choice and that their choice should depend on their own preferences."[34] When fully informed of the risks and benefits, only one of five severely symptomatic men actually chose prostate surgery.

DEATH AND CHOICE

Our cover story in the United States is choice. But the payment system, reinforced by fear of death, is actually the dominant force driving the American health sector. The same engine drives medical services in Japan and the United Kingdom, but in different directions. A country's economic ideology and its cultural beliefs concerning death will be reflected in its informed consent laws. Where individualism is highly prized and medical care is seen as a market good, legal doctrine will place a high premium on information disclosure to facilitate patient-consumer choices, especially among treatment alternatives. Countries like England and Japan with more collective notions about health care, and in which citizens are more likely to defer to authority, will be less interested in choice and thus less inclined to emphasize full disclosure or truth-telling. Instead, the content of disclosure will generally be discretionary with physicians.

Nonetheless, in all countries, informed consent probably gets more attention than it deserves with regard to treatment alternatives; physicians in fact make decisions about therapy for their patients rather than with them. This may be inevitable given information asymmetry, and it may be what even American courts mean when they designate the doctor–patient relationship as a trust or a fiduciary relationship. The medical profession does get to set its own standards for practice in the last analysis, and for most diseases physician treatment preferences leave room for little real patient choice. It will take a radical restructuring of information collection, analysis, and availability to change this.

Choice, at least the choice to forgo treatment altogether, seems to be most contested and most necessary at the end of life. In Japan, where few or no heroic efforts are made to prolong the life of dying patients, there is little interest in the right-to-die movement. In the United States, however, following cases like those of Karen Ann Quinlan and Nancy Cruzan, the right to refuse treatment has become central to the self-determination debate and is likely to be dominant in future resource allocation controversies as well. With this in mind, taking informed consent more seriously with regard to prognosis should help to make health systems more responsive to the true preferences of their respective patient populations.

There is no justification for forcing unwanted, and often expensive and ultimately useless, treatment on citizens at life's end. Nor will most patients demand futile, painful and expensive therapy once they are fully informed. Thus, informed consent, especially regarding the truth about prognosis, may be the only way the United States can, consistent with cultural expectations about patient autonomy, limit the use of expensive and ineffective treatment at the end of life. It may also be one of the few ways we can avoid massive new expenditures in order to underwrite universal access. This chapter opened with some thoughts from a British novelist; and it seems appropriate to close with the views of an American, William S. Burroughs, who ends his novel on our search for immortality, *The Western Lands*, by asking: "How long does it take a man to learn that he does not, cannot want what he 'wants'?" In the next chapter I explore the lamentable case of Baby K, a sad struggle between a mother and her anencephalic child's physicians and hospital involving mistrust and miscommunication that led to futile, expensive, and intensive care.

CHAPTER SEVEN

Treating the Untreatable

When treatment is not possible, should there still a choice about whether or not to treat? And if a technological intervention is characterized as a choice, whose choice is it—the patient's, the physician's, or someone else's such as a judge's? The case of a child known as Baby K can be used to explore these questions in an extreme context.[1] Whether or not it is ultimately concluded that there actually is a choice, and the decisionmaker is identified, there is little doubt that it is some choice.

Almost two decades ago *New England Journal of Medicine* editor Franz J. Ingelfinger predicted that if physicians kept turning to the courts "to resolve essentially medical matters," the medical profession's unfortunate "dependence on the lawyer in reaching essentially medical decisions will continue."[2] We can argue about what decisions or choices are "essentially medical," but the trend that worried Ingelfinger has continued, and perhaps reached its logical conclusion when physicians and a hospital sought legal and judicial guidance about how to treat an anencephalic infant known as Baby K.

TREATING BABY K

Baby K was born by cesarean section on October 13, 1992, at Fairfax Hospital in Falls Church, Virginia. Anencephaly (the absence of any higher brain) was diagnosed prenatally, and her mother decided to continue the pregnancy despite recommendations for abortion from both her obstetrician and neonatologist. The newborn had difficulty breathing at birth, and mechanical ventilation was begun. Within days the physicians began urging the mother (the father was only distantly involved) to agree to discontinue ventilation, since it served no therapeutic or palliative purpose and was therefore medically inappropriate. The mother refused. The physicians turned to the hospital's ethics committee and met with a subcommittee composed of a family practitioner, a psychiatrist, and a minister. A week later, the subcommittee concluded that if the impasse between the physicians and the mother continued, legal resolution should be sought.

Baby K was transferred to a skilled nursing home six weeks later, when she was not dependent on mechanical ventilation. Her mother agreed to the transfer on condition that the hospital would take Baby K back if her respiratory difficulties recurred. Approximately two months later, Baby K returned to the hospital for ventilatory support. She returned at least five times before her death in 1995. She may have been the longest-lived anencephalic in medical history.[3]

When Baby K was in the nursing home, Fairfax Hospital went to federal court seeking a ruling that it was not obligated to render "inappropriate" medical treatment to Baby K under existing federal and state law should Baby K again come to their emergency department in respiratory distress. Her mother's position was that "all human life has value, including her anencephalic daughter's life." She has "a firm Christian faith . . . [and] believes that God will work a miracle if that is his will . . . God, and not other humans, should decide the moment of her daughter's death." The hospital, the guardian ad litem appointed by the court, and Baby K's father all believed that further ventilatory assistance to Baby K was medically and ethically inappropriate.

THE TRIAL COURT

The trial judge, District Court Judge Claude Hilton, focused almost exclusively on antidiscrimination legislation in his opinion. Under the federal Emergency Medical Treatment and Active Labor Act (EMTALA) enacted by Congress to prevent the arbitrary refusal of treatment to uninsured people ("patient dumping"), all hospitals with emergency departments that receive Medicare funds must treat any person who arrives with an emergency medical condition and must continue appropriate treatment until the person's condition is stabilized and the person can be safely transferred.[4] Fairfax Hospital conceded that respiratory distress was an emergency condition but argued that the statute should be interpreted to include an exception for treatment deemed "futile" or "inhumane" by the hospital physicians. The judge disagreed for two reasons: First, the statute does not contain this exception; and second, even if it did, the exception would not apply to Baby K because her breathing could be restored. Therefore the mechanical ventilation could not be considered either futile or inhumane. The judge added: "To hold otherwise would allow hospitals to deny emergency treatment to numerous classes of patients, such as accident victims who have terminal cancer or AIDS, on the grounds that they eventually will die anyway from those diseases and that emergency care for them would therefore be futile."[5]

Judge Hilton also ruled that section 504 of the Rehabilitation Act[6] and the Americans with Disabilities Act both prohibited discrimination against Baby K based on her anencephaly. Finally, the judge ruled that as a general matter of law, "absent a finding of neglect or abuse" parents have the right to make medical treatment decisions for their children. When parents disagree with each other, the judge concluded that courts should support the parent who decides "in favor of life."

THE COURT OF APPEALS

In February 1994, the U.S. Court of Appeals, in a 2–1 opinion, affirmed the judgment of the trial court.[7] The appeals court, however, examined only one question in reaching its decision: Did Congress, in passing EMTALA, provide an exception for anencephalic infants (or anyone else) in respiratory distress? The court found the language of the statute clear and unambiguous: Hospitals are required to stabilize the medical condition creating the emergency. In the court's words, "a straightforward application of the statute obligates the hospital to provide respiratory support to Baby K when she arrives at the emergency department of the hospital in respiratory distress and treatment is requested on her behalf."

In making its case, the hospital suggested four reasons why the rule should not apply to Baby K, all of which were rejected. Two of the reasons merit discussion. The first was that Baby K's emergency condition was not respiratory distress, but anencephaly. The court disagreed, noting that it was her respiratory distress, not her anencephaly, that brought her to the emergency department. Second, the hospital argued that Congress did not "intend to require physicians to provide medical treatment outside the prevailing standard of medical care" in passing EMTALA. The appeals court seemed to agree with the hospital that the "prevailing standard of medical care for infants with anencephaly is to provide only warmth, nutrition, and hydration." Nonetheless, the court held that the statutory language was "unambiguous" and included no such limitation on the hospital's responsibility to stabilize emergency conditions:

> We recognize the dilemma facing physicians who are requested to provide treatment they consider morally and ethically inappropriate, but we cannot ignore the plain language of the statute because to do so would transcend our judicial function. . . . The appropriate branch to redress the policy concerns of the hospital is Congress.

Later in its decision the appeals court reiterated the point: "It is beyond the limits of the court's judicial function to address the moral or ethical propriety of providing emergency stabilizing medical treatment to anencephalic infants." The court concluded that EMTALA makes no exception either for such infants or for "comatose patients, those with lung cancer, or those with muscular dystrophy— all of whom may repeatedly seek emergency stabilizing treatment for respiratory distress and also possess an underlying medical condition that severely affects their quality of life and ultimately may result in their death."

The dissenting justice argued that EMTALA was enacted to prevent patients from being dumped for economic reasons and that since dumping was not an issue with Baby K, the statute was irrelevant. He also argued that it was wrong to consider Baby K's treatment as involving a series of discrete emergency conditions; rather, her care should be "regarded as a continuum," since there is "no medical treatment that can improve her condition [of permanent unconsciousness]."

MIXED MESSAGES AND CONFUSED ROLES

Many misjudgments were made in this case, but all relate to the failure to distinguish among medical standards, ethical precepts, and legal requirements. After birth, Baby K was given mechanical ventilation. This was a medical misjudgment (assuming the physicians really believed it was medically inappropriate), and giving the mother the choice of ventilation may have given her the impression that the doctors would provide medically inappropriate treatment to her child if she so desired. Since the physicians had known for months that she would be delivering an anencephalic baby, the issue of mechanical ventilation should have been resolved with the mother before the birth. If the physicians believed (on the basis of good and accepted medical standards) that mechanical ventilation was contraindicated, the mother should have been informed that it would not be used and given an opportunity to find alternate care givers.[8] If ventilation was to be used, the goal of this intervention (e.g., to confirm the diagnosis) should have been clearly specified, and support should have continued only until the goal was reached or was found to be unattainable.

Law Professor Charles DiSalvo has gone further, arguing that use of medical technologies like the ventilator have become so automatic that "from the start, there is no choice, no independent human volition, no reasoned decisionmaking." He also quotes physician Eric Cassell, who argues that medical technology can so radically transform the doctor–patient relationship that "for the patient, the technology becomes the doctor and for the doctor, the technology becomes the patient." As for Baby K's mother, DiSalvo believes her faith in God was in fact "an idolatry of physical life" founded on faith in medical technology.[9]

The ethics subcommittee at the hospital also misconstrued its role. It seems to have discussed nothing ethical at all. Composed of two physicians and a minister, it gave advice on medical practice and legal strategy, concluding that if the physicians could not reach agreement with the mother, the hospital should seek judicial relief. The subcommittee should have insisted that discussion with the mother continue until a resolution was reached, and it should have tried to facilitate this communication.

The hospital's administrators and attorney overreacted, though much more predictably. Instead of supporting their physicians in their application of existing medical standards or encouraging further discussion with the mother, they decided to go to court. They saw Baby K's ventilatory support as a legal issue that might affect the institution, rather than a question of medical practice or medical ethics.

The chief misjudgment by the trial judge was to try to act like a physician. His opinion can best be understood as that of a medical consultant who believes he has been asked one technical question: Can ventilatory support help an anencephalic infant in respiratory distress breath more easily? His answer was yes. The judge viewed this as a case of arbitrary discrimination by physicians against a mentally handicapped patient. He was correct that hospitals with emergency departments must provide medically appropriate treatment to stabilize the condition of all emergency patients. The physicians' desire not to give Baby K ventilatory support was, however, explained not by prejudice or financial concern, but instead by adherence to reasonable medical standards. Thus, the judge is chillingly wrong to equate Baby K (and anencephalic infants as a class) with patients with cancer or AIDS who are injured in automobile accidents. It is because of her anencephaly itself that Baby K cannot benefit from any medical intervention. Patients with AIDS or cancer can, of course, benefit from emergency treatment.

To treat Baby K is not, however, inhumane (as the physicians argued), since she can neither feel pain nor suffer. But it is degrading to treat her for either our own symbolic purposes or those of her mother, because to do so is to treat her as an object—as a means to someone else's ends.[10] If the mere maintenance of biologic functioning in the absence of cortical function (vitalism) were a reasonable medical goal, physicians would be prohibited from ever discontinuing cardiopulmonary resuscitation in any patient, since it maintains circulation and ventilation. Nor has the judgment about treating anencephalic infants been made only by physicians. Congress and the executive branch have also been involved—the Baby Doe rules, for example, specifically recognized limits on care of anencephalic infants and the role of reasonable medical judgment in setting those limits.[11] The regulations themselves specified, and Surgeon General C. Everett Koop agreed, that a decision not to treat an anencephalic newborn is not discriminatory if based on a "legitimate medical judgment" that treatment would be "futile" because such treatment would "do no more than temporarily prolong the act of dying."[12] A parental request for treatment does not alter the physician's obligation to exercise reasonable medical judgment. The Child Abuse Amendments of 1984 are also consistent with this view.

By the time the case reached the rarefied atmosphere of the Court of Appeals, the outcome was predictable. In answering its narrow question about the reach of EMTALA, the appeals court was correct: Congress provided no exceptions for anencephalic infants. On the other hand, I think the hospital was also correct in asserting that Congress did not intend to require physicians to provide emergency care "outside the prevailing standard of medical care." Certainly neither side could point to any statute by which Congress has ever required physicians to violate existing standards of medical care. Nor is there any evidence that Congress intended to amend or in any way change the Baby Doe rules with EMTALA. The appeals court seems to have simply believed that the trial court had not acted unreasonably in favoring a mother who wanted her child treated over a hospital that wanted the child to die sooner rather than later.

MEDICAL STANDARDS

The logic of EMTALA as interpreted by these courts, although understandable in context, is incorrect because the technological imperative is limitless. To avoid cases like this one, Congress should have included the phrase "consistent with reasonable medical standards" in its requirement for patient stabilization in the emergency department. If the legal rule really were that hospitals and physicians have to provide any and all life-saving treatments for anencephalic infants that are wanted by the parents, they could be required to provide not only ventilatory support, but also other types of support, such as kidney dialysis for renal failure, and ultimately a heart-assist device when the child's heart begins deteriorating. As the dissenting judge properly argued, the focus must be on the patient as a person, not on the patient as an assemblage of disconnected organ systems.

It is true that parents have (and should have) wide discretion in choosing among treatment options for their children. In the absence of evidence that a particular choice constitutes child abuse or neglect, we should presume that families can make the best decisions for their children. But it does not follow that physicians must do whatever parents (or adult patients themselves) order them to do regardless of standards of medical practice. Parents can choose among medically reasonable treatment alternatives, but they cannot prescribe treatment or demand that they or their children be mistreated.[13]

In the leading Supreme Court case cited by the trial judge, the Court upheld a state statute that permitted parents to commit a minor child to a mental institution without first providing the child with a court hearing.[14] But it did so only because the Court believed that the psychiatrist would make an independent medical assessment that institutionalized care was in the child's best interests. In another case, the Court ruled that retarded persons in state custody have a constitutional right to habilitation, but the content of that right should be left to the judgment of medical professionals.[15] Thus, it is not the law that physicians must do whatever parents want. Rather, the law that parents should usually consent to treatment decisions made for their children is based on the premise that physicians will exercise independent medical judgment and not follow parental decisions if the physician believes they are not in the best interest of the child. In passing EMTALA, Congress was responding to situations in which physicians were refusing to treat patients in emergencies for economic reasons—not because of any exercise of medical judgment or standards of medical practice.

Because contemporary medicine is often mischaracterized as a consumer good, and because many physicians and hospitals treat medicine as a business in which medical services are provided on the basis of patient desire rather than medical indications, it is becoming more and more difficult for physicians to refuse to do whatever patients and their families demand. Thus, for example, it is impossible for physicians to credibly argue that treating patients in persistent vegetative states is contrary to standards of medical practice, because most physicians actually provide continuing treatment for permanently unconscious patients if the family insists.[16] Treating medical care as a consumer good is a central reason why medical costs are out of control and why managed care plans that give physicians financial incentives not to treat seem so attractive to many employers and policymakers.

After the Baby K case was decided, a survey of 43 childrens hospitals was done with responses obtained from all neonatal intensive care unit directors, all ethics committee chairpersons, and 22 emergency department directors. None of these respondents could recall that their hospital had ever ventilated an anencephalic infant upon parental demand. Nonetheless, the surveyors concluded from their phone interviews that because of the possibility of "unwanted litigation and adverse publicity," these hospitals would have done the same thing as Fairfax Hospital did in the face of a mother who insisted on treatment. The surveyors thus concluded that the status quo is to provide futile treatment on demand and that this "does nothing more than confirm that physicians will do whatever patients and families want, regardless of the treatments' benefits."[17] Thus is the illusion of patient choice preserved, even in the face of medical futility. Some choice.

WHAT SHOULD BE DONE?

Before the case of Baby K, the medical standard of practice was not to provide artificial ventilation to anencephalic infants. Now physicians in emergency departments are legally obligated to provide medical assistance, ventilatory and otherwise, to anencephalic infants who need it to survive. Emergency physicians can live with this rule because a case like Baby K is not likely to occur again. There are three possible future scenarios. In the first, physicians will do whatever patients want (as long as they can pay for it), because medicine will be seen as a consumer commodity like breakfast cereal and toothpaste. This will make medicine even more unbearably expensive than it is. Therefore, the second scenario, a variation of Ingelfinger's vision, is more likely. The task of defining "appropriate medical care" will be removed from physicians altogether and put in the hands of payors and government regulators who will decide the content of medicine, at least partially based on outcomes data.

To avoid either of these scenarios, physicians must work toward a third, in which they not only set standards for medical practice but also follow them. Physicians cannot expect parents, trial court judges, insurance companies, or government regulators to take medical practice standards more seriously than they do themselves. If physicians cannot set standards for the treatment of anencephalic infants and adhere to them, standard-setting by physicians is a dead issue. In the next chapter I continue the discussion of medical standard setting by examining patient and physician choice of an outlawed therapy: medical marijuana.

CHAPTER EIGHT

Outlawed Choices

Marijuana is unique among illegal drugs in its political symbolism, its safety, and its wide use.[1] More than 65 million Americans have tried marijuana, with no associated increase in mortality.[2] Since the federal government first tried to tax it out of existence in 1937, at least partly in response to the 1936 film *Reefer Madness*, marijuana has remained at the center of controversy. Now physicians are becoming more actively involved. Most recently, the federal drug policy against any use of marijuana has been challenged by California's attempt to legalize its use by certain patients on the recommendation of their physicians. The federal government responded by threatening California physicians who recommend marijuana to their sick patients with investigation and loss of their prescription privileges under Drug Enforcement Administration (DEA) regulations.[3]

The editor in chief of the *New England Journal of Medicine*, Jerome Kassirer, wrote that prohibiting physicians from helping their suffering patients by suggesting that they use marijuana is "misguided, heavy-handed, and inhumane."[4] He recommended that marijuana be reclassified as a Schedule II drug and made available by prescription without the usual requirement of controlled clinical trials. Most states had previously passed laws that permitted their citizens to use marijuana for medicinal purposes under some circumstances. California's law seems to have engendered a uniquely harsh federal response because California is a large, trend-setting state; because its new marijuana law is very broad compared to others; and because it was passed by popular referendum. In this chapter I explore the reaction to the new California law and its implications for the choice of marijuana as an adjuvant treatment of serious illnesses, especially cancer and AIDS.

THE CALIFORNIA MARIJUANA PROPOSITION

In the fall of 1996, California voters approved the Medical Marijuana Initiative (Proposition 215) by a vote of 56 to 44%. The law is entitled the Compassionate Use Act of 1996, and its purpose is to give Californians the right to possess and cultivate marijuana for medical purposes "where that medical use is deemed appropriate and has been recommended by a physician who has determined that the person's health would benefit from the use of marijuana in the treatment of cancer, anorexia, AIDS, chronic pain, spasticity, glaucoma, arthritis, migraine, or any other illness for which marijuana provides relief." Nothing in the act permits persons using marijuana for medical purposes to engage in conduct that endangers others (such as driving under the influence), condones "the diversion of marijuana for nonmedical purposes," or permits the buying or selling of marijuana. The two operative sections of the law are:

(c) Notwithstanding any other provision of law, no physician in this state shall be punished, or denied any right or privilege, for having recommended marijuana to a patient for medical purposes.

(d) [existing California law] . . . relating to the possession of marijuana . . . [and the] cultivation of marijuana, shall not apply to a patient, or to a patient's primary caregiver [the person who has consistently assumed responsibility for the patient's housing, health, or safety] who possesses or cultivates marijuana for the personal medical purposes of the patient upon the written or oral recommendation or approval of a physician.[5]

The primary purpose of this law is to provide a specified group of patients with an affirmative defense to the charge of possession and cultivation of marijuana, the defense of medical necessity. To use this defense, the patient must be able to show that his or her physician recommended or approved of the use of marijuana either orally or in writing. Obviously, a note from a physician is better evidence than a simple assertion that "my doctor said this would be good for me," and most patients will want a written statement to help protect them from problems with the police. Nothing in this law changes current law against buying or selling marijuana or affects federal law; it merely provides that qualified patients and their primary caregivers can possess and cultivate their own marijuana for personal medicinal purposes without violating state drug laws.

COMPASSION AND USE OF UNAPPROVED DRUGS

The federal government has been in the business of regulating drugs for almost a century, and few exceptions have ever been made to basic rules of the Food and Drug Administration (FDA), even for patients with cancer or AIDS. In 1979, for example, the FDA was successful in convincing a unanimous U.S. Supreme Court that Congress intended no exception for terminally ill cancer patients who sought to take laetrile, an unapproved drug, for cancer. The FDA's primary rationale was that use of this unapproved and useless drug could prevent patients from seeking conventional cancer treatments that offered them at least some chance of a cure.[6] Under President Ronald Reagan, however, the FDA responded with a great deal more flexibility to the AIDS epidemic and permitted the use and sale of drugs not approved (but in use in ongoing clinical trials) if, among other things, "the drug [was] intended to treat a serious or immediately life-threatening disease."[7] More surprisingly, the FDA also permitted individual patients to import unapproved drugs from other countries for their personal, medical use. These regulations were almost purely political, had no scientific basis, and tended to conflate treatment and research and to undermine the very purpose of clinical trials.[8] The theory used to justify these exceptions to federal drug laws was the very one rejected by the Supreme Court in the laetrile case: Terminally ill patients have "nothing to lose" and should not be deprived of the hope (even false hope) that they might escape death.

Given this history, it is not surprising that the advocates of the medicinal use of marijuana concentrate their reform efforts on helping patients with cancer ameliorate the adverse effects of chemotherapy and helping patients with AIDS counteract weight loss and fight their disease. Virtually no one thinks it is reasonable to initiate criminal prosecution of patients with cancer or AIDS who use marijuana on the advice of their physicians to help them through conventional medical treatment for their disease. Anecdotal evidence of the effectiveness of smoked marijuana abounds.[9] Perhaps the most convincing is the account of Harvard professor and author Stephen Jay Gould, one of the world's first survivors of abdominal mesothelioma. When Gould started intravenous chemotherapy, he writes:

> Absolutely nothing in the available arsenal of anti-emetics worked at all. I was miserable and came to dread the frequent treatments with an almost perverse intensity. I had heard that marijuana often worked well against nausea. I was reluctant to try it because I have never smoked any substance habitually (and didn't even know how to inhale). Moreover, I had tried marijuana twice [in the sixties] . . . and had hated it . . . marijuana worked like a charm. . . . [T]he sheer bliss of not experiencing nausea—and not having to fear it for all the days intervening between treatments—was the greatest boost I received in all my year of treatment, and surely the most important effect upon my eventual cure.[10]

Similarly, in patients with AIDS, marijuana has been credited with counteracting such side effects of treatment as severe nausea, vomiting, loss of appetite, and fatigue, as well as stimulating the appetite to help prevent weight loss.

WHITE HOUSE PRESS CONFERENCE

Had the California proposition been limited to the use of marijuana for terminal illnesses such as cancer and AIDS, it would probably have caused much less concern. Arizona passed a much broader initiative that permitted physicians to prescribe any drug on Schedule I, but in April 1997 the Arizona legislature amended the law to apply only to drugs approved by the FDA, thus effectively repealing it.[11] The California law applies only to marijuana but makes it available for a wide range of medical conditions, including anorexia, pain, spasticity, glaucoma, arthritis, migraine "or any other illness for which marijuana provides relief." This very broad definition of the potential medicinal uses of marijuana seemed an explicit endorsement of the drug itself, which the Clinton administration and others believed to be sending the wrong message to America's youth. Two months later the Clinton administration announced that it would vigorously oppose the implementation of the California proposition and the Arizona law.

General Barry McCaffrey, director of the Office of National Drug Control Policy, announced at a White House news conference on December 30, 1996, that "Nothing has changed. Federal law is unaffected by these propositions." McCaffrey expressed concern that marijuana is a "gateway drug" for children and that the law might have potential impact on them. As for the potential medicinal uses of marijuana, he said:

> This is not a medical proposition. This is the legalization of drugs that we're concerned about. Here's what the medical advisor in the state of California saw as the potential uses of marijuana [shows a slide] . . . it includes recalling forgotten memories, cough suppressants, Parkinson's disease, writer's cramp. *This is not medicine. This is a Cheech and Chong show.* And now what we are committed to doing is to look in a scientific way at any proposition that would bring a new medicine to the assistance of the American medical establishment [emphasis added].

Secretary of Health and Human Services Donna Shalala said that the initiatives reinforced the growing belief among Americans that marijuana is not harmful, whereas the administration remained "opposed to the legalization of marijuana [because] all available research has concluded that marijuana is dangerous to our health." Nonetheless, she did say that the National Institutes of Health (NIH) would continue to support and review "peer-reviewed" and "scientifically valid" research on "the possible usefulness of smoked marijuana in the limited circumstances where available medications have failed to provide relief for individual patients."

Finally, Attorney General Janet Reno announced that physicians who followed the terms of the California law would be the new targets of federal law enforcement (instead of drug dealers) and threatened physicians with loss of their registrations with the Drug Enforcement Agency (DEA) and with exclusion from participation in Medicare and Medicaid. She stated:

> federal law still applies . . . U.S. attorneys in both states will continue to review cases for prosecution and DEA officials will review cases as they have to determine whether to revoke the registration of any physician who recommends or prescribes so-called Schedule I controlled substances. *We will not turn a blind eye toward our responsibility to enforce federal law and to preserve the integrity*

of medical and scientific process to determine if drugs have medical value before allowing them to be used [emphasis added].

DOCTOR–PATIENT CONVERSATIONS

Two basic issues are raised by the administration's position. One involves government regulation of doctor–patient conversations, and the other involves the quality of evidence necessary to make marijuana available by prescription. A group of California physicians filed suit against McCaffrey, Reno, and Shalala, arguing that the threats of prosecution against physicians for talking to their patients violate their 1st Amendment rights and interfere with their ability as physicians to use "their best medical judgment in the context of a bona fide physician–patient relationship."[12]

In the only comparable case to reach the U.S. Supreme Court, the Court narrowly upheld a gag rule related to discussing abortion in federally funded Title X family-planning clinics.[13] The Court upheld the gag rule because Congress could reasonably limit the types of medical services available at federally funded facilities. The Court was able to sidestep the 1st Amendment issue because patients (at least in theory) had access to other doctors who had an obligation to furnish them with full information, and the doctor–patient relationship in a Title X clinic was characterized as not "all-encompassing" but rather limited only to preconception counseling:

> The Title X program regulations do not significantly impinge upon the doctor–patient relationship. Nothing in them requires a doctor to represent as his own any opinion that he does not in fact hold. Nor is the doctor–patient relationship established by expectation on the part of the patient of comprehensive medical advice. The program does not provide post-conception medical care, and therefore a doctor's silence with regard to abortion cannot reasonably be thought to mislead a client into thinking that the doctor does not consider abortion an appropriate option for her.[14]

Even if one accepts this unconvincing rationale, it is impossible to apply it to California physicians who believe that marijuana would be beneficial for their patients and who are providing their overall health care. Patients receiving care for cancer and AIDS rightfully and reasonably expect and are entitled to full disclosure and discussion of available treatment options. The California physicians are on strong legal ground with their lawsuit and should prevail. In April 1997 U.S. District Court Judge Fern M. Smith granted a preliminary injunction prohibiting the DEA from carrying out its threats against California physicians and encouraged the litigants to try to work out a settlement of the dispute.[15]

In response to the lawsuit and growing opposition to its threats to physicians, the administration issued a clarifying letter, essentially stating that physicians may discuss marijuana with their patients so long as they do not recommend its use.[16] This provides no guidance at all. Of course doctors can talk to patients; the question is what they can say to them. The real subject of dispute remains whether physicians can recommend marijuana (and thereby grant their patients immunity from state prosecution), as the California proposition provides. Would, for example, telling a patient with cancer that other physicians have reported that marijuana has given their patients relief from nausea constitute a recommendation?

Judge Smith made it clear that the 1st Amendment protects physician–patient communications and that the government has no authority to determine the content of physician speech. She also concluded that the federal statements regarding threatened prosecution were vague and thus lead to physician censuring their own speech to avoid possible federal prosecution. On the other hand, she noted (correctly) that the 1st Amendment does not protect "speech that is itself criminal because [the speech is] too intertwined with illegal activity." Under federal drug laws, which cannot be affected by legislation in California, it remains a crime for physicians to aid, abet, or conspire—by speech or action—to violate federal criminal statutes. Thus, it is not a violation of the 1st Amendment for the federal government to prosecute or threaten to prosecute physicians who specifically intend to aid, abet, or conspire with their patients to violate federal drug laws.

Judge Smith could have added that to prevail in such a case the government will have to prove more than simply that the physician recommended marijuana to a patient as worth trying for a medical condition. The more will include evidence that the physician "associated himself with the venture" of illegally purchasing marijuana "as something he wished to bring about and sought by his actions to make succeed."[17] This should require at least that the physician identify a source of the marijuana, and some connection between that source and the physician.[18] It is only speech short of this that the injunction covers. Of course, this formulation still leaves it uncertain exactly how far physicians may go in recommending marijuana use before the federal government is justified in prosecuting them for criminal behavior. Judge Smith concluded with an understatement: "This injunction does not provide physicians with the level of certainty for which they had hoped."

MARIJUANA AS MEDICINE

Attempts to have marijuana reassigned from Schedule I to Schedule II began almost immediately after Congress passed the Uniform Controlled Substances Act of 1970, which established the current system of drug classifications. The following findings must be made to place a drug in Schedule I: "(A) The drug . . . has a high potential for abuse; (B) The drug . . . has no currently accepted medical use in treatment in the United States; and (C) there is a lack of accepted safety for use of the drug under medical supervision." Schedule II's part (A) is identical; the other requirements are: "(B) The drug . . . has a currently accepted medical use in treatment in the United States . . . and (C) Abuse of the drug . . . may lead to severe psychological or physical dependence."

In 1988, after two years of hearings, DEA Judge Francis Young recommended shifting marijuana to Schedule II on the grounds that it was safe and had a "currently accepted medical use in treatment." Specifically, Judge Young found that "marijuana, in its natural form, is one of the safest therapeutically active substances known to man. . . . At present it is estimated that marijuana's LD-50 [median lethal dose] is around 1:20,000 or 1:40,000. In layman's terms. . . . A smoker would theoretically have to consume 20,000 to 40,000 times as much marijuana as is contained in one marijuana cigarette . . . nearly 1500 pounds of marijuana within about fifteen minutes to induce a lethal response." As for medical use, the judge concluded that marijuana "has a currently accepted medical use in treatment in the United States for nausea and vomiting resulting from chemotherapy treatments."[19] The DEA administrator rejected Young's recommendation. Further attempts to get the courts to reschedule marijuana have been unsuccessful.

In reaction to a DEA suggestion that only a "fringe group" of oncologists accepted marijuana as an antiemetic agent, a survey of a random sample of the members of the American Society of Clinical Oncology was undertaken in 1990. More than 1,000 oncologists responded to the survey, and 44% of them reported that they had recommended marijuana to at least one patient. Marijuana was believed to be more effective than oral dronabinol (Marinol) by the respondents: Of those who believed they had sufficient information to compare the two drugs directly, 44% believed marijuana more effective, and only 13% believed Marinol more effective.[20] Of course, nothing in the FDA regulations requires a drug to be more effective than an existing one for it to be approved. Nonetheless, in the current antimarijuana climate, NIH has consistently refused to fund research on smoked marijuana. In the wake of the California proposition, this position is no longer tenable.

An NIH panel, after a two-day workshop in February 1997, recommended research on marijuana in the area of wasting associated with AIDS, nausea due to cancer chemotherapy, glaucoma, and neuropathic pain.[21] This list seems reasonable, especially since objective criteria such as weight gain, intraocular pressure, and the frequency of vomiting can be used to determine the drug's effectiveness. Such research may be difficult to do, but it is possible to compare orally administered Marinol with smoked marijuana. Although smoking is not the administration route for any other drug, smoking marijuana may be better for many reasons—including speed of absorption, dose titration, and inability to swallow.[22]

Because symptoms of nausea are so subjective and "extremely difficult to quantify in controlled experiments" some have also argued that marijuana should be available as a prescription drug on a compassionate basis; and current FDA regulations permit this while clinical studies proceed. Other support for its compassionate use would appear to come from the Clinton administration's solicitor general, Walter Dellinger, who argued before the Supreme Court less than two weeks after the McCaffrey–Reno press conference that the administration believed that Americans had a weak constitutional right "not to suffer." Although Dellinger said he did not believe this right was broad enough to prohibit the states from making physician-assisted suicide for terminally ill patients a crime (see Chapter 21), it should certainly be broad enough to prohibit the federal government from denying patients with cancer and AIDS access to drugs that could help them withstand potentially life-saving treatments.

WHAT ABOUT THE CHILDREN?

The final argument that the administration has made against any medical use of marijuana is that approval would send the "wrong message" to children, who would then use this "gateway drug" and get hooked on much more harmful substances, like cocaine and heroin. There are two responses to this argument. The first is provided by *Boston Globe* columnist Ellen Goodman, who asks, "What is the infamous signal being sent to [children]. . . . If you hurry up and get cancer, you, too, can get high?"[23]

The second response relates to the gateway issue itself: A 1994 survey did find that 17% of current marijuana users said they had tried cocaine and only 0.2% of those who had not used marijuana had tried cocaine. One way to interpret this data is that children who smoke marijuana are 85 times more likely as others to try cocaine; another is that 83% of pot smokers, or five out of six, never try cocaine.[24] Honesty is likely to make a greater and more lasting impression on our children than political posturing and hysteria. Many people want to make marijuana legal for everyone. But opposition to the legalization of marijuana generally is not a good reason to keep it from patients who are suffering. Making marijuana a Schedule II drug does not make it widely acceptable or available any more than classifying medicinal cocaine as a Schedule II drug made it more acceptable or available.

Doctors are not the enemy in the war on drugs; ignorance and hypocrisy are. Research should go on, and while it does, marijuana should be available to all patients who need it to help them undergo treatment for life-threatening illnesses. There already is sufficient scientific evidence to reclassify marijuana as a Schedule II drug. Unlike quack remedies such as laetrile, marijuana is not claimed to be a treatment itself; instead, it is used to help patients withstand the effects of accepted treatment that can lead to a cure or amelioration of their condition. As long as a therapy is safe and has not been proven ineffective, seriously ill patients (and their physicians) should have access to whatever they need to fight for their lives. The current choice patients now face really is some choice—between forgoing a potentially effective drug, and using the drug and risking criminal prosecution.

Medicinal marijuana will never be something all patients will want or need. Genetic information, however, is something all of us will soon be confronted with. Whether or not the "new genetics" actually revolutionizes the practice of medicine, it will confront all of us with new choices—including the choice of whether to undergo genetic testing at all. In the next chapter and the final one on treatment choices, I examine the implications of the genetics revolution for future choices.

CHAPTER NINE

Genetic Prophecy and Genetic Privacy

One of the few aspects of our lives over which we have no choice is our genetic inheritance, our genes.[1] We had no choice in the selection of our parents or in the combination of their genetic material that went into forming our own DNA. The next era in medicine is likely to be the era of molecular biology, and the human genome project is in the process of deciphering the entire genetic code. The co-discoverer of the structure of DNA, James Watson, has said, "We used to think our future was in the stars, now we know our future is in our genes." Actually, the opposite of this provocative statement is true: We used to *know* our future was in the stars, now we *think* our future is in our genes.

Knowledge of our own genetic composition can multiply our choices by prophesying our likely genetic future and providing treatment and prevention opportunities. But unless we agree on and enforce reasonable privacy rules related to genetic information, the price for using the new genetics in medicine may be privacy itself. Choices about our future could be made by others rather than by us. The genetic information gleaned from an analysis of an individual's DNA is similar to information contained in medical records. The DNA molecule itself, however, holds much currently indecipherable information and may usefully be analogized to one's "future diary" written in a code we have not yet broken.

DNA DATABANKS

Storing DNA molecules, or future diaries, in a "DNA bank" for future analysis presents novel privacy issues that merit widespread discussion and early action.[2] When the DNA bank contains information derived from the DNA sample, it becomes a "DNA databank." James Watson has also said that "The idea that there will be a huge databank of genetic information on millions of people is repulsive."[3] Why is such a databank repulsive, and what action can effectively safeguard the genetic privacy of individuals in our coming genetic age?

Increasingly precise genetic information has the potential to radically alter our life choices because control of and access to the information contained in our individual genome gives others potential power over our personal lives by providing a basis not only for counseling but also for stigmatization and discrimination. Genetic information also has unique privacy implications, since genetic information is immutable and provides information about the individual's parents, siblings, and children.[4] Finally, genetic information has been grossly misused in the past, especially in the eugenics movement and Nazi Germany's program of racial hygiene.[5] The uniqueness of genetic information, coupled with computer technology and a general distrust of large, bureaucratic record-keeping systems, requires credible privacy controls if DNA databanks are to be permitted.

Current policies and practices governing the privacy and confidentiality of medical information are woefully inadequate to protect personal privacy and liberty in the new age of genetics. Therefore, new rules for both genetic information in medical records and DNA databanks are needed now to help minimize the harm to individual privacy and liberty that the collection, storage, and distribution of genomic information could produce, and to permit the socially useful medical and epidemiological applications of genetic information.[6] In this chapter I outline the major privacy choices at stake in collecting, storing, and analyzing DNA, the problems inherent in "preventive treatment" of genetic predispositions, and legislation to protect some genetic choice.

MEDICAL RECORDS LAW

Since genetic information is most analogous to medical information, it is useful to begin with a summary of current protections of medical records. More than 20 years ago Justice William Brennan, concurring in a case upholding the constitutionality of a New York law that required the storage of drug prescriptions in a central computer (for the purpose of identifying prescription misuse) expressed his growing concern over the privacy implications of computerized medical information: "The central storage and easy accessibility of computerized data vastly increase the potential for abuse of that information, and I am not prepared to say that future developments will not demonstrate the necessity of some curb on such technology."[7] That time has arrived. There have been major changes in computerization that make medical records more accessible without corresponding changes in legal protections.

Almost all of the law dealing with access to medical records by persons other than the patient can be categorized under the headings of confidentiality, privilege, and privacy. Confidentiality presupposes that something secret will be told by someone to a second party (such as a physician) who will not repeat it to a third party (such as an employer). In the doctor–patient context, confidentiality is understood as an expressed or implied agreement that the doctor will not disclose the information received from the patient to anyone not directly involved in the patient's care and treatment.[8]

A communication is privileged if the person to whom the information is given is forbidden by law from disclosing it in a court proceeding without the consent of the person who provided it. Privilege, sometimes called testimonial privilege, is a legal rule of evidence, applying only in the judicial context. The privilege belongs to the patient, not to the professional, although the hospital, physician or databank may have a duty to assert it on behalf of the patient.

There are at least four senses in which the term privacy is generally used. The first three describe aspects of the constitutional right of privacy. The central one, found in the liberty interests protected by the 14th Amendment, is the right of privacy that forms the basis for the opinions by the U.S. Supreme Court limiting state interference with intimate, individual decisions, such as those involving birth control and abortion.[9] The second and third types of constitutional privacy protect certain relationships, like the husband–wife, parent–child, and doctor–patient relationships, and certain places, such as the bedroom, from governmental intrusion. There is also a fourth sense of privacy, the common law right of privacy, that applies to private actions: "the right to be let alone," to be free of prying, peeping, and snooping, the right to keep personal information inaccessible by others.[10]

Political scientist Alan Westin has defined privacy as "the claim of individuals, groups, or institutions to determine for themselves when, how, and to what extent information about them is communicated to others."[11] Specific privacy protections were built into the Constitution by the framers in terms that were important to their era, which, of course, did not include genetic information. With the subsequent inventions of the telephone, radio, television, and computer systems, more sophisticated legal doctrines have been developed in an attempt to protect the informational privacy of the individual. The policy underlying the right of informational privacy is that, because of the potential severe consequences to individuals, certain "private" information about them (such as their HIV status) should not be repeated without their permission. In the words of one legal commentator, "the basic attribute of an effective right of privacy is the individual's ability to control the flow of information concerning or describing him."[12]

The phrase "data protection" describes informational privacy, especially in the realm of medical records, financial records, employment records, and criminal records. Nonetheless, the phrase is inadequate in the case of genetic information because three types of privacy—informational privacy, relational (family) privacy, and decisionmaking privacy—overlap. This, combined with DNA's coded "future diary" character, creates unique privacy concerns.

Concerns about informational privacy have historically centered on the use to which authoritarian governments can put personal data to control the lives of individual citizens. Thus Orwell's vision of "big brother" in *1984* provided a powerful call to action, as did Alexander Solzhenitsyn's vision of authoritarianism in *Cancer Ward*:

> As every man goes through life he fills in a number of forms for the record. . . . A man's answer to one question on one form becomes a little thread, permanently connecting him to the local center of personnel records administration. There are thus hundreds of little threads radiating from every man. . . . They are not visible, they are not material, but every man is constantly aware of their existence. . . . Each man, permanently aware of his own invisible threads, naturally develops a respect for the people who manipulate the threads . . . and for these people's authority.[13]

The loss of individuality and control over one's life has been a theme of data protection, as have the horror stories of false data being stored in one's government profile.[14] DNA databanks will be developed not only by governmental agencies, however, but also by private corporations, hospitals, and physician researchers. It is thus useful to examine both governmental and private DNA databanks. Moreover, we will be equally concerned with protecting accurate information and with preventing false information. It is also important to distinguish between collection and storage of the DNA sample itself, and storage and distribution of information derived from analysis of the DNA sample, although most DNA databanks will likely do both.

DNA AS A FUTURE DIARY

DNA databanks, both governmental and private, contain information that may be considered unique and significantly more personal and private than medical records.[15] A medical record can be analogized in privacy terms to a diary; but a DNA molecule (as distinguished from information already derived and recorded from the DNA sample) is much more sensitive. It is in a real sense a future diary (although a probabilistic one), and it is written in a code that we have not yet cracked. But the code is being broken piece by piece, such that holders of a sample of an individual's DNA will be able to learn more and more about that individual and his or her family in the future as the code is broken. Of course, such predictions will not be precise, because the expression of genetic characteristics will vary from never expressed to expressed in an extreme manner, and individuals with the same genetic expression will respond differently. Nonetheless, this is information individuals, physicians, insurance companies, employers, and others will want and on which they will base decisions affecting the individual. Health insurance companies, for example, may wish to deny coverage to applicants with genetic predispositions to serious, potentially expensive, diseases.[16]

Medical researchers and epidemiologists will want access to the information stored in large DNA databanks to search for genetic connections to disease. One can even envision law enforcement or child protection agencies looking for children with genetic conditions to make sure their parents are providing them with proper medical care or prevention strategies. Although it seems far-fetched today, assuming that a gene that predisposes a person to skin cancer is discovered in the future and that such cancer is preventable if one stays out of the sun, one could envision searching DNA databases to identify these individuals, and then counseling them about their risks. If this is seen as reasonable, the next step would be to identify children at risk and require that their parents protect them from this genetic hazard by keeping them out of the sun and away from the beach. Similar scenarios can be constructed for virtually all diseases that have genetic predispositions. Although one can counter that similar arguments can be made for high blood pressure and high cholesterol, the identification of a genetic link will make prediction seem more scientific and prevention seem more important.

It seems reasonable to conclude that the mere existence of the technology to decode DNA will lead us to radically alter our view of informational privacy. In the past we have put special emphasis on information that is potentially embarrassing and sensitive (such as sexually transmitted diseases) and on information that is uniquely personal (such as a photograph of one's face). Genetic information is both potentially embarrassing and uniquely personal. The existence of such decodable information could either impel us to take privacy much more seriously in the genetic realm than we have in the medical and criminal realms or lead us to give up on maintaining personal privacy altogether. This latter response seems defeatist and unlikely, although one leading medical geneticist has already suggested that "we must prepare for others to know."[17] Is this true, or can genetic privacy be protected? The issue of genetic privacy revolves around choice in discovering and exposing personal genetic information, as well as choice in determining whether and how to treat "genetic predispositions."

PREDISPOSITION TO DISEASE AS DISEASE

In the continuing national debate about health care, surprisingly little attention has been focused on what medical services health care insurance should cover. Historically, discussions of this topic have focused on concepts such as a basic health care and medically necessary care. When medicine's power of diagnosis and treatment was limited, the content of these terms had boundaries as well. As medicine's diagnostic prowess increases, especially in the area of genetic diagnosis, terms like basic and necessary have become open-ended invitations for physicians and their patients to make their own choices by defining these terms according to their own values and desires. Although it does not provide an answer to the problem of defining disease, or genetic or predisposition-to-disease coverage, a dispute resolved by the Nebraska Supreme Court illustrates the issues that courts will more frequently confront.[18]

Blue Cross/Blue Shield of Nebraska refused to pay for Sindie Katskee's surgery to remove her ovaries and uterus on the basis that removal was not medically necessary and thus not covered by her insurance policy. The policy, like most, defined medically necessary services as those used in the diagnosis or treatment of the insured's illness, injury, or pregnancy, which are:

1. Appropriate for the symptoms and diagnosis of the patient's illness, injury or pregnancy; and
2. Provided in the most appropriate setting and at the most appropriate level of services; and
3. Consistent with the standards of good medical practice in the medical community of the state of Nebraska; and
4. Not provided primarily for the convenience of any of the following:
    a. the covered person;
    b. the physician;
    c. the covered person's family;
    d. any other person or health care provider; and
5. Not considered to be unnecessarily repetitive when performed in combination with other diagnoses or treatment procedures.

Blue Cross/Blue Shield denied coverage because it determined that the insured's condition did not constitute an illness, and therefore the treatment she had obtained for it was not medically necessary. In 1990 Ms. Katskee, following the recommendation of her gynecologist, consulted with Henry T. Lynch, an expert in hereditary cancer, concerning her family history of breast and ovarian cancer. Ms. Katskee's mother and aunt had both died of ovarian cancer; one was diagnosed at the age of 47, the other at 48. Because of this family history, it was estimated that Ms. Katskee (and her two sisters) had a 50% probability of developing breast or ovarian cancer sometime in her life. In the absence of a family history, the risk of developing ovarian cancer was put at about 1.5%. Dr. Lynch believed that a total abdominal hysterectomy and bilateral salpingo-oophorectomy was, under the circumstances, "a prophylactic procedure for a genetically predisposed disease"—and recommended it. He also described Ms. Katskee's condition as "hereditary ovarian cancer-proneness" and as a "genetic predisposition to an illness" and as "breast/ovarian carcinoma syndrome."[19]

Blue Cross/Blue Shield denied coverage for the surgery (which was performed by another physician) on the basis that familial breast/ovarian carcinoma syndrome was not an illness at the time of the surgery, and therefore the surgery was not medically necessary. Blue Cross/Blue Shield's decision was made by its medical director, who made his decision without consulting either any medical experts or any medical literature or research regarding breast–ovarian carcinoma syndrome.

The trial judge granted Blue Cross/Blue Shield's motion for summary judgment on the basis that Ms. Katskee "did not have a bodily disorder or disease only the potential therefore and [consequently] the surgery performed . . . although warranted as a prophylactic measure did not come within the coverage" of the policy. Katskee appealed.

The Supreme Court of Nebraska characterized this as a dispute over the meaning of the language used in an insurance contract. In such disputes contracts are interpreted so as "to give effect to the parties' intentions at the time the contract was made." The Nebraska court found that the words illness, sickness, and disease are often used interchangeably, and cited with approval a definition of disease in *Dorland's Illustrated Medical Dictionary* (27th ed. 1988): "Any deviation from or interruption of the normal structure or function of any part, organ, or system . . . of the body that is manifested by a characteristic set of symptoms and signs and whose etiology, pathology, and prognosis may be known or unknown."

The court also cited with approval the definition adopted by the Iowa Supreme Court (which found the terms illness, sickness, and disease were used synonymously in the context of an insurance policy): "a morbid condition of the body, a deviation from the healthy or normal condition of any of the functions or tissues of the body."[20] Based on these and other definitions in common use, the court concluded that the language of the policy was not ambiguous, but rather adopted the "plain and ordinary meaning" of the word illness to encompass:

> Any abnormal condition of the body or its components of such a degree that in its natural progression would be expected to be problematic; a deviation from the healthy or normal state affecting the functions or tissues of the body; an inherent defect of the body; or a morbid physical or mental state which deviates from or interrupts the normal structure or function of any part, organ, or system of the body and which is manifested by a characteristic set of symptoms and signs.

Once the court adopted this definition, the only remaining question was whether breast–ovarian carcinoma syndrome qualified as an illness. The court found that it did. In reaching this decision it relied heavily on Lynch's deposition, especially his statements that the surgery is prophylactic to prevent the onset of cancer and that the at-risk condition itself is the result of a genetic deviation from the normal, healthy state. In the court's words, "the recommended surgery treats that condition by eliminating or significantly reducing the presence of the condition and its likely development." The court was also influenced by the fact that Blue Cross/Blue Shield offered no evidence to dispute the genetic origin of the condition or disputed that it was likely to produce "devastating results" in its "natural development." The court concluded that the patient suffered from an illness within the meaning of the policy, because her

> condition is a deviation from what is considered a normal, healthy physical state or structure. The abnormality or deviation from a normal state arises, in part, from the genetic makeup of the woman. The existence of this unhealthy state results in

the woman's being at substantial risk of developing cancer. The recommended surgery is intended to correct that morbid state by reducing or eliminating that risk.

The court concluded that even though there was no "detectable physical evidence" of the illness, she nonetheless did "suffer from a different or abnormal genetic constitution." On the other hand, the court noted that not every condition that "itself constitutes a predisposition to another illness is necessarily [itself] an illness"—only one in which it is "such that in its probable and natural progression may be expected to be a source of mischief." In this regard, the court cited with approval an opinion of Justice Cardozo, who ruled that a "peasized ulcer" that developed because of a severe blow to the deceased's stomach was not a disease or infirmity within the meaning of an exclusionary clause of an accident insurance policy because if left unattended "the ulcer would only have been as harmful as a tiny scratch."[21]

PREVENTIVE INTERVENTIONS

It is easy to understand the court's sympathy for the patient in this dispute. She had a real fear of developing cancer that two close relatives had died of, her two sisters had had prophylactic hysterectomies and oophorectomies, and her physicians put her own risk of cancer at 50%. Moreover, Blue Cross/Blue Shield made no effort to determine the medical or scientific basis of her claim but rejected it in a seemingly arbitrary manner. Most importantly, the language of the insurance policy was general and seemingly open-ended, permitting the court to interpret it in the patient's favor. Nonetheless, although understandable, following the opinion to its logical conclusion would lead to undesirable consequences.

The patient and her physicians believed that her treatment was necessary. Although Blue Cross/Blue Shield's policy stated that a treatment is not automatically medically necessary because a physician says it is, it is difficult to come up with a much better definition of medically necessary, and this definition is, of course, circular and thus not helpful. The patient and her physicians, for example, concluded that surgery was necessary to prevent ovarian cancer but not necessary to prevent breast cancer. Since the risk of these two cancers was equal (about 50%), what accounts for the difference? In his deposition, Lynch testified that the primary distinction was that there was a method for early detection for breast cancer (mammography) that did not exist for ovarian cancer. Given this, he said, he only recommended prophylactic bilateral mastectomy in a woman who is "cancer-phobic" to such an extent that it significantly disrupts her life. Since it was not an issue in this case, there was no discussion of whether a prophylactic bilaterial mastectomy would have been considered medically necessary or whether breast implants following such surgery would also have been medically necessary. Nonetheless, there is nothing in the opinion to suggest the court would not have found both of these procedures covered by the policy had the patient and physician agreed they were necessary.

How should we decide whether prophylactic medical and surgical treatments should be covered by health insurance in a country that is rapidly developing diagnostic tests for genetic sequences that predispose individuals to serious diseases? These genetic tests will, of course, be much more specific than the family history used in the Nebraska case and pedigrees based on genetic markers currently used in genetic research protocols.[22] There are many possible avenues to explore, but none that seem inherently superior. The first is to let the physician decide when treatment of a genetic predisposition is medically necessary. This is very imprecise, and obviously physicians will disagree. Lynch, for example, had no hesitation in describing his recommendation as a necessary "life-saving potential procedure." Others might think it either always unnecessary, or that its necessity would be a function of the patient's age and child-bearing wishes.[23]

Another alternative is to let the patient decide what prophylactic treatments are medically necessary. But this, of course, defeats the purpose of having an insurance contract altogether. The patient must consent to prophylactic treatment; but it would be strange indeed if the patient could demand that her insurance company pay for it based primarily on either fear (of cancer or death) or desire. There should be safer, cheaper, and more effective interventions to deal with these states of mind, and no intervention can ever eliminate all risks of cancer or death.

A more attractive alternative might be based on a cost-effectiveness analysis which also attempts to include anxiety and fear as a surrogate for quality of life as one factor in the determination of necessity.[24] In this regard it might be seen as reasonable to perform surgery on any woman with a greater than 50% risk of developing a lethal cancer in early or midlife, but not with a smaller risk or a late-life onset likelihood. Any cutoff percentage, age designation, or combination of the two will be arbitrary, and perhaps ultimately politically unacceptable.[25] But it should be seen as unreasonable to pay for prophylactic mastectomies for any woman at the general population risk (12%) of developing breast cancer in their lifetime. Likewise, it would be foolish for a national health system to provide everyone with an artificial heart (when and if they become safe and effective) based on a general population risk of dying of heart disease (50%) and a patient's desire or fear.

Finally, if we decide that a genetic predisposition to a disease is (at least sometimes) itself a disease, is it a pre-existing condition that could be used as an exclusion or disqualification in an individual health insurance policy? To be consistent, the Nebraska court would have to conclude that a genetic "syndrome" is a preexisting condition, the treatment of which could be excluded from coverage on this basis. Since everyone carries a number of genetic predispositions that are likely to manifest themselves if we live long enough, this would require us to conclude that we are all conceived diseased. Although this seems silly, if one agrees with the logic of the Nebraska court, we are all genetically "ill," no matter what our physical condition.

Although the Nebraska case primarily raises questions about "preventive treatment" for genetic predispositions, it does help clarify some major issues. The first is that courts will continue to be called on to decide individual disputes. Moreover, courts will likely side with the physician and patient whenever the language of the insurance policy permits.[26] If disputes are rare events, this is workable; but as the number of genetic diagnostic tests for asymptomatic conditions increases, an increase in such disputes is inevitable, and a clear policy on coverage is desirable. Second, we must come to grips with what we mean by prevention, as opposed, for example, to predictive medicine, and decide when preventive surgery is appropriate. Use of the term "medical necessity" will no longer help us. As Daniel Callahan has insightfully noted, "We want to avoid sickness and death. We require whatever it takes to do so. Those are our needs."[27] But since we will all die of something, and since this something will have a genetic component if we live long enough, we all have genetic predispositions to terminal illnesses: We just don't have the power to diagnose or treat them yet.[28] Medicine may run out of diseases, but medicine will never run out of risk factors. The power of the new genetics may thus do much more to make us refocus our attention from the question of what medical interventions we should cover to the much more significant one of why medical interventions should be used in the first place.

KNOWLEDGE AS DISABLING

We like to think that knowledge is power and that the more knowledge we have about our health the more choices we will be able to make to enhance our quantity and quality of life. But is this always true? Would you really want to know how (or when) you are likely to die or to lose your mind? And even if you do, would you want your family, your clients, your employer, or your life or health insurance company to have this information?

In a September 1995 cover story in the Sunday *New York Times Magazine* Charles Siebert writes about his own personal confrontation with these questions. Siebert's family has a history of hypertropic cardiomyopathy (HCM), an incurable type of heart disease characterized by a thickening of the heart walls that usually leads to an early death. Geneticists cannot treat this condition, but by examining the DNA of family members (doing a pedigree) they can identify those who carry genes that indicate whether or not a person is likely to suffer from this condition. Siebert went to the National Institutes of Health in Bethesda, Maryland, thinking he would probably volunteer to be part of the research project looking for this gene. But as he learned more and more about genetics, he began to reconsider. Genes predispose, but they do not dictate our futures. We are all made up of genes, but genes are not all that we are. Environmental factors may determine our future as much as our genes; and our interaction with our environment is unpredictable. Siebert's father, for example, had died of HCM; but his cousin had been killed by a falling piece of scaffolding long before the disease could manifest itself.

Siebert wondered whether having a physician prepare a "genetic report card" on a person is always a good thing and learned that genetic information can be "toxic" and undermine our ability to go on with our lives and plan our futures. In the end he decided not to have a genetic test for the HCM that runs in his family; he decided he "didn't need to know." In his words:

> I would drive all night to get back home—to get back, in a sense to my own unknown. I had a right to that. And not simply for the privilege of hope but of pessimism as well—my own rendition, however misguided, of how and when I'm going to die.[29]

Charles Siebert's choice is still unusual; but it is one all of us will confront within the next few years as the new genetics produces bushelbaskets of new genetic screening tests which will soon invade both medicine and public health. Indeed, the new genetics is the centerpiece of breathless predictions of both a new medicine and a new public health. Molecular medicine, based on deciphering the genes of a patient instead of diagnosing the patient based on signs and symptoms, is said to be just around the corner. And using genetic screening in large populations to detect potentially preventable problems, such as breast cancer, is the dream of many public health professionals. But it will be some time, if ever, before either treatments or preventive measures for genetic predispositions are available. In the meantime, most genetic information will be used primarily to identify and possibly stigmatize individuals like Charles Siebert, who carry genes that likely increase their risk of developing specific diseases, not only HCM, but also cancer and dementia, in the future.

The privacy issues involved in the new genetics can be illustrated by considering genes that code for early onset Alzheimer's disease. People who carry these genes are not only very likely to develop Alzheimer's disease, but are likely to begin to experience symptoms in their 40s. There is currently no way to prevent the disease from manifesting itself and no treatment for the disease. Of course, the hope is that once the genes responsible for creating the bodily conditions that permit or encourage Alzheimer's disease are identified, it will be easier to find treatments and prevention strategies. We would all welcome these developments. But in the meantime, of what use is the knowledge that one carries an early onset Alzheimer's gene?

Also of great interest are genes that predispose one to cancers of various types. The first genes that are likely to be promoted for large-scale screening are the two breast cancer genes that have been identified to date, BRCA1 and BRCA2. A woman who carries one of these two genes will not necessarily develop breast

cancer, but her risk is high, perhaps over 50%, that she will. Since there is no way
to prevent this disease, what good is knowing you will probably get it in the future? Charles Siebert decided against HCM testing. What should women do? Historian of science Robert Proctor highlights the psychological issues presented by
screening for cancer genes:

> No one knows what the psychological impact of such tests may be: there is a novel
> element, insofar as these are diagnostic technologies being developed in the ab-
> sence of any appropriate therapy (short of watchful waiting or prophylactic
> coloectomy, ovariectomy, and mastectomy). Will women found not to have a breast
> cancer gene feel themselves not to be at risk? Will people not predisposed to colon
> cancer feel not obliged to exercise or cut down on fat and increase dietary fiber?[30]

Moreover, since genetic tests can be performed at any age (all one needs is a
DNA sample), the question of fetuses, newborns, and minor children must also
be faced. Disputes about the appropriateness of testing children for late-onset
diseases that cannot be prevented have already broken out. In one survey, for
example, only 2 of 49 geneticists said they would test a 5-year-old for the Hun-
tington disease (HD) gene at the request of the child's parents, whereas more than
50% (100 of 189) of pediatricians would comply with this request.[31] There seems
little to gain for the child (who will be labeled as already "sick" and lose his or
her right to decide whether to be tested for the HD gene). Nonetheless, the pediatricians seem to believe that testing children is justified by the potential benefits
to parents (enabling them to "adjust" to the implications of likely future disease
in their offspring).

The American public is as confused as its medical professionals. In a May 1995
Harris poll, for example, although only 27% claimed to have read or heard "quite
a lot" about genetic tests, 68% said they would be either "very likely" or "somewhat likely" to undergo genetic testing even for diseases "for which there is pres-
ently no cure or treatment." Perhaps most astonishing, 56% found it either "very"
or "somewhat acceptable" to develop a governmental computerized DNA bank
with samples taken from all newborns, in which their names would be attached to
the samples.[32] Although this survey reflects uninformed opinion, it raises serious
privacy concerns that the public may ignore at its own peril. What can be done to
safeguard the genetic privacy of individuals in the genetic age?

One laissez-faire strategy is to simply let the market determine what genetic
tests are done and have breaches of privacy remedied in civil lawsuits. The problem with this approach is that lawsuits for breaches of privacy have not been often
pursued (because the private information is usually made known to even more
people in the process) and that we should use the law to prevent predictable harms
if we can. I believe that we can achieve consensus when these issues are understood and that we can and should act on this consensus to protect the genetic privacy of all Americans while it is still possible to do so.

One way to protect genetic privacy is to codify rules for gene banks and computerized records based on genetic analysis, but this is too narrow. Although rules for gene banks are needed, it is very difficult to define what a gene bank is, and regulation at this level alone permits genetic analysis to be done, and information to be disclosed, in settings which do not involve the storage of DNA samples. The law has already begun to take action on a number of levels. Regulatory approaches that have been adopted to date include an Equal Employment Opportunity Commission (EEOC) guideline on genetic discrimination and a handful of state statutes that seek to limit the use of genetic information.

THE GENETIC PRIVACY ACT

For the short term a state-by-state approach is likely. But genetic information cannot be confined by state borders, and we will need federal legislation to effectively protect genetic privacy. My colleagues Leonard Glantz and Winnie Roche and I believe that we not only need uniform rules for the collection, analysis, and storage of DNA samples, but also that we need rules for storing and disclosing information derived from DNA samples, and that these rules must cover adults, children, incompetent persons, dead bodies, and fetuses and embryos. To codify rules for genetic privacy and make them uniform throughout the United States, we have drafted a proposed federal law, The Genetic Privacy Act (GPA),[33] the core of which protects "private genetic information" defined as:

> any information about an identifiable individual that is derived from the presence, absence, alteration, or mutation of a gene or genes, or the presence or absence of a specific DNA marker or markers, and which has been obtained:
> (1) from an analysis of the individual's DNA; or
> (2) from an analysis of the DNA of a person to whom the individual is related.

The GPA prohibits individuals from analyzing DNA samples unless they have verified that written authorization for the analysis has been given by the individual or the individual's representative.

The individual has the right to:

- Determine who may collect and analyze DNA
- Determine the purposes for which a DNA sample can be analyzed
- Know what information can reasonably be expected to be derived from the genetic analysis
- Order the destruction of DNA samples
- Delegate authority to another individual to order the destruction of the DNA sample after death
- Refuse to permit the use of the DNA sample for research or commercial activities
- Inspect and obtain copies of records containing information derived from genetic analysis of the DNA sample

A written summary of these principles must be supplied to the individual by the person who collects the DNA sample. The GPA requires that the person who holds private genetic information in the ordinary course of business keep such information confidential and prohibits the disclosure of private genetic information unless the individual has authorized the disclosure in writing or the disclosure is limited to access by specified researchers for compiling data.

The GPA deals explicitly with three areas which are likely to breed the most controversy and consequently the most litigation: the genetic testing of children, research using identifiable stored DNA samples, and informing relatives of their increased risk of genetic disease based on the diagnosis of a genetically-related person. Specifically, the GPA protects the privacy of children by not permitting the genetic analysis of a child under the age of 16 unless:

(1) there is an effective intervention that will prevent or delay the onset or ameliorate the severity of the disease; and
(2) the intervention must be initiated before the age of 16 to be effective, and
(3) the [minor's parent or guardian] . . . has received the disclosures required . . . and signed the authorization . . . Sec. 141(a).

Minors age 16 and 17 must themselves consent to any analysis of their DNA and must be "accompanied by a parent or other adult family member" when they are counseled regarding the DNA analysis and its possible consequences. Research on identifiable DNA samples stored in a genetic databank or gene bank (often no more than a collection of DNA samples in a clinic) cannot be conducted without specific authorization of the person if the sample can be traced back to that individual. If the sample has been stripped of all identifiers such that it is impossible to link the sample to the person, however, research can be conducted on the sample without specific authorization.

As to the issue of the geneticist's "duty to protect" other family members by informing them of a condition discovered in a patient, the GPA opts for protecting privacy by prohibiting disclosures to others. The policy reasons for this provision are both philosophical and practical. Philosophically, the genetic information is and should remain private; people in this sense have what Charles Siebert exercised, a right not to know as well as a right to be the only one who knows. Moreover, carrying a particular gene does not put anyone else at risk. Family members do have a moral obligation to other family members, and should be encouraged to share genetic information that may have an impact on other family members. But their obligation is not legal, and should not be made so by statute. As a practical matter, defining the scope of such a duty would be virtually impossible. Would it only be related to reproductive decisions? Would it only include genetic conditions for which there were treatments? How would it work, for example, in the area of breast cancer and colon cancer genes? In regard to the gene for early Alzheimer's? I believe it is good social policy to assume that family members will act benevolently toward each other in these circumstances, even if there will be some instances where this is not the case. There is not, and should not be, a professional obligation to disclose genetic information to relatives.

Regarding a broader social policy issue, the GPA itself does not prohibit the use of genetic information by employers and insurance companies (because this is a separate problem from privacy). It is, however, reasonable public policy to prohibit both employers and health insurance companies from using genetic information in making hiring and coverage decisions. Congress should act now to protect genetic privacy. While we wait for Congressional action, states should enact protective legislation and private companies and physicians should voluntarily adopt these privacy rules as their own.

The gene has become more than a piece of information; it has become "a cultural icon, a symbol, almost a magical force. DNA seems to be the locus of the true self, therefore relevant to the problems of personal authenticity posed by a culture in which the 'fashioned self' is the body manipulated and adorned with the intent to mislead."[34] To the extent that we accord special status to our genes and what they reveal, genetic information is uniquely powerful and uniquely personal, and thus merits unique privacy protection. We know the privacy and policy issues that come with the new genetics. The challenge is to act to maximize the benefits and minimize the harm that will come to all of us from our choices regarding new genetic knowledge.

The following section, which addresses illusory choices, opens with an examination of the health of presidents and presidential candidates. The opening chapter includes a brief discussion of the president's own right to genetic privacy.

PART III

Illusory Choices

CHAPTER TEN

Choosing a (Healthy) President

Bob Woodward entitled his book about the 1996 presidential election simply *The Choice*.[1] Although voting for president is a choice Americans get to make every four years, Americans have become so cynical about our presidential choices that fewer than half of eligible voters actually vote.[2] The general obsession Americans have with health nonetheless manifests itself in our intense interest in the health of presidential candidates.

In July 1995, candidate Robert Dole celebrated his 72nd birthday by releasing a detailed nine-page summary of his medical records. His personal physician told the press that despite Dole's serious World War II wounds, which left his right arm paralyzed and required one kidney to be removed, and his 1991 surgery for prostate cancer, his health was excellent. Dole was also photographed on his treadmill, which he used several times a week for 45 minutes and on weekends for an hour and a half.[3]

Since 1972, when George McGovern was forced to replace his vice-presidential running mate, Thomas Eagleton, after it was disclosed that Eagleton had been hospitalized for depression, the health status of presidential candidates has been seen as fair game by the press. In the 1976 presidential campaign, virtually all presidential candidates, except Eugene McCarthy, supplied summaries of medical histories to the press.[4] McCarthy argued that medical records were private, and in 1992 candidate Bill Clinton also appealed to privacy when he initially refused to release detailed medical information. But the day after physician–reporter Lawrence Altman wrote a front page story in the *New York Times* asserting that "Mr. Clinton has been less forthcoming about his health than any presidential nominees in the last 20 years," Clinton promised to make more medical informa-

tion available to the press.[5] Ross Perot, however, released no medical information during the campaign.

Every presidential campaign season we re-ask the question: How much information about the health of a presidential candidate does the public have a right
to? Clinton had promised to open his medical records should he be elected president, and this poses a related question: How much does the public have a right to
know about the health of the president?

MEDICAL PRIVACY AND THE PRESIDENT

As discussed in the previous chapter, it is a central legal and ethical rule that physicians not disclose private medical information to people not involved in a patient's
care without the patient's authorization. The doctor–patient relationship is a confidential one, and a breach of confidentiality is illegal unless it is necessary to
protect the public's health.[6] There is no exception to this rule for presidents or
presidential candidates. This does not, of course, mean that presidential physicians can ethically or legally mislead the public about the health of the president.
Nonetheless, many have done so, and these actions have led to increasing public
and press concern about the health of the president. President Franklin Roosevelt,
for example, was a sick man during his third term, and serious illness and death
only months into his fourth term was predicted by his physicians before his 1944
reelection. Some of President Eisenhower's physician thought he had only about
a 50:50 chance to survive a full second term. President Kennedy's Addison's disease was purposely obfuscated prior to the election. And the extent of President
Reagan's health problems during his first term was not publicized until after he
completed his second term.[7]

Presidents have not always been pleased with the disclosures their physicians
have made, even when they had authorized "complete disclosure." Eisenhower,
for example, was greatly embarrassed when, after his first heart attack, his physicians announced that he had had "a good bowel movement."[8] And President
Reagan remained upset for years after one of his NIH physicians announced that
"The President has cancer," after his colon cancer operation, instead of saying,
"The President had cancer."[9] Presidential campaigns, of course, are not so much
based on descriptions of the present as on predictions about the future. And this is
what makes them especially troubling in terms of health information.

In the 1992 presidential election campaign, Paul Tsongas' history of cancer
was a central issue in his candidacy for the Democratic Party's nomination. Both
he and two of his physicians said he was "cancer free" after his 1986 bone marrow transplant for lymphoma at the Dana-Farber Cancer Institute in Boston.
Tsongas was the first candidate for president to announce that he had had cancer.
A major question was whether the American public would accept a cancer survivor as a candidate. After Tsongas suspended his unsuccessful campaign, he and

his Dana-Farber physicians told the press that he had suffered a recurrence of lymphoma in 1987, which was successfully treated with radiation. Shortly after this announcement Tsongas wrote that if he should rejoin the campaign he would make "all" his medical records available for "public inspection" even though he thought that this would set a precedent "that all candidates will have to follow." He wrote further that if there was any doubt remaining, he would "submit to an examination by an independent group of doctors," something he thought other candidates would then be forced to do as well.[10]

In fact, Tsongas never rejoined the race, and shortly after the election announced that he was suffering a recurrence of his lymphoma. He underwent treatment just before Bill Clinton's inauguration. Tsongas called upon President-elect Clinton to appoint a special commission to define what should constitute full medical disclosure for presidential candidates.[11] President Clinton has taken no action on this or any other recommendation regarding making medical information about presidential candidates public. Tsongas died in January 1997, at age 55, and it seems he would have survived almost one full term as president had he been elected. He died of myelodysplasia, a blood disorder he developed that was a delayed complication of treatment of his cancer.

Commenting on the December 1992 Tsongas disclosures, Lawrence Altman wrote, "No less than the outcome of the 1992 presidential primaries, and thus the election itself, could have been influenced by the Dana Farber doctors' withholding of critical information." Tsongas had won the New Hampshire primary, and Altman opined that other candidates might have performed better and "emerged in a stronger position to challenge Bill Clinton for the nomination" had the disclosure of cancer recurrence been made.[12] This seems unlikely, although there is no way to know. Nonetheless, Dana Farber responded by developing a new medical disclosure policy for public figures. It involves preparing a written summary of the patient's medical history which the patient can review, but may not edit. If the patient approves, the statement is made available to the press, and a hospital spokesperson familiar with the area of medicine—not one of the treating physicians (who might have a real or perceived conflict of interest with full disclosure)—is made available to the press to comment on the statement. Although it involves presidential candidates and other public figures, this procedure is not too different from the one followed by George Washington University Hospital after the attempted assassination of President Reagan. There was no contingency plan for an attempted assassination, so with the approval of White House officials, the hospital appointed a sole spokesperson to give medical bulletins on the president's health to the press. Reagan's White House physician reviewed these 27 press releases but made virtually no changes in them.[13]

Whatever one thinks of the medical privacy of candidates for the presidency, both the Eisenhower heart attack and the attempt on Reagan's life illustrate that candidate Clinton was correct to assert that the health of the president is a more legitimate public concern. This does not, however, mean that the president's medical records or physician should be made available to the public, only that adequate and accurate information should be supplied to the public when illness or injury strikes the president. Rumors spread quickly when facts are not made available, as Boris Yeltsin discovered during his 1995 hospitalizations and 1996 heart surgery. Moreover, the provisions of the 25th Amendment to the U.S. Constitution apply to the president.

THE 25TH AMENDMENT

The transition of authority from president to vice president for cases other than death or resignation, as well as the ability of the president and Congress to fill a vacancy in the office of Vice President, was not dealt with until the passage of the 25th Amendment to the U.S. Constitution. Serious work on this amendment began after President Eisenhower's heart attack, but it was not passed until shortly after the assassination of President John Kennedy. The 25th Amendment provides that when there is a vacancy in the office of Vice President, the president "shall nominate a Vice President who shall take office upon confirmation by a majority vote of both Houses of Congress." This procedure was followed when President Richard Nixon nominated Gerald Ford to replace Spiro Agnew and again when President Gerald Ford nominated Nelson Rockefeller to fill the vacancy left when Ford himself became president. Both vacancies resulted from resignations in disgrace because of illegal activities, not death or disability. Two other sections of the amendment deal with the temporary transfer of power to the vice president when the president is "unable to discharge the powers and duties of the office." This can be done voluntarily or involuntarily.

The voluntary provision, section 3, applies when the president will predictably be temporarily unable to perform his duties, such as when he is out of communication with his subordinates (with satellite communications, this no longer seems to be an issue) or under or recovering from general anesthesia. When the president transmits to the House and the Senate his written declaration to this effect, the vice president shall be the "Acting President" until the president later transmits a written declaration to the contrary. The only time this provision was used was when President Reagan underwent surgery for colon cancer. Vice President Bush was acting president for approximately eight hours.[14] President Reagan's letter to Congress unfortunately questioned whether the 25th Amendment was applicable to "brief and temporary periods of incapacity" like his situation, although his was just the type of situation the amendment was meant to cover.[15]

Most of the controversy over presidential health has involved discussions of when a president's power can be involuntarily removed because of a disability. Specifically, section 4 provides that a declaration of inability be transmitted to the House and the Senate by "a majority of either the principal officers of the executive departments or of such other body as Congress may by law provide." The vice president becomes the acting president until the president submits a written declaration that he is able to resume his duties.

Physician commentators generally seem to favor getting physicians more directly involved in monitoring the health of the president. It has been suggested, for example, that Congress should use its authority under the amendment to set up a blue ribbon national panel of physicians to monitor the president's health, and to make the disability referral to Congress. This might have the advantage of taking the initiation of a referral out of the political realm where it may look like a betrayal by an unloyal vice president and his supporters. But this is its disadvantage as well. Taking away the powers of the president involuntarily, even temporarily, is an issue that should be decided in the political arena—because this is the arena in which we determine who should be president. Nevertheless, most involuntary suspensions will likely involve cases of mental instability or dementia, and medical expertise in these areas will be essential to making a reasonable evaluation of the President's condition.

Proposals have accordingly also been made that a mental health unit be formed in the White House as part of the medical office "to assist the White House physician in diagnosing and treating psychological problems."[16] The desirability of such a unit has been described as "indisputable—and a political impossibility."[17] Americans still seem unable to accept a president who has had occasion to consult a psychiatrist. Other proposals to monitor the president's health have also been widely discussed. One is for Congress to create a standing "inability commission" of respected medical experts, as well as other senior government officials. This proposal, however, lost much of its momentum in 1958 when Chief Justice Earl Warren sent a letter to Congress advising against putting any member of the Supreme Court on such a commission.[18]

In 1997 an Ad Hoc Working Group on Disability in U.S. Presidents, after two years of meetings and deliberations, concluded that the 25th Amendment "does not require revision or augmentation by another constitutional amendment." The group nonetheless did agree on a series of recommendations, including that "a formal contingency plan for the implementation of the amendment should be in place before the inauguration of every President," (Bush adopted the first such plan) and that the president should appoint a "Senior physician in the White House" who is responsible for the president's medical care and for the military medical unit, and will be "the source of medical disclosure when considering imminent or existing impairment according to the provisions of the 25th Amendment."[19]

THE WHITE HOUSE PHYSICIAN

What role should the president's White House physician play in making health information about the president available to the public in general and in making a disability determination in particular? In terms of what should be disclosed to the public, I agree with those who believe the Senior White House physician should act as the president's personal physician and as such should be bound by the same rules of confidentiality as all other physicians. Exceptions designed to protect the public seem unnecessary, as his closest advisers and senior cabinet members will certainly be aware of the ability of the president to function mentally.

It has been suggested that the physician to a national leader might have an obligation to disclose

> when the leader is not competent to decide his own fate, as for example in circumstances of dementia or severe functional psychiatric disorders, such as mania or severe depression; when the leader is about to commit a major act of illegality because of medical impairment; and when the leader is about to commit a grossly immoral act because of medical impairment.[20]

Although the first of these three is potentially compatible with both medical ethics and the 25th Amendment, it is unnecessary, and the latter two are outside the role and expertise of physicians. They involve interpreting the law and acting as a judge of the president's morals, areas where medical expertise is not useful.

The White House medical unit was significantly restructured under President Bush to include four physicians (a physician to the president and three White House physicians) as well as five physician assistants and five nurses.[21] Like President Bush, President Clinton has developed a detailed contingency plan for implementing the 25th Amendment, which spells out the role of the physician to the president in this process. The plan is classified. It is, of course, good to have such a plan; the fact that it is classified, however, makes it impossible to tell how sound the plan is. In any event, the primary role of the physician to the president, who is usually chosen more for political connections than medical prowess, should be in assembling the appropriate specialists needed to make an accurate diagnosis and prognosis of the president's condition. It is not the physician's job to determine whether the condition makes the president unable to discharge his duties. If his senior staff and Cabinet members believe he can perform his duties, who is the president's physician to disagree? This is different from the situation in which the physician is treating an airline pilot or school bus driver, and the physician is the only one aware that the patient's medical condition poses a risk to the public. In such a case if the patient will not voluntarily cease his dangerous activities, the physician may disclose only that information to his employer that is necessary to protect the public.

Although physicians cannot predict how a candidate's medical condition will affect the candidate's ability to perform politically to any degree of certainty, the public may take medical views very seriously concerning the prediction of death or disability in office. President Eisenhower, for example, had to make a decision about running for a second term following his heart attack. His most famous cardiac consultant, Paul Dudly White, found himself in a position where he could likely have had veto power over the decision by saying publicly that Eisenhower should not run for reelection because of his health. White did try to privately persuade Eisenhower not to run (and instead become an ambassador for peace) but ultimately accepted that the final decision should be the president's, not the president's physicians.[22] Eisenhower had many medical problems during his second term but survived them all and lived another eight years after he left office.

The first clear signs of bladder cancer were not found in Hubert Humphrey until 1969, after he had lost the 1968 presidential election to Richard Nixon. It has been suggested that had molecular diagnostic techniques been available, they could have detected the aggressive cancer by May 1967, and had Humphrey known about it "he might have withdrawn from the presidential race."[23] Whether to withdraw, however, should have been Vice President Humphrey's decision, not that of his physicians. Humphrey died in 1978.

LIMITS ON PUBLIC CURIOSITY?

Candidate Tsongas suggested that by disclosing all medical records and submitting to a medical examination by an expert medical panel, any presidential candidate could force all the other presidential candidates to do the same things. To the extent Tsongas was right, presidential candidates wind up playing a public game of chicken with their medical records and thus their medical privacy. President Clinton's position is the proper one: There should be limits on what presidential candidates should be expected to expose regarding their physical and mental health. These limits cannot be imposed by law (since the candidates could always make voluntary disclosures) but must be imposed by the candidates themselves and their advisers and physicians. If these limits are seen as reasonable, they will be respected by the public even if challenged by the press, which seems much more interested in private medical information than the public. The public will learn much more about a candidate's fitness for the presidency by the candidate's performance in the campaign than by a release of medical records.[24] Moreover, the public is likely to be much better served by candidates and presidents who seek medical care and psychiatric treatment when they need it without fear that this will jeopardize their political future.

Some medical information is trivial and its disclosure is probably harmless. Both Clinton and Dole, for example, happily disclosed their cholesterol levels, weight, and blood pressure; these numbers were used in presidential politics. Senator Dole remarked at the July 1995 meeting of the National Governors Association, "My weight is lower than Clinton's. My cholesterol is lower than Clinton's.

My blood pressure is lower than Clinton's. But I am not going to make health an issue in 1996." Clinton, who spoke to the same gathering a few hours later, said that he believed his resting pulse rate was actually lower than Dole's, but that this was not Dole's "fault [because] I don't have to deal with Phil Gramm every day."[25] To the extent that cholesterol levels and weight are proxies for virtue, however, all of this is nonsense and is likely to distract us from focusing on the substantive policy differences between the candidates.

Much more serious issues are raised by sensitive medical information that is inherently embarrassing or invites irrational prejudice. Consulting a psychiatrist is one such area, and I believe this should not be disclosed by candidates. Institutional mental health care is even more prejudicial, as the Eagleton case illustrates. We should encourage our leaders to seek such help whenever they feel they need it, both for their own sakes and for ours, and protecting their medical privacy is essential to do this. Three other types of sensitive information also deserve attention. The first is abortion. Since there have been few women candidates for the presidency this has not yet come up; we should agree now that it never should. The second is HIV status. Presidential candidates may, of course, wish to know their own HIV status, but there seems no reason anyone other than their personal physician and their sex partner should know this. Of course, at some point an HIV-positive person will develop AIDS, and this will be difficult if not impossible to keep secret. The only suggested rationale for presidential candidates getting an HIV test is that this is routine in the military and the president will be the commander in chief. But the military reasons (saving on disability benefits and—incredibly—the possibility of a battlefield transfusion) do not apply to the president.

Third, and perhaps most importantly, there is, as discussed in detail in the last chapter, an entire new set of tests, genetic tests, that will soon become available and will be able to make at least some probabilistic (but not definitive) estimates of odds of a person developing a certain disease, such as early onset Alzheimer's, breast cancer, and colon cancer.[26] These tests have the potential to inflict much harm on presidential candidates and presidential politics, since their results can be used to play to the fears and prejudices of the electorate, even though by themselves they cannot accurately predict how good or bad a president a candidate will be, or even whether the person will be able to do the job. Since everyone will die, and if they live long enough will die of a genetically influenced disease, we all carry at least some genes predisposing us to death and mental disability. It is pointless and hopelessly distracting to search for those that evoke the most fear in the electorate, since this is a reflection not of the fitness of a person for the presidency but of our own fears of death and disability. A good rule to adopt now is for candidates (and their physicians and physician advisers) to put genetic tests off limits in any disclosures of the health status of a candidate or of a president.

THE NEXT CAMPAIGN

Senator Eugene McCarthy was right to protect his medical privacy in the 1976 presidential campaign. He was also right to insist that a president be elected "on the basis of his or her record of service, of thought about the issues and programs to deal with them, and not on the basis of any private status such as that of patient."[27] U.S. presidents have always been more likely to be killed or disabled by assassins than by diseases, and the Secret Service thus has more to do with the president's health and safety than the president's physicians. In fact the only president ever to die in office of a preexisting medical condition that made his death in office likely was Franklin Roosevelt.

The things we want to know about the health of presidents and presidential candidates tell us much more about ourselves than the presidents and would-be presidents. They tell us about what we fear and what we hope for. Reasonable medical disclosures are now taken for granted, and may not be too harmful. But we are rapidly approaching diminishing returns, and unless we want to discourage our presidents, presidential candidates, and possible presidential candidates from seeking medical assistance in times of physical and psychological distress, we must show at least some respect for their medical privacy by setting strict limits to expected disclosures. There is no simple legal or procedural rule that can ensure this. The 25th Amendment is probably as good as we can do regarding temporary presidential disability. Presidents will have to disclose the details of actual injuries and illnesses they suffer in office.

The 1996 election provided an opportunity for us to begin to curb our tabloid-press-fed curiosity about private medical information of presidential candidates. That opportunity was missed by a White House that seems to have gone out of its way not to take the medical privacy of presidential candidates seriously. Perhaps this is because the contest was never really close, and Dole's age became a surrogate for his health. Nonetheless, President Clinton struggled with the issue of releasing his medical records almost up to election day.

In a comical press conference on September 12, 1996, for example, White House Press Secretary Mike McCurry engaged in the following bizarre exchanges relating to President Clinton's medical records:

> Q: So there's nothing in any of these medical records that a normal person might consider embarrassing to the President?
>
> McCurry: I wouldn't say that . . . all of us undergo tests that I'm not sure any of us would want to have spread out and printed on the front page of the newspaper.
>
> Q: But only a few of us are running for President . . .
>
> Q: But, Mike, can you characterize a test that you think would be embarrassing? . . .
>
> Q: Does he have a sexually transmitted disease? I mean . . .
>
> Q: Jesus!
>
> McCurry: Good God, do you really want to ask that question?

Q: No, I'm just asking what's embarrassing.

McCurry: That's an astonishing question to have just been posed here in the White House . . .

Q: Mike, you seem to be saying that even taking the test—let's say an HIV positive—taking the test for HIV, or some other sexually transmitted disease, just taking the test is in and of itself embarrassing.

McCurry: Look, I'm trying to keep some level of dignity here. I'm talking about things like rectal exams, OK. Do you want to have all those things spread out there. All right, enough on this subject, I think.

Q: We really have reached a new low.

McCurry: You guys are really bored. It's hard to know that there is a campaign underway here.

McCurry was right. Not much was going Dole's way in the campaign, which was run without any issues, and the press seemed to be looking for something to write about. The *Wall Street Journal*, for example, editorialized on the basis of that press conference that although the president certainly seemed physically healthy, "his long-standing resistance [to releasing his medical records] to scrutiny suggests that something embarrassing lurks in his medical history—if not relating to sex perhaps to depression or even, like his brother, drugs."[28] Of course such baseless and politically motivated speculation can make things appear much worse than they are.

Under these conditions, it was not surprising for President Clinton to grant *New York Times* reporter Lawrence Altman a long interview on his health on October 13, 1996. Asked why he did not submit to this interview sooner the president replied, "I don't know; I can't say. I don't remember my staff saying anything about it one way or another." Altman is a skilled interviewer and asked many questions, especially about HIV tests and urine tests for illicit drugs, that I think should be out of bounds.[29] But the president answered them. Finally, Altman asked Clinton about the position I had taken in an earlier version of this chapter (urging journalists to curb their curiosity about private medical information of presidential candidates). In Altman's words, "Asked about such criticism, President Clinton said he did not regard the interview about his health as an invasion of privacy and that 'the public has right to know the condition of the President's health.'"[30] The president was right about the limit of the public's right to know, but wrong to conclude that none of Altman's questions could legitimately be considered invasions of privacy.

One year later, in the fall of 1997, President Clinton, after his annual physical examination, and in connection with a lawsuit against him by Paula Jones alleging sexual harassment, went even further in shedding his privacy and dignity. He authorized his physician to disclose, through his lawyer, on national TV, that regarding his penis, "in terms of size, shape, direction, whatever the devious mind wants to concoct, the President is a normal man." Even acerbic columnist Maureen

Dowd had to conclude that this was just too much information. In her words, "I feel sorry for him [and] maybe I simply feel sorry for us, not only for the lost dignity of the Presidency but for the lost dignity of the citizenry. The President of the United States should not be publicly strip searched."[31]

The good news is that since his election to a second term President Clinton has recognized the importance of genetic privacy; the bad news is that neither the president nor the press takes the medical privacy of presidents seriously. The press simply cannot control itself; and the more private medical information presidents provide, the more the press wants. Of course, that is the president's choice; but as President Clinton seems to understand by his often-conflicting statements, it's some choice.

CHAPTER ELEVEN

A Woman's Choice at Work

The choice between Bill Clinton and Bob Dole was decided by the women's vote, although not by the celebrated suburban "soccer moms."[1] The soccer moms comprised only 10% of all women who voted for president. Instead, the most influential block of women who voted to reelect the president were what have been called "waitress moms," low-wage, blue-collar workers. These women gave Clinton 55% of their votes, with only 28% going to Dole; among unmarried women the gap was even higher, 62% to 28%.

As Republican pollster Kellyanne Fitzpatrick, put it, "For lower wage women the government is the co-pilot or insurer. . . . Soccer moms lost control of their lives by choice, blue-collar moms have no control."[2] It is, of course, one thing for a woman to choose not to work. It is another thing for a woman who must work to support her family to have her choices of jobs and job conditions limited simply because she is a woman. In this regard the law has at least begun to support a woman's right to choose occupations, regardless of whether employers or others believe the occupation is not "woman's work" because they think the job would expose the woman to toxic chemicals that might affect a fetus.

Employers have historically sought to limit women's access to traditionally male, high-paying jobs. In one famous case, the U.S. Supreme Court upheld an Oregon law that forbade the hiring of women for factory jobs that required more than 10 hours a day. The chief justice explained that this restriction was reasonable because "healthy mothers are essential to vigorous offspring" and preserving the physical well-being of women helps "preserve the strength and vigor of the race."[3] This rationale was never particularly persuasive, and women's hours have not been limited in traditionally female, low-paid employment, such as nursing. Although such blatant sex discrimination in employment is a thing of the past, in the mid-1980s the average man earned almost 50% more per hour than the average women, and even in 1997 the median earnings for full-time working women were just under 75% of the men's median (down from 77% in 1993).[4]

The contemporary legal question is: Can employers substitute concern for fetal health for concern for women's health to limit job opportunities for women? The U.S. Supreme Court decided in March 1991 that the answer is no: Federal law prohibits employers from excluding women from job categories on the basis that they are or might become pregnant. All nine justices agreed that the fetal protection policy adopted by Johnson Controls to restrict battery manufacturing to men and sterile women was a violation of law, and six of the nine agreed that federal law prohibits any discrimination solely on the basis of pregnancy. The ruling applies to all employers engaged in interstate commerce, including hospitals and clinics.

Title VII of the Civil Rights Act of 1964 forbids employers from discriminating on the basis of race, color, religion, sex, or national origin. Explicit discrimination on the basis of religion, sex, or national origin can only be justified if the characteristic is a "bona fida occupational qualification" (BFOQ). The Pregnancy Discrimination Act of 1978 made it clear that sex discrimination includes discrimination "on the basis of pregnancy, childbirth, or related medical conditions."[5]

THE FETAL PROTECTION POLICY

Beginning in 1977, Johnson Controls advised women who expected to have children not to take jobs involving lead exposure, warned women who took such jobs of the risks of having a child while being exposed to lead, and advised workers to consult their family doctor for counsel. The risks were said to involve a higher rate of abortion as well as unspecified potential risks to the fetus. Between 1979 and 1983 eight employees became pregnant while maintaining blood lead levels in excess of 30 mg/dl (a level the Centers for Disease Control had designated as excessive for children). Although there was no evidence of harm to any of children of the employees from lead exposure, a medical consultant for the company said that he thought hyperactivity in one of the children "could very well and probably was due to the lead he had."[6]

Apparently following medical consultation on the dangers of lead exposure to the fetus, the company changed from a policy of warning to a policy of exclusion in 1982: "women who are pregnant or who are capable of bearing children will not be placed into jobs involving lead exposure or which could expose them to lead through the exercise of job bidding, bumping, transfer or promotion rights." The policy defined women capable of bearing children as all women except those who "have medical confirmation that they cannot bear children."

In 1984, a class action was brought challenging the policy as a violation of Title VII. In 1988, a federal district court granted summary judgment in favor of

Johnson Controls, primarily on the basis of depositions and affidavits from physicians and environmental toxicologists on the potential damage lead exposure could cause to developing fetuses, children, adults, and animals.[7] The U.S. Court of Appeals affirmed this decision in 1989 in a 7 to 4 opinion. The majority based its opinion primarily on the medical evidence of potential harm to the fetus, and on their view that federal law permitted employers to take this potential harm into account in developing employment policies.

THE U.S. SUPREME COURT DECISION

The U.S. Supreme Court unanimously reversed in a decision written by Justice Harry Blackmun. The Court had no trouble finding that the bias in the policy was "obvious," since "fertile men, but not fertile women, are given a choice as to whether they wish to risk their reproductive health for a particular job."[8] The Court noted that the company did not seek to protect all unconceived children, only those of its female employees. The policy was pregnancy-based, and accordingly directly in conflict with the Pregnancy Discrimination Act of 1978. The key to the case was determining whether nonpregnancy or nonpotential pregnancy was a BFOQ for battery making.

Employment discrimination is permitted "in those certain instances where religion, sex, or national origin is a bona fide occupational qualification reasonably necessary to the normal operation of that particular business or enterprise." The Court's approach was to determine if Johnson Controls' fetal protection policy came within the scope of those "certain instances." The statutory language requires that the "occupational qualification" affect "an employee's ability to do the job." The Court determined that the defense was available only when it went to the "essence of the business" or was "the core of the employee's job performance."

The Court had previously allowed a maximum security male prison to refuse to hire women guards because "the employment of a female guard would create real risks of safety to others if violence broke out because the guard was a woman." Thus sex was seen as reasonably related to the essence of the guard's job: maintaining prison security. Similarly, other courts had permitted airlines to lay off pregnant flight attendants if necessary to protect the safety of passengers. The Court agreed that protecting customer safety or security went to the essence of the business and was legitimate.

Unconceived fetuses, however, did not fit into either category. In the Court's words, "No one can disregard the possibility of injury to future children; the BFOQ, however, is not so broad that it transforms this deep social concern into an essential aspect of battery making." Limitations involving pregnancy or sex "must relate to ability to perform the duties of the job . . . women as capable of doing their jobs as their male counterparts may not be forced to choose between having a child and having a job." The Court concluded that Congress had left the welfare of the next generation to parents, not employers: "Decisions about the welfare of future children must be left to the parents who conceive, bear, support, and raise them rather than to the employers who hire those parents."

The Court finally addressed potential tort liability should a fetus be injured by its mother's occupational exposure and later sue the company. The Court opined that since the Occupational Safety and Health Administration (OSHA) had concluded that there was no basis for excluding women of childbearing age from the minimal lead exposure permitted under OSHA guidelines, the likelihood of fetal injury was slight. And even should injury occur, the injured child would have to prove that the employer was negligent. If the employer followed OSHA guidelines, and fully informed its workers of the risks involved, the Court concluded that liability seemed "remote at best." Thus just as speculation about risks to children not yet conceived has nothing to do with job performance, speculation about future tort liability—at least one step further removed from fetal harm—is not job-related.

THE CONCURRING OPINIONS

Justice Byron White wrote the main concurring opinion for himself, Chief Justice William Rehnquist, and Justice Anthony Kennedy. Although they agreed with the outcome in this case, they dissented from the BFOQ analysis as it applied to tort liability and warned that the case could be used to undercut the privacy rights of patients and other customers. These three Justices believed that under some circumstances it should be permissible for employers to exclude women on the basis that their fetuses could be injured and sue the employers. (The women themselves could not sue because they are covered by workers' compensation as their exclusive remedy.) Their logic was that parents cannot waive the rights of their children to sue, that the parents' negligence will not be imputed to the children, and that even in the absence of negligence, "it is possible that employers will be held strictly liable, if, for example, their manufacturing process is considered." Avoiding such liability, was, in the view of these Justices, a safety issue relevant to the BFOQ standard.

The other point made by these three concurring Justices was relegated to a footnote but is of substantial interest. They argued that the Court's opinion could be read to outlaw considerations of privacy as a basis for sex-based employment discrimination because privacy considerations would not directly relate to the employees' ability to do the job or to customer safety. They specifically cited cases in which the privacy wishes of some patients for nurses and nurses aides of the same sex had been upheld as a BFOQ, including the sex of nurses' aides in a retirement home,[9] and a policy excluding male nurses from obstetrics practice in a hospital.[10] The Justices in the majority reacted by saying simply, "we have never addressed privacy-based-sex discrimination and shall not do so here because the sex-based discrimination at issue today does not involve the privacy interests of

Johnson Controls' customers." This issue is left for another day, but it should be noted that the obstetrical nurse case rests on very shaky grounds.[11]

CHOICE OR CONTROL?

The Court took the language of the Pregnancy Discrimination Act seriously, correctly observing that "concern for a woman's existing or potential offspring historically has been the excuse for denying women equal employment opportunities." The purpose of the Act was to end such employment discrimination, and *Johnson Controls* holds that recasting sex discrimination in the name of fetal protection is illegal. Johnson Controls had argued that their policy was ethical and socially responsible, and meant only to prevent exposing the fetus to avoidable risk. Judge Easterbrook probably had the most articulate response to this concern in his dissent to the Appeals Court decision:

> There is a strong correlation between the health of the infant and prenatal medical care; there is also a powerful link between the parents' income and infants' health, for higher income means better nutrition, among other things. . . . Removing women from well-paying jobs (and the attendant health insurance), or denying women access to these jobs, may reduce the risk from lead while also reducing levels of medical care and quality of nutrition.

Judge Easterbrook argued that ultimately fetal protection cannot be about "zero risk," but must be about reasonable risk. He correctly noted that it is good and reasonable to worry about the health of workers and their future children. But, "to insist on zero risk . . . is to exclude women from industrial jobs that have been a male preserve. By all means let society bend its energies to improving the prospects of those who come after us. Demanding zero risk produces not progress but paralysis."

The same zero risk analysis can, of course, be applied to the possibility of tort liability as seen from the industry perspective. The industry would like its risk to be zero. Six of the nine Justices agree that it is close to zero, and at least remote. As a factual matter, there has only been one recorded case of a child bringing a lawsuit for injuries suffered while its mother was pregnant and continued to work. In this case, the jury found in favor of the employer, even though there was evidence that the employer had violated OSHA safety standards.[12] Two-thirds of the Justices ruled that state tort liability is preempted so long as the employer follows federal law, informs workers of the risks, and is not negligent. Added to this is the extraordinarily difficult issue of causation, even if the employer is negligent. Putting the two together may not yield zero risk, but it yields as close to zero risk as is reasonable to expect.

It has been persuasively suggested that fetal protection policies that affect only women are based on the view that women are "primarily biologic actors" and not economic ones and that men are only economic actors who have no "biologic connections and responsibilities to their families."[13] *Johnson Controls* continues the legal and social movement to provide equality of opportunity in the workplace. It does not eliminate the duty to minimize workplace exposures to toxic substances. Indeed, it would be a hollow victory for women to gain the "right" to choose to be exposed to the same mutagens and other toxic substances that men get exposed to. Some choice. The real public policy challenge remains to get the focus off new methods of sex discrimination and onto new ways to reduce workplace hazards.

Elizabeth Perle McKenna has usefully put the issue another way: "The unfinished women's revolution continues. For all this country's talk about valuing families, we all still work in a world where we're best rewarded if we pretend we don't have any."[14] McKenna goes on to argue that the more women work, the more women will bring their values with them and will help "humanize" the workplace. The humanization she hopes to see includes a work environment that is not just safe for women but also one in which "careers aren't traumatized by the birth of a child, where 'flex time' and 'job sharing' aren't synonyms for 'mommy track,' [and where] balance, meaning and connection become as important as money, power and prestige."

Employers must reduce exposure to harmful toxic substances in the workplace for all workers (by replacing such agents with others, reducing their volume, and encouraging the use of protective gear), both men and women, warn all workers about health risks of exposures that cannot be avoided, and encourage workers to be monitored for the early signs of damage. Personal physicians should continue to take an occupational history and be able to tell their patients about the risks of exposure to various substances, including what is known about their mutagenicity and teratogenicity. Armed with this information, workers, both men and women, will be able to make an informed decision about their jobs and the risks they are willing to run to keep them, as well as to intelligently pressure management to make the workplace safer.

Congress and the Court have made very strong statements about the use of fetal protection as a rationale to control or restrict the activities and decisions of women: The ultimate decisionmaker must be the woman worker. These statements are consistent with good medical practice as well, such as the policy of the American College of Obstetrics and Gynecology on maternal–fetal conflicts.[15] Obstetricians have learned that women do not lose their constitutional right to choose and make decisions for themselves by becoming pregnant or deciding to continue a pregnancy. To paraphrase Justice Blackmun: It is no more appropriate for physicians than it is for the courts or individual employers to attempt to control women's opportunities and choices based on their reproductive role. In the next chapter I turn to a group of workers who have even fewer choices than women: soldiers in the U.S. military.

CHAPTER TWELVE

A Soldier's Choice

In his classic treatise *On War*, Karl von Clausewitz emphasizes that courage is the "first quality of the warrior."[1] He defines two types of courage: "courage in the presence of danger to the person, and next, courage in the presence of responsibility, whether before the judgment seat of an external authority, or before that of the internal authority which is conscience."[2] Both were involved in the U.S. military's decision to seek a waiver of informed consent requirements for the use of investigational drugs and vaccines on our troops in the Persian Gulf War. The danger of chemical and biological warfare was seen as demanding this waiver, while the Nuremberg Code, medical ethics, and respect for the human rights of American soldiers cautioned against it. The legal maneuvering to revise consent regulations for wartime conditions provides a case study illustrating how the boundary line between therapy and experimentation can become hopelessly blurred, the differences between law and ethics, and the ethical obligations of military physicians.

THE NUREMBERG CODE AND THE U.S. ARMY

The Nuremberg Code was promulgated by U.S. judges acting under the authority of the U.S. Army at Nuremberg in 1947.[3] The defendants in the Doctors' Trial were charged with war crimes and crimes against humanity for performing both lethal and nonlethal experiments on concentration camp prisoners. Most were found guilty, and seven were hanged. The judges also enunciated the Nuremberg Code, a ten point declaration governing human experimentation based on "principles of the law of nations as they result from the usages established among civilized peoples, from the laws of humanity, and from the dictates of public conscience." The first and central principle provides that the voluntary, competent, informed, and understanding consent of the subject is "absolutely essential." There are no exceptions for soldiers or for wartime, and until the Gulf War, the U.S. military had accepted the Nuremberg Code as their guide. The military had never argued that there should be any exception to the Code's informed consent requirement. Current U.S. statutory law also requires that informed consent be obtained for all "investigational use" of drugs, except where the investigator deems it "not feasible, or in their professional judgment, contrary to the best interests of [the subjects]."[4]

In the fall of 1990, following the invasion of Kuwait by Iraq, the Department of Defense (DoD) sought a waiver of the informed consent requirements of existing human experimentation regulations from the Food and Drug Administration (FDA) to authorize the military use of investigational drugs and vaccines on soldiers involved in the Gulf War without their informed consent. The basis of the waiver request was military expediency. In DoD's words: "In all peace time applications, we believe strongly in informed consent and ethical foundations . . . but military combat is different." The DoD's rationale was that informed consent under combat conditions was "not feasible" because some troops might refuse to consent, and the military could not tolerate such refusals because of "military combat exigencies."[5] The FDA granted the request and issued a new general regulation, Rule 23(d), that permits drug-by-drug waiver approval on the basis that consent is "not feasible" in a specific military operation involving combat or the immediate threat of combat."[6]

THE DISTRICT COURT

Shortly after the regulation was promulgated, and just prior to Desert Storm, Sidney Wolfe's Health Research Group (a part of Public Citizen) brought suit on behalf of an unnamed soldier (John Doe) and his wife to enjoin the DoD from using Rule 23(d) drugs on troops in the Gulf without consent. The FDA had granted Rule 23(d) waivers for the use of two agents, pyridostigmine bromide 30 mg tablets (for use as a "pretreatment" prior to nerve gas attack) and pentavalent botulinum toxoid vaccine (to protect against botulism in biological warfare), and these were the only waivers that have ever been granted under the rule.

U.S. District Judge Stanley Harris made it clear that he had no desire to get involved with military matters. In his words, "The DoD's decision to use unapproved drugs is precisely the type of military decision that courts have repeatedly refused to second-guess."[7] He characterized the decision as one to protect individual servicemen, and as "strategic" in nature, and thus not reviewable by a court. He went on, however, to say that if he thought he had the authority to review the decision, he would uphold it.

Consistent with the Nuremberg Code, the Defense Authorization Act prohibits DoD from using any of its funds "for any research involving a human being as an experimental subject" unless the subject's informed consent has been obtained. This Congressional restriction was in reaction to U.S. Army experiments on servicemen using both radiation and LSD at the beginning of the cold war. Judge Harris, however, decided that "the primary purpose of administering the drugs is military, not scientific," and therefore the statutory prohibition was inapplicable.

The "not feasible" exception had previously applied only to subjects who were unable to communicate, unconscious, or incompetent. Nonetheless, Judge Harris decided the FDA could reinterpret this exception as long as its interpretation was not "arbitrary, capricious or manifestly contrary to the statute." Finally, Judge Harris rejected the claim that forced administration of unapproved drugs violates the 5th Amendment liberty interest of servicemen. Instead he found that the military's interests in trying to prevent injury to troops and "successfully accomplishing the military goals of Operation Desert Storm" were sufficient to justify the exception to informed consent. The Nuremberg Code was not mentioned in the decision.

THE COURT OF APPEALS

John Doe appealed. At the hearing, held after the war was over (in March 1991), a letter from DoD to FDA, saying that the military requirements for use of the two agents without informed consent had ended, was introduced into evidence. DoD also informed FDA: "Central Command has recently reported that the military command in the theatre of operations decided to administer the [botulinum] vaccine on a voluntary basis. The pyridostigmine tablets were used without prior informed consent." On the basis of the end of the war and the DoD letter, the Justice Department argued that the case was moot and should be dismissed.

The majority of the court, in a 2 to 1 opinion written by Judge Ruth Bader Ginsburg (now Justice Ginsburg) in July 1991, disagreed.[8] The court concluded that even though DoD had withdrawn its two specific waivers, Rule 23(b) remained in effect, and therefore the required use of unapproved agents was both capable of repetition and evading review. The Court of Appeals relied heavily on government reports concerning the proliferation of nuclear, chemical, and biological weapons systems, especially among third world nations like Iraq. On the merits, the court disagreed with the lower court that the case was beyond court review because it was military in nature. Instead the Court of Appeals defined the issue as a challenge to FDA's authority to issue a waiver of its consent regulations to DoD, not as an action challenging military decisions. The Court of Appeals did, however, agree with all the other conclusions of the lower court. Again, no mention was made of the Nuremberg Code.

Judge Clarence Thomas (now Justice Thomas) dissented. He agreed with the Justice Department, arguing that because the war was over, and because it was virtually impossible for John Doe himself to be subjected to the rule again, the case should be dismissed as moot. He said that the majority "surely overstates" the risk of future chemical warfare, noting that "after all, American soldiers have not been the victims of organized chemical attack since the First World War." He also stressed that there was no "reasonable likelihood that John Doe *personally*" will be involved in any future war using chemical weapons. In his words, "The majority focuses on Rule 23(b) in the abstract—and in the process forgets about Doe, the plaintiff."

THE COURTS AND WAR

Since the time of Cicero it has been said that *inter arma leges silentae sunt*—amid the clash of arms the laws are silent.[9] This was certainly true of the forced internment of Japanese–Americans during World War II, and was true of the courts here as well. While troops are in the field, courts are unlikely to make any decisions that make them appear to be interfering with the military decisionmaking. This realpolitik is disturbing because it undermines progress in human rights, but nonetheless remains consistent. The brief history of international human rights has, after all, been written primarily in the aftermath of war: the founding of the United Nations in 1946, the Universal Declaration of Human Rights in 1948, and current efforts to foster human rights in the wake of the cold war. Neither of these two courts could acknowledge (let alone discuss) the Nuremberg Code. The waiver rule permits direct violations of the Nuremberg Code, and acknowledging this could have embarrassed the United States by making us look hypocritical internationally. This is because members of the Bush administration were calling for a "Nuremberg-like" tribunal to try Saddam Hussein and his military leaders for violations of international law at the time these cases were heard in our own courts. International human rights laws must, of course, apply to both victors and vanquished.

Even though Rule 23(d) authorizes the violation of the consent requirements of the Nuremberg Code, it can be reasonably argued that the Code itself was not actually violated in the Gulf War. The argument is that the Code applies only to human experimentation or research on human beings and that DoD was not actually conducting research. What was at stake with the pyridostigmine bromide tablets was the use of an approved and licensed drug for an unapproved use. This can be justified if there is good scientific evidence to support its safety, and could even be considered treatment or "pretreatment" if nerve agent attack appears imminent, as it did to the commander of the XVIII Airborne Corps whose 41,650 soldiers took the drug in tablet form for one to seven days at eight-hour intervals.[10] Members of the military (unlike civilians) have no right to refuse any medical *treatment* that can make them fit for combat or return them to active duty. Thus, if pyridostigmine can reasonably be considered treatment, it needs no exception to Nuremberg: Nuremberg is simply inapplicable.[11] I think this argument is correct. But this means that the military was simply wrong to ask for a waiver of the requirement of informed consent to administer this agent in a research trial. The Court of Appeals should have used this rationale for its decision. If the drug is really a treatment, no waiver of consent is necessary; if it is experimental, no waiver of consent should be permitted. The Army, Navy, and Air Force seem to have agreed with this, and were prepared to use pyridostigmine long before the waiver was even sought.[12]

It is much more difficult, however, to make this argument regarding botulinum toxoid vaccine. This vaccine had been used by about 3,000 laboratory workers in the past, but its use was discontinued briefly in the mid-1970s (before sufficient safety or efficacy data had been gathered to qualify it for licensure), and few laboratory workers have used it since. It remains an experimental agent, and the Centers for Disease Control has an elaborate consent form that explains its experimental nature under their IND (investigational new drug) protocol. This is why a U.S. Army IRB at Fort Dietrich voted, in October 1990, to require consent for this vaccine if used in the Gulf.[13] The reason the military may not have violated the Nuremberg Code by using this vaccine on troops is not because it can be legitimately considered treatment or therapy, but because the military appears to have ultimately decided to give our troops in the Gulf information about the vaccine and the right to refuse to be vaccinated. We can be somewhat skeptical about the meaning of "voluntary" under imminent combat conditions. Nonetheless, this decision merits commendation, and one would like to know more about how and why military commanders in the field chose not to take advantage of the legal authority they had to use this vaccine on their troops without consent.[14] No matter what their motivation, however, they did the right thing and took the principles of the Nuremberg Code more seriously than DoD, FDA, or these two courts did.

As the Court of Appeals noted, DoD had argued in court that these agents had not been previously tested in controlled clinical trials "because humans cannot intentionally be exposed to chemical or biological [warfare] agents in order to test the effectiveness of a drug." This is true, but only because it violates another dictate of the Nuremberg Code: "No experiment should be conducted where there is an *a priori* reason to believe that death or disabling injury will occur." General Norman Schwartzkoff and his medical command seem to have understood that one cannot pick and choose which provisions of the Nuremberg Code to take seriously without being hypocritical.

Immediately after the war I opined (wrongly, it turns out) that the risk of chemical and biological warfare in the Gulf had been overstated. Likewise, the DoD assured the nation until 1996 that there were no troops exposed to Iraqi chemical weapons. In mid-1997, however, the Pentagon admitted that as many as 100,000 U.S. troops may have been exposed to low levels of the nerve agent sarin after the war when American combat engineers exploded the Kamisiyaw ammunition depot.[15] There are at least two explanations for covering up these exposures. First, pyridostigmine bromide is designed as a pretreatment to a soman attack (followed by atropine and 2-PAM in the event of attack), but it may be contraindicated for sarin, another agent held by Iraq.[16] Therefore, use of pyrido-stigmine may either indicate a breakdown of intelligence before the war, or acknowledge an inability to protect troops against both sarin and soman at the same time. Second, even a small exposure to sarin could produce delayed nerve damage, especially in concert with other exposures, including pyridostigmine itself.[17] There is likely no single cause of Gulf War syndrome, but such an exposure could be one.[18]

ROLE OF MILITARY PHYSICIANS

What should physicians in the military do when asked to administer investigational agents without the informed consent of the soldiers? Even if such administration is legal (as the courts have ruled), it is unethical and following orders is no excuse for unethical conduct, even in combat. It would seem that the only justification a physician could have for participating in the administration of experimental or investigational agents without consent is that the physician sincerely believes that the agents are therapeutic under combat conditions. This is a difficult position to defend, since war does not change the investigational nature of a drug or vaccine. Such a decision would also be contrary to military regulations which are that although a serviceperson must accept standard medical treatment or face court martial, soldiers have no obligation to accept interventions that are not generally recognized by the medical profession as standard procedures.[19]

A related question is whether the military physician is primarily responsible for the health and well-being of the soldiers under the physician's care (as in civilian life) or must subordinate the medical interests of the soldier–patients to the military mission. Remarkably there is no written policy or standard view on this question in the military. This issue deserves critical attention in peacetime, since it is not susceptible to rational thought during wartime. An unequivocal policy upholding traditional patient-centered ethics, although not legally required, seems the most responsible position for U.S. military physicians to take.

SHOULD THE NUREMBERG CODE APPLY TO THE MILITARY?

The United States is and should remain at the forefront of the worldwide human rights movement. In crafting exceptions for the military, even in wartime, we do more damage to ourselves than to our enemies, because any major retreat from supporting human rights is destructive to both our credibility and to the cause of human rights. It is also simply not true that members of the U.S. military cannot understand or appreciate military missions to such an extent that informed consent is "not feasible" in combat situations. According to DoD itself, this turned out not to be true in Desert Storm, nor in Korea or Vietnam. Although the U.S. Supreme Court has ruled that U.S. soldiers cannot sue the military for money damages for violation of the Nuremberg Code, all of the Justices have said that an injunction against such violations can be sought in a civilian court (as the plaintiff in the Desert Storm case did).[20] Unfortunately, during war, courts ignore human rights, and thus our soldiers are left without a remedy as a practical matter. Our military must have the courage to continue to take the Nuremberg Code seriously in its own ranks, since no court will second-guess last-minute rule rewriting or impose Nuremberg's legal and ethical dictates on the military in wartime.

The U.S. military is interested in the possible combat-related use of approximately 20 vaccines which are currently investigational.[21] There is a clear need for a policy on their use. The Gulf War experience should reinforce the lessons of the Nuremberg Code: Except where the agent has had extensive enough human testing to have been proven safe, no agent should be used on American troops without their informed consent. Investigational agents can be used in combat; but soldiers must get to make the decision based on what is known about their risks and benefits. The pyridostigmine experience provides a useful example. Although pyridostigmine tablets were ordered to be taken, there was no real way to monitor their use, and as the military investigators noted, "full compliance with an every-eight-hour regimen would be unlikely when soldiers themselves believed the nerve agent threat was low." Nonetheless, at the beginning of hostilities in January, compliance seems to have been "well over 99%."[22] In short, it is not only ethically wrong to force compliance on soldiers, it is impossible and militarily unnecessary.

In December 1995 I was invited to participate in a meeting on Rule 23(d) sponsored by the Presidential Advisory Committee on Gulf War Veterans' Illnesses. During the meeting the DoD representative continually referred to American soldiers as "the kids" and the responsibility of DoD to protect "the kids." I probably waited too long to tell him that I found this offensive, and he apologized for his choice of words. Nonetheless, the words are telling: Rule 23(d) treats American soldiers like kids by applying the basic rules for research on children to them with regard to consent—someone else makes the decision for them because they are seen as too immature to make it for themselves. For an adult this is, of course, always an affront to human dignity and disrespectful of personhood. In this regard Rule 23(d) is a mistake and an aberration. As General Dennis Reimer, the Army's Chief of Staff, has emphasized, the Army is committed to treating all its troops "with dignity and respect."[23]

Soldiers are not pieces of equipment. They have numbers, but they retain their humanity and basic human rights. The DoD should have exercised a third kind of courage—the courage to admit its mistake—and asked the FDA to rescind Rule 23(d) and remove this pointless blot on our military laws. Instead, when the FDA was petitioned by Public Citizen to revoke the rule in 1996, the DoD supported continuing the waiver of consent rule as "fully consistent with law and ethics." In mid-1997 the FDA finally asked for public comments on what should become of the rule.[24] The answer remains simple: It should be rescinded because it violates every code and ethical principle developed since World War II to regulate research with human subjects, and it is unacceptable to permit commanders to turn soldiers into human subjects. The field commanders in Desert Storm seem to have realized this instinctively. Soldiers who fight to protect basic human rights must be protected by them.

The next two chapters address broader issues of research with human subjects. The first explores government-sponsored research aimed not at insuring military superiority, but at developing a genetically perfect human and an immortal human. The second, Chapter 14, confronts the problem of ambiguity and duplicity in more everyday medical research and how these problems affect the research subject's choices.

CHAPTER THIRTEEN

Our Most Important Product

The following minutes from an October 1994 meeting of a top secret federal inter-agency group known as Perfect People 2020 (PP2020) were mistakenly provided to the author following a Freedom of Information request. When the mistake was discovered, the U.S. Attorney General attempted to recover the document alleging that its dissemination would violate national security interests. A federal judge reviewed the document and personally excised all material that could affect national security. What follows is representative of both the entire document and the overall research strategy of PP2020. The group apparently meets once every five years to assess their progress.

MINUTES PP2020

The meeting began at 1800 hours on 31 October 1994 and opened with a general discussion of the events of the past five years. All present agreed that with the end of the cold war the overall goals of Perfect People 2020 (PP2020) should be modified. From its post-WWII inception, the group's primary goal had been to develop the perfect soldier—one who could survive illness, injury, or capture and continue to function effectively as a fighting man. In the mid-1960s the group also decided to work toward developing the perfect astronaut for space flights. Although real progress has been made toward attaining both of these goals (see below), the group agreed that they are too narrowly defined. Instead, the group adopted as its new goals the same goals that are currently being pursued by noncovert researchers in America's academic medical centers: human immortality and the genetically perfect human.

It was noted that there may soon be no further need of PP2020 since it now appears that the public is willing to accept virtually *any* experiment on a human being that promises either to lengthen life or to alter or eliminate genetic defects. A 1992 public opinion poll, for example, found that although 86% of Americans know "little" or "nothing" about gene therapy, 89% approve its use in both therapy and research.

It was also noted that although the 1947 Nuremberg Code requires protecting both the rights and the welfare of human subjects, most contemporary researchers and bioethicists seem content to approve any experiment in which either the welfare of the subject is protected by prior peer review *or* the rights of the subject are protected by required consent to the experiment. In the case of terminally ill subjects, the researcher's assertion of trying to save the life of the subject seems sufficient in virtually all instances.

It was agreed that the trend of treating all research as therapy is one PP2020 should actively encourage. We will therefore continue to financially support both ACT-UP and the *Wall Street Journal* as long as they continue their campaigns to destroy the distinction between experimentation and treatment. [national security deletions]

PAST EXPERIMENTS

There was considerable debate over which experiment or series of experiments that the various divisions of PP2020 have sponsored since WWII should be considered prototypes for future work. Much support was voiced for joint CIA/US Army mind control experiments. The members agreed that it was unfortunate that these experiments, most conducted in the 1950s, have become public. All members were heartened, however, by the U.S. Supreme Court's 1987 decision that experimental subjects who are members of the U.S. armed forces cannot sue experimenters or their bosses who cause them permanent injury, even if there was neither informed consent nor prior peer review of the experiment. This opinion makes members of the active-duty U.S. military ideal subjects for risky experiments. [national security deletions] It was the consensus of the group that whenever possible members of the military should be used as experimental subjects when healthy volunteers are required. The U.S. courts also proved very helpful and supportive of our efforts in Desert Storm when they approved of our scheme to use experimental drugs and vaccines on our troops without their consent—although we did agree to have the protocols reviewed at the Department of Defense prior to commencing our experiments. The group did not speculate on how soon we can count on another shooting war, but group members all agreed to have new biological and chemical warfare experiments ready to go in the event that the opportunity arises in the near future.

The other candidates for best prototype were more closely related to the new goals of PP2020. Perhaps the most spectacular was the 1971–84 experiment with

David, also known as the bubble boy. He lived almost his entire life in the sterile plastic bubble and provided a tremendous amount of information for both our space travel and our immortality studies. X2 expressed (as he had at our last meeting five years ago) astonishment that the American public accepted this experiment—he had urged that it be conducted in secret. It is now X2's view that if it is societally acceptable to raise a human being in a laboratory—to live a completely artificial life—then anything goes in American experimental medicine already, and PP2020 is unnecessary. Other members of the group thought we just got lucky with the bubble boy. Instead of considering his bubble a cage or a prison, for example, most Americans (those who thought about it at all) considered it a life-saving device. Paul Simon also helped with his song about miracles and wonders, complete with examples: "the boy in the bubble and the baby with the baboon heart." The Baby Fae experiment was not sponsored by PP2020, but the group strongly approved of the experiment—although none of the members believed that it should have been done on a child. Instead, PP2020 has been encouraging researchers to do xenografts as bridges to human organ transplants on adults. Although the use of pig livers as bridges has gotten some bad press, the group considered these experiments a scientific success and will continue to fund xenograft work across the country. More funding will also be made available for work on transgenic pigs, as well as on pig cloning.

The xenograft goal is to produce a virtually infinite supply of replacement organs so that the lifespan of chosen individuals can be significantly extended. This is a short-term goal. Long term, all members of the group believe that artificial organs will be the ultimate replacement parts and that the overall goal (discussed below) must be production of a totally artificial body which will act as a permanent enclosure to protect the human brain. [national security deletions.] The general assessment of the artificial heart program was that it was on track. X12 was congratulated all around for his exemplary work on the Institute of Medicine's artificial heart assessment panel, which endorsed continued research on the artificial heart in the face of NIH criticism.

Some of the most exciting work is currently being done in the field of cryonics. We have established that the human embryo can be frozen and thawed out later for implantation without damage to the resulting child. This work has won wide public support, and the group believes that most of it will continue with existing private funding. We have also been extraordinarily successful in launching the Human Genome Project (HGP) as a cover for our genetic engineering research program. We were also successful in getting the HGP to fund our friends the bioethicists. No intellectual development in America has been as helpful to our programs as the bioethics community, and they deserve our support. Our goal of producing a grass-eating human who is resistant to radiation and chemical and biological warfare toxins now seems doable by 2020.

We will also continue to support research designed to experiment on extracorporeal human embryos with identified genetic disorders, such as cystic fibrosis, to see if defective genes can be suppressed or replaced. In this regard the work of X3 with NIH's Recombinant DNA Advisory Committee has been very effective. The consensus was that, at least in genetics if not in all areas, we will not have to force our experiments on the population—the American people can easily be made to demand genetic perfection as their right with simple advertising. Cosmetic surgery provides a useful model here. Experimental medicine aimed at enhancement really is a consumer good.

E8 observed that the public has already begun to demand whole body cryo-preservation as a right. A California male, dying of a brain tumor, went to court to seek a declaratory judgment that he had the legal right to be frozen prior to death. Although the judges failed to grant his petition, his request got lots of publicity. It won't be long until our own private foundations (established to cryo-preserve individuals and attempt to revive them in the future) will be open for business. This will be great. Although the group decided not to initiate legislation on this issue now, we will support any individual or group that does so in the future. We will also continue our support for all state aid in dying and physician-assisted suicide referendums with a view to amend them to include predeath cryopreservation.

NEW AND CONTINUING PROJECTS

L103. There was some sentiment to shut down our citizen monitoring projects which have been concentrated on the development of unremovable devices. When New Jersey canceled its parole program using ankle monitors, it was a body blow to the future to these devices. Nonetheless, our new concept of an employee smart card ID, which the employer can use to monitor where the employee is, with whom, and for how long, got some support. The project will continue and work on audio-visual feedback will be added.

X7 asked for group approval to begin his project to implant nonremovable monitoring devices at the base of the brain of neonates in three hospitals (L103B). The implantations would be done by nurses trained by our agents. The devices would not only permit us to locate all the implantees at any time but could be programmed in the future to broadcast the sound around them and to play subliminal messages directly to their brains. The experiment was approved, subject to review in five years. [national security deletions]

L195. G3 reported that his organization was having trouble recruiting surrogate mothers for his genetic experiments. He proposes setting up a new institute (akin to Will Gaylin's neomortuary) which would house women who are in persistent vegetative states. The uteruses of these women would be hormonally prepared and used to incubate embryos that we have genetically altered. This would have many advantages. The most clear one is that when the children are born, they would have no living parents who knew or cared about them. Thus we could continue our experiments on the children without having to worry about unwanted publicity. Until our artificial uterus is constructed (and this project [A18] is way behind schedule) this seems a viable option. The members generally agreed, although the group required that the facility be located outside the United States and have a self-destruct mechanism that could be activated by the chair at any time. [national security deletions] Long-term plans call for the genetic alteration of all female embryos (a sonic mutator that can be placed in prenatal clinics is under consideration) to disable the fallopian tubes. This will, of course, require that these women (eventually all women) use IVF to have children, which will in turn give us access to their embryos. The ultimate plan is to screen all human embryos and enhance desirable genetic characteristics. Defective embryos would, of course, be discarded. Our project to crossbreed a chimpanzee and a human [A35] was eliminated as no longer necessary. The living offspring will be sacrificed.

L96 & 97. A lively discussion followed the suggestion that we shut down the human gill adaptation program (GAP) and the human wing adaptation program (WAP). These programs are designed to use human fetuses that are aborted alive as subjects for grafting gill slits and wings. So far the results have been terrible, although one fetus did survive more than a week under water and the gills did function. Therefore we know it can be done. None of the grafted wings have functioned. Since the ocean will have to be used for human habitation within two or three centuries, it was decided that GAP should continue. WAP will be shelved until GAP is successful. The bionic wheel project [A26] was also suspended, although artificial wheels have been successfully attached to two Department of Veterans Affairs patients who were double amputees. The general feeling in the room was that although the bionic wheel will be much more efficient for space travel, astronauts may want to walk on the destination planet.

COORDINATION

There was basic agreement that all projects for the next five-year period should be coordinated by two leaders: a principal investigator for immortality (PII) and a principal investigator for the perfect human (PIPH). The immortality project will concentrate on cryonics. It will perfect ways to freeze and store embryos, fetuses, and live (but near-death) children and adults. In addition, this project will continue its development of a totally artificial body that can serve as a receptacle for a human brain. The existing portions of the project will be shifted away from the goal of creating the ultimate fighting machine to the goal of creating the immortal citizen. [national security deletions]

The perfect human project will devote all of its efforts for the next five years to (1) the detection of genetic diseases in the early human embryo and (2) the enhancement of human characteristics in the early human embryo. We will be looking to genetically engineer a taller, stronger, smarter, and more beautiful human with a longer lifespan. We will be kept informed of all developments at all labs sponsored in whole or in part by the NIH/DOE Human Genome Project. In this regard G5 reported that his Liberty Project has been more successful than anyone could have hoped. Not only did the project successfully convince the last two administrations to viciously attack the constitutional notion of privacy (and replace it with liberty), but we have also been successful in getting two people who share our views on the U.S. Supreme Court: Justices Antonin Scalia and Clarence Thomas. G5 thinks it is overly optimistic to conclude that privacy is a dead issue, but he does think its influence will wilt to such an extent that the concept will have little power to deter our genetics program.

THE HUMAN GENOME DIVERSITY PROJECT

The group got copies of an internal memorandum prepared earlier this year by ETHCON LTD, an ethics consulting group specializing in helping multinational corporations with scientific research projects. ETHCON was hired to help revive the stalled Human Genome Diversity Project. The text is as follows:

> The Human Genome Project has been able to flourish both because it has well-defined scientific goals and because it has taken ethical concerns seriously enough to allocate up to 5% of its annual US budget to explore ethical issues. The much less ambitious Human Genome Diversity Project has faltered and seems in danger of collapse. This is because the project lacks a clear scientific goal, and the ethical issues inherent in collecting DNA samples from the world's vanishing tribes have not been seriously addressed.
>
> Indigenous peoples, especially those that have remained geographically isolated, carry genes that may hold the key to documenting prehistoric migrations, patterns of natural selection, as well as information on the social structure of populations and the frequency and types of mutations our species have experienced. This information could provide invaluable clues to the evolutionary and migration patterns of our species, as well as insights into both anthropology and archeology. Such genomes can, for example, help provide independent verification for the work of geochronologists. The Human Genome Project is aimed at mapping and sequencing the 3 billion base pairs that make up the DNA of the typical human being. But as important as similarities are to understanding genetic function, an understanding of human genetic diversity is at least equally important. Studying diversity will require genetic samples from as many diverse human groups as possible, and could lead to the establishment of what has been termed a fundamental database, a planetary encyclopedia of genomes.
>
> Many unique groups of indigenous peoples are in danger of extinction from deforestation, economic pressures, wars, and assimilation, and many of them will likely soon become extinct. If humanity is not to lose the benefit of their genetic information, steps must be taken immediately to collect it. As has been noted, "Humans are an endangered species from the point of view of genetic history . . . [and only] international collaboration . . . [can] save the vanishing information

on the history of *Homo sapiens* from extinction."* (The recognition of this threat of loss of genetic knowledge which "harbors the clues to the evolution of our species" provided the impetus for a call for a worldwide survey of human genetic diversity in 1991.[†] The tepid response the Human Genome Diversity Project has evoked is unfortunate. There have been logistical challenges. The proposal calls for collecting blood, saliva and hair samples from each of 25 unrelated men and women of approximately 500 of the world's most "exceptionally interesting and unique populations . . . [those that] cry for immortalization."[†] Difficulty has been encountered in collecting blood samples and transporting them in liquid nitrogen to an appropriate laboratory facility where immortal cell lines can be produced.

There has also been the challenge of identifying the groups to be sampled of the estimated 7,000 candidates worldwide. Given sufficient funding, as many groups as feasible should be included, since any useful survey should be both worldwide and geographically comprehensive. The original proposal mentioned the peoples of Africa; the Etas of Japan; insular populations of Malaysia and southeastern Asia; ethnic minorities in China; the Polynesians; the aborigines of Australia and Melanesia; the Kurds of eastern Turkey; the peoples of the Caucasus; the Lapps; the Basques, and many of the native American populations. Special efforts, of course, would be made to immediately target tribes thought to be on the verge of extinction, including the Pkenan of Sarawak, the Tawahka Sumu of Honduras, the Bushmen of Namibia, the Yanomami and Awa-Guaja Indians of the Amazon, the Hadza of Tansania, the Yukaghir of Siberia, and the Orge and Greater Andamanese of Malaysia.*

The major challenges to the project, however, are not logistical or tactical, but scientific and ethical. Gene researchers themselves are not responsible for the fact that many of these tribes and groups are becoming extinct. But by taking from them the only thing they possess that the world values—their DNA—genetic researchers could be seen as at least indirectly contributing to their destruction. From a scientific point of view, collecting genetic samples is also second best. It is scientifically far superior to be able to have the individuals from whom samples are collected available for further study should unique genetic characteristics be discovered. In collecting DNA samples only, without the possibility of follow-up studies on the source person, researchers are acting more like butterfly or plant collectors than scientists. Equally important from a scientific perspective, the project has lacked a coherent hypothesis.

Although the proponents of the project have argued that the indigenous populations "cry for immortalization," in fact the project's goal is simply to immortalize cells. This mining of a group's genetic resources is a kind of neocolonialism, which might be termed "genocolonialism." The DNA of indigenous populations is collected for the benefit of the dominant culture, and both the knowledge and profits from the collected DNA are expropriated for the sole benefit of the dominant culture. To the extent that patents are sought on cell lines and DNA sequences, the practice has been termed "biopiracy." Informed consent provides no justification because no people or tribe is likely to willingly cooperate in its own extinc-

---

*Bowcock, A. M., Cavalli-Sforza, L. L., The Study of Variation in the Human Genome, *Genomics* 1991; 11:491–498.

[†]Cavalli-Sforza, L. L., Wilson, A. C., Cantor, C. R., Cook-Deegan, R. M., King, M. C., Call for a Worldwide Survey of Human Genetic Diversity: A Vanishing Opportunity for the Human Genome Project, *Genomics* 1991; 11:490–491.

tion by donating the only resource the rest of the world believes makes the tribe itself worth trying to save. It has also been suggested that the project might reinforce racism by emphasizing genetic differences among ethnic groups.

1993 was the United Nation's International Year of the World's Indigenous People. Unfortunately, neither the UN nor the indigenous peoples embraced the project. Instead, the World Council of Indigenous Peoples unanimously voted to "categorically reject and condemn the Human Genome Diversity Project as it applies to our rights, lives, and dignity" in December 1993. John Liddle, the Director of the Central Australian Aboriginal Congress lamented: "Over the last 200 years, nonAboriginal people have taken our land, language, culture, health—even our children. Now they want to take the genetic material which makes us Aboriginal people as well."

Fortunately there are straightforward ethical, scientific, and public relations strategies that should permit this project to regain its momentum while inspiring cooperation among the world's scientists and funding agencies, including UNESCO, WHO and UNIDO. The core strategy is to offer the vanishing tribes internationally-guaranteed sanctuary. Since this is not possible where they now live, twenty-five males and females from each of the chosen vanishing tribes or groups can be relocated to a suitable island which could be purchased by a worldwide consortium of funders. Given the large number of tribes from rain forest areas, Madagascar and Sumatra immediately suggest themselves as possible sites for the sanctuaries. Each tribe would, of course, have its own individual sanctuary, as it would be important both to them and to the project to keep their individual gene pools uncontaminated. To help compensate them for their relocation, they could receive first world vaccinations and other medical care.

Although the sanctuaries will require significant funding during the development phase, they could eventually become self-supporting. A number of revenue sources can be envisioned. For example, the tribes involved can be permitted to retain a portion of the royalties (perhaps 10%) generated on their cell lines that produce useful products and are patented by the funding agencies and various multinational corporations. The US has already evidenced interest in patenting cell lines obtained from a Guaymi woman from Panama; an individual from Papua New Guinea, and a Solomon Islander. A conference center and theme park could be constructed on the island. Traditional arts and crafts could also be sold through mail order catalogs.

It is essential that population control over the endangered tribes in the sanctuary be strictly maintained, since land resources available to them will be limited. To that end, contraception would be heavily emphasized through means traditional to each society as well as through other Western methods, such as latex condoms, cervical shields, and abstinence. Should these methods of population control fail and the population excess threaten a tribe's continued survival, excess members could conceivably be sacrificed, but only as a last resort.

The project will also be much more attractive to the general public if it holds out the promise of curing serious diseases. Accordingly, medical progress through understanding genetic diversity should be adopted as one of the project's primary goals. To help assure the international community that ethics is being taken seriously, all medical research conducted at the sanctuary should be reviewed and approved by an international ethics commission made up of leading genetic scientists, as well as a representative from the endangered tribes. Phase I of the project should adopt as its scientific hypothesis that all vanishing tribes carry an extinction gene. Project scientists will try to identify this gene, along with its environmental triggers.

This proposal has the great advantage of addressing the scientific and ethical problems inherent in the diversity project head on. Only something like this proposal can save the Human Genome Diversity Project by replacing its ethical vacuum with a realistic ethical framework. An argument can also be made that this proposal is consistent with the UN's draft Declaration on the Rights of Indigenous Peoples since it provides tribes likely to become extinct soon with a realistic chance of long-term survival, and therefore prevents rather than promotes both ethnicide and cultural genocide. Consistent with the Declaration, the project should promise that there will be no relocation without the free and informed consent of the indigenous peoples themselves or their community leaders as well as assurance that consent will be obtained in a culturally-sensitive manner. Moreover, within each sanctuary, individual tribes will be guaranteed the rights under the Declaration, including "the right to revitalize, use, develop, and transmit to future generations their languages, oral traditions, writing systems and literature's, and to designate and maintain their own names for communities, places and persons."

A detailed blueprint for obtaining informed consent, determining which members of vanishing tribes should be transported, and governance procedures for the sanctuaries, is under preparation. In the meantime, a concerted public relations campaign dedicated to characterizing the project as a truly cooperative attempt to understand human history and to discover cures for serious human diseases should commence. A summary of our new approach should be published in *Science* and *Nature*. Finally, to reflect its new emphasis, the project's name should be changed to the Human Fellowship Project.

The group voted to authorize purchase a block of ETHCON stock and to encourage their fine work on behalf of human progress.

PUBLIC RELATIONS

The meeting ended with a discussion of the possible reaction to PP2020 by the president if he finds out about it. G7 noted that since WWII only Truman (who started the program) and Kennedy (who found out about it a week before he was assassinated) ever learned of PP2020. It is unlikely Clinton will ever hear of it. If he does, he will probably initially respond with horror. The group predicted a typical "Frankenstein reaction" in which the president says we are overstepping ourselves, fooling with things that belong to God and not to man, and that we should end the project before its results turn on us and destroy us the way Frankenstein's monster eventually destroyed him and his family.

X4 played a surveillance tape of a 1984 conversation between the Secretary of Health and Human Services, his speechwriter, and an unidentified physician. [*The transcript of this tape was previously obtained by the author from a member of PP2020 in 1990, and my source, who has been reassigned, speculates that SX4 (the surveillance unit) purposely planted the minutes of the PP2020 meeting in the FOI files as a payback for his earlier disclosure. The two transcripts are iden-*

tical except that the unnamed physician is now identified as "Country Doc" and all references to President Reagan were deleted.]

IN SERVICE: HEALTH DEPT/EXEC 3.1.84 VOICE ACTIVATED TAPE FILE 84: HEAL75932EX

Secretary: I need something good for openers with the Senate Finance Committee. Those guys wanted a management whiz type in this job, not a country doctor. They're stuck with me for now, but they probably don't like it much. The [inaudible] wants me to be friendly; act like just plain folks on the Hill. Hell, I don't know how to do that, but I owe it to him to keep on the Senate's good side.

Speechwriter: I think I've got an angle. I think we can make the Senators sit up and take notice of a new presence in town, a manager with vision and imagination. Let me lay it out. There's a lot of paranoia in the country that the whole works is going down the tubes—that the average guy's got nothing to say because of a gigantic bureaucracy in Washington that has lost touch with everything but power. Individuality is out, conformity is in. The art of medicine is going to hell. What the country needs is someone to tell them about the good things progress has given us to renew their faith in government. Now here's my plan. Everyone's half crazy worrying about 1984. We get 1984 this and 1984 that, it's enough to make you throw up. You put it on the line. Here we are in 1984. Orwell predicted this and that; well it hasn't happened. In fact, as far as our medical and scientific community goes, we've continued to work to foster individual freedom and initiative. And you pledge that you will foster this tradition, and the benefits of medical progress will be available to all citizens.

Secretary: Not bad. It would certainly play in Peoria, but will it go over on the Hill?

Country Doc: Don't underestimate the folks in Peoria.

Secretary: OK, OK, you're right. The Midwest is still the source of 90% of the original ideas in this country. But spell it out for me. It's been a long time since I've read *1984*. [inaudible]

Speechwriter: Orwell envisions this highly structured society, the ultimate totalitarian dictatorship with Big Brother at the helm. Big Brother broadcasts his constant messages and watches his subjects by means of telescreens in every room and every public place. The citizens' activities are directed by slogans that tend to negate thought process, and the language is constantly being simplified to eliminate thought altogether. The principal slogans are "War is Peace," "Freedom is Slavery," and "Ignorance is Strength." All books have been destroyed and the news is completely managed. If Big Brother wants to change history, he merely rewrites the newspapers in his archives—the only permanent record in existence. People who don't conform to the wishes of the government are imprisoned, tortured, put through painful brainwashing, and released only after their will to resist has been completely destroyed. It is total government founded on fear.

Secretary: What does all that have to do with the United States? Other than the use of slogans, I don't see any parallel. [inaudible] And what's wrong with "Health is Happiness"?

Speechwriter: That's the point, chief. All this 1984 jazz has been blown way out of proportion. People shouldn't be worried about it. It's like punting on third down.

We're doing a great job, and everything is under control. Take Orwell's concept of doublethink, the ability to hold two contradictory beliefs simultaneously, and accept both of them. The good party member does this at all times. Thus when the party alters history or changes its interpretation of an event or belief, there can be an immediate acceptance of the new line. Doublethink has the advantage of divorcing thought completely from reality, letting one live in an imaginary world. In such a world citizens do not attempt to influence or change the real one. Fact reversal becomes a prime tool of government. The Ministry of Peace concerns itself with War, the Ministry of Truth with lies, the Ministry of Love with torture, and the Ministry of Plenty with starvation.

Country Doc: I get it. Like our Department of Defense is really a War Department, our Department of Agriculture is working to keep land out of production, and, hell, our own Health Department is really concerned only with disease.

Speechwriter: Let's forget the doublethink. How about *1984*'s main slogan, "Big Brother is Watching You." Big Brother is all around you and you better watch what you're doing 'cause he is and you'll be out of the ball game if he catches you. Now that's the guts of the book, and we don't have anything like that.

Secretary: I'm glad you're not in my planning department. Back in 1980 HHS awarded a contract to develop a cheap and efficient computer that could be used by physicians. Within the decade all physicians and hospitals who get payments from the national health program—and that'll be 95% of 'em—will have to use this computer to enter complete patient history, diagnosis, and each and every test and result. We'll keep it all confidential, of course, but we'll be able to profile every doc in the country. We'll know the names and conditions of all his patients, his patterns of practice, his diagnostic techniques, his frequency of surgery for certain indications, and his success rates. Hell, we'll probably be able to tell when he goes to the bathroom. The computer will also be linked to public health and law enforcement agencies to permit instant reporting of gunshot wounds, child abuse, drug abuse, VD, and the like. And if it's the only thing I do as Secretary, I'm going to put the marginal practitioners out of business: Those docs who don't know the difference between mono and leukemia, or those who still routinely treat sore throats with cloromyseeten [ph].

Country Doc: Wait a minute. They could do that in the book, but this is the United States. You don't have the power to restrict the practice of private physicians.

Secretary: I'm going to let you spend a week with my legal girls. They'll tell you a thing or two. Part of the national health legislation is a section that will turn all licensing authority over to my department in five years. We're developing a set of implementing regulations right now that would permit our own Quality Assurance Panel to pull the license of any physician in the lower 5% of the nation on any of about 500 categories that measure quality of care on a combination process–outcome scale. We're also going to be able to draw a computer map of the country based on medical specialty and population density and tell doctors where they can and can't practice for the national health program.

Country Doc: [inaudible] I thought we were going to use positive incentives, education and all that.

Secretary: That didn't work. I want to put the fear of the Lord in them. That works every time. The next phase will be to allocate all expensive medical treatment by computer.

Speechwriter: Gee, chief, maybe the *1984* bit's no good. But I'm used to changing strategy at half-time. My fallback position is to have you talk about *Brave New World*. Huxley saw it about 600 years in the future, although he later changed that estimate to a century or so. It involves control of the population by a combination of genetic engineering, operant conditioning, and psychotropic drugs. Anyone who doesn't conform is labeled sick and treated. Unlike *1984*, where the goal of society is power, the goal of *Brave New World* is happiness. Instead of mind-altering drugs being illegal, their use is encouraged. The analogy he uses is life in a large insect community, like a beehive or anthill, where liberty is unnecessary and all work for the collective good. Now we've got nothing like that on the drawing boards, and the Senators might get a kick out of looking at how Huxley went wrong in imagining man's future.

Secretary: They might. That is if I could keep myself from thinking about the embryo development experiments that the Army Medical Corps is doing around the world, and the Armed Forces Behavior Modification Program, Top Secret, of course, which makes basic training look like a cub scout jamboree weekend. As for drugs, Huxley's got it right. If we ever get into another era of confrontation politics one of the most effective things he could do is to make barbiturates and amphetamines over-the-counter items. A drugged citizen is a happy citizen, and they'll be happy to drug themselves with a little encouragement from the Department of Health.

Speechwriter: Dammit, another fumble. I thought I had it. Guess I just don't have the hang of this health stuff yet. Let me think on it some more. Maybe there's something in Zamiatin's [ph] *We* that you can use. That one's based on a mission to subjugate the inhabitants of other planets to mathematically faultless happiness.

Secretary: That's it! Forget *1984*. Our theme will be *1999*. You know, after that space program that used to be on TV. People love to talk about space gadgets, ray guns, and creatures from other planets. My theme will be space-age technology in medicine and how we can retain and retrain the old family doctor to be a super healer. You know, a sort of Leonard McCoy [*Star Trek*] or Helena Russell [*Space 1999*] for every citizen. Hell, I might even hold out the prospect of bringing back home visits—by telescreens, of course.

There was a brief discussion of the implications of the tape and the meddling in health policy by neophyte political appointees. It was noted that Beverly Crusher [*Star Trek: The Next Generation*] was the proper model now and that the TV space programs had done a terrific job in preparing the American population for novel experiments. Some concern was also expressed at the decision taken at the last meeting to cancel the soma experiments [L.284-89] on the basis that the underclass in the United States was already using far more mood-altering drugs voluntarily, both legal and illegal, than we could ever hope to induce them to use through our methods. On the other hand, the short supply of some of these drugs, especially heroin and cocaine, has greatly contributed to the crime rate in the cities. PIPH agreed to financially support groups dedicated to decriminalizing the use of mind-altering drugs. It was agreed that William F. Buckley should receive any financial support he needs to continue his drug decriminalization campaign, as should the ACLU.

Discussion then returned to dealing with the president should he discover the existence of PP2020. It was agreed that our response should be that, unlike Frankenstein, we are not lone rangers. We are not working for ourselves, but for the good of the human race. We are not out for our own glory (all our work is secret and even the scientists and physicians we fund do not even know our real names), but for the glory of America. Moreover, all of our projects have built-in self-destruct mechanisms and can be destroyed before anything we create can destroy us. It was easier to justify our work when we could just say, "The Russians are doing it, and we have to beat them to it." On the other hand, PIPH suggested that we can now use the real reason: Immortality and genetic perfectibility are the most important frontiers in science, and we either go forward and try to conquer them, or we stagnate at our current level and ultimately perish. If this doesn't work, the group discussed making the president watch *Blade Runner*. If that doesn't work, maybe he could read the Burroughs screenplay of the same title. If that doesn't work, we'll tell him we're shutting down and continue business as usual. Experimentation is too important to leave to the commander-in-chief.

The meeting came to a close at midnight.[1]

CHAPTER FOURTEEN

Plagued by Dreams

Contemporary physicians and scientists often describe their experiments as part of a search for the "Holy Grail."[1] Sometimes this quest is expressed more specifically, as when the Human Genome Project is described as a search for the "Holy Grail of biology." This rhetoric suggests that experimental work is holy, God's work, and that the results will prove miraculous and good for everyone. But this type of blind devotion produces uncritical action that can ultimately destroy values essential to human dignity. As Tennyson tells us in his poem, "The Holy Grail," "an excessively zealous pursuit after spiritual truth can be as destructive to social order as an indulgence in the materialistic qualities of life."[2] In Tennyson's poem, for example, a monk tells the questing Sir Percivale that forsaking his life at court for the hardship of the search was a choice he made at a time Percivale thought he could have both, a double life, but that his dream of a better life was also a plague:

> but O the pity
> To find thine own first love once more—to hold,
> Hold her a wealthy bride within thine arms,
> Or all but hold, and then—cast her aside, Forgoing
> all her sweetness, like a weed!
> For we that want the warmth of a double life,
> We are plagued with dreams of something sweet
> Beyond all sweetness in a life so rich,—

Contemporary medical researchers often lead double lives in pursuit of their research goals, exhibiting the same determination and desperation as the questing knights of the Holy Grail. Like the knights of old, their quest for the good, whether progress in general or a cure for AIDS or cancer specifically, can lead to the destruction of those human values such as dignity and liberty that we hold central to a civilized life.[3]

153

Doubling and duplicity in both language and action have become hallmarks of experimentation on humans in the United States and most of the developed world. We have come to this pass, like Arthur's knights, with good intentions and worthy goals. Neither our intentions nor our goals, however, can justify the duplicitous use of language in human experimentation, nor the betrayal of the Hippocratic ethic of "do no harm" in the physician (researcher)–patient (subject) relationship.

This chapter explores the evolution of the rationales physicians have used to justify experiments on their patient/subjects from the Nazi doctors to contemporary experimenters with the goal of articulating the destruction concealed by duplicitous language, especially the rhetoric of choice, including role ambiguity and overt deception. Although the scale and justification for research on humans is different when sponsored by the government or by private industry, the language distortions and role ambiguities have infected both. This will be demonstrated by examining both past government-sponsored, war-justified experiments (as exemplified by the radiation experiments) and current drug-company-sponsored, profit-justified experiments (as exemplified by cancer and AIDS experiments).

A POSTMODERN CRITIQUE

Most scholars date postmodernism from Hiroshima and the Holocaust, one an instantaneous annihilation and the other a systematic one. Together they represent the death of our civilization's dream of moral and scientific progress that had characterized the modern age. The postmodern world is much more ambiguous and uncertain. Postmodern criticism itself seeks to subvert our culture and our beliefs. Nonetheless, by seeing culture and beliefs as subjects worthy of study and critique, it simultaneously legitimizes them. It is this "doubleness" that "prevents any possible critical urge to ignore or trivialize historical-political questions."[4] The double discourse of the postmodern is both illustrated and illuminated in our post–World War II discourse on human experimentation, a discourse that simultaneously condemns the Nazi experiments as barbaric while demanding access to contemporary experiments as a human right. Use of a double discourse in this context obscures what should be illuminated, and marginalizes what should be privileged. Exposing the pervasiveness of the double discourse at least gives us the option of confronting the ambiguities in our motivation and our actions, and (re)forming or at least (re)framing current rules governing research on humans.

The concepts of doubling and doublethink both live in contemporary human experimentation. Robert Jay Lifton has suggested, for example, that the way in which the Nazi physicians at Auschwitz could continue to see themselves as healers while killing concentration camp inmates was through a process of "doubling." He describes it as "the division of the self into two functioning wholes, so that a part-self acts as an entire self."[5] Lifton's psychological description of the Nazi doctors need not be accepted. Nonetheless, there is a long history of the double in literature, including, for example, *Frankenstein* (between the creator and his creature) and *Dr. Jekyll and Mr. Hyde*. As Jekyll puts it, although his nature was split, he was not:

> Though so profound a double-dealer, I was in no sense a hypocrite; both sides of me were in dead earnest. . . . With every day and from both sides of my intelligence, the moral and the intellectual, I thus drew steadily nearer to that truth, by whose partial discovery I have been doomed to such a dreadful shipwreck: that man is not truly one, but truly two.

Doubling, of course, produces double standards; even double thinking. This latter concept is well described in George Orwell's *1984* where power, "the capacity to inflict unlimited pain and suffering on another human being," is an end in itself. Orwell was writing primarily about totalitarian dictatorships, such as the USSR under Stalin and Germany under Hitler. In his view, the key to a successful totalitarian system is abolishing truth as objective reality. When successful, "anyone who is a minority of one must be convinced that he is insane." The dominant mode of thinking in this type of a society is denoted doublethink, which means "the power of holding two contradictory beliefs in one's mind simultaneously, and accepting both of them."[6] The party's slogans in *1984* illustrate this concept: "War is Peace, Freedom is Slavery, and Ignorance is Strength." We recognize these pairings as nonsensical and think we could never be victims of such blatant propagandistic sloganeering. But even a cursory history of modern human experimentation demonstrates the pervasiveness of three doublespeak concepts: experimentation is treatment, researchers are physicians, and subjects are patients. Indeed, we have encapsulated all three into a "newspeak" word, "therapeuticresearch" (although we retain a space between the c and the r).

This doublespeak allows us to use double standards as they suit our purposes, that is, it permits us to treat truth as negotiable and then to act irrationally. We act in the best interest of patients. The experiment is justified as therapy, or potential therapy. But if it produces harm, it was, after all only an experiment, and was thus necessarily a "success," because we learned something from it that could benefit others. It should be of only slight comfort that the term therapeutic research was not invented by a totalitarian government but rather by physicians who were responding to a legal condemnation of experiments performed under the authority of a totalitarian government: the Nuremberg Code.

THE NUREMBERG CODE AND THE DECLARATION OF HELSINKI

The Nuremberg Code was formulated by United States judges at the end of the 1946–47 trial of 23 Nazi physicians and experimenters. The Nazi experiments involved murder and torture, systematic and barbarous acts with death often the planned endpoint. The subjects of these experiments were concentration camp prisoners, mostly Jews, Gypsies, and Slavs. The Nuremberg Code itself was thus articulated in response to horrendous nontherapeutic, nonconsensual prison research. Nonetheless, the judges meant its application to be universal; and the Nuremberg Code remains the most authoritative legal and ethical document governing international research standards, and one of the premier human rights documents in world history.[7]

The judges based the Nuremberg Code on natural law theory. They derived it, with the help of expert witnesses, from universal moral, ethical, and legal concepts. The Code protects individual subjects first by protecting their rights. Voluntary, informed, competent, and understanding consent is required by the first principle of the Code, and principle 9 gives the subject the right to withdraw from the experiment. The consent of the subject is necessary under the Nuremberg Code, but consent alone is not sufficient. The other eight provisions of the Code are related to the welfare of subjects, and must be satisfied *before* consent is even sought from the subject. The subject cannot waive these provisions. The requirements of these eight welfare provisions include a valid research design to procure information important for the good of society that cannot be obtained in other ways; the avoidance of unnecessary physical and mental suffering and injury; the absence of an *a priori* reason to believe that death or disabling injury will occur; risks that never exceed benefits; and the presence of a qualified researcher who is prepared to terminate the experiment if it "is likely to result in the injury, disability, or death" of the subject.[8]

Physician–researchers viewed the Nuremberg Code as confining and inapplicable to their practices because it was promulgated as a human rights document by judges at a criminal trial and because the judges made no attempt to deal with clinical research on children, healthy volunteers, patients, or mentally impaired people. The Code, afterall, applied only to Nazis. Moreover, the Code has no explicit rules for many modern research agendas. The answer to the first concern is that the Code is universal, and the response to the second lies in interpretation of the Code rather than in its abandonment. A reasonable analogy is the way we interpret the U.S. Constitution to apply it to changes in technology.

The World Medical Association, nonetheless, has consistently tried to displace the Code with The Declaration of Helsinki, a more permissive alternative document, first promulgated in 1964, and amended four times since. This document is subtitled "Recommendations Guiding Doctors in Clinical Research" and is just that, recommendations by physicians to physicians. The Declaration's goal is to replace the human rights-based agenda of the Nuremberg Code with a more lenient medical ethics model that permits paternalism. U.S. researcher Henry Beecher probably best expressed medicine's delight with the Declaration of Helsinki's ascendancy when he said in 1970: "The Nuremberg Code presents a rigid act of legalistic demands. . . . The Declaration of Helsinki, on the other hand, presents a set of guides. It is an ethical as opposed to a legalistic document and is thus more broadly useful [to physicians] than the one formulated at Nuremberg."[9]

The core of the Declaration of Helsinki is a doubling, dividing research into therapeutic ("Medical Research Combined with Professional Care") and non-therapeutic, thus blurring the line between treatment and research. The physician (researcher?) need not obtain the subject's (patient's?) informed consent to "medical research combined with professional care" if the physician submits the reasons for not obtaining consent to the independent review committee. The current trend seems to seek to go even further, abolishing the distinction between research and therapy, researcher and physician, and subject and patient altogether. In this new regime, research becomes treatment, the researcher becomes the healer, and the subject becomes a patient. The way language is used to obscure the truth and justify the unjustifiable can be illustrated by some cold war radiation experiments performed in the United States in the 1940s, 1950s, and 1960s and by contemporary experiments on terminally ill cancer and AIDS patients.

THE COLD WAR RADIATION EXPERIMENTS

In 1986, Representative Edward J. Markey (D–Massachusetts) released a report from the House Subcommittee on Energy Conservation and Power entitled *American Nuclear Guinea Pigs*. The report detailed 31 experiments conducted on more than 700 Americans by the federal government from the 1940s to the 1970s, most designed to test the effect on the human body of exposure to radiation. The experiments included injection of plutonium or uranium into terminally ill patients; irradiation of the testicles of prisoners to study the impact of radiation on fertility; exposure of nursing home residents to radium or thorium, either injected or ingested, to measure the passage of these radioactive substances through the body; and feeding radioactive fallout to human subjects to see how the body would excrete it. Although the 1986 report was carefully documented and cited specific published reports of the studies, it went virtually unrecognized and unheralded, primarily because the administration of President Ronald Reagan dismissed it as overblown.[10]

Under the administration of President Bill Clinton, the reaction to similar disclosures involving thousands of Americans was dramatically different. In October 1993 reporter Eileen Welsome of the *Albuquerque Tribune* wrote a series of articles about five individuals who, without their knowledge or consent, had been injected with plutonium in 1945–47 as part of an Atomic Energy Commission (AEC) study of the impact of plutonium on human beings. The information was sought to help determine how to treat workers and scientists exposed to plutonium at weapons development and production plants. In one case, plutonium was injected into the leg of a 36-year-old man who was thought to have bone cancer. His leg was then amputated for study. As a result of the amputation, the man could no longer work and was dependent upon his wife to support him. He died 45 years later, in 1991. Another subject was misdiagnosed as having stomach cancer and was injected with plutonium in 1945. He lived to age 79, dying in 1966. The subjects were not told the purpose of the experiments, either at the time or when follow-up studies were conducted later.[11]

When these stories became public, Secretary Hazel O'Leary of the U.S. Department of Energy (DOE, successor to the AEC), said she was "appalled and shocked" by the plutonium experiments.[12] She took steps to begin an investigation of other radiation experiments conducted by the AEC and suggested that a way should be found to compensate the victims. This reaction was shared by President Clinton, and an interagency task force was created to conduct a similar review of all federal agencies that might have been involved in radiation experiments during the cold war. The president also formed an advisory committee to the task force, which issued its final report in October 1995.[13] Their 900-page report detailed a number of specific experiments and made a number of recommendations regarding radiation experiments in particular and research on human beings in general. Two specific experiments, one dealt with superficially by the advisory committee, the other in detail, illustrate the pervasive problems in the government-sponsored radiation experiments.

The first experiment was funded by the AEC and conducted at Boston's Massachusetts General Hospital in the mid-1950s. The experiment was designed to find the dose of uranium that could be tolerated by humans. The primary published report involved six terminally ill patients with brain tumors who were injected with uranium (U^{235}). Five of the six were semicomatose or in a coma at the time; most died within two months, but one lived for 17 months. There is no evidence of consent by anyone, although permission to perform an autopsy was refused by the family of the only woman in the study. The published report of the experiment, which indicated that the subjects had been exposed to a range of 10% to 30% of a lethal dose of uranium, concluded, "Of the common laboratory animals, man appears to correspond most closely to the rat in regards to intravenous tolerance to uranium."[14]

Human subjects were used in this case because they were captive and available. No consent was sought or obtained, apparently because the researchers believed that terminally ill individuals could not be harmed. No disrespect to the subjects is intended by noting that they were treated no better than laboratory rats would have been. This was apparently not unusual in the 1950s. As one eminent physician, Louis Lasagna, told the committee's investigators in an oral history interview, "Mostly, I'm ashamed to say, it was as if, and I'm putting this very crudely purposely, as if you'd ordered a bunch of rats from a laboratory and you had experimental subjects available to you."[15]

The advisory committee concluded that even if one of the purposes of the study had been to see if large doses of uranium localized in brain tumors, one of the patients had no such tumor, and "Even for the patient–subjects with brain cancer, there was no expectation on the part of investigators that the experiment would benefit the subjects themselves." The committee concluded that even though these patients were dying (and thus presumably were "not likely to live long enough to be harmed"), this did not "justify failing to respect them as people." Although it could find no evidence that informed consent was obtained from the subjects (it clearly could not be from those who were comatose) the committee nonetheless stopped short of condemning the experiment, saying simply, "Unless these patients [subjects?], or the families of comatose or incompetent patients, understood that the injections were not for their benefit and still agreed to the injections, this experiment was unethical." But more could (and should) be said. Treating people like rats is unethical even if relatives think it is acceptable, and there are limits to what even dying patients can consent to if one takes the eight welfare principles of the Nuremberg Code seriously.[16]

The second experiment was conducted a decade later, and by then simply asserting that the patient was dying anyway was no longer seen as sufficient justification for using them for your own purposes: The Cincinnati Whole Body Radiation Experiment. The experiment, which involved 88 subjects from 1960 to 1971, is described in a 1973 medical report by the investigators. It was financed by the U.S. Defense Project Support Agency to determine whether amino acids in the urine could be used as "an indicator of biological response of humans to irradiation." Like the Massachusetts General Hospital study, this one was an experiment designed to test a hypothesis for the U.S. military on subjects selected primarily because they were available and thought to be terminally ill with cancer.

In the medical literature, this military research study was transformed into a civilian treatment series. As the researcher described it in the first sentence: "The purpose of these investigations has been to improve the treatment and general clinical management and if possible the length of survival of patients with advanced cancer." It was alleged that, "All patients gave informed consent." The patients were "eligible for this form of treatment if they had advanced cancer for which cure could not be anticipated." Later in the article the experimental protocol itself is transformed into "the therapeutic regime." Whether therapy or experimentation, however, serious problems were apparent even in this self-serving rendition: Eight subjects (almost 10%) could have died directly from the radiation exposure; none were told of the risk of death, nor of the common and devastating side effect of nausea and vomiting (56% experienced it), and most patients were poor, black, and at least 12% had IQs under 70.[17]

Although the principal investigator, Eugene Saenger, continues to defend this experiment as therapy, saying that total body irradiation—TBI—"treatments" were given as a "palliative cancer therapy" for people for whom there was no better alternative,"[18] this assertion is simply not credible.[19] The advisory committee seems to have had considerable difficulty in deciding whether these patients were subjects, whether this was an innovative treatment (or an experiment), and whether the physicians were trying to help their patients. These are, of course, the ambiguities in research that are attenuated by duplicitous language. Nonetheless, the committee ultimately did conclude:

> The impact of the research protocol on the care of the patient-subjects cannot be construed as beneficial to the patients; in addition, there is evidence of the subordination of the ends of medicine to the ends of research. The decisions to withhold information about possible acute side effects of TBI as well as to forgo pretreatment with antiemetics were irrefutably linked to advancing the research interests of the DOD. To the extent that this deviated from standard care, and caused unnecessary suffering and discomfort, it was morally unconscionable.[20]

The committee went on to raise, but not answer, a question at the core of our inquiry: "Whether the ends of research (understood as discovering new knowledge) and the ends of medicine (understood as serving the interests of the patient) necessarily conflict and how the conflict should be resolved when it occurs are still today open and vexing issues."

Before the committee's *Final Report* was issued, a federal judge, relying on the Nuremberg Code, permitted a lawsuit by the families of these subjects against the researchers to proceed, saying:

> The allegations in this case indicate that the government of the United States, aided by officials of the City of Cincinnati, treated at least eighty-seven of its citizens as though they were laboratory animals. If the Constitution has not clearly established a right under which these Plaintiffs may attempt to prove their case, than a gaping hole in that document has been exposed. *The subject of experimentation who has not volunteered is merely an object* [emphasis supplied].[21]

The lawsuit has since been settled.

CANCER AND AIDS

Susan Sontag has noted that cancer and AIDS have become linked as perhaps the two most feared ways to die in the developed world. In her words, "AIDS, like cancer, leads to a hard death. . . . The most terrifying illnesses are those perceived not just as lethal but as dehumanizing, literally so."[22] Philosopher Michel Foucault was not speaking of the medicalization of death by cancer and AIDS, but he could have been when he chronicled how the power of government over life and death has shifted in the past two centuries. "Now it is over life, throughout its unfolding, that power establishes its domination; death is power's limit, the moment that escapes it."[23] In human experimentation on the terminally ill we have Foucault's vision of public power played out in private: researchers take charge of the bodies of the dying in an attempt to take charge of the patient's lives and prevent their own personal deaths, and death itself.

The Nazi doctors' chief defense at Nuremberg was that experimentation was necessary to support the war effort.[24] Now, as detailed in Chapter 4, we frequently use the military metaphor as combating disease has itself become a "war" and we

speak of a "war on cancer" and a "war on AIDS." And in that war patients, especially terminally ill patients, are conscripted as soldiers. As former editor of the
New England Journal of Medicine Franz Ingelfinger put it: "[T]he thumb screws
of coercion are most relentlessly applied" to "the most used and useful of all experimental subjects, the patient with disease."[25] But as Sontag reminds us, war
metaphors are dangerous in disease because they encourage authoritarianism,
overmobilization, and stigmatization. In her words:

> No, it is not desirable for medicine, any more than for war, to be "total." Neither
> is the crisis created by AIDS a "total" anything. We are not being invaded. The
> body is not a battlefield. The ill are neither unavoidable casualties nor the enemy.
> We—medicine, society—are not authorized to fight back by any means whatever.[26]

The self-deception inherent in seeing experimentation as treatment, especially
in terminally ill cancer patients, is well-illustrated by contemporary phase 1 drug
studies with anticancer agents. Are they research or therapy? Food and Drug
Administration (FDA) regulations state that phase 1 studies are intended to have
no therapeutic content, but are to determine "toxicity, metabolism, absorption,
elimination, and other pharmacological action, preferred route of administration,
and safe dosage range." Nonetheless, National Cancer Institute (NCI) researchers
insist on calling them "potentially therapeutic."[27]

The self-deception problem is that in a terminally ill person, virtually any intervention, even a placebo, can be described as "potentially therapeutic," and once
this misleading label is applied, the nonbeneficial phase 1 study is de facto eliminated and transformed into therapy, now labeled "experimental therapy." Any
distinction between experimentation and therapy is lost, and a new choice seems
to exist. This "phase 1 doublespeak" has invaded even pediatric research, even
though no cures or remissions for longer than a year have been documented in
phase 1 studies, and even remissions occur less than 6% of the time and most last
less than two months.[28] Thus the conclusion that "Administration of chemotherapy
in phase 1 pediatric oncology trials should be considered a *therapeutic research*
intervention, because there is some likelihood of modest benefits accruing to
participating subjects,"[29] is untenable. Parents consenting on behalf of their
dying children seem to be doing so because they are provided with false hope and
unrealistic expectations. Moreover, 94% of investigators concede that adult patients enroll in phase 1 studies "mostly for the possibility of medical benefit."[30]

Self-deception permits both researchers and subjects to double themselves: It
permits researchers to see themselves as physicians and subjects to see themselves,
and their children, as patients. It is unlikely that patients can ever draw the distinction between physician and researcher when these two conflicting roles are
merged in one person, because most simply do not believe that their physician
would either knowingly do something harmful to them or would knowingly use
them simply as a means for their own ends. Because of this almost blind trust in
physicians by their patients, the Helsinki Declaration's theoretical division be-

tween therapeutic and nontherapeutic research is meaningless. This is, of course, clearest for terminally ill patients who have "exhausted" all therapeutic "choices."

AIDS has always been perceived as the disease in which there literally is *no* distinction between treatment and experimentation. This is because, even though we are moving toward making AIDS a chronic condition, there is still no cure for AIDS. The disease primarily strikes the young, leading to a death that is premature by virtually any calculation, and existing treatments that can prolong life are far from satisfactory. ACT-UP's (AIDS Coalition to Unleash Power) political slogan, "A drug trial is health care, too," for example, serves to duplicitously conflate experimentation with therapy and to encourage people with AIDS to seek out experimentation as treatment, and physician–researchers to see AIDS patients as potential subjects who have "nothing to lose." Under this rationale all types of experiments are performed under the guise of treatment. At the extreme are the experiments of Henry Heimlich in China, using malaria infection to stimulate the immune system of AIDS patients. Anthony Fauci characterizes the experiment as "quite dangerous and scientifically unsound." Heimlich, on the other hand, says it is "safe for patients," and he gets their consent.[31]

The most potentially far-reaching work in human experimentation is in the area of genetics. French Anderson, one of the leaders in the field, has argued that even the initial genetic experiments on humans should really be regarded as therapy:

> There exists a fundamental difference between the responses of clinicians [physicians] and basic scientists [researchers] to the question: Are we ready to carry out a human gene therapy clinical protocol? . . . The basic scientist objectively analyzes the preclinical data and finds it wanting. . . . Clinicians look at the situation from a different perspective. Every day they are expected to provide their patients with the *best treatments for disease*. When they deal with incurable diseases, they must watch their patients die. . . . The urge to do something, anything, if it might help is very strong. . . . A clinician's reaction to a *new therapy protocol* tends to be: If it is relatively safe, and it might work better, then let's try it. Historically, much of medical innovation has resulted from trial and error experimentation. . . . What's the rush? The rush is the daily necessity to help sick people. Their (our) illnesses will not wait for a more convenient time. We need help when we are sick.[32]

Anderson concludes his argument: "It will take many years of clinical studies before gene therapy can be a widely used treatment procedure. The sooner we begin, the sooner patients will be helped." The distinction between experimentation and treatment is lost in this discussion, with the ethics of the inapplicable doctor–patient treatment model dominating the scientist–subject model. Likewise, the use of a baboon heart in the Baby Fae transplant was considered lifesaving therapy by the surgeon, even though it was the first operation of its kind in the world.[33] It should be obvious that the fact that the patient is dying does not transform experimental intervention into standard treatment modalities and does not eliminate the necessity for informed consent. It is the nature of the intervention and the data that support its use, not the medical status of the patient or the intent of the physician–researcher, that determine the nature of the intervention.

Likewise, consent comes after a justifiable research protocol has been developed. Just as consent is no justification for the torture or exploitation of human beings, it is no justification for improper research. We must stop treating terminally ill cancer and AIDS patients as subhuman by irrationally offering them questionable experiments in the guise of treatment. We cannot justify this behavior on the basis of either their demand for it or our belief that the ultimate good of mankind will be served by it. Researchers who believe their subjects cannot be hurt by experimental interventions should be disqualified from doing research on human subjects on the basis that they cannot appropriately protect their subjects' welfare with such a view. Likewise, subjects who believe they have "nothing to lose" and are desperate because of their terminal illness should also be disqualified as potential research subjects because they are unable to provide voluntary, competent, informed, or understanding consent to the experimental intervention with such a view.[34] It should be emphasized that these are proposed *research* rules that would not necessarily apply to treatment in a doctor–patient relationship untainted by research conflicts of interests.

WHY LANGUAGE MATTERS

One theme of this book is that language can clarify, but it can also obscure. The project of at least some leading medical researchers since Nuremberg seems to have been to use language to obscure: to blur or eliminate the distinctions between research and therapy, scientist and physician, and subject and patient. This doublethink is the essence of "therapeutic research," a concept that has been used to disguise the true nature of experimental protocols and to obscure the ideology of science (which follows a protocol to test a hypothesis) with the ideology of medicine (which uses treatments in the best interests of individual patients).[35] Disguising the distinction between interventions done to test a hypothesis to gain generalizable knowledge and those done for the benefit of the individual patient seems to have been done to lower the standards for obtaining informed consent. To the extent to which physicians have been given the benefit of the doubt in withholding certain risk information from patients under the therapeutic privilege, this view has received at least some legal sanction. But modern informed consent doctrine is meant to safeguard the patient's interest in both decisionmaking autonomy (liberty) and dignity. It is thus inappropriate to have separate disclosure requirements for therapy and research in any event, and whatever differences currently exist in practice should be abolished, since the rationale for information disclosure (and choice) is identical in both cases.

There should be only one standard of informed consent, applying to both research and therapy; and it should be as set forth in article 1 of the Nuremberg Code:

voluntary, competent, informed, and understanding. Courts have seemed to place the emphasis in the treatment arena on disclosure alone (i.e., the "informed" part of informed consent) rather than on the understanding of the information by the patient. Nonetheless, since the test of competence is the ability to understand and appreciate the information needed to give informed consent,[36] it is fair to conclude that the requirement of understanding the material information has always been an implicit part of the informed consent doctrine in any event.

Nor should it matter if the research or treatment is government-funded or privately funded. Consent requirements should also include all of the elements spelled out in both the leading informed consent cases, such as *Cobbs v. Grant* and its progeny (discussed in chapters 5 and 6), and the federal rules for research on human beings. Of course special rules should apply to those individuals who cannot consent for themselves, and these rules of substituted consent should be uniform as well. In this way researchers should not be tempted to see their work as treatment to avoid the requirements of informed consent.

Informed consent is necessary in both contexts to protect the rights of the individual, but it is not sufficient. Consent, for example, has been transformed from a shield to protect subjects into a sword to be used against them in contemporary research. The consent (or demand) of the research subject is now often seen as sufficient justification in itself to perform the experiment on a human being.[37] But the consent of the research subject does not transform an experimental protocol into a therapeutic intervention. Consent speaks to liberty and dignity, not to reasonableness or risks and benefits. As has been illustrated over and over again, however, choice has been so reified in our society that we seldom ask, "Choice for what purpose?" Choice itself seems its own justification. Is it then any wonder that Americans want to "choose" experimental, first-of-their-kind interventions? Consent alone cannot, however, justify an otherwise-unjustifiable experiment. In the scientific research context more is needed to protect the welfare of individual subjects. The more is, at minimum, the eight subject welfare precepts of the Nuremberg Code that doublethink language seeks to obscure.

MARKET IDEOLOGY

Two ideologies have been explored: the ideology of science (which puts the requirements of the research protocol designed to objectively test a hypothesis as the highest priority) and the ideology of medicine (which puts the best interests of the patient as the highest priority). Medicine is currently, however, faced with a new dominant ideology: the ideology of the marketplace, which puts profit-making (sometimes denoted by its method, cost-containment) as its highest priority. It is no secret that the most consistently profitable industry since World War II has been the pharmaceutical industry.[38] Now, however, as competition in this industry has heated up, and as the new biotechnology industry is emerging with great promises of future profits, the role of a successful clinical experiment has become central to the profitability of an entire industry. In this domain both scientific truth and the best interests of patient–subjects can often find themselves sacrificed in the name of the bottom line. As one observer of the new biotechnology noted of the current state of medical science in the United States: "To do science you need money, but to raise money competitively you need to project illusions that are the antithesis of science."[39] Selling illusions to investors has supplemented selling illusions to patients.

A contemporary example combining cancer research and U.S. atomic research usefully illustrates the continuing pervasiveness of doublethink and its dangers to human subjects in an atmosphere governed not by war metaphors but by market metaphors. The Brookhaven National Laboratory recently pursued an experimental protocol to redo (in a more sophisticated manner) an experiment conducted between 1951 and 1960 to test the use of a boron compound delivered to the brain in a stream of neutrons with the hope that the boron will become radioactive and deliver its radiation selectively to a brain tumor. This approach, termed boron neutron capture therapy, proved either useless or fatal in the 1950s.[40]

The first subject, Joann Magnus, who had a terminal brain tumor, a glioblastoma, was admitted to the new experimental protocol before it was ready (in September 1994) because she had strong political connections. As Ms. Magnus herself said, "I had nothing to lose." Her physician said, "I do what I think is best for each individual patient . . . without this treatment, she'd be dead."[41] Reporter Andrew Lawler, who described this first of its kind experiment in *Science*, exemplifies the victory of doublethink best. In his words, what happened involved "an improved version of a therapy"; an "updated treatment"; and simply, "the therapy." Although only two subjects (of a planned protocol of 28) had undergone this experiment, Brookhaven Laboratory was described as "bracing for a flood of requests from dying patients," having to devise "a lottery to choose from among those who meet stringent initial requirements for treatments," and as seeing "the procedure" as "a tremendous cash cow" for the laboratory.[42]

In our postmodern world it seems to have struck no one as strange that the very person who demanded a serious and sustained investigation into cold war radiation experiments, DOE Secretary Hazel O'Leary, was also the person who sponsored the first subject for this U.S. government experiment. In this case O'Leary adopted the rationale of treatment of a terminally ill patient, saying, "There's a passion in the hearts of people who know they are terminal with a disease for which there seems to be no cure."[43] But this is about research, not treatment, and about giving the nuclear reactors made irrelevant by the end of the cold war a new lease on life by engaging them in what O'Leary terms "the positive side of nuclear technology." Just how positive this procedure is, of course, remains to be seen.[44] What is obscured in this language is the experiment itself, and that the "requirements" are those of science, not medicine. Moreover, in that Ms. Magnus' personal physician saw this experiment as a last resort therapy demonstrates the continuing ambiguity in postmodern experimentation on the terminally ill.[45]

Although the advisory committee decided not to explore contemporary radiation experiments like the one at Brookhaven, the committee did do the most comprehensive study to date on current research practices in America. Specifically, the committee reviewed a random sample of 84 research protocols consent forms and IRB deliberations involving ionizing radiation funded from 1990 through 1993 and compared them with a sample of 41 nonionizing radiation studies from the same period. In a separate study, 1,900 patients at medical institutions across the country were interviewed. Advisory committee member Professor Jay Katz of Yale did an independent review of 93 of the proposals. No significant differences were found between radiation and nonradiation protocols or consent forms. Of the 125 total studies, 78 were rated as involving greater than minimal risk. Of these, the panel concluded that about half raised serious or moderate ethical concerns, mostly affecting such things as ability to understand the experiment, to know that participation is voluntary, and to understand the potential risks involved. Katz's separate study of 93 proposals identified 41 that posed greater than minimal risk. Of these, Katz identified 30 (or 73%) that raised serious ethical concerns, 10 borderline and 20 more serious. In the panel's words:

> Katz found that the most striking element of the troublesome consent forms was the lack of a forthright and repeated acknowledgment that patient-subjects were *invited* to participate in human experimentation. All too quickly the language shifted to *treatment* and *therapy* when the latter was not the purpose and was only, at best, a by-product of the research.[46]

Katz describes his own reaction to his study and the report in a "statement" in the body of the committee's *Final Report*. Among other things he says, in examining informed consent process,

> I had expected to discover problems, but I was stunned by their extent . . . the obfuscation of treatment and research, illustrated most strikingly in Phase I studies, but by no means limited to them; the lack of disclosure in randomized clinical trials about the different consequences to patient-subjects' well being if assigned to one research arm or the other; the administration of highly toxic agents in the 'scientific' belief that only the knowledge gained from 'total therapy' will *eventually* lead to cures, but without disclosure of the impact of such radical interventions on quality of life or longevity.[47]

Katz concludes, among other things, that although we all officially acknowledge that informed consent is central to the protection of subjects, we have "failed to take responsibility for making these requirements meaningful ones."

The message from this study is clear: The IRB and informed consent mechanisms adopted in response to Nuremberg and as a way around the Nuremberg Code's "rigid" requirements have failed. In almost half of all cases, this failure can be documented by a review of records alone—one shudders to think what a review of actual consent discussion with the subject would disclose. In their patient interview and survey, for example, the committee found direct evidence of language choices being used to deceive potential research subjects. The patients were asked to compare the terms clinical trial, clinical investigation, medical study and medical experiment with medical research.

It will probably surprise no one who has read this chapter to this point that the term medical experiment "evoked the most striking and negative associations" and was the only term ranked worse than medical research. "Clinical investigation" and "clinical trial" were somewhat better than "medical research;" but the term "medical study" got the best ratings of all, as such studies were viewed as "less risky, as less likely to involve unproven treatments, and as offering a greater chance at medical benefit." The study also indicated that many patients conflate research with treatment. In short, for many, if not most research subjects, deception or self-deception is inherent in our current research endeavors. Patients desperately want to believe they have at least some choice.

SOME SUGGESTIONS

It is no wonder that Americans demand experimentation as treatment and insist that their insurance companies and health care plans pay for any experimental intervention that exists. There is, of course, a continuum from (scientific) experiment to (therapeutic) treatment,[48] but few interventions are in the gray zone, and an objective distinction can almost always be made between an experimental intervention and a treatment. An experiment, for example, does not become therapy simply because no conventional (validated or unvalidated) intervention exists, any more than subjects become patients simply because they are given a terminal diagnosis. I have proposed that we adopt special regulations to protect the rights and welfare of terminally ill patients from exploitative experimentation.[49] I continue to believe that this is necessary. Like the Nuremberg Code's consent requirement, however, it is not sufficient.

To confront not only our mortality, but also our morality, we must use language to clarify rather than obscure what we do to one another. At a minimum, we must correctly identify and describe roles and responsibilities in human experimentation. In our postmodern world, it may not be realistic to think we can always distinguish research from therapy, physicians from scientists, or subjects from patients. Nonetheless, it is a moral imperative to use language to clarify differences because ignoring these differences undermines the integrity of scientific research, the medical profession, and the rights and welfare of patients and subjects.

This conclusion seems unremarkable and is not likely to be controversial. Putting it into practice, however, will require changes in the way we conduct contemporary experiments on humans that will likely cause controversy. Nonetheless, if we take the dignity, rights, and welfare of the subjects of human experimentation seriously in the clinical medicine arena, we should take at least the following steps:

1. Research must always be identified as research, and its purpose (to gain generalizable knowledge) must always be spelled out and differentiated from medical treatment designed only to benefit the patient.
2. Patients should always continue to be patients, even if they also volunteer to serve as research subjects. It is unlikely that it will ever be possible, in our death-denying and death-defying world, for patients not to indulge in self-deception by imagining that research is really treatment, and that they are patients, not research subjects. We cannot separate the subject into two persons. But we can assure that the subject–patient always has a physician whose only obligation is to look out for the best interests of the patient. Thus we can and should prohibit physicians from performing more than minimal-risk research on their patients and as a corollary only permit physician–researchers to recruit the patients of other physicians for their research protocols. In this way, at least the "doubling" of physician and researcher can be physically, and perhaps psychologically, eliminated.[50]
3. There should be strict disqualification rules for both subjects and researchers to engage in the research enterprise. At the extremes, for example, subjects who believe they have "nothing to lose" should be disqualified from participation since they are unable to give understanding and voluntary consent, and researchers who feel subjects have "nothing to lose" by participating should also be disqualified from doing research on them since they are not able to protect the dignity and welfare of their prospective research subjects with this attitude.[51]
4. The term "therapeutic research" and all of its progeny, such as "experimental treatment," "unvalidated treatment" should be abolished from research protocols and informed consent processes and forms. Research is research (designed to test a hypothesis and performed based on the rules of the protocol); treatment is something else (designed to benefit a patient and subject to change whenever change is seen in the patient's best interest). Confusing research and treatment confuses both the researcher and subject and permits self-interested self-deception by both of them by making the research seem like just another choice. The doubling and doublethink phenomena are difficult enough to control even when language is not used to disguise ambiguity.
5. To help expose the new market ideology of experimentation, the researcher should be required to disclose any and all financial incentives involved in the research to both the IRB and to the potential subjects. This information should be presented to the subject in a separate, written, disclosure form so that the

subject knows what financial incentives may be affecting the scientific judgment or medical judgment of the researcher.[52]

6. Institutional Review Boards should be radically overhauled. We now have 20 years of experience with them, and they continue to support both doublethink and the double nature of the researcher-physician. In this regard they have primarily engaged in legitimizing ambiguity and deception and have betrayed the research subjects they are charged to protect. The explanation may be found in both the federal regulations that govern IRBs and in the membership of these bodies. Reform on at least three levels is required. We need to (1) form a national human research agency to set the rules for research on humans, monitor their enforcement, and punish those who fail to follow them;[53] (2) rewrite current research rules to reflect the problems of doubling outlined in this article; and (3) restructure IRBs so that their role is to protect the subjects of research (not the researcher) and so that they are accountable to a national body (the proposed national human experimentation agency, also discussed in chapter 1), not their own institution. At a minimum this will require democratizing the IRBs by requiring a majority of members be community members and opening all meetings to the public.

Changing our ways in our postmodern world will not be easy. Our quest for the Holy Grail of medicine (immortality and genetic perfection?), as honorable as it may seem in theory, can become destructive in practice. As Bertolt Brecht has Galileo say in the version of the play he rewrote following Hiroshima:

> I take it that the intent of science is to ease human existence. . . . Should you, then, in time, discover all there is to be discovered, your progress must become a progress away from the bulk of humanity. The gulf might even grow so wide that the sound of your cheering at some new achievement would be echoed by a universal howl of horror.

PART IV

Toxic Choices

CHAPTER FIFTEEN

AIDS and TB Choices

AIDS and TB (tuberculosis) have become the two primary examples that critics of a public health vision that takes human rights seriously have used to argue that putting rights first promotes contagion and death.[1] This view, however, finds little support in fact and contemporary public health officials mostly agree that taking human rights seriously is a necessary component of an effective public health strategy. In this chapter I begin a section on the notion of toxic choices, not from the perspective of the individual, but rather from the perspective of government officials charged with protecting the public's health.

Ideas govern actions in both private and public realms, and language molds ideas. This is easy to see in the global context of the cold war, where a U.S. policy based on containment and deterrence led to the development of a vast nuclear weapons arsenal, an unsustainable arms race, and the ultimate destabilization of many of the world's countries. Not only did U.S. nuclear policy spawn its own peculiar strategies (such as mutually assured destruction), it also created new phrases to manage its discourse, such as windows of vulnerability, collateral damage, surgical strikes, and crisis management, all used to make nuclear war seem clean and controllable.[2] As discussed in chapter 4, metaphors matter. It makes all the difference whether in adopting a global AIDS strategy nations adopt the war-containment-escalation discourse (the war on AIDS strategy) in which control is viewed as an end in itself, and the infected body becomes a battlefield; or the human rights discourse, in which our collective futures and the values of human flourishing and the right to humane treatment are paramount.

In this chapter I examine the destructiveness of a militarized HIV containment strategy as pursued at a U.S. military base in Cuba, and a human-rights-based public health strategy, currently being pursued in response to the TB epidemic in the

United States. The purpose is to expose the power of discourse models to affect the choices public health officials make, and how these choices affect both the lives of real people and the global course of the AIDS and TB epidemics, and thus all of our futures.

HAITIAN REFUGEES AT GUANTÁNAMO

After the military overthrow of President Jean-Bertrand Aristide in September 1991, human rights violations by the Haitian military, including murder, torture, and arbitrary arrest, prompted approximately 40,000 Haitians to flee their country. Approximately 10,500 such refugees were found to have a "credible fear" of return and were granted admission into the United States; about 25,000 others were returned to Haiti. In the fall of 1991 the U.S. Immigration and Naturalization Service began testing "screened in" refugees for HIV, and in February 1992 those testing positive were interviewed and required to meet a higher standard to establish that they had a "well-founded fear" of persecution. The Immigration and Naturalization Service denied requests by the refugees' attorneys to be present at these interviews.

Haitians interdicted on the high seas were taken to the U.S. naval base at Guantánamo Bay for processing. "Screened out" refugees are not entitled to appeal or to legal representation under the Constitution. But once "screened in," the Haitian's fundamental legal and human rights status is changed vis-à-vis the United States government. Those HIV-positive refugees who successfully completed the interview were housed at a separate facility at Guantánamo Bay, Camp Bulkeley. In a lawsuit brought on behalf of the HIV detainees, Judge Sterling Johnson, Jr., of the U.S. District Court, described this camp as follows when it housed approximately 200 HIV-positive Haitian refugees:

> They live in camps surrounded by razor barbed wire. They tie plastic garbage bags to the sides of the building to keep the rain out. They sleep on cots and hang sheets to create some semblance of privacy. They are guarded by the military and are not permitted to leave the camp, except under military escort. The Haitian detainees have been subjected to pre-dawn military sweeps as they sleep by as many as 400 soldiers dressed in full riot gear. They are confined like prisoners and are subject to detention in the brig without a hearing for camp rule infractions.[3]

Although the military physicians were capable of providing general medical care to the Haitian detainees at Guantánamo, the facilities were inadequate to provide medical care to detainees with HIV infection and AIDS. The physicians themselves first raised this issue in May 1992, requesting that specific HIV-positive patients be evacuated to the United States because adequate medical care could not be provided for them at Guantánamo. Some of these requests were denied by the Immigration and Naturalization Service. At the trial, the United States conceded that the medical facilities at Guantánamo were insufficient to treat patients with AIDS "under the medical care standard applicable within the United States itself." Judge Johnson himself described what the Immigration and Naturalization Service euphemistically called a humanitarian camp as "nothing more than an HIV prison camp."

The judge was asked to find that the medical conditions in the camp violated the U.S. constitutional due process requirement that the government provide its prisoners with adequate medical care and safe conditions—an issue that had not been raised in previous cases involving the Haitian refugees. Although American citizens still have no explicit right to health care, since 1976 American prisoners have been entitled to protection under the 8th Amendment of the U.S. Constitution (which forbids cruel and unusual punishment) from "deliberate indifference to serious medical needs."[4] Judge Johnson found that "deliberate indifference" included "denial or delay of detainees' access to medical care, interfering with treatment once prescribed, [and] lack of response to detainees' medical needs."

Closely related to the issue of adequate medical care was the prospect of detaining the HIV-positive Haitians at Guantánamo indefinitely. Judge Johnson found that the detention was not due to any act committed by the Haitians, but to government actions. For example, 115 Haitians who had met the well-founded fear standard had been detained for almost two years, with no indication of when, if ever, they would be released (although they had been told that they could be there for 10 to 20 years or until a cure for AIDS was found). At the time of the judge's final decision in June 1993, there were 158 refugees in the camp: 143 HIV-positive adults, 2 HIV-negative adults, and 13 children who had not been tested. The court concluded, in terms that invoke universal human rights:

> [The] detained Haitians are neither criminals nor national security risks. Some are pregnant women and others are children. Simply put, they are merely the unfortunate victims of a fatal disease. . . . Where detention no longer serves a legitimate purpose, the detainees must be released. The Haitian camp at Guantánamo is the only known refugee camp in the world composed entirely of HIV positive refugees. The Haitians' plight is a tragedy of immense proportion and their continued detainment is totally unacceptable to this Court.[5]

The judge ruled that the attorney general had kept the Haitians in detention "solely because they are Haitian and have tested HIV-positive." Federal regulations do not permit medical status and HIV infection to be used as criteria for continued detention, and Congress had not provided for mandatory exclusion of persons with HIV infection from either "parole [the means by which interdicted aliens who are screened in are brought to the United States in order to pursue their asylum claims] or the grant of asylum in the United States." Under these circumstances, the judge concluded that further imprisonment of the HIV-positive Haitians "serves no purpose other than to punish them for being sick."

Judge Johnson, among other things, permanently enjoined the processing of Haitians with well-founded fear; held unlawful the attorney general's denial of parole to the screened-in Haitians; and ordered that the screened-in HIV-positive Haitians "be immediately released (to anywhere but Haiti) from . . . detention." The Clinton administration announced it would comply with the court's order and the 158 Haitians held at Camp Bulkeley were almost immediately released and entered the United States. Once in the United States, a number of organizations, including New York's Haitian Women's Project and the Haitian Centers Council, helped the refugees make contact with friends and relatives and obtained housing and Medicaid for them. About 60% of the HIV-positive refugees took up residence in New York and most of the rest in Miami and Boston.[6] New York, which invited the HIV-positive Haitians to live there, is also the primary site of the resurgence of multidrug-resistant tuberculosis.[7]

TUBERCULOSIS CONTROL

In their history of tuberculosis, *The White Plague*, René and Jean Dubos note that the first national movement to control tuberculosis in the United States came from the Medico-Legal Society of the City of New York, a group of lawyers, scientists, and physicians devoted to solving social problems.[8] At a meeting in 1900 to organize an American Congress on Tuberculosis, the group drafted legislation designed to prevent the spread of the disease. Even though almost every state in the United States eventually passed tuberculosis control laws, it was not the passage of legislation, or even the development of effective treatment, that led to the decline of tuberculosis in the United States, but improvement in living conditions. The decline in the disease was so impressive that by the 1980s predictions were made that tuberculosis would soon be eradicated in the United States. With the increasing incidence of tuberculosis and the rise of multidrug-resistant tuberculosis, especially among those with HIV infection, that optimism has disappeared.[9]

The inherent governmental power to act to protect the public's health and safety is referred to as the police power, and in the United States it resides in the individual states. In most of the rest of the world this power resides at the national level. This is why public health issues have almost always been dealt with at the state level in the United States, with state departments of public health taking the lead. And the state's powers are broad. When, for example, the state's power to permit local communities to require vaccination against smallpox was challenged at the beginning of the century, the U.S. Supreme Court ruled in *Jacobson v. Massachusetts* that "the safety and the health of the people of Massachusetts are, in the first instance, for the Commonwealth to guard and protect. They are matters that do not ordinarily concern the national government." Using military metaphors, the Court ruled as a general matter that "upon the principle of self-defense, of paramount necessity, a community has the right to protect itself against an epidemic of disease which threatens the safety of its members."[10] Actions designed to contain an epidemic will be upheld as constitutional as long as they are not arbitrary or unreasonable and are rationally related to the goal of protecting the public's health. A responsible public health approach to infectious epidemics requires surveillance, reporting, intervention, and the education of health professionals. All four must be coordinated or their efficacy will drastically decrease. But an effective public health strategy does not require a military response, or the trampling of basic human rights.

States have the legal authority to identify infectious diseases through screening programs, and they have the legal authority to require physicians and others to report the names of persons with infectious diseases to the state. Screening and reporting are legitimate public health methods designed to protect the health and safety of citizens. Steps must, of course, be taken to protect the confidentiality of medical records and reports so that only public health officials with a legitimate need to know the identity of individual patients (such as officials responsible for monitoring or contact tracing) have access to their names.[11] More difficult human rights questions are raised by treatment of disease. Although involuntary confinement should only be used as a last resort, its availability as a legal option merits discussion because it illustrates both the broad scope of the state's public health powers and ways to restrain it.

QUARANTINE

Many court cases, including *Jacobson*, provide legal authority for states to enact and enforce statutes that permit the confinement (at home, in a hospital room, or at a special facility or residence) of a patient with active tuberculosis who is a danger to others. If a state wishes to deprive such patients of their liberty on the grounds that they are a danger to others, however, the patients are now entitled to considerably more due process than they would have had at the beginning of the century.

The closest legal analogy is provided by court cases that have reviewed the constitutionality of state statutes permitting the involuntary commitment of mental patients on the basis that they have a disease that causes them to be dangerous. The Supreme Court has held, for example, that illness alone is an insufficient justification for confinement if the patient is "dangerous to no one and can live safely in freedom."[12] Nor is "mere public intolerance or animosity" sufficient "constitutionally [to] justify the deprivation of a person's physical liberty." The Court has repeatedly held that "civil commitment for any purpose constitutes a significant deprivation of liberty that requires due process protection." For example, the minimal standard of proof that the state must meet to commit a person involuntarily to a facility is that there is "clear and convincing evidence" of his or her dangerousness (this is less stringent than the criminal standard "beyond a reasonable doubt," but more stringent than the usual civil standard of "preponderance of the evidence").[13]

The following due process rights, outlined by a West Virginia court in a case that involved the involuntary commitment of a patient with tuberculosis for treatment, are likely to be found constitutionally required by most U.S. courts (and should be required in all cases):

> (1) an adequate written notice detailing the grounds and underlying facts on which commitment is sought; (2) the right to counsel and, if indigent, the right to appointed counsel; (3) the right to be present, to cross-examine, to confront and to present witnesses; (4) the standard of proof by clear, cogent and convincing evidence; and (5) the right to a verbatim transcript of the proceedings for purposes of appeal.[14]

Although these safeguards may seem impressive, in fact the only issues likely to concern a judge in a tuberculosis (or HIV) commitment proceeding are two factual ones: Does the person have active tuberculosis, and does the person present a danger of spreading it to others? Since it is unlikely that any case will be brought by public health officials when the diagnosis is in doubt, the primary issues will be the danger the patient presents to others and the existence of less restrictive alternatives to confinement that might protect the public equally well.

Under these circumstances, the burden of involuntary confinement falls most heavily on the homeless and those who live in crowded, inadequate housing, because they have no place to "confine themselves" during treatment for active tuberculosis. Since the rationale for involuntary commitment is danger to others based on the contagiousness of the patient's disease, under existing state statutes (written before multidrug-resistant tuberculosis was identified as dangerous to the public) patients have a right to be released when their tuberculosis is no longer communicable and they are therefore no longer a danger to others.

The possibility of acquiring and spreading multidrug-resistant tuberculosis poses a particularly difficult problem. Even though not currently a danger to others, the patient whose tuberculosis is inactive but not yet cured might be a danger in the future. This could happen if a treatment regimen is not followed and if, instead, the patient takes drugs in such a way as to transform tuberculosis into a multidrug-resistant variety (for instance, by starting the course of treatment but not finishing it, thus encouraging resistant organisms to arise), which later becomes active and communicable. Because clear and convincing evidence is required to prove dangerousness, the fact that a person *might* be a risk to others in the future is insufficient reason alone, under current law, for confinement until cure.

DIRECTLY OBSERVED THERAPY

Current discussion is properly focused not on quarantine but on less intrusive interventions such as routine and universal directly observed therapy. This methadone maintenance mode of treatment delivery is now considered standard of care by many commentators, but controversy remains. Although the data is incomplete, it appears that in the United States more than 80% of all tuberculosis patients completed 12 continuous months of drug therapy from 1976 to 1990.[15] The completion figure is much lower for New York, but it is still a majority. There is an understandable egalitarian desire to try to treat everyone the same by subjecting everyone to directly observed therapy. There is, however, insufficient justification for requiring this annoying and inconvenient mode of treatment for those patients who pose virtually no risk of not taking their tuberculosis medications and thus pose no public health risk.

This is not a matter of conflict between public health and civil rights. It is a matter of common sense. As René and Jean Dubos rightly observed, measures to prevent the spread of tuberculosis generally do not require legal compulsion because they "have acquired the compelling strength of common sense." Requiring all persons to undergo directly observed therapy because it is necessary for some is wasteful, inefficient, and gratuitously annoying; it also undercuts strategies that individualize treatment and use the least restrictive and intrusive public health interventions. Moreover, in many if not most cases, reasonable discharge planning (including housing for the homeless) and counseling will greatly improve voluntary compliance. Of course, it can be difficult to accurately predict compliance for some patients, and individualized case management strategies and monitoring will be necessary.

Directly observed therapy is preferable to quarantine, and efforts to deliver therapy on an outpatient basis should be diligently and imaginatively tried before involuntary confinement is contemplated. Both of these legal interventions, however, concentrate on the victims of societal neglect rather than on the real sources of the new tuberculosis epidemic. This is understandable (because poverty is a much more difficult problem to address), but the evidence from the history of tuberculosis is that controlling tuberculosis depends much more on the general standard of living than specific medical or legal interventions.

AIDS AND HUMAN RIGHTS

The reactions of both individuals and governments to people with HIV infection and AIDS have not, as one would expect in a "war," always been benign, and challenging discriminatory actions in court has become almost commonplace in the United States. Such challenges have been largely successful and helped prod the U.S. Congress to pass the Americans with Disabilities Act, which applies to virtually all diseases and handicaps. The AIDS epidemic has also prompted renewed interest in human rights with regard to health, especially in the international arena. There has, for example, been wide support in the public health community for unrestricted international travel by people with AIDS and HIV infection, and discrimination on the basis of disease has been denounced. This was symbolized by the decision to move the 1992 World AIDS Conference out of the United States to protest U.S. immigration policy toward people with HIV infection.

Judge Johnson was correct in saying that Guantánamo had the only refugee prison camp exclusively for HIV-positive persons, but he had only to look more closely at Cuba itself to find the world's only facility where HIV-positive citizens are placed in mandatory quarantine. Located in a suburb of Havana, Cuba's main quarantine facility is largely fenced in and is composed of barracks housing hundreds of people.[16] Since inspectors from other nations have not been permitted to report on conditions in the quarantine facility, it is difficult to know how much better or worse they are than those at Guantánamo. We do know, however, that the liberty of those living there is extremely restricted and that they are separated from their families.[17] Unlike the United States, however, Cuba has no constitution guaranteeing individual rights and no independent court system to which the inmates in the Cuban facility can appeal for release.

As the United States and other countries become more and more concerned with immigration problems, it is likely that more draconian steps will be taken to restrict immigration worldwide. In the United States, for example, Congress voted in 1993 to ban immigration by those infected with HIV, and this bill was signed into law by President Clinton. The justification used was twofold: There is the cost of caring for those with HIV infection and AIDS, and there is the risk of spreading HIV to others. Both are legitimate areas of concern. But here the military metaphor of containment and defense counsels one action (barring entry) while the future-oriented human rights metaphor counsels another (building a world community).

The cost of caring for immigrants with HIV infection should be viewed in the same manner as the cost of caring for patients with any other expensive illness including, in appropriate circumstances, requiring people to demonstrate sufficient ability to pay for their care. Likewise, the risk of spreading infection is a legitimate public health concern—one that justifies, for example, confining patients with active tuberculosis who refuse to cooperate with treatment and voluntary measures of infection control. But to avoid violations of human rights, the risk of a person's spreading the disease in question must be real, and its assessment must not be based primarily on irrational fear or prejudice.

Discrimination based solely on disease status has not yet received sufficient attention as a human rights violation. When governments sponsor such discrimination, the courts can responsibly respond by speaking clearly and strongly in support of fundamental human rights. When discrimination also adversely affects medical care, physicians and lawyers should work together to defend and promote the interests of the sick, both in their own countries and internationally.[18] Using military metaphors in medicine and public health is ultimately destructive. Future-oriented views of a flourishing international community based on human rights provides a much more constructive model—and the AIDS epidemic is helping the law, and all of us, to move, albeit painfully slowly, beyond the military metaphor and toward a sustainable international community.

CHAPTER SIXTEEN

Tobacco Choices

The figures have become familiar.[1] Tobacco use has been declared "the single most important preventable cause of [premature] death in the United States, accounting for one of every six deaths, or some 390,000 deaths annually."[2] The health goals of the nation call for reducing cigarette smoking prevalence to 15% of adults (a 48% decrease from the current 29%, and reducing the initiation rate of smoking in teenagers to 15% (a 50% decrease from its current rate of 30%).[3] The goal of reducing smoking in the United States is not controversial from a medical or public health viewpoint. But controversy continues as to the most effective methods and the role tort law should play in discouraging or controlling smoking.

Product liability litigation has been instrumental in encouraging automobile manufacturers to make safer cars and drug manufacturers to test products carefully, and in increasing safety awareness in industry generally. To date, however, product liability lawsuits in smoking have been notoriously unsuccessful. Although there have been hundreds of cases filed against cigarette manufacturers for harms caused by smoking, the companies have yet to pay one cent in awards to smokers.[4] In fact, in only two cases to date has any jury ever awarded any damages at all. *Cipollone* is by far the most important tobacco product liability case, and the decision of the U.S. Supreme Court both sets the rules for future lawsuits and illustrates the difficulties faced by injured cigarette smokers and their families who pursue them.[5]

THE CASE OF ROSE CIPOLLONE

Rose Cipollone began smoking in 1942 when she was 17. She smoked Chesterfields until 1955, L & M filters from 1955 to 1968, Virginia Slims and Parlia-

ments from 1968 to 1974, and Trues until 1982, when part of her lung was removed because of lung cancer. She finally stopped smoking in 1983, and died in
1984 of metastatic cancer. Throughout her smoking career she smoked between
one and two packs a day, and she based her brand-switching choices primarily on
her views of the safety of the brands which she learned about from cigarette advertisements. In August 1983, Mrs. Cipollone and her husband filed suit against the
manufacturers of these brands, Liggett, Philip Morris, and Lorillard, for damages
caused by her lung cancer. Following the death of Mrs. Cipollone, her husband continued the suit both individually and as executor of her estate. And following her
husband's death, their son continued the lawsuit as the executor of their estates.

Prior to trial the Circuit Court of Appeals had ruled that most causes of action
against cigarette manufacturers after 1965 were preempted by federal statutes that
mandated health warnings on cigarette packages.[6] After a four-month trial in 1988,
a jury concluded that Liggett did breach its pre-1966 duty to warn of health hazards but that Mrs. Cipollone was nonetheless 80% at fault for her injuries because
"she voluntarily and unreasonably encountered a known danger by smoking cigarettes." The jury, however, awarded $400,000 to Mr. Cipollone to compensate him
for damages he sustained (because of his wife's cancer) from Liggett's breach of
express warranty. Both parties appealed.

The Appeals Court reversed on technical grounds and remanded the case for
a new trial.[7] The case was accepted by the U.S. Supreme Court to resolve a question that had been decided differently by state supreme courts and U.S. Circuit
Courts of Appeal: Does the preemption language in the 1965 federal Cigarette
Labeling and Advertising Act and the Public Health Cigarette Smoking Act of
1969 bar smokers and their families from suing cigarette manufacturers on the
basis of state tort laws? Put another way, were the mandatory warnings one of the
best things that ever happened to the tobacco companies?

PREEMPTION

The U.S. Constitution grants the federal government some exclusive powers (such
as coining money and raising an army). In other cases, such as nuclear power, the
federal government can, at its option, exercise exclusive authority over a subject
matter and eliminate or "preempt" the state's power to regulate in that area. This
power to take over or preempt a specific area of the law is provided for in the
Supremacy Clause of the U.S. Constitution, which provides that federal laws shall
be the supreme law of the land, any laws of the states notwithstanding. There is
no question that Congress can preempt (exert exclusive authority over) the area
of regulating smoking and health labeling and advertising under its interstate commerce powers. The question before the Court was how much of this area Congress
had actually preempted, and thus what powers, if any, remained with the states.

The 1965 Act required all cigarette packages to contain the following label: CAUTION: CIGARETTE SMOKING MAY BE HAZARDOUS TO YOUR HEALTH. In regard to preemption, the Act provided that no other statement "relating to smoking and health" could be required on any cigarette package. The 1969 Act amended the 1965 Act by requiring a statement that cigarette smoking "is dangerous" and banned cigarette advertising in any medium of electronic communication subject to FCC jurisdiction. Its preemption language stated: "No requirement or prohibition based on smoking and health shall be imposed under State law with respect to the advertising or promotion of any cigarettes the packages of which are labeled in conformity with the provisions of this Act."[8]

The Federal Trade Commission extended the warning label requirement to print advertisements for cigarettes in 1972, and Congress required four rotational warnings in print advertisements and packages in their 1984 Comprehensive Smoking Education Act. The question of the effect of the 1969 preemption clause was so difficult for the Court to determine that no interpretation of this clause won five adherents. Instead the Court split into three opinions: a four Justice plurality, and two concurring in part, dissenting in part opinions (three Justices in one, and two in the other). Writers of both concurring opinions, although disagreeing with each other, agreed that the plurality's opinion would be extremely difficult for lower courts to understand and implement.

THE U.S. SUPREME COURT

Justice John Paul Stevens wrote the plurality opinion for himself and Justices Rehnquist, O'Connor, and White. In former cases the Court generally decided what was preempted on the basis of the language of the entire statute in question, sometimes called the "statutory scheme," and often used the statute's legislative history as well to help it to determine Congressional intent. If this was not clear, preemption could be implied by irresolvable conflicts between federal and state law, state law acting as an obstacle to federal law, and the nature of the subject matter itself.

The plurality, however, issued a new and narrow rule of statutory interpretation regarding preemption: When Congress includes a preemption provision in a statute, that language alone should be used to determine the scope of preemption, keeping in mind the strong presumption against preemption. Under this approach, the plurality concluded that the 1965 Act only prohibited the states from "mandating particular cautionary statements . . . in cigarette advertisements," so as to avoid "diverse, nonuniform, and confusing labeling and advertising regulations." The Cipollones had four basic causes of action against the cigarette manufacturers: the plurality's rule required the judges to examine each to determine if the preemption language of the 1969 Act (quoted above) applied.

As to failure to warn, the plurality decided that any state law that established a duty to warn consumers of health hazards in order to make the product reasonably safe was preempted by the "no requirement or prohibition" language in the 1969 Act. In other words, after 1969 no lawsuits alleging failure by cigarette companies to include additional or clearer health warnings than those required by Congress on cigarettes could succeed because any legal requirement for additional warnings was preempted by the 1969 Act.

The claim of breach of express warranty is one that holds the seller responsible for any "affirmation of fact or promise" made to the buyer. The plurality decided that these promises are not imposed by state law, but are "voluntarily undertaken" and made by the seller. Therefore they are *not* preempted by the 1969 Act. Fraudulent misrepresentation was alleged on two bases: (1) that advertising neutralized the effect of the federally mandated warnings and (2) that the manufacturers falsely misrepresented and concealed material facts related to smoking and health. As to the first, the plurality found it "inextricably related" to the failure-to-warn allegation, and thus preempted as well. As to the second, however, the plurality found it *not* preempted, primarily because it was not a rule "based on smoking and health." Rather, "state law proscriptions on intentional fraud rely only on single uniform standard: falsity." Thus claims based on fraud by concealing or misrepresenting material facts are not preempted. For the same reason, the plurality concluded that conspiracy to misrepresent or conceal material facts was not preempted either.

CONCURRING AND DISSENTING OPINIONS

Justice Harry Blackmun wrote for himself and Justices Kennedy and Souter. Blackmun argued that given the plurality's insistence on reading preemptive language narrowly out of respect for state sovereignty, their conclusion that some common law damage claim rights were preempted was "little short of baffling." In Blackmun's opinion, it is not possible to properly interpret words in isolation; the statute must be read as a whole. Moreover, Blackmun noted that the Court had previously distinguished statutory prohibitions from common law actions; noting that the effects of the former were direct, and the latter indirect. Essentially, Blackmun read the 1969 amendments as simply clarifying the 1965 Act. And, using legislative history, Blackmun found no indication that Congress meant to leave consumers without any remedy at all for injuries suffered by smoking. He would have thus found *none* of the state's common law remedies preempted by the 1969 Act.

In contrast to the Blackmun opinion, Justice Scalia, joined by Justice Thomas, would have found all of the common law tort claims at issue preempted by the 1969 language. Scalia argued that the proper rule for interpreting preemption provisions should be the same as the general rule of all statutory interpretation:

"Their language should be given its ordinary meaning." Of course, if this were as easy as it sounds it would have been considerably easier to get agreement as to the meaning of statute's language. In his view both the 1965 and the 1969 language is broader than the other two opinions concluded. Moreover, he suggested an alternate way to determine whether specific state rules or common law actions are preempted: the "proximate application" methodology which asks, "whatever the source of the duty [statute or common law] does it impose an obligation in this case because of the effect of smoking on health?"

Because of the way the Court split, whenever the Stevens plurality decided a common law cause of action was preempted, it had six votes for this position (its four and Justices Scalia and Thomas); and whenever it determined that a common law cause of action was not preempted, it had seven votes (its four and Justices Blackmun, Souter, and Kennedy). Thus, although it is still unclear whether the Court will ever adopt the plurality's "new" method of interpreting Congress' preemption language, the Court's conclusion on the availability of state tort remedies for smokers and their families is beyond dispute: Lawsuits can be filed against cigarette manufacturers which allege breach of express warranty, intentional fraud and misrepresentation, and conspiracy under state law. Lawsuits that are preempted, and thus cannot be brought against cigarette manufacturers, are those alleging failure to warn of the dangers of smoking, and the inadequacy of federally mandated warnings to the extent that those claims rely on statements made in or omitted from advertising or promotions.

FUTURE TOBACCO LAWSUITS

The fact that smokers can bring lawsuits against cigarette manufacturers does not, of course, mean that they will win. Two serious hurdles remain. The first is proof of fraud or misrepresentation. In a related case, the trial judge in *Cipollone*, H. Lee Sarokin, was removed from hearing the rest of the case (and ultimately from rehearing *Cipollone* as well) because of his apparent bias on this issue. In a February 1992 pretrial determination that the cigarette manufacturers were not entitled to use the attorney–client privilege to shield certain documents from discovery Judge Sarokin wrote:

> All too often in the choice between the physical health of consumers and the financial well-being of business, concealment is chosen over disclosure, sales over safety, and money over morality. Who are these persons who knowingly and secretly decide to put the buying public at risk solely for the purpose of making profits and who believe that illness and death of consumers is an appropriate cost of their own prosperity! As the following facts disclose, despite some rising pretenders, *the tobacco industry may be the king of concealment and disinformation* [emphasis added].[9]

An appeals court later ruled that these words constituted at least the appearance of bias against the cigarette companies, and removed him from the case. Later

Cippolone's lawyers decided they could not afford to continue the lawsuit, and it was dropped. Although judicially intemperate, many (perhaps most) physicians and public health professionals will agree with Judge Sarokin's assessment and applaud his statement. And Judge Sarokin's conclusion seems reasonable:

> A jury might reasonably conclude that the industry's [1954] announcement [continued to 1970] of proposed independent research [Council for Tobacco Research] into the dangers of smoking and its promise to disclose its findings was nothing but a public relations ploy—a fraud—to deflect the growing evidence against the industry, to encourage smokers to continue and non-smokers to begin, and to reassure the public that adverse information would be disclosed.

Injured smokers face a second hurdle as well—one Rose Cipollone could not overcome—convincing the jury that they smoked or continued to smoke not by choice but *because* they relied upon the representations of the cigarette companies and would *not* have smoked or continued to smoke had there not been misrepresentations or concealment by the tobacco companies. This is perhaps the chief obstacle to a successful suit against a cigarette manufacturer. Nonetheless, there seems to be no valid reason to deny individuals their right to a jury trial on this issue in cases where their smoking, and thus their damages, were caused by fraud and misrepresentation. For people who began smoking after the Congressionally required warning labels were introduced, proving that they did not know smoking was harmful is probably impossible. In this sense the warning labels are one of the best things that ever happened to the tobacco industry.

Tort law provides remedies for past harms. Public health strategies are much more effective when designed to prevent harm in the first place. Tort suits should certainly be available to consumers in the cases of breach of express warranty and fraud, regardless of the existence of required warning labels, as the U.S. Supreme Court has affirmed. It is unreasonable to suggest that Congress meant to immunize cigarette manufacturers from damages caused by fraud and deceit when Congress required health warning labels on cigarette packages. Such suits, however, are very limited. Both Rose Cipollone and her husband died long before their lawsuit was resolved. It is probably the fact that physicians and public health professionals have been so successful at publicizing the health risks of smoking, and encouraging smokers to stop, that all members of an average jury will know the health risks. Nonsmoking jury members will not be impressed by an argument that advertising makes people smoke, smokers who have stopped with little difficulty may find it hard to believe smoking is addictive, and smokers will likely know the risks they have decided to continue to take. Thus it is unrealistic for the medical and public health community to think that private tort litigation by smokers and former smokers against tobacco companies is ever likely to be so successful that it would force them to stop manufacturing and selling cigarettes.

Given all of the publicized health risks, it is unlikely that warning labels have any impact at all on a decision to smoke or not to smoke, and thus even blunter warnings, such as "smoking is addictive" and "smoking causes cancer" will not curtail smoking. This is not to say that health warnings should be abandoned— only that, no matter how harshly they are phrased, they have probably long ago reached their peak of effectiveness. Reducing tobacco use will require more effective interventions. Primarily these should be focused on discouraging teenagers from smoking and making it difficult for them to smoke. In this effort it is unrealistic to expect any support from the tobacco industry. As one fictional cigarette industry executive puts in a California antismoking TV ad: "We're not in this business for our health."[10]

Antismoking ads work. The major focus of public health professionals, however, has been on prosmoking ads. The next chapter details the legal strategy to eliminate tobacco advertising to teenagers, and drastically reduce it to adults. Because of the protections of the 1st Amendment, Congress is limited in how far it can go to restrict the tobacco industry's advertising choices.

CHAPTER SEVENTEEN

Cowboys and Camels

The Marlboro Man and Joe Camel have become public health enemies number one and two, and removing their friendly faces from the gaze of young people has become a goal of President Bill Clinton and his health officials.[1] The strategy of limiting the exposure of children to tobacco advertising is based on the fact that almost all regular smokers begin smoking in their teens and is made politically possible because almost all Americans believe that tobacco companies should be prohibited from targeting children in their advertising.[2]

Shortly before the 1996 Democratic National Convention the president announced that he had approved regulations drafted by the U.S. Food and Drug Administration (FDA) to restrict the advertising of tobacco products to children. At the convention itself, Vice President Al Gore told the delegates: "Until I draw my last breath, I will pour my heart and soul into the cause of protecting our children from the dangers of smoking."[3] At a press conference in the White House immediately following the announcement, Secretary of Health and Human Services Donna Shalala said, "This is the most important public health initiative in a generation. It ranks with everything from polio to penicillin. I mean this is huge in terms of its impact."[4]

No one doubts that a significant reduction in teenage smoking would mean a significant reduction in adult smoking when these teenagers grow up, and this would have a major impact on the health and longevity. Since almost 50 million Americans smoke, reducing this number substantially would be "huge in terms of its impact." The real question is not the goal, but whether the means proposed to reach that goal are likely to be effective. In this regard the FDA regulations could fail for either of two related reasons: (1) Some of the proposed regulations could be found unconstitutional as a violation of the 1st Amendment, or (2) implementation of the regulations may not affect the initiation of teenage smoking.

FDA'S ANTISMOKING REGULATIONS

The FDA's new regulations are designed to lower the demand for tobacco products by teenagers to cut underage smoking by half in seven years.[5] The FDA, which has never before asserted jurisdiction over cigarettes and smokeless tobacco, bases its jurisdiction over these two products on its authority to regulate medical devices, defining cigarettes as a "drug-delivery device." Of course, this means that the FDA also defines nicotine as a drug. The regulations apply to sellers, distributors, and manufacturers. Sellers may not sell cigarettes or smokeless tobacco to anyone under the age of 18 and must verify the age of purchasers under 26 by a photo identification in a "direct, face-to-face exchange." Exceptions are mail orders and vending machines located in facilities that persons under the age of 18 are not permitted to enter at any time. The distribution of free samples is also outlawed, as is the sale of cigarettes in packs of fewer than 20 (so-called "kiddie packs"). All cigarettes and smokeless tobacco products must bear the following statement: NICOTINE-DELIVERY DEVICES FOR PERSONS 18 OR OLDER.

The most controversial portions of the regulations deal with advertising. One section outlaws all outdoor advertising within 1,000 feet of public playgrounds and elementary and secondary schools. Advertising in certain places is restricted to "only black text on a white background." This restriction applies to all billboards but does not apply to "adult publications." These adult publications are defined by the regulations as "any newspaper, magazine, periodical or other publication . . . whose readers younger than 18 years of age constitute 15 percent or less of the total readership as measured by competent and reliable survey evidence; and that is read by fewer than 2 million persons younger than 18 years of age." Other advertising restrictions prohibit tobacco manufacturers and distributors from marketing any item (other than cigarettes or smokeless tobacco) that bears any brand name used for any brand of cigarettes or smokeless tobacco and from offering any gift to anyone purchasing cigarettes or smokeless tobacco products. Finally, "no manufacturer, distributor, or retailer may sponsor or cause to be sponsored any athletic, musical, artistic, or other social or cultural event, or any entry or team in any event, in the brand name (alone or in conjunction with any other words)." Such events may, however, be sponsored in the name of the corporation which manufacturers the tobacco product provided that the corporate name existed prior to 1995 and does not include any tobacco brand name.

Tobacco companies filed suit to enjoin enforcement of the regulations. According to former FDA Commissioner David Kessler, the FDA decided to assert jurisdiction over cigarettes when a scientific consensus developed that the nicotine in tobacco products is addictive and that the tobacco companies were likely manipulating the levels of nicotine to maintain their market of addicted users. Under the FDA's enabling legislation, a drug is any product "intended to affect the structure or any function of the body." The FDA contends that cigarettes and smokeless tobacco can be properly viewed as a drug-delivery device for the drug nicotine because they meet all three independent tests: "a reasonable manufacturer would foresee that the product will be used for pharmacologic purposes, that consumers actually use it for such purposes [and] . . . the manufacturer expects or designs the product to be used in such a manner."[6]

The primary argument of the tobacco companies is that Congress has consistently refused to give the FDA jurisdiction over tobacco products, and the FDA itself has, until these regulations, consistently said that it has no jurisdiction over tobacco products. Moreover, the companies assert that if the FDA had authority over cigarettes as a drug or a drug-delivery device, FDA would have to ban them as not "safe," and this is something Congress has also repeatedly refused to do or permit. Their second argument, which is the focus of this chapter, is that the regulations violate the 1st Amendment by restricting the right to free speech in advertising. Congress could vote to give the FDA authority over tobacco, but cannot, of course, change the 1st Amendment.

THE FIRST AMENDMENT AND COMMERCIAL SPEECH

The basic test for whether or not the government can ban commercial speech is set out in the 1980 U.S. Supreme Court *Central Hudson* opinion.[7] This case involved a regulation that prohibited electrical utilities from advertising to promote the use of electricity. The Court adopted a four-step test to determine whether this regulation was constitutional: (1) to be protected by the 1st Amendment, the expression must concern a lawful activity and be accurate; (2) the state's interest in banning a protected expression must be "substantial"; (3) the ban must "directly advance" the state interest; and (4) the ban must be no more extensive than necessary to further the state's interest. In *Central Hudson* the Court concluded that although the state had a substantial interest in energy conservation that was advanced by the advertising ban, the ban nonetheless failed the fourth test. The ban failed the fourth test because it was overbroad in that it prohibited the promotion of potentially energy-saving electric services, and there was no proof that a more limited restriction of commercial expression could not have achieved the same goal. The Court suggested, as an example, that a less broad regulation could have required "that the advertisements include information about the relative efficiency and expense of the offered services."

In 1986, in *Posadas*, the Court upheld a ban on advertising casino gambling to the Puerto Rico public. The Court held that this ban met the four tests of *Central Hudson*. The Court added that the government could ban advertising for any activity that it could outlaw, saying, "It would be a strange constitutional doctrine which would concede to the legislature the authority to totally ban a product or activity, but deny to the legislature the authority to forbid the stimulation of demand for the product or activity through advertising."[8] The Court gave a number of other "sin" examples, including cigarettes, alcoholic beverages, and prostitution—examples that struck many in the public health community as good areas in which to restrict advertising. Of course, fashions change, and many states now promote and advertise gambling, in the form of lotteries and casinos, as good for the financial health of the government. Nonetheless, following the most recent and most complete commercial speech case, decided in 1996, it is unlikely that *Posadas* will any longer be followed, and that the four-part test of *Central Hudson* will be very strictly applied in the future.

THE 44 LIQUORMART CASE

44 Liquormart v. Rhode Island[9] involved a challenge by a liquor retailer to Rhode Island laws that banned all retail liquor price advertising except at the place of sale and prohibited the media from publishing any such ads, even in other states. 44 Liquormart placed an advertisement identifying various brands of liquor that included the word "wow" in large letters next to pictures of vodka and rum bottles. An enforcement action against them resulted in a $400 fine. After paying the fine, 44 Liquormart appealed seeking a declaratory judgment that the two statutes and the implementing regulations promulgated under them violated the 1st Amendment.

The U.S. District Court declared the ban on price competition unconstitutional because it did not directly advance the state's interest in reducing alcohol consumption and was "more extensive than necessary to serve that interest."[10] The Court of Appeals reversed, finding inherent merit in the state's submission that competitive price advertising would lower prices and that lower prices would induce more sales.[11] In reviewing these decisions, the U.S. Supreme Court unanimously concluded that the laws violated the 1st Amendment, but no rationale for this opinion obtained more than four votes. Justice John Paul Stevens (who wrote the principal opinion) began his discussion by quoting from an earlier case involving advertising the price of prescription drugs:

> Advertising, however tasteless and excessive it sometimes may seem, is nonetheless dissemination of information as to who is producing and selling what product, for what reason, and at what price. So long as we preserve a predominantly free enterprise economy, the allocation of our resources in large measure will be made through numerous private economic decisions. It is a matter or public interest that those decisions, in the aggregate, be intelligent and well informed. To this end, the free flow of commercial information is indispensable.

Justice Stevens went on to note that "complete speech bans, unlike content-neutral restrictions on the time, place, or manner of expression . . . are particularly dangerous because they all but foreclose alternative means of disseminating certain information." Bans unrelated to consumer protection, Stevens noted further, should be treated with special skepticism when they "seek to keep people in the dark for what the government perceives to be their own good." Stevens then applied *Central Hudson's* four-point test. He concluded that "there is no question that Rhode Island's price advertising ban constitutes a blanket prohibition against truthful, nonmisleading speech about a lawful product." Stevens also seemed to concede that the state has a substantial interest in "promoting temperance."

But can the state meet part three of the test by showing that the ban is effective in advancing this interest? Four Justices defined the third test as requiring the state to "bear the burden of showing not merely that its regulation will advance its interest, but also that it will do so 'to a material degree.'" This is because of the "drastic nature" the state has chosen: "the wholesale suppression of truthful, nonmisleading information." Justice Stevens concluded that Rhode Island did not meet this burden, and could not without any findings of fact or other evidence. The commonsense notion that prohibitions against price advertising will lead to higher prices and thus less consumption (a conclusion simply accepted in *Central Hudson*) was found insufficient to support a finding that their speech prohibition would "significantly reduce market-wide consumption." "Speculation or conjecture" does not suffice.

As to the fourth test, Justice Stevens concluded that the Rhode Island ban also fails because Rhode Island did not show that alternative forms of regulation—such as limiting per capita purchases, or using educational campaigns focused on the problem of excessive drinking—could not be equally or more effective in reducing consumption. All nine Justices agreed with this conclusion. Finally, Justice Stevens (again for four Justices) argued that in *Posadas* the Court wrongly concluded that the state's ability to ban a product or activity meant that it could ban advertising about it. He argued that the 1st Amendment was much stronger than that case had implied, noting, "we think it quite clear that banning speech may sometimes prove far more intrusive than banning conduct" and thus it is not true that "the power to prohibit an activity is necessarily 'greater' than the power to suppress speech about it. . . . The text of the 1st Amendment makes clear that the Constitution presumes that attempts to regulate speech are more dangerous than attempts to regulate conduct." Stevens also rejected the idea that "vice" activities have less 1st Amendment protection than other commercial activities, noting that "a vice exception" would be "difficult, if not impossible, to define." Moreover, prohibiting speech about an activity while not prohibiting the commercial behavior at issue, "fails to provide a principled justification for the regulation of commercial speech about that activity."

FREE SPEECH AND THE FDA REGULATIONS

Selling cigarettes and smokeless tobacco to those under the age of 18 is illegal in all states, so advertising to this age group is not protected by the 1st Amendment. Nor is there any 1st Amendment problem in outlawing vending machines that children have access to. Because the FDA regulations try to apply only to children and do not foreclose all alternative sources of information, it is impossible to predict with certainty how the U.S. Supreme Court will respond to a 1st Amendment challenge (assuming the Court finds that the FDA has authority in this area). Nonetheless, the areas of primary concern can be identified.

Bans will be subject to a higher standard of review than restrictions. Bans include the distribution of products (other than cigarettes and smokeless tobacco) with the tobacco brand name or insignia on them, billboards within 1,000 feet of playgrounds and elementary and secondary schools, and use of brand names for sporting and cultural events. If the Court adopts the strict version of the third prong of *Central Hudson*, the FDA must present evidence that these bans will reduce underage smoking "to a material degree." Moreover, to meet the fourth prong, which all members of the Court found could not be met in *44 Liquormart*, the FDA must also show that no other less restrictive method, such as antismoking advertising or better enforcement of existing laws, would work as well. This will be difficult, especially since the FDA commissioner has already indicated that the FDA believes that antismoking advertising is effective in helping young people understand the risks of smoking and that FDA plans, after the publication of its rule, "to notify the major cigarette and smokeless-tobacco companies that it will begin discussing a requirement that they fund an education program in the mass media." The Court could find that this strategy should have been tried first.

Restrictions on advertising may be easier to uphold, but even restrictions are not obviously permissible. The tobacco companies spend $6 billion a year in advertising and promotion, about $700 million of which is on magazine ads.[12] The core antiadvertising regulation requires that ads on all billboards and in publications that have a readership of either 15% under the age of 18 or two million children under the age of 18 be limited to black on white text. This is a restriction (not a ban) and does not prohibit the inclusion of any objective factual information (such is the price of liquor at issue in *44 Liquormart*). The rationale for these rules is that the images portrayed in bright colors, of which Joe Camel is the primary example, entice children to smoke or continue to smoke. Since no objective information is being banned or restricted, the Court may find such a restriction need only meet a commonsense test.[13] If, however, the Court takes a more sophisticated view of advertising—which is largely image rather than text focused in the United States—it may well hold that the same rules apply and that therefore the burden of proof is on the FDA to demonstrate that such a restriction would reduce underage smoking "to a material degree." No study has yet been able to show this. Consistent with the view that pop art should be protected at least as much as text is the view that they are art forms designed to elicit certain responses—and as such entitled to at least as much 1st Amendment protection as objective text information.

Drastic advertising restrictions may also either not work at all or be counter-productive. In Britain, for example, where both Joe Camel and the Marlboro Man are outlawed, and tobacco advertisers are prohibited from using anything that implies health, fresh air, or beauty, creative advertisers have launched a variety of ad campaigns. One for the brand Silk Cut features various images of silk being cut (by, for example, scissors dancing a cancan in purple silk skirts, and a rhinoc-eros whose horn pierces a purple silk cap), and Marlboro ads portray bleak and forbidding Western U.S. landscapes with the tagline, "WELCOME TO MARLBORO COUN-TRY." It has been suggested that by using surreal scenes such as desert landscapes and cutting silk, tobacco advertisers may be appealing to images of death and sexual violence that have a powerful (if unconscious) appeal to consumers.[14] Such im-agery may actually have greater appeal to teenagers than Joe Camel. U.S. adver-tising agencies have already been asked to come up with black and white text-only ads and have suggested that the required phrase, "A nicotine-delivery device," can be used in conjunction with a cyberspace-evocative line like "pleasure.com" and a sideways-smiling face formed from a colon, a hyphen, and a closed paren-thesis [:-)] to powerfully suggest that nicotine is a modern-age pleasure.[15]

The FDA knows it has a 1st Amendment problem here. In its comments ac-companying the regulations, the FDA argues that it is not required to "conclu-sively prove by rigorous empirical studies that advertising causes initial consump-tion of cigarettes and smokeless tobacco." In fact, the FDA says it is impossible to prove this. Instead, the FDA argues it need only demonstrate that there is "more than adequate evidence" that "tobacco advertising has an effect on young people's tobacco use behavior if it affects initiation, maintenance, or attempts at quitting." The FDA's position follows the conclusion of the Institute of Medicine:

> portraying a deadly addiction as a healthful and sensual experience tugs against the nation's efforts to promote a tobacco-free norm and to discourage tobacco use by children and youths. This warrants legislation restricting the features of adver-tising and promotion that make tobacco use attractive to youths. The question is not, "Are advertising and promotion the causes of youth initiation?" but rather, "Does the preponderance of evidence suggest that features of advertising and promotion tend to encourage youths to smoke?" The answer is yes and this is a sufficient basis for action, even in the absence of a precise and definitive causal chain.[16]

The Surgeon General has also reached a similar conclusion:

> Cigarette advertising uses images rather than information to portray the attrac-tiveness and function of smoking. Human models and cartoon characters in ciga-

rette advertising convey independence, healthfulness, adventure-seeking, and youthful activities—themes correlated with psychosocial factors that appeal to young people.[17]

The Court may make an exception for tobacco ads because of their clear health hazards and use of restrictions instead of bans, but the contours of the restrictions will have to be justified. In this regard, the 15% young-reader rule for publications is more difficult to justify as either not arbitrary or not more restrictive than necessary. The FDA admits, for example, that its rule would require the following magazines to use text-only, black and white ads: *Sports Illustrated* (18%), *Car and Driver* (18%), *Motor Trend* (22%), *Road and Track* (21%), *Rolling Stone* (18%), *Vogue* (18%), *Mademoiselle* (20%), and *Glamour* (17%). The FDA seems particularly offended by "a cardboard Joe Camel pop-out" holding concert tickets in the center of *Rolling Stone* (and while some Americans might prefer to censure the naked Brooke Shields on the cover of the October 1996 issue, her image is clearly protected by the 1st Amendment). A 20% rule, for example, would exempt most of these magazines, all of which have an over 80% adult readership.

The FDA justifies using a 15% rule (rather than any other number) because of its view that "if the percentage of young readers of a publication is greater than the percentage of young people in the general population, the publication can be viewed as having particular appeal to young readers." The FDA says it found that young people between the ages of five and 17 constitute approximately 15% of the U.S. population and that this number justifies the 15% rate (five- and six-year-olds building in a margin of error). A similar analysis can, of course, be pursued regarding sporting and cultural events—some of which may have very few young people in attendance. On the other hand, the billboard restrictions seem to be on solid ground.

Tobacco companies profit handsomely by selling products that cause significant health problems and contribute to the deaths of millions of Americans. There is also little doubt that nicotine is addictive and that it is in the interest of tobacco companies to get children addicted early, since very few people take up smoking after the age of 18. The FDA admits, however, that it cannot prove that cigarette advertising causes children to begin to smoke, and it has not tried alternatives such as strictly enforcing current laws that prohibit sales to minors and engaging in a broad-based antismoking advertising campaign to reduce the number of children who smoke. Until the FDA can either prove the causal link or try methods of discouraging smoking that do not implicate the 1st Amendment, total bans on speech and restrictions on advertising raise enough significant 1st Amendment problems to insure that they could be tied up in court for years.

The 1st Amendment, of course, only applies to government action. Tobacco companies can voluntarily stop using images in their advertising that the public finds offensive (and would seem to be foolish not to). In May 1997 the Federal Trade Commission decided to look again at the issue of whether Joe Camel was designed specifically to target underage smokers. Partly in response to this, and partly to help encourage a global settlement of all the lawsuits against them, R. J. Reynolds Tobacco announced in July 1997 that it would be phasing out Joe Camel from their advertising.[18]

Since sex sells, perhaps better than cartoon characters, the company plans to replace Joe with sexy women who, for example, puff away "as smoke curls up into the shape of a camel, with the tag line, 'what you're looking for.'"[19] It seems unlikely that this new advertising strategy will be any less distressing to public health advocates who want to see smoking ended in the U.S. As David Kessler has put it, "the industry must agree not to encourage smoking, either directly or indirectly."[20] To the extent that Kessler, and others who agree, are taken at their word, their real objection all along was never to Joe Camel or the Marlboro Man; it is to tobacco advertising itself.

Truthful advertising cannot be banned in the United States because it is protected by the 1st Amendment. Nonetheless, advertising can be drastically limited voluntarily or under terms of a settlement agreement. The major settlement proposed to date has the industry agreeing to abide by the terms of the FDA advertising rules described in this chapter and pay money in exchange for immunity from class action lawsuits and punitive damages. How lawsuits drove the tobacco industry to consider making such an agreement, and what it could ultimately look like, are the subjects I address in the next chapter.

CHAPTER EIGHTEEN

Smoking with the Devil

Tobacco companies have become the personification of the devil, and strategies to exorcise tobacco smoking from the United States proliferate.[1] Tobacco's demonic status is reflected in popular fiction. John Grisham's best-seller *The Runaway Jury*, for example, is a broadside attack on tobacco companies. He opens the book by noting that tobacco companies "had been thoroughly isolated and vilified by consumer groups, doctors, even politicians." This was bad; but it was getting worse; "now the lawyers were after them."[2]

Physicians often see trial lawyers as predators, but in choosing sides between lawyers and big tobacco, medicine's choice of devils has recently seemed easy. The American Medical Association, for example, endorses "all avenues" of litigation against the tobacco companies as a public health strategy.[3] As *New York Times* reporter Philip J. Hilts has put it, "The natural end for a tangle like the tobacco wars is in court."[4]

Lawsuits against tobacco companies are not a new phenomenon, but until 1996 they seemed singularly impotent. Chroniclers of tobacco litigation identify three "waves" of litigation.[5] The first dates from the time medical research first demonstrated the risks of cancer from smoking and continued until the early 1970s (1954–73). The second wave (1983–92) began in the early 1980s and ended with the dropping of the *Cipollone* case, the subject of chapter 16. Tobacco companies paid nothing to claimants in any of these lawsuits, ultimately winning them all by relying on three arguments: Smoking is a free choice; there is no conclusive proof that tobacco causes disease; and the industry supports research on the effects of smoking on health.[6] The third wave, which dates from 1994, was seen as much more likely to succeed because of the discovery of a vast array of previously secret industry documents that undercut their own arguments, including documents indicating that the industry knew nicotine was addictive and used this knowledge to hook users.[7] Moreover, while previously plaintiff lawyers have been totally outgunned financially by tobacco companies willing to pay virtually any price not to lose a case, the third wave have been brought by teams of law firms in one major case, and by state attorneys general with the help of private lawyers in others. The playing field has been leveled to such an extent that discussions soon began on how Congress might act to "settle" all tobacco lawsuits.

THIRD-WAVE CLASS ACTION SUITS

The class action that can be said to have marked the beginning of the third wave is *Castano v. American Tobacco Company*, filed in March 1994 in federal district court in Louisiana. Represented by more than 60 law firms, the class sought damages from the tobacco companies only for the somewhat ambiguous "injury of nicotine addiction." The trial court defined the class broadly to include:

(a) All nicotine-dependent persons in the United States . . . who have purchased and smoked cigarettes manufactured by the defendants;

(b) the estates, representatives, and administrators of these nicotine-dependent cigarette smokers; and

(c) the spouses, children, relatives and 'significant others' of those nicotine-dependent cigarette smokers as their heirs or survivors.[8]

A nicotine-dependent person was defined as any smoker "who has been diagnosed by a medical practitioner as nicotine-dependent," or any "regular cigarette smoker" who has been "advised by a medical practitioner that smoking has had or will have adverse health consequences" and who thereafter did not quit smoking. This is, of course, a potentially giant class, comprising millions of people. To be certified as a class under the *Federal Rules of Civil Procedure*, the court must find, among other things, that "the questions of law or fact common to the members of the class predominate over any questions affecting only individual members, and that a class action is superior to other available methods for the fair and efficient adjudication of the controversy."[9] The trial court so found; but the case was reversed on appeal, and the class decertified.

As described by the appeals court, the key to the plaintiffs' complaint is the "wholly untested theory" that the tobacco companies "fraudulently failed to inform consumers that nicotine is addictive and manipulated the level of nicotine in cigarettes to sustain their addictive nature." Specific allegations included fraud and deceit, intentional infliction of emotional distress, violation of state consumer-protection statutes, breach of warranty, and strict product liability. The remedy sought was compensatory and punitive damages, attorneys fees, an admission of wrongdoing, and use of profits for restitution and to establish a medical monitoring fund. The appeals court refused to certify this as a class action primarily because it did not believe that the trial court had considered how variations in the laws of the various states would affect the outcome of individual cases; and the trial court had not properly considered how a trial on the merits of the cases would actually be conducted.

Concerning the state law issues, the appeals court noted that "in a multi-state class action, variations in state law may swamp any common issue" because states have different legal rules, "including matters of causation, comparative fault, and the types of damages available." Specifically, the court noted that the class members had used different tobacco products, for different amounts of time, and over different time periods. Knowledge of danger differed from person to person, as did the reason for use of the product in the first place. The appeals court found the idea of millions of individual cases formidable, but concluded, "Absent considered judgment on the manageability of the class, a comparison to millions of trials is meaningless." The court concluded, "The collective wisdom of individual juries is necessary before this court commits the fate of an entire industry or indeed, the fate of a class of millions, to a single jury." This May 1996 decision was a serious blow to all tobacco-related class action lawsuits. Nonetheless, the plaintiffs almost immediately set about to file separate class actions in individual states.[10]

STATE REIMBURSEMENT SUITS

Potentially more important than private class action suits are the state medical-cost reimbursement suits in which individual states and more than a dozen cities, including New York City, have sued the tobacco companies on behalf of taxpayers to recover the share of Medicaid costs for the uninsured attributable to tobacco-induced disease. The states are aided by outside private counsel working on a contingency fee basis. All of the state lawsuits include fraud and addiction allegations, but the state claims themselves vary.[11] The first case to be brought, for example, was filed in May 1994 by Mississippi Attorney General Mike Moore. The Mississippi lawsuit, which was the first set for trial and the first ultimately settled (in July 1997), was based on theories of unjust enrichment and restitution on the basis that the state's taxpayers had been injured directly by the tobacco industry by having to pay for the medical costs of the illnesses induced by tobacco products through Medicaid.

The second suit, filed by Minnesota Attorney General Hubert H. Humphrey III, alleges both antitrust conspiracy and consumer fraud in engaging in an "unified campaign of deceit and misrepresentation" to conceal information about addictiveness from the public. In October 1996 Humphrey filed a newly discovered 1980 internal memorandum from the British-American Tobacco Co., which he characterized as "an astounding disclosure" of a point in time where the tobacco companies decided to choose to continue their "deadly cover-up" instead of admitting the truth for the sake of their "integrity." The memo argued that acknowledging that cigarettes cause cancer would put the tobacco companies in a more credible position, positioning it "alongside the liquor industry as being so-cially responsible, in that we acknowledge our products can be harmful in excess." The memo also contained a warning, "If the prediction of the U.S. lawyers are correct, we could lose a cancer suit, and this could lead to a new 'industry' in America and elsewhere, that of suing tobacco companies, costing a lot of money."[12]

These cases mark the first time states had sued anyone on the basis that the defendant had injured people for whom the state was in turn obligated to pay medical bills. Robert I. Rabin of Stanford Law School has said that given their novelty, it is impossible to predict how the cases will fare in court, noting, "It is possible that with all the revelations [of company wrongdoing] there will be a much greater likelihood of overcoming the freedom of choice argument."[13] As of May 1998, four state cases had been settled (Mississippi, Florida, Texas, and Minnesota). But how should harm to the states be measured? Of the smokers who die of smoking-related illnesses, most do not die until they become eligible for Medicare. Thus the cost of their final illness (other than long-term care expenses) is likely to be borne not by the city or state but by the federal government. More-over, to the extent that the individual smoker dies earlier than he or she would have otherwise died, the federal government may even get a net savings from Social Security and Medicare. The extent to which federal financial burdens and ben-efits should be factored into state level judgments, or whether the federal govern-ment should be a party to these cases, remains unresolved.

INDIVIDUAL SMOKER LAWSUITS

Although class actions and state-sponsored lawsuits are the major characteristics of the third wave of tobacco litigation, individual lawsuits have been given new life by the discovery of industry documents, like those uncovered by Humphrey, concerning addiction, concealment of research, and obfuscation. For the first time, a jury awarded damages ($750,000) to a smoker, Grady Carter of Jacksonville, Florida, in August, 1996 (in *Cipollone* the damages were awarded to the smoker's spouse and another case involved allegations of asbestos contaminating the fil-ters of Kent cigarettes). Mr. Carter, age 66, developed lung cancer after smoking for 44 years. The jury found that Brown and Williamson, the makers of Lucky Strike, had failed to properly warn Carter of the risks of smoking prior to the time warning labels were required by federal law. The case was the first in which in-ternal Brown and Williams documents were admitted into evidence, and the jury seems to have been persuaded that the company should have informed the public about the addictiveness of nicotine. Interviews with 3 of the 6 jurors revealed that two of them were angry at what they saw as the company's hypocritical defense: The company had accumulated "reams of evidence" that smoking was harmful but continued to tell the public that the hazards of smoking were not proved. The jury also seems to have been impressed that Mr. Carter admitted some responsibility for continuing to smoke (he picked a physician who smoked so he wouldn't be pressured by his doctor to quit), sought a relatively small amount of money ($1.5 million), and did not ask for punitive damages.[14]

In reaction to the Carter case, the stock price of Philip Morris dropped 14% and RJR Nabisco dropped 13% in one day, even though these tobacco companies were not directly involved in the litigation. Their stock prices later recovered, however, and the entire industry breathed a bit easier (and their stock prices rose) when a jury returned a defense verdict in a later Indiana case in which the company's internal documents were not admitted into evidence.[15] The Florida verdict rekindled interest in pursuing individual lawsuits, and a long string of even relatively small victories could go a long way toward putting the tobacco companies out of business, as their shareholders seem to realize.

POSSIBLE "GLOBAL" SETTLEMENTS

In March 1996 the Liggett Group, the smallest of the major American tobacco companies, offered to settle four of the five then-pending state suits and the *Castano* class action. Liggett offered to pay each state (Florida, Massachusetts, Mississippi and West Virginia) $4 million over ten years and between 2 and 7% of its pretax income over 24 years, and to settle *Castano* by paying another 5% of pretax income for 25 years for smoking cessation programs. The company also agreed not to give out free samples or use cartoon characters in its ads. The deal was originally proposed by Bennett S. LeBow and included the right of any company Liggett merged with to make the same deal. LeBow's goal was to influence the RJR Nabisco shareholders to vote for a merger with his company. Liggett retained the right to withdraw from the agreement if the other tobacco makers won their suits on the merits, and could terminate the *Castano* portion if the class certification was reversed on appeal (as it was). The deal would have cost Liggett approximately $31 million over 25 years, far less than it would likely spend on legal fees.[16]

Liggett did settle with the states, and agreed to pay each $1 million. But the merger did not succeed and no other company joined Liggett. LeBow indicated that his company, Liggett, "just can't afford a scorched-earth litigation policy.... One major judgment against Liggett would put us out of business." He continued to encourage the larger tobacco companies to pursue a global settlement.[17]

One such global settlement proposal was floated in August 1996 by attorney Richard Scruggs, who was working with Mississippi's attorney general and apparently with the backing of Scruggs' brother-in-law, Senate Majority Leader Trent Lott. Under the proposal, the tobacco companies would have paid about $6 billion in the form of grants to the 50 states in 1997, the cost for each company based on the number of cigarettes each company sells in the U.S.[18] Thereafter, the manufacturers would have contributed about $100 billion over 15 years, or between 30 and 40 cents for every pack sold. In addition to dismissing all the state suits, Congress would take jurisdiction over tobacco and adopt the FDA's youth advertising regulations as law. Jurisdiction would, however, return to the FDA if youth smoking rates failed to decline within a specified period of time (the industry was said to see this as a "deal breaker"). Lawsuits would be drastically curtailed for the next 15 years, although specific details were not made public. Pending lawsuits would be permitted to go forward, but damages would be limited, with a proposed cap of $1 million per plaintiff.[19]

Richard Kluger, the author of *Ashes to Ashes*, had earlier suggested an alternate global settlement:

1. Congress would [grant blanket] . . . immunity to the tobacco companies against all pending and future product liability claims. . . .
2. The FDA would be given regulatory oversight of the manufacture and packaging of cigarettes, including the power to set maximum levels for their hazardous ingredients.
3. Health warning labels would be enlarged to occupy the entire back of all cigarette packs and would carry far more informative language.
4. . . . OSHA regulations restricting smoking at most work places . . . and FDA [regulations regarding advertising would be promptly implemented] . . .
5. The federal cigarette tax would be doubled to 48 cents to pay for enforcing these new regulations. An additional 2 cents a pack tax would pay for an antismoking advertising campaign.[20]

It is hard to imagine that more specific or larger warning labels would have much of an impact on smokers. Raising the tax on cigarettes may discourage young smokers, but strikes hardest at addicted low-income smokers.[21] Moreover, there seems no rationale for granting the tobacco companies blanket immunity for past wrongdoings—at least for lawsuits in which fraud can be proven. On the other hand, limited immunity may be a price worth paying for FDA regulatory authority over tobacco that has a real chance to lead to cigarettes that are safer and contain progressively lower levels of nicotine, and a large amount of money for public health programs. Both of these settlement proposals had serious shortcomings, but their existence itself was novel, and the search for some global settlement continued to gain ground as litigation intensified and the public's disgust with the tobacco industry grew.

The CEO of RJR Nabisco, attorney Steven F. Goldstone, gave up cigarette smoking at his physician's insistence almost 20 years ago. Goldstone, however, is happy to have his customers risk their health with his tobacco products. In his words, "Not to be too red-white-and-blue about it, but taking risks is what this country is about." And preventing unnecessary illness and injury is what public health is all about.[22] One risk Goldstone does not seem willing to take, however, is that society's increasing disgust with the tobacco companies will hold the stock price of his company down. Thus in an October 1996 interview concerning third-quarter earnings he said he was looking for a negotiated settlement to the legal war on tobacco, declaring, "I have to believe that both the industry and Congress—

no matter who's in Congress—will be willing to talk about it. I'm confident President Clinton will as well."[23]

In June 1997 the attorneys general and the tobacco industry announced that they had reached a settlement. However, since the settlement terms required the approval of Congress, what the two sides had really agreed to was to work together for legislation that embodied the terms of their settlement. The settlement agreement, not in legislative language, runs some 68 single-spaced pages. Its primary provisions include an agreement by the tobacco companies to pay the states $368 billion over 25 years to compensate them for paying the medical bills of injured smokers, to abide by the proposed FDA advertising restrictions (discussed in the previous chapter); an agreement to FDA jurisdiction over nicotine and the ingredients in cigarettes (but FDA would be prohibited from outlawing nicotine for at least 12 years, and before it could even require lower nicotine content it would have to show that this would not result in a black market); an agreement that warnings would be made more severe and larger (e.g., "Smoking can kill you"); targets for the reduction of teenage smoking; and penalties if teen smoking did not decline 30% after five years, 50% after seven years, and 60% after 10 years (although most of this money would be returned if the tobacco companies had made a good-faith effort to follow the rules). From the tobacco companies' point of view, the most important provisions would eliminate class action suits and punitive damages, and limit the total amount of money annually that could be paid to individual litigants (33% of the annual industry base payment).[24]

The settlement would ensure the financial health of the tobacco industry well into the future (its total costs under the settlement could be met by a 62 cent increase per pack, and all payments would be tax deductible) and provide significant revenues to the states. Individuals who continue to smoke or who begin to smoke in the future, would, of course, pay for the settlement by paying the higher prices for cigarettes. It was a settlement by lawyers, and many would soon allege primarily for lawyers, who stood to make billions in fees.

By the fall of 1997 it was clear that the "settlement" could not pass Congress as proposed, and President Clinton announced "five key elements" any settlement must contain: (1) reduce teen smoking; (2) give FDA full authority to regulate tobacco products; (3) methods to hold the industry accountable for marketing to children; (4) reduce second-hand smoke and expand smoking prevention and cessation programs; and (5) protect tobacco farmers.[25]

The public health community could not articulate a vision of what they wanted from a settlement, at least in part because many seemed to want to outlaw smoking altogether or destroy the tobacco industry, two goals that were not on the settlement table because the tobacco companies could never agree to their self-destruction. Former FDA Commissioner David Kessler, who had advanced the FDA rules on marketing, insisted on three other "key" elements: (1) raise the price of cigarettes enough to reduce smoking by 50%; (2) abandon all advertising, and use the best technology available to make a safer cigarette; and (3) full disclosure of all tobacco industry documents. To these three (really four) issues he added two more, reduction in secondhand smoke and no preemption of state or local tobacco control efforts.[26]

In early 1998 Kessler determined that even this list was insufficient, and that no deal should be made with this "shameless rogue industry" that has fraudulently marketed a product whose use "is the ultimate underlying cause of nearly 1 in every 5 deaths in the United States year after year." Together with former surgeon general C. Everett Koop and JAMA editor George Lundberg, he urged Congress not to make any liability concessions to the tobacco industry that would protect them from lawsuits "against any past, present, or future wrongdoing."[27] Without such protection, of course, there is nothing for the tobacco companies to bargain for, and no necessity for Congressional action. Shortly thereafter, Senator John McCain's (R-Arizona) Commerce Committee voted 19 to 1 to approve legislation that would raise $516 billion and provide no immunity, only a yearly cap on total lawsuit payouts. This proposal led the tobacco companies to pull out of the settlement process on the grounds that it would drive them into bankruptcy.

It is extremely difficult, if not impossible, for anyone dedicated to protecting the public's health to either take money from an industry responsible for such a deadly product or take part in a settlement agreement that essentially lets the industry pay protection money to states to continue to market their deadly product. If tobacco really kills millions of people, how can the states protect and profit from its sale? This is what continues to leave public health professionals on the sidelines. The deal is seriously flawed. But short of outlawing tobacco products altogether, if the FDA is given authority over tobacco products (it will have to be a new authority, because as a drug, nicotine would have to be banned as an ingredient in cigarettes because it is not a "safe" drug under current FDA law) and has the will and ability to require safer cigarettes with lower nicotine levels, and if effective ways to prevent teen smoking can be devised, funded, and implemented, a deal is probably worth making.

Congress has always had the authority to raise the tax on tobacco as high as it wants to help curtail smoking (and could do so today in the absence of any deal), but it has not. Congress has also always had the power to give the FDA regulatory authority over tobacco, but it has not. Big tobacco has always had friends in Congress and has always contributed heavily to them. The class action lawsuits got the attention of the tobacco industry; and the companies are willing to give almost all of what public health professionals have said they wanted (e.g., the FDA's proposed marketing restrictions, which are otherwise vulnerable to 1st Amendment attack). Perhaps more class action suits and the threat of punitive damages could win more, but it seems unlikely. As Philadelphia lawyer John Shubb said after a U.S. District Court threw out his class action suit (on behalf of all Pennsylvania smokers, seeking a health monitoring program valued at $2 billion), "It's not as easy to beat big tobacco as some of the zealots think."[28]

The acceptability of any global settlement will, of course, depend upon one's goals in the tobacco wars. The public believes (quite rightly) that Congress is much more interested in increasing tax revenues than reducing teenage smoking; 70% believe raising the price of cigarettes is to get additional tax revenues, only 20% think it is to cut teen smoking.[29] Protecting individual choice while minimizing health hazards seems reasonable, as does putting tobacco under FDA jurisdiction. The 1980 internal tobacco company memorandums had it right: Cigarettes are a hazardous product that like alcohol should be recognized and regulated as such. Prohibition has not and will not work—and to the extent that the proposed OSHA workplace rules would amount to a total prohibition on smoking in all workplaces, they will not work either as the attempt by California to eliminate smoking in bars demonstrates. The twin goals of reducing smoking and making smoking itself less addictive and safer are attractive. Tobacco smoking in the United States seems unlikely to engage more than its current 25% of adults, and it will most likely continue to decrease, as smoking becomes even more socially unacceptable. It is also reasonable to restrict access and ban advertising of cigarettes to children—something the tobacco companies can and should do voluntarily. Increasing taxes on cigarettes to fund antismoking and smoking cessation programs also seems reasonable, although using this regressive tax for other social programs is unfair to addicted smokers.

The key to public health action on the tobacco front seems to lie in combining strategies to discourage children from smoking and to produce a much safer cigarette for those who cannot, or will not, resist the temptation to smoke. Development of a much safer cigarette will obviously have worldwide benefit, not just for U.S. smokers. Litigation has many problems; but to the extent that litigation has made a global settlement at least possible, it is time for Congress to determine reasonable terms.

Death (from cancer) and taxes are at the center of the tobacco debate, as is the possible death of an industry. Responding to the McCain proposal in April 1998, the chairman of Brown and Williamson Tobacco Corporation said, "Congress wants us to sign a suicide note. We won't do that."[30] The next section explores the choice to commit suicide, often as a response to incurable cancer, and whether it is a choice society can reasonably sponsor.

PART V

Choices in Dying

CHAPTER NINETEEN

The Kevorkian Syndrome

Lewis Thomas has tellingly observed that doctors "are as frightened and bewildered by the act of death as everyone else."[1] "Death is shocking, dismaying, even terrifying." Thomas continued, "A dying patient is a kind of freak . . . an offense against nature itself."[2] It is thus not surprising that physicians have difficulty talking candidly with dying patients and caring for them, a reaction that often results in undermedication for pain and expensive and ineffective overtreatment.

Americans know this, and although death is a culture-wide enemy, and death-denial a cultural trait, many Americans fear the process of dying in the impersonal modern hospital more than death itself. Americans say they want to die at home, quickly, painlessly, and in the company of friends and family. Most, however, die in hospitals, slowly, often in pain, and surrounded by strangers. Discussions of assisted suicide, publication of self-help suicide books, and fascination with suicide machines are all symptoms of the problem modern medicine has with the dying, rather than solutions.[3] The state of Michigan has been struggling with these symptoms in an effort to stop Jack Kevorkian for almost a decade. That unsuccessful struggle continues; in this chapter I explain how it began.

THE SUICIDE MACHINE

Jack Kevorkian decided to test his suicide machine in Michigan because he was convinced that Michigan had no laws against assisted suicide.[4] This belief was based on his own reading of two Michigan cases, *People v. Roberts*[5] and *People v. Campbell.*[6] The first is a 1920 case in which Frank Roberts pleaded guilty to the charge of murder for killing his wife, Katie. Katie Roberts was terminally ill, practically helpless, and suffering from multiple sclerosis. According to Roberts,

209

it was at his wife's request that he mixed a quantity of paris green (which contains arsenic) in a drink and placed it within his wife's reach. Katie Roberts drank the potion with the intention of taking her own life and died a few hours later. After being sentenced to life imprisonment on the basis of his guilty plea, a sentence required under Michigan law for murder "perpetrated by means of poison," Roberts appealed. His primary argument was that since suicide was not a crime in Michigan, there could be no crime of being an accessory before the fact to suicide—that is, since Katie Roberts committed no crime in killing herself, Frank Roberts could have committed no crime in helping her. The Michigan Supreme Court agreed that if there is no crime of suicide there can be no crime of being an accessory to suicide. Roberts, however, was not charged with being an accessory to suicide, but with murder, to which he pled guilty. The court concluded that the facts supported a guilty finding of murder by poison.[7]

In 1983, the Michigan Court of Appeals dismissed the indictment of Steven Paul Campbell on the charge of murder in connection with the suicide of Kevin Basnaw. On the night of his suicide, Basnaw had been drinking heavily with Campbell. Just two weeks earlier, Campbell had caught Basnaw in bed with Campbell's wife. Basnaw talked about suicide but said he didn't have a gun. Campbell offered to sell him one and ridiculed him. Finally, the men drove to the home of Campbell's parents to get a gun and bullets, after which Campbell left Basnaw at home. The next morning Basnaw was found dead with a self-inflicted gunshot wound to the temple. The prosecutor relied upon *Roberts* to justify a charge of first-degree murder against Campbell. The appeals court agreed that the case could not be distinguished from *Roberts* but ruled that *Roberts* was no longer good law. The court found that "the term suicide excludes by definition a homicide. Simply put, the defendant here did not kill another person." The court invited the legislature to pass a statute against this type of conduct, which it said laws in other states had characterized as crimes ranging from negligent homicide to voluntary manslaughter, but not murder. The court concluded that Campbell's conduct, although "morally reprehensible," was not "criminal under the present state of the law."

By 1998, Kevorkian, according to his attorney, had been involved in "nearly 100 cases" of assisted suicide,[8] mostly involving women, using two suicide machines, one with drugs and another using carbon monoxide. The drug-based suicide machine consists of three hanging bottles connected to an intravenous line. When the line is in place, it delivers a saline solution. The subject can then push a button that switches to the second bottle, containing the sedative thiopental. A third bottle, containing potassium chloride, is later activated automatically by a timer, and death follows within minutes.

After this method was used by Janet Adkins in June 1990, I observed that the "suicide machine stands as a hybrid between medical and nonmedical technology," and that if Kevorkian had used a noose or helped Adkins "point a gun at her head and indicated when to pull the trigger, there seems little doubt that he would have been charged with and convicted of manslaughter (the reckless endangerment of another's life), if not murder."[9] Kevorkian was in fact charged with murder in the death of Adkins, but the medical trappings of the machine seemed to help persuade the trial judge that Kevorkian's acts were medical in nature, and thus presumptively benign. Relying on *Campbell*, Judge Gerald McNally dismissed all charges, ruling that Adkins had caused her own death and that Michigan had no specific law against assisting a suicide.[10]

In February 1991, a permanent court injunction was issued barring use of the suicide machine. In November 1991, Kevorkian's license to practice medicine in Michigan was suspended, and in April 1993, his license to practice medicine in California was also suspended. Kevorkian, a pathologist, had trouble starting the intravenous line in Janet Adkins, and had to make five attempts to enter a vein. With his second subject, Sherry Miller, he tried unsuccessfully four times to start the infusion, and eventually returned home to get a cylinder of carbon monoxide. Later that same day he was successful in starting an intravenous line in Marjorie Wantz, but thereafter he abandoned his drug-based suicide machine and has since relied exclusively on carbon monoxide. Murder charges were also brought in connection with the deaths of Sherry Miller and Marjorie Wantz, but the prosecution could not obtain a conviction. On December 15, 1992, the day Kevorkian supplied carbon monoxide to his seventh and eighth subjects (who, like all the earlier subjects, were women), Governor John Engler signed Michigan's anti–assisted suicide bill, which was to become effective in March 1993. Kevorkian stepped up his activities, however, and after his list of cases grew quickly to 15, Michigan's legislature made the statute effective immediately (on February 25, 1993) and also clarified the exceptions to the new crime of assisted to suicide.[11]

MICHIGAN'S ANTI–ASSISTED SUICIDE LAW

Michigan's anti–assisted suicide law had two basic provisions. The first established a 22-member Commission on Death and Dying, composed of individuals recommended by 22 different interest groups in Michigan, including the state's medical society, hospital association, Hemlock society, and right-to-life organization. This commission was given 15 months to "develop and submit to the legislature recommendations as to legislation concerning the voluntary self-termination of life," a task that turned out to be impossible.

The second part of the statute temporarily criminalized assisted suicide (for a maximum of 21 months) and was automatically repealed 6 months after the commission's deadline to make recommendations to the legislature. The statute stated:

> (1) A person who has knowledge that another person intends to commit or attempt to commit suicide and who intentionally does either of the following is guilty of criminal assistance to suicide, a felony punishable by imprisonment for not more than 4 years or by a fine of not more than $2,000.00, or both:

(a) Provides the physical means by which the other person attempts or commits suicide.

(b) Participates in a physical act by which the other person attempts or commits suicide.

(2) Subsection (1) shall not apply to withholding or withdrawing medical treatment.

(3) Subsection (1) *does not apply to prescribing, dispensing, or administering medications or procedures if the intent is to relieve pain or discomfort* and not to cause death, even if the medication or procedure may hasten or increase the risk of death [emphasis added].[12]

This statute was, of course, a direct response to Kevorkian's activities, but it covered other types of assistance in suicide as well. Kevorkian's actions meet the requirements of both parts (a) and (b) in that, with knowledge that a person intends to commit suicide, he "provides the physical means" and "participates in [the] physical act." And since his intent is "to cause death," his action does not fall within the exception in subsection (3). A case like that in *Campbell*, in which a person provides a gun and bullets to someone who expresses a desire to kill himself or herself, would be covered by part (a), as would the act of providing poison, as in *Roberts*. The statute was attacked as unconstitutionally interfering with the right of privacy, but given its exceptions, that challenge did not succeed.[13] I will discuss the more well known constitutional challenges to assisted suicide statutes that were decided by the U.S. Supreme Court in 1997 in detail in chapter 21.

On the surface, the statute might seem to criminalize actions like those described by Timothy Quill in the *New England Journal of Medicine*. Quill, whose case is also described in more detail in chapter 21, prescribed barbiturates to a terminally ill patient with cancer who said she might use them to kill herself at some indeterminate future time.[14] Assuming, however, that a Michigan physician writes a prescription for drugs that have a legitimate medical use (but also could be used to commit suicide) with the intent "to relieve pain and discomfort and not to cause death," the physician's action should qualify as a exception under subsection (3).

The existence of a long-term doctor–patient relationship seems necessary to argue such a defense credibly in a case like that described by Quill. This is because making a medical judgment about the appropriateness of a drug prescription requires knowledge of the patient and the patient's condition. Prosecutors must also contend with the fact that unlike the defendants in *Roberts* and *Campbell*, physicians who write prescriptions do not provide the "physical means" to commit suicide any more than someone who gives a person money to fill the prescription or a car to go and get it filled at the pharmacy would have provided the physical means. A drug prescription is a piece of paper and cannot be used to commit suicide. All elements of a crime must, of course, be proven to a jury, which must find the physician guilty of each element beyond a reasonable doubt.

The concern that the statute might bar either the withdrawal of life-sustaining medical treatment or the provision of sufficient pain medicine to relieve suffering, even if this would hasten death, is misplaced. Subsections (2) and (3) provide that the statute does not apply to withholding and withdrawing medical treatment and that the principle of the double effect provides a legal defense to prescription, dispensing, or administration of medication for the purpose of relieving pain or discomfort, even if such action does in fact hasten death. These exceptions cover not only health care professionals but also the family and friends of the patient. No physician should fail to provide pain medication out of fear of legal consequences, because, as the Massachusetts Board of Registration in Medicine has put it, "no patient should ever wish for death because of a physician's reluctance to use opioid analgesics."[15]

DISTINGUISHING QUILL AND KEVORKIAN

There is no evidence, other than the language of the statute, that the Michigan legislature sought to distinguish between actions of Jack Kevorkian and Timothy Quill. But in determining legal, ethical, and medical policy, it is important to distinguish between these two types of cases. What is at stake is the proper role of the criminal law in medical practice, and Kevorkian seems correct when he asserts that he is "not practicing medicine."[16] Similarly, the AMA is simply wrong to equate the actions of Kevorkian and Quill, and to adopt an idiosyncratic, overly broad, and vague definition of physician-assisted suicide to cover them both.

In the AMA's definition, "assisted suicide occurs when a physician facilitates a patient's death by providing the necessary means and/or information to enable the patient to perform the life-ending act (e.g., the physician provides sleeping pills and information about the lethal dose, while aware that the patient may commit suicide)."[17] This definition is much broader than in the Michigan statute, which does not prohibit any information sharing at all, and which requires not only providing the means, but also doing so with the knowledge that another person intends to commit suicide. The AMA, moreover, seems unable or unwilling to distinguish physician-assisted suicide from killing by a physician, saying that both are "contrary to the prohibition against using the tools of medicine to cause a patient's death." But the tools of medicine are used all the time with the knowledge that they may cause death—in surgery, for example. Such use is acceptable because the *intent* is to benefit the patient. Risking death on the operating table is not the same as intending that death occur.

The crucial legal and ethical distinctions lie not just in the nature of the tools but also in the intent of the physician using them. Quill's actions can be compared with those of the gynecology resident described in "It's Over Debbie,"[18] who gave a lethal injection to a 20-year-old patient with ovarian cancer whom he did not know and who had said only, "Let's get this over with." Making this comparison, New York's medical licensing board concluded, "One [Quill] is legally and ethically appropriate, and the other, as reported, is not."[19] A Kevorkian-type physician intends and ensures the deaths of his subjects. A Quill-type physician intends to alleviate the pain and suffering of his patients' final weeks or months of life, even if this risks suicide.

THE SLIPPERY SLOPE

The most powerful argument against legislative expansion of the power of physicians to assist patients in suicide is the danger that greater legal latitude will result in abuses that disproportionately affect especially vulnerable populations—the poor, the elderly, women, and minorities. In a country that treats the dying as "freaks," already-marginalized members of society could be deprived of their human rights by making them appear somehow less than fully human. This is especially true in the context of cost containment and economic constraints.

Kevorkian is fond of describing his detractors as Nazis. The Nazi analogy should not be used promiscuously. But his own actions suggest that we need to examine the Nazi experience. Kevorkian's primary method of inducing death, for example, is carbon monoxide poisoning. This was the method personally chosen by Adolf Hitler at the outset of the Nazi euthanasia program on the advice of his medical adviser, Werner Heyde. Heyde conducted an experiment in 1940 on various ways to kill people and concluded that carbon monoxide gassing was the most humane. Even though it was difficult to see gas poisoning as a medical act, the Nazi physicians nonetheless persisted in stressing that "only doctors should carry out the gassing."[20] It is remarkable how much commentary has been devoted to Kevorkian's early drug-based suicide machine and how little to his routine use of carbon monoxide gas. There is nothing medical about the latter method, as carbon monoxide gas has no legitimate medical use; nonetheless, many people seem to accept the idea, as did the Germans, that if a physician performs the act it must be medical, and if it is medical, it must be beneficent and therefore acceptable.

For similar reasons, state-ordered executions in the United States are moving from the gas chamber to lethal injection. Medical organizations throughout the world have quite properly declared that participation of physicians in executions is unethical.[21] The primary reason is that physicians should not permit their caring profession to be subverted for the nonbeneficent goals of the state. The medicalization of executions makes them appear more humane and thus much more acceptable to society.

The same may be said about assisted suicide. If suicide is assisted by a physician, instead of a relative or friend (even using poison gas), society is much more likely to see this assistance as acceptable, even expected. Although proponents currently insist on contemporaneous competent, voluntary, and informed consent, the terms "physician-assisted suicide" and "euthanasia" are routinely used almost interchangeably. This linkage indicates that it will be as difficult to retain personal consent at the time of death as a prerequisite to physician-assisted death in the United States as it has proved to be in the Netherlands, where almost half of all lethal injections given to incompetent patients are given in cases in which the patient has never expressed a wish for euthanasia.[22] When we decide to rely on substituted judgment, our own definition of another person's best interests, or proxy consent, we quickly move from assisted suicide to direct killing by physicians.[23]

Michigan had to try to stop Kevorkian. And so far Michigan has failed, although 'attempts to pass new legislative curbs on Kevorkian (and his would-be clones) continue. But stopping or failing to stop one aberrant physician is not what the debate over physician-assisted suicide is about. Kevorkian is a symptom of a medical care system gone seriously wrong at the end of life. Dying continues to be treated as an "offense against nature," even though it is as integral a part of our nature as birth and life itself.

Kevorkian says, in effect, that medicine cannot change and that society must therefore accept his methods as another choice. Some choice. The Michigan legislature properly rejected his approach. But the real issues are related to medical practice, not the law, and the challenge Kevorkian presents to modern medicine is real. As will be discussed more in the next two chapters, physicians must respond by listening to their dying patients, comforting them, providing them with continuity of care and freedom from pain (even to the extent of providing them with prescriptions for drugs despite the risk of suicide), and bringing hospice care into mainstream medicine. If physicians fail to meet this challenge, society will ultimately embrace the Kevorkian syndrome and thereby medicalize suicide the way we have already medicalized death.

In the next chapter I explore the actions of Oregon, the first and only state to make the mirror-opposite choice of Michigan by legalizing physician-assisted suicide by popular initiative.

Chapter Twenty

Oregon's Bloodless Choice

Americans are unable to accept death and consequently we are unable to deal with the physical, psychological, and spiritual approach of death.[1] The hour of death itself "is commonly tranquil," but "the serenity is usually bought at a fearful price— and the price is the process by which we reach that point"—a process that has been described as "a purgatory that may last for weeks."[2] Suicide has been seen as a rational way to avoid that purgatory, especially as a response to end-stage cancer and AIDS, and proposals to legalize physician-assisted suicide in well-defined cases have persisted. Kevorkian's actions resulted in anti–assisted suicide legislation in Michigan that I described in the previous chapter. Suicide advocates have also gone to court to challenge the constitutionality of laws against assisted suicide, and this is the subject of the next chapter. In addition to legislatures and courts, there is a third way to change state law: Almost half the states permit a direct vote by an initiative petition. Even though all three "death with dignity" initiatives to date have come from a single advocacy group, the Hemlock Society, they have struck a responsive cord with the public and deserve to be taken seriously.

Three initiatives that have been voted on so far include one in Washington in 1991 (Initiative 119), one in California in 1992 (Proposition 161), and one in Oregon in 1994 and again in 1997 (Ballot Measure 16). The drafters of the Oregon initiative learned from the defeat of the two previous measures. As a result of incorporating these lessons into their much-narrower proposal, their initiative was adopted by the voters by a 51 to 49% majority in November 1994. Due to continuing controversy, another vote on the measure was held in November 1997 and it was overwhelmingly readopted. A brief review of the Washington and California proposals help explain enigmas in the Oregon law. The next chapter explains why, although identical, the measure passed in 1997 almost trifling (since it followed the 1997 U.S. Supreme Court cases on assisted suicide), while the 1994 measure was much more revolutionary.

WASHINGTON'S INITIATIVE 119

Washington's initiative was written by the state chapter of the Hemlock Society as a series of amendments to Washington's 1979 Natural Death Act (the nation's second living will law). Initiative 119, however, went far beyond making it easier to refuse treatment in that it included both physician-assisted suicide and voluntary euthanasia in the purposely vague term "physician aid-in-dying." The official ballot question was phrased simply, "Shall adult patients who are in a medically terminal condition be permitted to request and receive from a physician aid-in-dying?" Aid-in-dying is a term that disguises more than it reveals, and few Washington voters likely had an accurate idea of what they were asked to vote on.[3] Initiative 119 defined physician aid-in-dying as "a medical service, provided in person by a physician, that will end the life of a conscious and mentally competent qualified patient in a dignified, painless, and humane manner, when requested voluntarily by the patient through a written directive."

Campaigns for and against 119 provided the public with little useful information. Proponents concentrated on a straight choice message, using statements from terminally ill cancer patients asking for the right to choose a humane and dignified death.[4] Opponents argued that Initiative 119 had no safeguards; their advertisements featured a nurse saying it would "let doctors kill my patients" and an elderly farmer saying it gave physicians too much power, "more or less a right to kill." Ultimately, the fear of a painful and degrading death was overcome by fear of killing by unaccountable physicians. Initiative 119 was defeated, receiving 46% of the 1.5 million votes cast.[5] Opponents did, however, agree to support long-overdue changes in the 1979 Natural Death Act, and in 1992 the legislature enacted provisions that broadened the ability of patients to use advance directives to order the withholding and withdrawal of treatment in the case of terminal illness or "a permanent unconscious condition." The experience with Initiative 119 also inspired a Hemlock-associated group called Compassion in Dying to challenge the constitutionality of the state's law prohibiting assisted suicide in the case of terminally ill persons. A federal district court judge, who also could not distinguish between refusal of treatment and suicide, ruled the statute unconstitutional because it denied equal protection of law to competent terminally ill patients who had no life-sustaining treatment to refuse.[6] This decision was ultimately reversed by the U.S. Supreme Court in a 1997 opinion described in detail in the next chapter.

CALIFORNIA'S PROPOSITION 161

California's 1992 death with dignity initiative was based on an earlier Hemlock Society proposal (The Humane and Dignified Death Act) that failed to qualify for the 1988 ballot. In its reincarnated form it was sponsored by a group called Californians against Human Suffering. It continued the use of the ambiguous phrase physician aid-in-dying, although it more clearly defined the phrase to encompass voluntary euthanasia and assisted suicide: "'Aid-in dying' means a medical procedure that will terminate the life of the qualified patient in a painless, humane and dignified manner, whether administered by the physician at the patient's choice or direction or whether the physician provides means to the patient for self-administration."

In addition to being clearer than Initiative 119, Proposition 161 attempted to incorporate more safeguards to prevent abuses. Special protection, for example, was given to patients in skilled nursing facilities, whose written directives were to be invalid unless witnessed by a patient advocate or ombudsman designated by the state department of aging for this purpose. In addition, hospitals and health providers were required to keep records and to file an annual report to the state department of health services that included each patient's age, type of illness, and the date on which the directive was carried out (but not the identity of the patient). The written directive itself was to be put into the patient's medical record "in each institution involved in the patient's care."

The patients who qualify for aid-in-dying were, like those covered by Washington's Initiative 119, only those who physicians believe have less than six months to live. Also like Initiative 119, Proposition 161 was defeated by a margin of 54% to 46%. Defeat was followed by renewed regulatory efforts to encourage physicians to deal more effectively with pain management, including a proposal to eliminate triplicate prescription forms for controlled substances, which are believed to inhibit physicians from prescribing the proper amounts of medication.[7]

OREGON'S BALLOT MEASURE 16

The Hemlock Society moved its national headquarters from California to Oregon in 1988. Nonetheless, it was not until 1994 that one of its initiatives, Ballot Measure 16, made it onto the Oregon ballot. The society's founder and former president, Derek Humphry, had difficulty locating a physician to supply lethal drugs he ultimately used to help his first wife, who was dying of cancer, end her life when he was still living in England. He expected Ballot Measure 16 to be successful, in large part because it is more limited than the Washington and California initiatives.[8] Specifically, although it has the same title as the previous two, the Oregon Death with Dignity Act is limited to permitting physicians to comply with the request of a competent adult patient with less than six months to live for a prescription for lethal drugs:

> An adult who is capable, is a resident of Oregon, and has been determined by the attending physician and consulting physician to be suffering from a terminal disease, and who has voluntarily expressed his or her wish to die, may make a written request for medication for the purpose of ending his or her life in a humane and dignified manner in accordance with this act.

As with requests for euthanasia under Initiative 119 and Proposition 161, Ballot Measure 16 requires that the request for a drug prescription be in writing and signed in the presence of at least two witnesses who agree that the patient is competent and acting voluntarily. Required contents of the form are also again specified. Residents of long-term care facilities must have at least one witness with qualifications specified by the state's department of human resources. At least two physicians must agree that the patient will likely die from a terminal illness within six months, the patient must be referred for counseling if a psychiatric or psychological disorder is suspected, and the attending physician must ask (but can't require) the patient to notify his or her next of kin about the request. Records must be maintained, and a sample of records must be reviewed annually by the state's health division (but not made public except in a statistical report).

Two waiting periods are built into the act. Two oral requests are required, the second no less than 15 days after the patient's original oral request, before the required written request can be accepted, and the prescription itself cannot be provided less than 48 hours after the written request. No physician is required to write a prescription upon request, but physicians are provided with immunity from "civil or criminal liability or professional disciplinary action" for "good faith compliance" with the act. This immunity specifically extends to "being present when a qualified patient takes the prescribed medication to end his or her life in a humane and dignified manner."

Ballot Measure 16 seems to have been written in response to the generally favorable public reaction to the case of Timothy Quill, who prescribed lethal drugs to his patient Diane, and to avoid the more negative public reaction to Jack Kevorkian, who uses carbon monoxide poisoning. The writers of Ballot Measure 16 implicitly repudiated Kevorkian and his methods and exclusively endorsed the Quill prescription method. This strategy is also consistent with Hemlock Society ideology, which teaches that a suicide by drugs is "peaceful, bloodless dying."[9]

CONTINUING CONTROVERSIES

Oregon governor and physician John Kitzhaber has said "I believe an individual should have control, should be able to make choices about the end of their life."[10] But both the control and choice Ballot Measure 16 provides may be illusory. Its narrower scope made Oregon's Ballot Measure 16 a much more reasonable initiative to put to a vote than either the Washington or California version. Nonetheless, several contentious issues remain. One is the persistent argument that physician-assisted suicide and killing by physicians (euthanasia) are essentially the same thing, so distinguishing between them, as Ballot Measure 16 does, is pointless.[11] This argument is powerful because physicians will likely be asked to be with their patients while they take the drugs, and to "finish them off" if the drugs to not induce death, or if the dying process takes longer than the family had anticipated. Nonetheless, physician presence is not required for suicide, and if they are present physicians can and should refuse to kill. Thus I find this argument ultimately not persuasive, since it ignores the identity of the person doing the actual killing by making no distinction between self-killing (suicide) and killing another (homicide). Those worried about the slippery slope, however, will take Derek Humphry seriously when he says that Ballot Measure 16 is just the first step and that when people become "comfortable with this form of assisted dying . . . we may be able to go the second step," which is euthanasia.[12]

It is essential to understand existing law before trying to change it. Is there a need for such a narrow law, or could it do more harm than good? Providing terminally ill patients with drugs they might use to kill themselves does not currently constitute assisted suicide, as discussed in the previous chapter, even if the patient actually uses them for suicide, unless it is the physician's intent that the patient so use them. Physicians legally can, and as a matter of good medical practice should, supply prescriptions for potentially lethal drugs that have an independent legitimate medical use to their terminally ill patients upon request if they believe that having these drugs is likely to permit the patient to live better. Thus, no changes in current law are needed to legalize the prescription of lethal drugs that have a legitimate medical use to terminally ill patients. Although the clear purpose of Ballot Measure 16 is to encourage this drug prescription practice, nonetheless, the act of putting this proposal into legislative language may itself create the erroneous impression that current legitimate prescription practices are illegal and must therefore be discontinued.

Ballot Measure 16 could also decrease the number of physicians who are willing to prescribe potentially lethal drugs because the patient must make a request for lethal medication not because he or she will feel more secure if it is available, and therefore be able to live longer and better, but only "for the purpose of ending his or her life." Likewise, the physician's intent in writing the prescription *must* be to end the patient's life. In short, under Ballot Measure 16, the physician must agree with an explicit plan of suicide by the patient and must participate in the suicide plan directly and unambiguously.

FEDERAL DRUG LAW

Even though Oregon adopted its state law legalizing the prescription of drugs for the purpose of committing suicide, state law cannot nullify federal regulations governing the prescription of drugs, as I discussed in chapter 8 on California's medical marijuana law. The types of drugs that would be prescribed for this lethal purpose are likely to be those which are regulated under the federal Controlled Substance Act. To be lawful, a prescription for a controlled substance "must be issued for a legitimate medical purpose by an individual practitioner acting in the usual course of his professional practice."[13] The question remains whether, under federal law, prescribing drugs for a patient to use to commit suicide would constitute a legitimate medical purpose. It is unclear whether, if a state authorizes a physician to engage in certain practices, they are considered "legitimate" under federal law, since the drafters of the federal statute certainly did not have this purpose in mind. What case law exists indicates that the physician must have nonlethal therapeutic purpose to prescribe lawfully.

Likewise, although the Food and Drug Administration is not required to certify drugs used in executing condemned prisoners as "safe and effective" for this purpose,[14] to gain immunity under Ballot Measure 16 a physician prescribing such drugs must act in "good faith." Since the physician is required to prescribe a drug regimen that induces death in a "humane and dignified manner," and since no drugs have been approved for this use, additional data could reasonably be required before concluding that any such drug is prescribed in good faith. All this is not to say that Ballot Measure 16 necessarily conflicts with federal law, only that it is unlikely to reassure physicians who do not already help their dying patients by prescribing potentially lethal drugs because of fear of potential legal entanglements.

PHARMACISTS

Pharmacists face similar quandaries, since it is the pharmacist who actually supplies the drugs to the individual patient. Pharmacists will have to decide not only whether they are violating federal law but also what their own ethical and professional standards demand in this situation. Pharmacists are not even mentioned in Ballot Measure 16, and it is doubtful that the drafters took pharmacists into consideration at all; rather, the authors of the proposal probably considered pharmacists simply as agents of the attending physician. This view may be reasonable when pharmacists are dispensing drugs to help patients live better or longer, but it is not tenable in this situation. Patients and their families will naturally have questions for pharmacists about how the drug is likely to act, how it should be taken, and how long it will take death to come, for example. What should the pharmacists' role be? What advice on suicide can and should they provide?

Enactment of Ballot Measure 16 also created a new paradox in our drug laws. Physicians are permitted to prescribe drugs with the intent that patients use them to kill themselves but are not permitted to prescribe the same or less dangerous drugs, such as marijuana (see chapter 8) and lysergic acid diethylamide (LSD), to prevent suicide. Drugs not only relieve depression and pain, they can also give patients a sense of control that permits them to live. One dramatic example is the most famous suicidal patient of the 1980s, Elizabeth Bouvia.[15] Quadriplegic and in pain, she abandoned her legal quest to commit suicide with medical assistance after she was given control over the administration of her own morphine and has continued to live ever since. A necessary prerequisite to legalizing suicide by prescription should be the ability to prescribe the same and similar drugs to prolong life. Of course, supporters of Ballot Measure 16 likely favor laws permitting the terminally ill to take any drugs their physicians believe might prevent them from committing suicide by enhancing the quality of their lives. However, this is not just a state issue, but a federal issue as well.

BETTER OR WORSE?

Since physicians want to be covered by the immunity provisions of Ballot Measure 16, those who now supply potentially lethal drugs to their patients will likely do so only in the manner prescribed by the measure (including the requirements for a minimal 17-day waiting period, the witnessed written request, record keeping, and involvement of a second physician). These requirements will make the practice of prescribing such drugs much more bureaucratic and burdensome and less private and accountable. It seems better to retain the current system—in which physicians can act to favor life, with therapeutic intent (accepting the risk of suicide), and with flexibility, while accepting responsibility for their actions—than to replace it with a more mechanical system in which physicians are not responsible for their actions and must specifically intend the deaths of their patients. This seems especially true since the explicit endorsement of the current system by the U.S. Supreme Court in 1997, which is detailed in the next chapter. The uselessness of the Oregon suicide scheme is further illustrated by the fact that 5 of the first 10 patients trying to qualify for a lethal prescription died during the waiting period.[16] Four years after the 1994 initiative and more than four months after the 1997 initiative, only one patient had actually used the law's mechanism to commit suicide.[17]

The Oregon choice is deciding whether prescribing lethal drugs to a few who cannot now get them from their physicians is sufficient reason to put disadvantaged Oregonians, who are already relegated to the country's only formally rationed medical service delivery system, at even higher risk of underservice, alienation, and abandonment. The New York Task Force on Life and the Law, for example, unanimously concluded that "ideal" cases, like that described by Quill, are an insufficient basis for changing public policy in a country where medicine continues to be practiced in the context of bias and social inequality and where hospice care is not generally available. They rightly concluded that in the real world, legalizing assisted suicide would "pose the greatest risks to those who are poor, elderly, members of a minority group, or without access to good medical care."[18]

THE INITIATIVE APPROACH

Initiatives let the public vote on issues about which elected representatives have no special expertise, and can circumvent legislatures that are unresponsive to the voters. On relatively simple questions this method is reasonable. But neither euthanasia nor physician-assisted suicide is a simple question, and legalizing either or both requires not only carefully worded legislation but also a thorough and detailed public debate and discussion. Contemporary initiative petitions tend to degenerate into televised sloganeering, and permit neither of these. That is probably why both the Washington and California initiatives went down to defeat, even though public opinion polls consistently showed large majorities in favor of them.

Opinion polls measure what people say, but they cannot measure what people mean unless very sophisticated and complete questions are asked. In the early stages of the debate over euthanasia, people may hold opinions that are inconsistent without even realizing it. Only as the public debate matures do "people's views become more integrated and thoughtful."[19] It is only then that public opinion can be accurately measured, and it is only then that it should be taken seriously.

In my view, Oregon's Ballot Measure 16 was deficient in 1994 because it was likely to do more harm than good for terminally ill patients. In 1997, after the U.S. Supreme Court decisions to which I now turn, the measure is unnecessary to address the suffering of terminally ill patients, and muleheadedly displaces attention from dying patients and their real suffering to their physicians and their unrealistic worry about legal liability.

CHAPTER TWENTY-ONE

The Bell Tolls

For Whom the Bell Tolls, Ernest Hemingway's novel of the Spanish Civil War, ends with its American hero, Robert Jordan, mortally wounded and trying to decide whether to commit suicide with a machine gun or risk capture by trying to retain consciousness long enough to cover the retreat of his comrades. Confronting his impending death Jordan thinks, "Dying is only bad when it takes a long time and hurts so much that it humiliates you." Hemingway, one of the most American of American writers, himself committed suicide with a shotgun. Most American suicides are committed with guns, but America has no monopoly over suicide. Only in America, however, have groups of physicians gone to the court to argue that suicide by drug overdose in the context of a doctor–patient relationship should have privileged status of a constitutional right.[1]

The physicians, like Hemingway, described suicide as a way to exercise control and assert autonomy. Many Americans die horrible deaths under medical care, and the overall debate about how to make death in America better for patients and their families is complicated, multifaceted, and perhaps unresolvable. The debate about a constitutional right to physician-assisted suicide, on the other hand, was abruptly ended on June 26, 1997, when the U.S. Supreme Court issued two 9 to 0 decisions ruling that there is no constitutional right to physician-assisted suicide.

PHYSICIANS AND PATIENTS

In the spring of 1996, within one month of each other, U.S. Circuit Courts of Appeals on both coasts ruled that state prohibitions against assisted suicide were unconstitutional when applied to physicians who prescribe overdoses of drugs for terminally ill, competent adults who wish to end their lives. The Ninth Circuit includes Alaska, Arizona, California, Hawaii, Idaho, Montana, Nevada, Oregon, and

Washington, and the Second Circuit includes New York, Connecticut, and Vermont. Both courts reached the same conclusion, but for different reasons.

In the Ninth Circuit (*Compassion in Dying v. Washington*),[2] four physicians and three patients (one dying of AIDS, one of cancer, and one of emphysema) challenged a Washington law that prohibits aiding another person to commit suicide. In the Second Circuit (*Quill v. Vacco*),[3] three physicians and three patients (two dying of AIDS and one of cancer) challenged New York laws that prohibit aiding another person to commit or attempt suicide. None of these patients were currently suicidal, but all wanted prescription drugs that they could take to end their lives if their suffering became unbearable. As I discussed in the last chapter, taking an overdose of prescription drugs is the suicide method that has long been advocated by Derek Humphry and his Hemlock Society.[4] All the physicians said that they felt unable to comply with the requests because of state laws against assisting suicide. (There are no laws against committing suicide or attempting to commit suicide.) Two primary stories by the physicians were used to illustrate their concerns about legal liability.

Harold Glucksberg, who the Ninth Circuit case was named after when it went to the U.S. Supreme Court, recounted the story of a 34-year-old AIDS patient of his in his affidavit. Glucksberg had been treating him during the last year of his life, and through four months of "excruciating pain." Wasting away, and in danger of becoming blind, the patient asked him "to prescribe drugs that he could take to hasten his inevitable death," because he did not want to enter a hospital and "linger in a drug-induced stupor." The patient was competent and the physician believed he "should" accommodate this request. However, Glucksberg writes, "because of the statute [prohibiting assisted suicide] I was unable to assist him in this way." The patient later committed suicide by "jumping from the West Seattle bridge," and the physician continues, because of his physical condition "it is my belief that he was aided by close family members."

The second story, by Timothy Quill, after whom the Second Circuit case was named, is much more famous because Quill wrote about his patient Diane in the *New England Journal of Medicine*.[5] Diane was suffering from cancer which if treated has a 25% chance of remission. She refused the cancer treatment, but was very concerned that she would die in terrible pain. She asked Quill for a prescription for drugs she could take to end her life if her suffering became unbearable. Unlike Glucksberg, Quill did write a prescription, instructing Diane to keep in touch. He also put her in touch with the Hemlock Society. A few months later Diane took the drugs and died. After Quill published an article about this case, a district attorney brought him before a grand jury, but it failed to indict him. The New York medical licensing board also investigated the case, but concluded that Quill followed good medical practice in his treatment of Diane.

Each of the Circuit Court cases presented the same two issues: Is there a constitutional right to the assistance of a physician in committing suicide? And if so, does the state nonetheless have a sufficient interest to prohibit the exercise of this right? Lurking in the background throughout was Jack Kevorkian—a former Michigan pathologist who continues to use carbon monoxide gas to assist in the suicides of his clients who may or may not be terminally ill, and who Michigan has failed to stop (discussed in chapter 19).

THE NINTH CIRCUIT OPINION

The Ninth Circuit adopted the term "physician-assisted suicide" to describe "the prescription of life-ending medication for use by terminally ill, competent adult patients who wish to hasten their deaths" but was not happy with it, saying, "We have serious doubts that the terms 'suicide' and 'assisted suicide' are appropriate legal descriptions of the specific conduct at issue here." Instead of simply ruling that the assisted suicide laws do not apply to such prescriptions, the court's ambitious 8 to 3 opinion, written by Judge Stephen Reinhardt, relied on a substantive due process approach to create a new constitutional right: the right to determine "the time and manner of one's own death."

This new right is broadly worded, but the court ruled that only a narrow category of patients may lawfully exercise it: competent, terminally ill adults who have "lived nearly a full measure" of life and who want to die with dignity. For such patients, "wracked by pain and deprived of all pleasure, a state-enforced prohibition on hastening their deaths condemns them to unrelieved misery or torture." Surely, the court concluded, choosing "whether to endure or avoid such an existence" is a liberty every bit as vital as that involved in deciding whether or not to proceed with a pregnancy. In the court's words, "Like the decision of whether or not to have an abortion, the decision of how and when to die is one of 'the most intimate and personal choices a person may make in a lifetime,' a choice 'central to personal dignity and autonomy.'" The court cited as "highly instructive" almost presumptive" Justice Kennedy's poetic language in *Casey*,[6] the U.S. Supreme Court's most recent abortion decision:

> At the heart of liberty is the right to define one's own concept of existence, of meaning, of the universe, and of the mystery of human life. Beliefs about these matters [personal decisions relating to marriage, procreation, contraception, family relationships, child rearing, and education] could not define the attributes of personhood were they formed under compulsion of the state.

The other analogy the Ninth Circuit relied on was the removal of feeding tubes. A majority of the U.S. Supreme Court had assumed that there was a constitutionally protected liberty interest in "refusing unwanted medical treatment" in the case of Nancy Cruzan, a young woman in a persistent vegetative state whose family sought to have a feeding tube discontinued on her behalf. Because Nancy Cruzan would die without a feeding tube, the Ninth Circuit characterized the decision in the *Cruzan*[7] case as having "necessarily recognize[d] a liberty interest in hastening one's own death," thus permitting "suicide by starvation." The court thought that "as part of the tradition of administering comfort care, doctors have been supplying the causal agent of patients' deaths for decades," and understood that physicians have justified this prescribing pattern on the basis of the "double effect—reduce the patient's pain and hasten death." But the court rejected the double-effect rationale, saying, "We see little, if any, difference for constitutional or ethical purposes between providing medication with a double effect and providing medication with a single effect . . . [or] between a doctor's pulling the plug on a respirator and . . . prescribing drugs which will permit a terminally ill patient to end [his or her] own life."

After this new constitutional right is defined, the only remaining question is whether the state has a sufficient interest to prohibit its exercise. The court concluded that it does not: "When patients are no longer able to pursue liberty or happiness and do not wish to pursue life, the state's interest in forcing them to remain alive is clearly less [than] compelling." The court did, however, call on states to regulate the practice, suggesting procedural safeguards—such as witnesses, waiting periods, second medical opinions, psychological examinations, and reporting procedures—to help avoid "abuse."

THE SECOND CIRCUIT OPINION

One month later, in April 1996, the Second Circuit summarily rejected the Ninth Circuit's entire substantive due process analysis, concluding simply, "The right to assisted suicide finds no cognizable basis in the Constitution's language or design, even in the very limited cases of those competent persons who, in the final stages of terminal illness, seek the right to hasten death." But the Second Circuit nonetheless found a new constitutional right to a doctor's lethal prescription, based on the Equal Protection Clause of the 14th Amendment. The Equal Protection Clause requires states to treat people who are similarly situated in a similar manner.

Although this is superficially a different constitutional approach from that of the Ninth Circuit, the Second Circuit also had to implicitly discover a new right (the right to hasten death) before it could conclude that the right was being protected unequally by the state because all persons in New York had the right to refuse treatment, and no one in New York had the right to assistance in suicide. The Second Circuit did this by making two related assertions: The right to refuse treatment is the same as the right to hasten death, and there is no distinction between a person who is dependent on life-support equipment and one who is not. Neither assertion is persuasive. As to the first, the court argued that New York treats similarly situated people unequally because its law permits people "in the final stages of terminal illness who are on life support systems . . . to hasten their deaths by directing the removal of such systems," but those

not receiving life support cannot hasten their deaths "by self-administering prescription drugs." The primary cases cited for this proposition are *Cruzan* and
Eichner,[8] even though neither of the patients in these two cases was competent
(both were in persistent vegetative states), terminally ill, or had expressed any
desire to commit suicide.

The patient in the *Eichner* case, Brother Joseph Fox, was an elderly Catholic
brother of the Society of Mary who had said to his friend, Father Phillip Eichner,
before hernia surgery, words to the effect, "If I wind up like Karen Quinlan pull
the plug." Since suicide is a mortal sin in the Catholic Church, it is likely that
Brother Fox would have been horrified at the notion that his prospective refusal
of a ventilator constituted suicide. As both *Eichner* and *Cruzan* make clear, both
the courts and the real people involved in these cases believe the right at stake in
these cases is the right to refuse treatment (even if refusal results in death), not the
right to commit suicide. Moreover, there is no legal requirement that a person be
terminally ill, suffering, or in pain to exercise the right to refuse treatment. Americans have never been obligated to accept any or all manner of medical treatment
available to prolong life; the essence of the legal right at stake is the right to be
free from unwanted bodily invasions, including the invasions of medicine.

Even more striking is the court's second assertion, which is based on its acceptance of Justice Antonin Scalia's strange concurring opinion in *Cruzan* (an
opinion no other Justice joined). Scalia argued that refusals of treatment that result in death are all suicides and that any notion that the patient dies a natural death
from the underlying disease is nonsense. The Second Circuit adopted Justice
Scalia's position, concluding that death after the removal of a ventilator is "not
natural in any sense"; rather it brings about "death through asphyxiation." Likewise, the Second Circuit stated that the removal of artificially delivered fluids and
nutrition causes "death by starvation . . . or dehydration." In the court's words,
"The ending of life by these means is nothing more nor less than assisted suicide."
Because it considered both refusing treatment and taking an overdose of drugs to
equally constitute suicide, the Second Circuit concluded that equal protection of
law requires the state to treat both acts the same. The court argued that because
doctors are permitted to "assist" patients being sustained by various life support
devices to commit suicide by removing them, patients who do not need these
medical interventions to continue to live should also be entitled to the assistance
of a physician to commit suicide.

As to the state's possible interests in distinguishing between these acts, the
court concluded that the state has no interest "in requiring the prolongation of a
life that is all but ended." The court continued, "What business is it of the state to
require the continuation of agony when the result is imminent and inevitable?"
The court did not believe it was giving physicians a new license to kill, since it
believed "physicians do not fulfill the role of 'killer' by prescribing drug [over-
doses] to hasten death any more than they do by disconnecting life support sys-

tems." The court did, however, specifically reject euthanasia, distinguishing it from assisted suicide: "In euthanasia one causes the death of another by direct and intentional acts. . . . Euthanasia falls within the definition of murder in New York."

DISTINGUISHING GOOD SUICIDES FROM BAD

Because avoiding the slippery slope to euthanasia is the primary state interest in prohibiting physician-assisted suicide, the ability to distinguish objectively between good and bad suicides is critical. The opinion of the Ninth Circuit overruled a 1995 decision in the same circuit in which Judge John Noonan, writing for a 2 to 1 panel, had concluded that any attempt to define the category of constitutionally protected assisted suicides is "inherently unstable," such that any right to assisted suicide would ultimately have to be available to all adults.[9] In contrast, the 1996 Ninth Circuit's decision, issued by a larger panel of 11 judges on that court, concluded that doctors can accurately distinguish worthy suicides from unworthy and irrational suicides. In the court's words:

> One of the heartaches of suicide is the senseless loss of a life ended prematurely. In the case of a terminally ill adult who ends his life in the final stages of an incurable and painful degenerative disease, in order to avoid debilitating pain and a humiliating death, the decision to commit suicide is not senseless, and death does not come too early. Unlike the depressed twenty-one year old, the romantically-devastated twenty-eight year old, the alcoholic forty-year-old . . . a terminally ill competent adult cannot be cured . . . [but] can only be maintained in a debilitated and deteriorating state, unable to enjoy the presence of family or friends.

The court found that frustrating the wishes of terminally ill patients is "cruel indeed" and quoted Kent's lines from *King Lear*, spoken immediately after Lear dies, to buttress its argument: "Vex not his ghost: O! let him pass; he hates him/ That would upon the rack of this tough world/Stretch him out longer." Courts almost never resort to quoting literature, and when they do it, it is usually because they have no legal argument to support their conclusion. I believe that is true here, and the court's misreading of *King Lear* only serves to emphasize how difficult it is to draw lines or make objective assessments about suicide. Thus, the seemingly marginal use of a literary quotation turns out to be central to understanding the entire opinion. Lear did not die because he was terminally ill or in severe pain. Rather, Lear is much more like the person who dies because of a personal emotional tragedy: In Lear's case he had just learned that his one faithful and loving daughter, Cordelia, had been murdered, and has just uttered his famous line over her dead body: "Why should a dog, a horse, a rat, have life,/And thou no breath at all?" Earlier that same day, Lear was prepared to spend many years in prison with Cordelia. But after her murder, Lear dies of a broken heart. There is no suicide and no assistance; instead (to the contemporary reader) Kent acts as Lear's health care agent and exercises Lear's right to refuse treatment by ordering that resuscitation not be attempted. No legal changes are needed to protect the right of someone in Lear's position to refuse treatment.

ABORTION AND ASSISTED SUICIDE

Taking a line out of context from *King Lear* parallels the way the Ninth Circuit also took a line out of context from *Casey* to use as the basis for the new constitutional right it enunciated. There are some striking similarities between abortion and assisted suicide. Perhaps the most notable is the tendency of proponents and opponents to use overblown language that obscures rather than clarifies. Thus in the abortion debate opponents use words like "killing babies" and "murder" and "right to life"; and similar language is used by opponents of physician-assisted suicide. Proponents, also adopt "prochoice" rhetoric to support assisted suicide, using words like "personal choice," "liberty," and "control" (over one's life) to express their views. Contrary to such political incantations, notions of control and choice are either illusory or incredibly limited at both ends of life. The other striking image is the use of suffering. The antiabortion camp tends to concentrate on the suffering of the fetus, such as in the film *Silent Scream* and descriptions of "partial birth" abortions, whereas the proponents of physician-assisted suicide focus on the suffering of the terminally ill person. Religion and religious beliefs also play a major role in both debates. The challenge is to get beyond the sloganeering, and even religious beliefs, to try to understand the real differences between abortion and suicide and their relevance to constitutional analysis.

The most important difference is the definition of the constitutional right involved. In abortion, it is the right to decide whether or not to continue a pregnancy. In contrast, although suicide has been decriminalized, there is no constitutional right to commit suicide, and it would be difficult to know what such a right would look like. Perhaps this is why neither the Ninth nor the Second Circuit discussed a right to suicide. Instead, both courts used phrases like a right to hasten death and a right to determine the time and manner of death. This is important because, as *Casey* teaches, the right of a physician to perform an abortion is entirely derivative from the right of the pregnant woman to have one. If there is no constitutional right to commit suicide, there can be no constitutional right to have a physician's assistance in committing suicide.

A second distinction involves the basis for the constitutional right at issue. To the extent that both are characterized as liberty rights found in the Due Process Clause of the 14th Amendment the parallel holds. However, no such parallel exists in an equal protection analysis. Abortion applies only to women, and pregnancy itself is sui generis. In this aspect abortion cannot be seen as parallel to suicide, since there is no issue of gender equality involved in suicide. Likewise, the right to terminate a pregnancy is limited to a narrow and very easily defined class of people: pregnant women. As previously discussed, there is no bright line that can limit the category of people to whom a right to commit suicide (or assistance in suicide) would apply.[10]

A third distinction involves the role of the physician. Abortion is a medical procedure. Because abortion endangers the life and health of women if performed by the woman herself or by unlicensed or back alley practitioners, the state has a sufficiently compelling interest in protecting women's health to require that only licensed physicians be permitted to perform abortions. No such rationale exists regarding suicide. Almost all competent adults are capable of committing suicide, and tens of thousands do so every year. Suicide is not a medical procedure, and there is no health or safety reason why physicians must be involved in an individual's suicide. Jack Kevorkian's use of carbon monoxide poisoning illustrates these points.

A fourth major distinction is what is being killed. The heart of what makes abortion a social policy, political, and religious issue is the belief that many hold that protectable human life begins at conception and that to purposely kill an embryo or a nonviable fetus is "murder." The U.S. Supreme Court (with no Justice ever disagreeing on this), however, has consistently ruled that a fetus does not become a person under the Constitution until birth (although it is so similar to a person at viability that the state has a compelling interest in protecting its life at this point). This is what makes near birth feticide so divisive. What is killed in pregnancy termination is human and alive, but it is not a person. On the other hand, the entity being killed (or killing him or herself) in physician-assisted suicide is always a person under the Constitution. And the state has a compelling interest in protecting the lives of all persons, including those who are suffering and near the end of life.

Reliance on *Cruzan* is as unpersuasive as relying on *Casey*. *Cruzan* involved the easily definable right to refuse treatment, not the indefinable right to hasten death. Nor did anyone involved, including her parents, the state of Missouri, the Missouri Supreme Court, and the U.S. Supreme Court see the refusal of artificial fluids and nutrition by Nancy Cruzan, or by her parents on their daughter's behalf, as a possible violation of Missouri's law against assisted suicide. Suicide and assisted suicide were simply not at issue in *Cruzan* because refusing treatment, even when the refusal will certainly end in death, has never been equated with suicide by courts, state legislatures, patients, or their families.

PHYSICIANS AND ASSISTED SUICIDE

The patients whose cases were presented to these two courts are all sympathetic, and it is not surprising that the courts wanted to help them. Cancer and AIDS often lead to "hard deaths,"[11] and patients dying of these two diseases make up the vast majority of patients in hospices as well as of those who seek the assistance of physicians in committing suicide,[12] probably because the final stages of these illnesses are relatively predictable. What is surprising is that these courts failed to explicitly acknowledge that it has never been illegal to prescribe pain medication that competent terminally ill patient *might* use to commit suicide, as long as the physician's *intent* is to foster the patient's well-being by giving them more control over their life, and the drugs have independent legitimate medical use.[13] Such prescriptions can legitimately be intended as suicide prevention rather than suicide assistance. Neither court could point to any case of a physician ever being criminally prosecuted for the conduct they approve of, and both courts would have been on much stronger ground if they had simply acknowledged that intent matters in criminal law and that prescriptions written under these very limited circumstances do not legally constitute assisted suicide by definition.

In this regard, it should be noted that the Ninth Circuit's restatement of the principle of the double effect, which treats pain relief and death as equally intended, is false: The principle is that treating the patient's pain is acceptable even if the treatment hastens death (which it will, of course, not always do). Providing medication to control pain has always been a legitimate and lawful medical act, even if death or suicide is risked; just as performing surgery is a legitimate and lawful medical act even if death is risked. There is a difference between an intended consequence and an unintended but foreseen and accepted consequence. Thus, no physician should have concluded on the basis of the Ninth Circuit opinion that providing pain medication that increases the risk of death is either assistance in suicide or homicide. As one of the dissenting judges in the Ninth Circuit, Judge Andrew Kleinfeld, properly noted, when General Dwight D. Eisenhower ordered American troops to the beaches in Normandy, he knew he was sending many to certain death, but his intent was to liberate Europe from the Nazis. Judge Kleinfeld continued, "The majority's theory of ethics would imply that this purpose was legally and ethically indistinguishable from a purpose of killing American soldiers." Intent really does matter.

Neither courts' logic about the cause of death after refusal of treatment is persuasive either. If one accepts that Nancy Cruzan "died of starvation" and not from the vegetative condition that made continued artificial feeding necessary for her survival, one would also have to accept the conclusion that when physicians stop attempted cardiopulmonary resuscitation (CPR) on a patient in cardiac arrest, what kills the patient is not the heart attack but rather the physician who intentionally stops compressing the heart. Since failure to perform CPR always hastens death, under each court's logic, patients who refuse CPR would always be committing suicide (and doctors who write "do not resuscitate" orders would always be assisting this suicide). But this is demented. The failure to distinguish real causes of death from various medical tools and techniques that may temporarily substitute for particular bodily functions is fatal to the logic of both opinions.

This logical failure also helps explain why neither court could define the right they had discovered or persuasively limit its exercise to prescriptions written by physicians for competent, terminally ill patients (limitations that have no basis in constitutional law).[14] *Cruzan* and *Eichner*, after all, support the proposition that the right to refuse treatment is not lost by incompetence but can be exercised in advance by a living will or the designation of a health care proxy, and also that an adult need not be terminally ill to refuse treatment. Of course, it is not possible to commit suicide by proxy. On the other hand, nothing in the logic of these opinions would prohibit physicians from actually injecting lethal doses into patients who meet their other criteria and who are physically unable to commit suicide themselves, although the Second Circuit explicitly prohibited this.

The Ninth Circuit (but not the Second) also explicitly protected family and friends working under direction of a physician, but never explained why either a physician or a drug prescription is constitutionally required. For example, neither court suggested any reason why a physician could not recommend suicide by gun and instruct a patient or family member where to aim it before the patient pulled the trigger. Since both courts admitted that there is no constitutional definition of terminal illness, the group of covered patients may encompass many with years to live (like Lear) whose lives no longer bring them joy or happiness, and certainly seems to include early HIV infection, Alzheimer's disease, and cancer. To the extent that states have an interest in protecting these persons from physicians who might encourage suicide for reasons other than unrelievable pain or suffering at the end of life, these opinions cannot prevent a slide down the slippery slope.

STATE REGULATIONS

Recognizing the dangerousness of the right they espouse, both courts called on states to regulate physician-assisted suicide. The Ninth Circuit also seemed to approve of Oregon Ballot Measure 16, which, as discussed in the last chapter, provides legal immunity to physicians who follow certain procedures when prescribing lethal drugs to terminally ill patients with the intent that they use them to commit suicide.[15] Under the Second Circuit's equal protection analysis, the state is permitted to adopt the same or substantially similar regulations for refusals of treatment that hasten death as for physician-assisted suicide. If states adopt such regulations, the hard-won rights that the great majority of patients can and do now exercise to refuse medical treatments are put at risk, since mandatory procedural safeguards can actually frustrate rather than foster patient self-determination.[16]

The opinions could also be read as undercutting all laws relating to Schedule I drugs, as well as regulation of medical experimentation, at least with regard to patients near the end of life. If laws against assisted suicide are unconstitutional because they deprive terminally ill patients of relief from suffering, how can laws that restrict their access to heroin or LSD be constitutional? Contrary to the actions of these courts, the Supreme Court has previously and unanimously endorsed the view of the Food and Drug Administration that drug laws that require demonstrated safety and efficacy forbid everyone, including the terminally ill, to obtain unapproved drugs.[17]

By ignoring the past two decades of jurisprudence concerning the right to refuse treatment (including the rulings by state supreme courts that explicitly hold that refusals of treatment are neither suicide nor homicide), and by failing to make such basic distinctions as those between the right to refuse treatment and the right to die, between suicide and assisted suicide, between law and ethics, and between ends and means, these courts virtually guaranteed that their decisions would not be the last word on the subject.

THE U.S. SUPREME COURT OPINIONS

The U.S. Supreme Court agreed to review both of these decisions in September 1996 and heard oral arguments on January 8, 1997. At the oral argument, which was widely anticipated and covered as potentially the most important case of the term before the Court, the advocates on behalf of physician-assisted suicide dramatically shifted their approach. Harvard law professor Lawrence Tribe, who argued for upholding *Quill*, centered his argument on an alleged medical practice that had not even been mentioned in either lower court: "terminal sedation." Tribe described terminal sedation as drugging a patient into a coma and then starving the patient to death by withholding fluids and nutrition. He argued that this practice was the same as assisting suicide (homicide?) since death is the intended end. Because this practice is legally permitted, Tribe argued that the state must also permit patients a choice of taking an overdose and dying at once (instead of forcing the patient to be subjected to this degrading procedure, which might undermine the patient's firmly held values and drain the meaning from his death). New York Attorney General Dennis Vacco argued that terminal sedation (which he termed "sedation in the imminently dying") is only legally permitted as a last resort, in extreme cases, after carefully titrating medication until it effectively eliminates pain or the other symptoms it is designed to treat. It is thus consistent with an intent to treat the patient, not an intent to kill, and is justified by the principle of the double effect.

Attorney Katherine Tucker, who represented Compassion in Dying, argued that physician-assisted suicide should be heavily regulated and limited only to those very near death. Asked specifically, by Justice Ruth Bader Ginsburg, if a suffering, terminally ill patient who met all of her qualifications but who could not physically take the drug overdose herself could be given an injection of lethal drugs by a physician, she replied no, saying that the drugs must be self-administered to insure that the decision is "authentic and voluntary." Justice Ginsburg also asked U.S. Solicitor General Walter Dellinger what he knew about doctors defying the law by using "winks and nods." Dellinger replied that he knew of no evidence to support this characterization of current medical practice.

The fundamental constitutional right proposed is exceptionally narrow, much narrower than that discovered by the two circuit courts. In the words of the *Quill* brief, authored primarily by Professor Tribe, it is the "Right of a terminally ill, mentally competent adult who is in the process of dying to end her own intolerable suffering, pain and physical disintegration by obtaining, within the context of the doctor–patient relationship, a prescription for medication that will allow her to end her own life."

The Justices were skeptical that such a right existed, and wondered, if it did and was so important, why it shouldn't apply to more people. They also indicated that they believed there was a real difference between suicide and refusing treatment, and that too little was known about the entire area of end-of-life care for the Court to take the issue away from the states and rule definitively on it for all U.S. citizens. Virtually all who observed the oral arguments agreed that it was likely that the Supreme Court would reverse both cases, and by a wide margin. Nonetheless, the overwhelming 9 to 0 opinions were stunning. Both opinions were written for the Court by Chief Justice William Rehnquist. Five Justices also wrote concurring opinions.

WASHINGTON V. GLUCKSBERG[18]

The question before the Court in the appeal from the Ninth Circuit was "whether the 'liberty' specially protected by the Due Process Clause [of the 14th Amendment] includes a right to commit suicide which itself includes a right to assistance in doing so." The Court's "established method" of defining a new fundamental constitutional right has two parts: The right must be "deeply rooted in this nation's history and tradition," or fundamental to ordered liberty, and must have a "careful description." The Court easily concluded there is no historic tradition of treating suicide as a fundamental right, observing that to find such a right the Court would instead "have to reverse centuries of legal doctrine and practice, and strike down the considered policy choice of almost every state." In a review of the history of laws against suicide and assisted suicide, the Court noted that suicide was decriminalized because it was impossible to punish the person who committed suicide, and because it was seen as "unfair to punish the suicide's family for his wrongdoing." Nonetheless, suicide "remained a grievous, though nonfelonious, wrong."

The Court also reviewed the Ninth Circuit's reliance on *Cruzan* and *Casey* as sources for a new right to commit suicide. The Court characterized the case of Nancy Cruzan (a young woman in a persistent vegetative state) whose parents wanted artificial feeding discontinued as a case which involved the constitutional right to refuse medical treatment. This right is supported in common law battery and informed consent doctrine and by "the long legal tradition protecting the decision to refuse unwanted medical treatment." In contrast, suicide "has never enjoyed similar legal protection" and the "two acts are widely and reasonably regarded as quite distinct." In *Cruzan*, the Court said, "we certainly gave no intimation" that the right to refuse treatment could be "somehow transmuted into a right to assistance in committing suicide." The Court dealt even more summarily with *Casey*, noting simply that the right to abortion did not support "the sweeping conclusion that any and all important, intimate, and personal decisions" are protected by the U.S. Constitution. Washington's assisted suicide law withstands constitutional review because it "does not violate the Fourteenth Amendment, either on its face or 'as applied to competent, terminally ill adults who wish to hasten their deaths by obtaining medication prescribed by their doctors.'"

Because the Court concluded that no fundamental constitutional right to suicide could be found in our nation's history or in the concept of ordered liberty, the state of Washington had only to demonstrate that its assisted suicide law was "rationally related to legitimate government interests." The Court concluded that "this requirement is unquestionably met here." The Court listed the following as legitimate governmental interests: (1) preserving human life, (2) preventing suicide, (3) protecting the integrity and ethics of the medical profession, (4) protecting vulnerable groups from abuse, neglect and mistakes, and (5) preventing a start "down the path to voluntary and perhaps even involuntary euthanasia." As to the slippery slope, the Court noted that the Ninth Circuit's opinion seemed to permit surrogate decisionmaking and "in some instances" lethal injection by a physician or family member. Therefore, the Court concluded, "it turns out that what is couched as a limited right to 'physician-assisted suicide' is likely, in effect, a much broader license, which could prove extremely difficult to police and contain. Washington's ban on assisting suicide prevents such erosion."

VACCO V. QUILL[19]

In the appeal from the Second Circuit the question was whether the state of New York violates the Equal Protection Clause of the 14th Amendment by making it a crime to aid another to commit suicide while permitting patients to refuse life-saving treatment. The Court held that "it does not."

Equal protection "embodies a general rule that States must treat like cases alike but may treat unlike cases accordingly." Unless the statute "burdens a fundamental right or targets a suspect class," it will be upheld as long as it bears "a rational relation to some legitimate end." As previously summarized, in *Washington v. Glucksberg* the Court concluded that statutes outlawing assisted suicide do not infringe fundamental rights or involve a suspect classification and are reasonably related to legitimate state interests. Therefore the only real question in *Vacco v. Quill* was whether there is a rational difference between assisting a competent patient to commit suicide and withdrawing life-sustaining treatment from a competent patient who refuses to consent to its continuation. The Court answered this question at the outset, stating that New York's laws treat all New York citizens the same: "Everyone, regardless of physical condition, is entitled, if competent, to refuse unwanted lifesaving medical treatment; no one is permitted to assist a suicide."

The lower court had concluded that since ending or refusing life-sustaining medical treatment is "nothing more nor less than assisting suicide," the anti–assisted suicide law prohibiting those terminally ill people who are not dependent on medical technologies from ending their lives with assistance denies them equal protection of laws. The Supreme Court emphatically disagreed, specifically upholding as rational the distinction between withdrawing life-sustaining treatment and assisting suicide, "a distinction widely recognized and endorsed in the medical profession and in our legal traditions."

The Court did not see as legally relevant the often-discussed distinctions between active and passive, or between artificial fluids and nutrition and other medical interventions. Instead, the Court explained that causation and intent are the two critical questions in this area of the criminal law. As to causation, the Court agreed with previous courts that had ruled that "when a patient refuses life-sustaining medical treatment, the patient dies from an underlying fatal disease or pathology; but if a patient ingests lethal medication prescribed by a physician he is killed by that medication." Since therapeutic medications, those prescribed for a legitimate medical use, can also carry a risk of death, the primary distinction in close cases is the physician's *intent* in prescribing or administering the medication. In the Court's words, when a physician provides palliative care, "in some cases, pain killing drugs may hasten a patient's death, but the physician's purpose and intent is, or may be, only to ease his patient's pain." On the other hand, a doctor who assists a suicide necessarily intends that the patient dies. Similarly, a patient who commits suicide with a doctor's aid "necessarily has the specific intent to end his or her own life, while a patient who refuses or discontinues treatment might not." The Court noted that the law has historically distinguished between actions done "because of" a given end and actions done "in spite of" their unintended but foreseen consequences. Intent matters. The Court quoted as authority Judge Andrew Kleinfeld's example of General Eisenhower ordering American soldiers to battle to liberate Europe, knowing many American soldiers would certainly die because of his order. If intent did not matter, only outcome, Eisenhower's orders would have been the moral equivalent of ordering the murder of American soldiers at the hands of the Nazis.

The Court observed that other courts have routinely made this distinction, citing 34 prior court decisions. Similarly, legislatures in virtually every state have also adopted the distinction between refusing treatment and committing suicide in their laws. Finally, the Court said that it itself, in *Cruzan*, had "also recognized, at least implicitly, the distinction between letting a patient die and making that patient die." *Cruzan*, the Court said, was not based on the recognition of any "general and abstract 'right to hasten death . . .' but on well-established, traditional rights to bodily integrity and freedom from unwanted touching." The Court therefore (unsurprisingly) concluded: "By permitting everyone to refuse unwanted medical treatment while prohibiting anyone from assisting a suicide, New York follows a long-standing and rational distinction."

The example on which the case was fought at the oral argument—terminal sedation—was relegated to a footnote. The Court's discussion of terminal sedation is important nonetheless, because the Court applied the reasoning of its opinion to that example. Even accepting the bizarre characterization of terminal sedation as "inducing barbiturate coma and then starving the person to death," the Court concluded that a state can legally countenance this form of palliative care if it is "based on informed consent and the double effect. Just as a state may prohibit assisting suicide while permitting patients to refuse unwanted lifesaving treatment, it may permit palliative care related to that refusal, which may have the foreseen but unintended 'double effect' of hastening the patients' death."

A RIGHT NOT TO SUFFER?

There were five votes for each of the Court's opinions (the Chief Justice and Justices O'Connor, Scalia, Kennedy, and Thomas). All nine Justices agreed that state laws prohibiting assisted suicide violate neither the Due Process nor the Equal Protection Clause of the 14th Amendment to the U.S. Constitution, even as applied to physicians who prescribe overdoses of medication to competent, terminally ill patients who want to commit suicide. Nonetheless, five Justices wrote concurring opinions to express additional or different reasons for this conclusion.

Justice O'Connor wrote a four-paragraph opinion, the only concurring opinion that any other Justice agreed with, that suggests she believes there might be a right to avoid "great" suffering near death. She made three points: (1) in Washington and New York states there is no legal barrier preventing "a patient who is experiencing great pain" from "obtaining medication, from qualified physicians, to alleviate that suffering, even to the point of causing unconsciousness and hastening death"; (2) the state's interests therefore justify prohibiting physician assisted suicide; and (3) state legislatures are the proper forum for an "extensive and serious evaluation of physician-assisted suicide and other related issues."

Justice Ruth Bader Ginsburg concurred with the Court's judgments in both opinions, "substantially for the reasons stated by Justice O'Connor." Justice Stephen Breyer also joined Justice O'Connor's opinion, "except insofar as it joins the majority." It is difficult to tell exactly what Justice Breyer meant, but he is concerned about dying patients who get insufficient pain medication. Breyer concluded that if a state ever did prohibit physicians from providing sufficient palliative care—"including the administration of drugs as needed to avoid pain at the end of life"—the Court would be presented with a different case, "and might have to revisit its conclusions in these cases."

Justices John Paul Stevens and David Souter each wrote much longer concurring opinions. Justice Stevens concluded that it is possible that some other particular case (which he does not describe) might impose "an intolerable intrusion on the patient's freedom" by outlawing "the only possible means of preserving a dying patient's dignity and alleviating her intolerable suffering." Justice Souter seems to favor something like a right to end one's life with dignity that would apply not only to a person dying in pain but also in unacceptable "dependency and helplessness." He nonetheless concluded that too little is known about the real world affect of such a right for the Court to act, noting that "the case for the slippery slope is fairly made out here" and that "legislatures have superior opportunities to obtain the facts necessary for a judgment about the present controversy."

WHY THE BELL TOLLED

In retrospect it is easy to see how the right to physician-assisted suicide failed to gain constitutional recognition in the Supreme Court. To find such a constitutional right, the Court had to find a constitutional right to suicide itself, and there is no historical or legal support for this. Second, the analogies the proponents relied on, abortion and the right to refuse treatment, were easily distinguishable. The Court itself remains deeply divided on abortion, and notwithstanding some expansive language, *Casey* limited the abortion rights articulated in *Roe v. Wade*, it did not expand them. The right to refuse treatment is deeply rooted in American law, and so are the principles of intent and causation in the criminal law—principles that distinguish suicide from treatment refusal and assisted suicide from withdrawing or withholding treatment. This distinction is one that virtually every court since *Quinlan* has made, as well as virtually every legislature that has passed living will and health care proxy legislation. The overwhelming acceptance by the public of the distinction between suicide and refusing medical treatment was dramatically illustrated just months after the Court's decisions. Beloved American author James Michener let it be known that he had chosen to stop the kidney dialysis that was keeping him alive. When he died one week later, the national press reported (correctly) that he had exercised his right to refuse treatment. There was no suggestion, nor should there have been, that Mr. Michener had committed suicide, nor that his death was in any way comparable to the suicide death of Ernest Hemingway. Third, to agree with the proponents the Court would have had to limit any constitutional right it found to a small group of citizens (competent, suffering, terminally ill people near death) and a particular method of suicide (overdosing on prescription drugs), limitations that have no constitutional precedent.

The Court only had to find the state interests in outlawing assisted suicide "rationally-related to a legitimate state interest" to uphold these statutes. Nonetheless, it seems reasonable to conclude that a majority of the Court would have permitted the states to continue to outlaw physician-assisted suicide even if the Justices thought it was a fundamental constitutional right, because at least some of these interests, especially avoiding the slippery slope to active euthanasia, are compelling. A state supreme court in the future could thus find a limited right to assistance in suicide in a state constitution but nonetheless uphold laws prohibiting assisted suicide because the state's interest in avoiding the inevitable slide to euthanasia from assisted suicide is compelling.

In the first test of this kind, and within a month of the Court's decisions, the Florida Supreme Court reversed a lower court's ruling that the right to privacy in Florida's Constitution includes a right to physician-assisted suicide at the end of life. In a 5 to 1 opinion, the Florida Supreme Court concluded that the privacy right is not this broad and that, in any event, the state has at least three compelling interests that "clearly outweigh" the petitioner's desire for assistance in committing suicide: the preservation of life, the prevention of suicide, and maintenance of the ethical integrity of the medical profession.[20]

DRUG PRESCRIPTIONS, CAUSATION, AND MORPHINE

Although the Court explicitly endorsed the principle of the double effect, the Court did not directly apply the double effect to writing drug prescriptions. Nonetheless, the logic of the opinion supports the conclusion that physicians can continue to write prescriptions for medically indicated drugs even with the knowledge that the patient might use the drugs to commit suicide, as long as the physician's intent is to prolong the patient's life or relieve pain. A physician who writes a drug prescription under these circumstances is not engaged in physician-assisted suicide by legal definition.

The opinions can also be read as a strong endorsement of the views of the New York Task Force on Life and the Law, whose report, *When Death is Sought,* is cited as authority at numerous points by the Justices.[21] The New York Task Force is important because it is the only long-standing, government-sponsored, multidisciplinary group that has carefully studied the issue of physician assisted suicide with a view toward proposing legislation, as well as the only authoritative group to report its conclusions both before and after the opinions of the Second and Ninth Circuits were handed down.[22] The Task Force has been especially critical of autonomy assertions to justify physician-assisted suicide. At oral argument, for example, Justice Anthony Kennedy quoted the Task Force's 1994 report with approval, noting that it had suggested that the autonomy that advocates seek is "illusory" and that legalized assisted suicide, because it puts the vulnerable, the mentally ill, and the poor at risk, could actually "diminish choices, not increase them . . . and will increase fear."

The Task Force wrote a supplement to its 1994 report in April 1997. None of the Justices cited this supplement, although their opinions are consistent with its logic and conclusions. Two points that the Task Force makes are worth emphasizing. The first relates to legal causation, which is used by courts to determine legal accountability, not simply to describe facts. In the context of a physician treating a dying patient, many causes may contribute to death. But, as the Task Force properly observes: "When a variety of factual causes are necessary, but not individually sufficient, to bring about a particular result, the determination of which among them are properly cited as causative for legal purposes becomes a policy judgment, reflecting underlying assumptions about rights, duties, and moral blame."[23] The judges' views of "rights, duties, and moral blame" help explain why we do not hold physicians accountable as causal agents for deaths that occur after life-sustaining treatments have been removed at the patient's insistence, or when a patient undergoing surgery dies on the operating table. Courts have always recognized that death under medical care does not take place in a moral vacuum.

The second point is one emphasized in all of the concurring opinions: "The effort to characterize morphine drips as a form of covert euthanasia is extremely misguided."[24] This effort is a mistake for two reasons. The first is a factual one: Morphine use is often necessary for proper medical care, and it is never necessary to accompany it with "winks and nods." Death is neither necessarily hastened nor intended by use of a morphine drip. "Properly titrated" morphine usually does not hasten death at all because of "the rapid development of tolerance to the respiratory depressant effects."[25] The second is that even in those cases where increasing the morphine dosage "may accelerate" the patient's death, this fact "does not make their use equivalent to assisted suicide or euthanasia." The question is, is the risk of death "justified in light of the paucity and undesirability of other options?" This point, and the centrality of the principle of the double effect, is well recognized in medical practice: "medical treatment sometimes requires significant trade-offs, and acceptance of negative consequences for legitimate medical purposes is not equivalent to causing those consequences for their own sake."[26]

DEATH AND CONSTITUTIONAL LAW

The quest for a constitutional right to physician-assisted suicide failed in the Supreme Court because it has no coherent basis in constitutional law. The right to refuse treatment, on the other hand, is a long-recognized right. It is not discretionary with physicians, who are legally and ethically required to honor it; patients have a right to insist that their bodies not be invaded without their consent. Likewise, the right to abortion is fundamentally different from the right to die: It protects (rather than ends) a pregnant woman's life, health, and future; it can be exercised by a clearly identifiable category of citizens, pregnant women; and physicians are needed to perform abortions because (unlike suicide) abortion is a medical procedure that cannot be safely or effectively performed by the woman herself.

No sympathy can be found in either of these opinions for the idea that physicians should be granted prospective legal immunity from criminal prosecution for writing drug prescriptions. The Court did not specifically deal with the affidavit of Harold Glucksberg in this regard, but perhaps by ignoring it the Court has made its comment. Unlike Quill, Glucksberg abandoned his dying AIDS patient, who he says then threw himself off a Seattle bridge with the help of his family. This is a shocking story, but not because it illustrates problems with the assisted suicide laws. Rather the shocking part is that Glucksberg sees himself as the victim in this case, not his former patient or the patient's family—this, even though no physician in the history of the United States has ever been indicted (let alone tried or convicted) or had his or her medical license suspended or revoked for complying with such a request.

It would have been more comforting for physicians had the Court more explicitly ruled that what the physicians wanted to do in these cases was not assisted suicide by definition, and thus the constitutionality of the statutes as applied to them did not even have to be adjudicated.[27] The avoidance of this central question, and the hand-wringing of the five Justices who wrote or joined in concurring opinions about hypothetical of cases of suffering, terminally ill patients, that were not before the Court, all indicate that the Justices—like all Americans, have a very difficult time coming to grips with the dying process. The abstract nature of all of the opinions can also be explained by the fact that there was no trial in either case, and thus there were only physician affidavits of fear of the law and the stories of already-dead patients before the Court.

In the wake of the Supreme Court's ruling, only physicians who really believe that there is no distinction between prescribing drugs that patients could use to commit suicide and giving them loaded guns with the intent that the patients use the gun to kill themselves need to change their behavior to comply with the laws against homicide and assisting suicide. Doctors who provide palliative care with the primary intent of relieving pain and suffering, and with the patient's consent, are strongly encouraged to continue to do so by the Court. Indeed, at least five members of the Court seem to think there is something akin to a right not to suffer, at least near death, and that states have no constitutional authority to prohibit or inhibit physicians from doing all in their medical power to prevent such suffering.

These opinions make no change in the states' authority to outlaw or decriminalize assisted suicide. The real issue has never been what the states can do, but what they *should* do. There are proposals for new pain relief laws, but these are not focused on the terminally ill, and no new laws are needed to improve the care of the dying. Moreover, to the extent that physicians go to state legislatures and ask for further regulation of prescriptions or the administration of medications near the end of life, treatment of dying is likely to get worse, not better.[28] There is no simple legal solution to our problems with dying.[29] The failed attempts to constitutionalize physician-assisted suicide should be seen in this context: as a symptom of the problems with death in America, not a solution.

CHANGING AMERICAN MEDICINE

There are real problems with the way Americans die, but the solution to these problems is not to be found in the U.S. Constitution or in making it even easier for patients to kill themselves. Thus, unless these cases help us to focus our efforts on taking care of real people instead of constructing illusory constitutional theory, they will have been a waste of time and a missed opportunity. Americans consistently say they want to die at home, with friends and family, quickly and without pain. Instead most Americans die in the hospital, surrounded by strangers, and in varying degrees of pain. There are many reasons for this (including denial on the part of dying patients), but I think the most important one is that patient rights are not taken seriously during life and therefore they are not likely to be taken seriously just before death.

Problems in dying exist in the extreme in the contemporary teaching hospital, in which patient care is often a distant third goal after teaching and research. In the high-tech, high-pressure environment, there is little room for thoughtfulness, for the intrusion of human values, or for conversation with the patient or family. The primary values are action- and technology-oriented; the imperative is to use all available medical technologies possible for the patient or for practice. As hospitals become more and more like large ICUs this impersonal technological emphasis has increased. Add the cost pressures of managed care to treat patients more quickly, and care of the dying in hospitals is getting worse, not better. Hospice care remains marginalized, and death is still seen as failure. Medical students and residents are taught that talking is a waste of time, distracting from the time available to do real medicine. And when doing "real medicine" cannot help the dying patient, students and residents quickly learn that the attending physicians are uninterested in having discussions with patients or families about death or pain, so these discussions must not be important.

These attitudes are such a pervasive part of contemporary medical culture that the only realistic way to improve the care of dying patients in the short run is to get them out of the hospital and to keep them from going to the hospital at the end of their life. One major study, for example, showed that an astonishing "41% experienced moderate or extremely severe pain most of the time" during their last three days of life in a hospital intensive care unit.[30] There is no excuse for this indifference to human suffering, which amounts to systematic patient abuse, and observing such callous "care" is at least one reason why physician-assisted suicide has been seen by the public as a reasonable option.

Medical sociologists teach that there are three basic ways to change professional behavior: convince the profession that it is in their best interests to change (rational); change the norms of the profession (normative); and change the incentives (coercive). The first strategy hardly ever works, since professionals generally think they know their own best interests better than any outsider. The second works, but takes a very long time. Perhaps we are now in a cultural lag period in medicine, but if so we are at the very beginning. The third produces much more rapid change, which is why changing the payment rules for hospital services has already drastically changed the role and nature of the hospital in medical care in the United States and will ultimately transform teaching hospitals into institutions that actually take patient-centered care seriously if they want to survive. Our payment rules should also encourage hospice care and home care, as Medicare rules now do, both of which place the patient in the center of the enterprise.

If we really want to enable patients in hospitals to have their pain properly treated and to exercise their right to refuse treatment near the end of life, we must have much stronger prevention methods and establish much more effective patient-centered interventions. Changing treatment incentives, rather than trying to develop new constitutional theories of suicide, is the most effective way to proceed. What is needed is not immunity for discretionary acts but incentives to actually care for patients and follow effective pain relief regimes. Medical licensing boards must make it clear to physicians that painful deaths are presumptively ones that are incompetently managed, and a pattern of such deaths should result in license suspension or revocation in the absence of a satisfactory justification.

A more effective way to use law than constitutional adjudication would be to establish a system of not-for-profit public-interest health care law firms whose sole mission is to promote patient rights by educating the public and the medical community about their rights and by bringing lawsuits on behalf of patients whose rights are not honored in the hospital setting. Patients would learn of the availability of law firms to help them through advertising, the Internet, a hotline, and paralegals who would act as patient advocates on request. The firms would take cases on a contingency fee basis, and all of the contingency fees would go to help fund the firm (whose lawyers would all be on salary). The firms would continue in existence until there were insufficient cases of patient abuse to support them, at which point one might be able to conclude that the culture of hospital-based medicine had changed sufficiently to honor patient refusals and keep patients pain free as routine matter.[31]

This plan would require a national network of public interest firms, but a pilot program could be started in three or four major cities and expanded from this base if it proved a successful model for enhancing patient rights in health care systems much more dedicated to their own interests and survival. Alternatively, established law firms could offer their services pro bono in this area. They could also work with the state attorneys general separately, or in concert in a manner analogous to the legal strategy the attorneys general adopted against the tobacco companies to fund Medicaid that recently led to a possible "settlement" by Congress (discussed in chapter 18). The problem of pain and suffering near death is pervasive in America, and only a very powerful challenge to existing medical practice is likely to change it. Lawyers are likely to get the ear of physicians, hospitals, and health plans that have been deaf to the pleas of patients, families, and nurses.

Resort to the courts means that the system has broken down, and lawyers should be primarily engaged in prevention. In addition to education and deployment of a system of patient advocates, it will also be helpful for patients if report cards are developed on both hospitals and physicians that include their attitudes and actions on informed consent and other patient rights and their actual track records in areas such as availability for discussions with the patient and family, adherence to advance directives, providing adequate pain management, writing DNR orders upon request, and keeping dying people out of the ICU.

Hemingway ends his novel with Robert Jordan waiting for an enemy "to reach the sunlit place where the first trees of the pine forest joined the green slope of the meadow" and feeling "his heart beating against the pine needle floor of the forest." It is only possible to romanticize war, killing, and death by turning away from them and describing something else. The bell has tolled for a constitutional right to physician-assisted suicide, but it should awaken us to the challenge that remains: to face and deal directly with death and dying.

PART VI

Global Choices

Toward a Globalization of Human Rights and Medical Ethics

I have argued both that bioethics in America is the creature of American law and legalistic inclinations, and that we have managed to trivialize autonomy, justice, and equality by camouflaging them with the rhetoric of choice. If I am right in this assessment, does it make any sense to try to export American bioethics or law? Perhaps remarkably, I think the answer is yes, but only if we can change our vocabulary and enlarge our vision. I think the way to do this is to return to the roots of American bioethics and the concepts of human rights. Human rights language is much richer and inclusive than choice language.

1997 was the 50th anniversary of the conclusion of the trial of Nazi physicians at Nuremberg, a trial which has been variously designated as the "Doctors' Trial" and the "Medical Case," and which is generally considered the inspiration for bioethics.[1] 1998 is the 50th anniversary of an even more important human rights document—the Universal Declaration of Human Rights. The primary product of the Doctors' Trial has come to be known as the Nuremberg Code, a judicial codification of ten prerequisites for moral and legal experimentation with human beings. The 1946–47 trial of the Nazi doctors documented the most extreme example of physician participation in human rights abuses, criminal activities, and murder. Hitler called upon physicians not only to help justify his racial hatred policies with a "scientific" rationale (racial hygiene) but also to direct his sterilization and euthanasia programs, experimentation programs, and ultimately his death camps.[2] Sixteen physicians and scientists were found guilty, and seven were executed. A universal standard of physician responsibility in human rights abuses involving experimentation on humans, the Nuremberg Code, was articulated and has been widely recognized, if not always followed, by the world community.

The Nuremberg Code was a response to the horrors of Nazi experimentation in the death camps—wide-scale experimentation, without consent, that often had the death of the prisoner–subject as its planned endpoint.[3] The Code has 10 provisions—two consent provisions designed to protect the rights of subjects of human experimentation and eight designed to protect their welfare.[4] Although the Nuremberg Code has never been formally adopted as a whole by the United Nations, a statement related to torture appears as Article 5 of the Universal Declaration of Human Rights. A second sentence added to the text of Article 5, which further reflects the concerns of the Nuremberg Code, appears as Article 7 in the United Nations International Covenant on Civil and Political Rights (adopted and opened for signature, ratification, and accession by the UN General Assembly in 1966; entered into force in 1976).

THE WORLD MEDICAL ASSOCIATION

In late 1946, 100 delegates from 32 national medical associations met in London to form the world's first international medical organization. The World Medical Association (WMA) was created to promote ties between national medical organizations and doctors of the world. Its objectives were:

- To promote closer ties among the national medical organizations and among the doctors of the world by personal contact and all other means available.
- To maintain the honour and protect the interests of the medical profession.
- To study and report on the professional problems which confront the medical profession in the different countries.
- To organize an exchange of information on matters of interest to the medical profession.
- To establish relations with, and to present the views of the medical profession to the World Health Organization, UNESCO, and other appropriate bodies.
- To assist all peoples of the world to attain the highest possible level of health.
- To promote world peace.[5]

In September 1947, shortly after the final judgment at the Doctors' Trial, the first official meeting of the WMA was held in Paris. The WMA formulated a new physician oath to promote and serve the health of humanity. This was followed by a discussion of the "principles of social security." Key principles adopted included:

- Freedom of physician to choose location and type of practice.
- All medical services to be controlled by physicians.
- That it is not in the public interest that doctors should be full-time salaried servants of government or social security bodies.
- Remuneration of medical services ought not to depend directly on the financial condition of the insurance organization.
- Freedom of choice of patient by doctor except in cases of emergency or humanitarian considerations.

To the WMA's credit, one of the first issues discussed by the 1947 general assembly was the "betrayal of the traditions of medicine" which occurred in Germany. The assembly asked, "why did these doctors lack moral or professional conscience and forget or ignore the humanitarian motives and ideals of medical service?" "How can a repetition of such crimes be averted?" and acknowledged the "widespread criminal conduct of the German medical profession since 1933." The WMA endorsed "the judicial action taken to punish those members of the medical profession who shared in the crimes, and it solemnly condemned the crimes and inhumanity committed by doctors in Germany and elsewhere against human beings."[6] The assembly continued: "We undertake to expel from our organization those members who have been personally guilty of the crimes. . . . We will exact from all our members a standard of conduct that recognizes the sanctity, moral liberty and personal dignity of every human being."

Nonetheless, consistent with its physician-protection goals, the WMA has always focused more on physician choice than patient choice. Through its Declaration of Helsinki in 1964, for example, it endorsed shifting the focus in medical research from the protection of human rights through informed consent to the protection of patient welfare through physician responsibility. The 1964 Declaration, for example, divided research into two types: research combined with professional care, and nontherapeutic research. Consent was required for the latter. But as to the former, the subject was transformed into a patient, and consent was simply urged: "If at all possible, consistent with patient psychology, the doctor *should* obtain the patient's freely given consent after the patient has been given a full explanation." The Declaration of Helsinki thus attempted to undermine the primacy of subject consent in the Nuremberg Code and displace it with the paternalistic values of the traditional doctor–patient relationship.

Although the WMA has issued a number of noble statements condemning physician involvement in torture and capital punishment, it has largely acted like other professional trade associations. Its primary interest is the members' welfare, with a secondary objective of issuing lofty ethical statements. With the exception of barring membership of Japanese and German physicians following World War II, the WMA has never sought or exercised any authority to identify, monitor, or punish either physicians or medical societies who violate their ethical principles. In fact, in 1992, the WMA irrevocably lost all claim to speak on behalf of the ethics of the world's physicians when it elected a Nazi physician as president: Hans-Joachim Sewering, a former member of the Nazi party and the Nazi SS.

During World War II Sewering was a physician at the Schönbrunn Institute for the Handicapped in the city of Danchau. During his tenure at the institute he transferred at least one 14-year-old girl with epilepsy to Eglfing-Haar Hospital. Three weeks later, in late 1943, this physically healthy girl was dead. Of 275 children who were admitted to Eglfing Haar from 1940 to 1942, 213 were killed. Sewering's 1992 election to the presidency of the WMA provoked public protests. Andre Wynen, fellow German physician and the secretary general of the WMA, defended him, saying that "we must accept that the young people of that time had the right to make mistakes." Sewering later acknowledged his Nazi past, but claimed no knowledge of or involvement in the euthanasia program. In January 1993, four nuns still living at the Schonbrunn Institute, who had worked there during the war, substantiated that from 1940 to 1944 more than 900 mentally and physically handicapped patients were sent to specific "healing centers."[7] The nuns said that they knew the patients would be exterminated at these centers as so-called "unworthy lives" and that Sewering, despite his denials, must also have known. If electing a Nazi physician involved in the euthanasia program as president does not disqualify an organization to set the ethical standards for the world's physicians, what would?

BRITISH MEDICAL ASSOCIATION REPORT

The 1992 report of the British Medical Association's working party on the participation of doctors in human rights abuses documents continued physician involvement in crimes against humanity throughout the world.[8] Physicians have been directly involved in the torture of prisoners, as well as in activities that indirectly facilitate torture. Physician involvement includes the examination and assessment of "fitness" of prisoners to be tortured, the monitoring of victims while being tortured, the resuscitation and medical treatment of prisoners during torture, as well as falsification of medical records and death certificates after torture.

The report documents examples of physician involvement in psychiatric "diagnosis" and commitment of political dissidents, forcible sterilizations, force feeding of hunger strikers, and supervision of amputation and other corporal punishments. Countries implicated span the globe, and include the former Soviet Union, the United States, the United Kingdom, China, India, South Africa, as well as countries in the Middle East and Central and South America. The working party notes the existence of international law and codes of ethics but acknowledges the lack of enforcement and inability to monitor compliance. The theme of the report is that neither medical associations nor international law has been effective in preventing physician involvement in crimes against humanity.

A PERMANENT NUREMBERG

In light of these problems and other ethical and human rights issues involving physicians, many have argued that the world needs an international tribunal with authority to judge and punish the physician violators of international norms of medical conduct, as well as an independent body to conduct ongoing surveillance and develop a rapid response capacity. Without these, the world is as before Nuremberg: international norms of medical conduct relegated solely to the domain of poorly defined medical ethics. In addition, the courts of individual countries, including the United States as discussed in chapter 14, have consistently proven incapable of either punishing those engaged in unlawful or unethical human experimentation or compensating the victims of such experimentation, primarily because such experimentation is often justified on the basis of national security or military necessity.

The International War Crimes Tribunal declared in 1946 that there were such things as war crimes and crimes against humanity and that those who committed these crimes could be punished for them (the "Nuremberg Principles"). The enumeration of these crimes followed from the concept of "inalienable rights," as expressed in such documents as the U.S. Declaration of Independence. The remaining or subsequent trials at Nuremberg, including the Doctors' Trial, were based on the legal precedent articulated by the International War Crimes Tribunal, but they were held exclusively under the control and jurisdiction of the U.S. Army. M. Cherif Bassiouni, Robert Drinan, Telford Taylor, and others have argued eloquently and persuasively that a permanent international tribunal is needed to judge and punish those accused of war crimes and crimes against humanity.[9] Nonetheless, although the rhetoric supporting such a tribunal has heated up, the international political will to form and support such a "permanent Nuremberg" is lacking. There has even been a lack of enthusiastic support for ad hoc war crime tribunals for Bosnia and Rwanda.

AN INTERNATIONAL MEDICAL TRIBUNAL

Medicine and law are often viewed as opponents, but in the promotion of human rights in health they have a common agenda. One way for the world's physicians and lawyers to work together is to form and support an International Medical Tribunal. Ideally such a body should be established with the sanction and authority of the United Nations. However, given the competing political agendas of the member states, initial failure to win UN approval and support should not doom this project. Even if unable to punish with criminal sanctions, a privately-sponsored tribunal could hear cases, develop an international code, and publicly condemn the actions of individual physicians who violate international standards of medical conduct. The establishment and support of such a tribunal is a worthy project for the world's physicians and lawyers.

The medical profession is the most promising candidate to take a leading role here because it has an apolitical history, it has consistently argued for at least some neutrality in wartime to aid the sick and wounded, it has a basic humanitarian purpose for its existence, and physician acts intended to destroy human health and life are a unique betrayal of both societal trust and the profession itself. It is also much easier for governments to adopt inherently evil and destructive policies if they are aided by the patina of legitimacy that physician participation provides.

To move forward, the establishment of such an International Medical Tribunal could be put on the agenda as an advocacy effort of all medical and legal associations around the world. Since the tribunal must be both authoritative and politically neutral, no one country or political philosophy can be permitted to dominate it, either by having a disproportionate representation on the tribunal, or by disproportionately funding it. The tribunal itself should be composed of a large panel of distinguished judges. Recruiting such judges (without which the court would have little credibility) will require a commitment from governments to permit the selected judges to take time off from their full-time judicial duties to hear these cases.

MEDICAL ETHICS AND HUMAN RIGHTS

It is, of course, not just torture and murder that must concern the world's lawyers and physicians. Human rights can help improve health in all of its aspects. Human rights and health, especially public health, are two complementary approaches, and languages, to address and advance human wellbeing. Human rights seeks to describe, and then promote and protect, the societal preconditions for human wellbeing in which all individuals can achieve their full potential. Modern human rights is a civilizational achievement to identify and agree upon what governments should assure to all people, and what governments should not do to people. Human rights are not provable statements; rather, they achieve their legitimacy from having been developed, shaped, and adopted by the nations of the world, and incorporated into the domain of international law.[10]

Public health has demonstrated that the achievement of health is usually dependent upon the social setting that in large measure determines health status. Thus assuring at least minimal conditions for healthy living is necessary to protect and enhance the public's health. It is in this regard that the Universal Declaration of Human Rights, through its focus on the societal determinants of wellbeing, can be seen as a fundamental document on the health and human rights nexis, even though the word health appears in the Declaration only once. Recognition of the dependency of health on societal factors, and the linkages between these factors and the protection of human rights, as illustrated in chapter 16, provides a new approach and framework to promoting health by promoting and protecting human rights.

The international debate on maternal-fetal HIV transmission prevention trials in Africa illustrates the how human rights concepts can move us beyond simple declarations of choice. The central ethical and human rights issue is when it is justified to do research with impoverished populations.[11] The central issue involved in doing research with impoverished populations is exploitation. Harold Varmus, speaking for the NIH, and David Satcher, speaking for the CDC realize this, and write that "trials that make use of impoverished populations to test drugs for use solely in developed countries violate our most basic understanding of ethical behavior."[12] Instead of trying to demonstrate how the study interventions, such as shorter course zidovudine, could actually be delivered to the populations of the countries in the studies, however, they assert that the studies can be justified because they will provide information that the host country can use to "make a sound judgment about the appropriateness and financial feasibility of providing the intervention." However, what these countries require is not good intentions, but a real plan to deliver the intervention should it be proven beneficial.

Unless the intervention being tested will actually be made available to impoverished populations used as research subjects, developed countries are simply exploiting these impoverished populations for their own benefit, since the knowledge gained, whether positive or negative, will be quickly utilized in the developed world. If the research reveals regimens of equal efficacy at less cost, these will surely be implemented in the developed world. If the research reveals the regimens to be less efficacious, these results will be added to the scientific literature and the developed world will not conduct those studies. Ethics and basic human rights principles require not a thin promise but a real plan as to how the intervention will actually be delivered. Actual delivery is also, of course, required to support even the utilitarian justification for the trials: to find a simple, inexpensive and feasible intervention in as short a time frame as possible because so many people are dying of AIDS. None of these justifications are supportable unless the intervention is actually made widely available to the relevant populations.

Neither NIH nor CDC (nor the host countries) has a plan that would make the interventions they are studying available in various African countries, a continent in which more than two-thirds of the people in the world infected with HIV reside. As an example, Varmus and Satcher point out that the wholesale cost of zidovudine in the 076 protocol (described in note 11) is estimated to be in excess of $800 per mother and infant and that this amount is far greater than most developing countries can pay for standard care. The Centers for Disease Control themselves estimate that the cost of the "short course" of zidovudine regimens being investigated to be roughly $50 per person. The cost of merely screening for HIV disease, a precondition for any course of therapy, is approximately $10 and all pregnant women must be screened to find the cases to treat. These costs must be compared to the total per capita health care expenditures of the countries where this research is being conducted, which is in the $5 to $22 range. Given this fact, these African countries (or some other funder) must make realistic assurances that if research proves effective in reducing mother to infant transmission of HIV, resources will be made available so that the women of these African countries will receive the regimen.

The mere assertion that the interventions will be feasible for use in the developing countries is simply not good enough, given our experience and knowledge of what happens in Africa now. We already know, for example, that effectively treating sexually transmitted diseases can drastically lower the incidence of HIV infection, and that there are simple and effective treatments for syphilis, gonorrhea and chancroid. But these inexpensive and effective treatments are not delivered to poor Africans. A recent study showed that improving the treatment of sexually transmitted diseases in rural Africa could reduce HIV infections by 40%. Nonetheless, this relatively inexpensive and effective intervention is not delivered. Vaccines against devastating diseases have also been developed using sub-Saharan African populations as test subjects. Nonetheless, even though vaccines like the group A meningococcal meningitis vaccine are inexpensive and effective, they are not adequately delivered to the relevant sub-Saharan African populations.[13] Choice language focuses on letting individuals in various countries do what they want. Human rights language focuses on the real lives of real people, and enlarges the discussion to include economics and living conditions as well as political rights.

International human rights law is similar to medical ethics in that both are universal and aspirational and both have so far been unenforceable (although publicity, embargos, and even military force have been used on occasion). A critical challenge is to make both meaningful, and this may be the most important legacy of the Nuremberg trials. For physicians, the challenge is to articulate and follow a universal medical ethic, based on human rights, and to guard this ethic, for the sake of humanity, against its subversion and corruption by governments and corporations that would use medicine for their own purposes. Examples of use of physicians for governmental purposes discussed in this book include cold war radiation experiments (chapter 14) and the authority to use investigational drugs on U.S. soldiers in the Gulf War without consent (chapter 12), both done in direct violation of the Nuremberg Code. Other examples include the use of physicians in lethal injection executions, using psychiatrists to drug prisoners for easier control, and using physicians in the military for nonmedical purposes. This list could also include government-sanctioned use of physicians for "euthanasia" of incompetent persons.[14]

Physicians need more than codes that proscribe putting their skills in the service of the nonmedical goals of governments, military establishments, and corporations. Physicians also need support for upholding medical ethics and human rights, and mechanisms to punish those who violate basic medical ethics and human rights in medicine. International human rights law and codes of medical ethics are necessary, but not sufficient, to prevent human rights abuses by physicians. Many physician groups are already active in promoting human rights globally, including International Physicians for the Prevention of Nuclear War (IPPNW) and its U.S. affiliate, Physicians for Social Responsibility (PSR), Physicians for Human Rights (PHR), *Médecin sans Frontières*, and *Médecins du Monde*. But physicians should not be expected to shoulder the cause of human rights alone.

Judges and lawyers were also tried separately at Nuremberg in "The Justice Case," for engaging in "an unholy masquerade of brutish tyranny disguised as justice, and converting the German judicial system to an engine of despotism, conquest, pillage, and slaughter."[15] As Professor Lon Fuller has described the rise of the Nazi state, "The first attacks on the established order were on ramparts which, if they were manned by anyone, were manned by lawyers and judges. These ramparts fell almost without a struggle."[16] Just as it took lawyers and physicians working together to bring the Nazi physicians to justice at Nuremberg, it will take the world's lawyers and physicians working together not only to prevent wholesale violations of human rights but also to proactively support the growth of human rights worldwide. The world's physicians and lawyers, because of their moral authority in defending life and justice and their privileged positions in society, have special obligations to humanity.

The world's physicians and lawyers can, for example, work together transnationally to identify, publicize, and isolate physicians, lawyers, and judges involved in human rights abuses. Even if these abuses are tolerated in the country in which the professional works, the professional can be effectively isolated and "imprisoned" within their own outlaw country. This can be done by refusing to license the outlaw physician or lawyer in any other country, by refusing to provide specialty or other training or access to professional meetings in any other country, and by refusing to publish any articles or research done by the outlaw professional physician in the world's professional literature. Lawyers should work with and defend physicians who resist subversion of their medical skills by representing them in court and other settings, including employment settings. Lawyers should also work to enact laws that protect physician autonomy in all cases in which physicians follow acceptable principles of medical ethics and protect and promote human rights, whether they act as healers or researchers. Perhaps more importantly, lawyers and physicians can work together for social justice, with the provision of adequate health care for all as a central goal.

To fulfill these obligations more effectively, my physician colleague Michael Grodin and I have founded Global Lawyers and Physicians (GLP), an organization whose purpose is to facilitate lawyers and physicians working together to promote human rights and health in all countries. The mission of GLP is to work collaboratively toward the global implementation of the health-related provisions of the Universal Declaration of Human Rights, the Covenant on Civil and Political Rights, and the Covenant on Economic, Social, and Cultural Rights with a focus on health care ethics, patient rights, medical research, and human experimentation. Specific goals of the organization include providing information and resources about human rights and health, serving as a network and referral source for professionals working on health-related human rights issues, and providing support and assistance in developing, implementing, and advocating public policies and legal remedies which protect and enhance human rights in health.[17]

UNIVERSAL DECLARATION OF HUMAN RIGHTS

Article 25

1. Everyone has the right to a standard of living adequate for the health and well-being of himself and of his family, including food, clothing, housing and medical care and necessary social services, and the right to security in the event of unemployment, sickness, disability, widowhood, old age or other lack of livelihood in circumstances beyond his control.

2. Motherhood and childhood are entitled to special care and assistance. All children, whether born in or out of wedlock, shall enjoy the same social protection.

INTERNATIONAL COVENANT ON CIVIL AND POLITICAL RIGHTS

Article 7

No one shall be subjected to torture or to cruel, inhuman or degrading treatment or punishment. In particular, no one shall be subjected without his free consent to medical or scientific experimentation.

INTERNATIONAL COVENANT ON ECONOMIC, SOCIAL, AND CULTURAL RIGHTS

Article 12

1. The States Parties to the present Covenant recognize the right to everyone of the enjoyment of the highest attainable standard of physical and mental health.

2. The steps to be taken by the States Parties to the present Covenant to achieve the full realization of this right shall include those necessary for:

    a. The provision for the reduction of the stillbirth-rate and of infant mortality and for the health development of the child;

    b. The improvement of all aspects of environmental and industrial hygiene;

    c. The prevention, treatment and control of epidemic, endemic, occupational and other diseases;

    d. The creation of conditions which would assure to all medical services and medical attention in the event of sickness.

What lessons have we learned from the dominant role of law in American bio-ethics, the Doctors' Trial, and the trivialization of choice? Three stand out: (1) Statements, even authoritative statements, of medical ethics are not self-enforcing and require active promulgation, education, and enforcement. (2) Human experimentation and torture are important areas where violations of human rights and medical practice occur, but they are too narrow in themselves to provide guidance for physicians and the public on the broad range of physician involvement in human rights abuses around the world. (3) There is no effective mechanism to promulgate and enforce basic medical ethics and human rights principles in the world.

The legacy of Nuremberg and the Doctors' Trial is that physicians and lawyers have special obligations to use their power to protect human rights. Medical ethics devoid of human rights are no more than hollow words. Bioethics must move beyond law and economics, and beyond cloning choice clichés, to be challenging and even subversive. Arthur Schlesinger has said, "The American identity will never be fixed and final; it will always be in the making."[18] American bioethics should be actively involved in "the making"; but it can no longer just be American; it must be global. We should be about fashioning a bioethics that moves beyond the laws of individual countries and into the realm universal inalienable rights—the realm of human rights. A synthesis of medical ethics and human rights could tap into the reason why most physicians and lawyers joined their profession in the first place: to help make the world a better place for everyone.

NOTES

INTRODUCTION

1. *See also* Annas, G. J., The Dominance of American Law (and Market Values) Over American Bioethics, (In) Grodin, Michael A. ed., *Meta Medical Ethics: The Philosophical Foundations of Bioethics*, Dordrecht: Kluwar Academic, 1995, pp. 83–96; and Grodin, M. A., Annas, G. J., Legacies of Nuremberg: Medical Ethics and Human Rights, *JAMA* 1996; 276:1682–1683.

2. *See, e.g.*, Schlesinger, Arthur Jr., *The Disuniting of America: Reflections on a Multicultural Society*, New York: W.W. Norton, 1982; Wills, Gary, *Inventing America: Jefferson's Declaration of Independence*, New York: Vintage Books, 1978.

3. Purdy, J. S., The God of the Digerati, *American Prospect*, March/April 1998, 86–90.

4. Gaylin, Willard, and Jennings, Bruce, *The Perversion of Autonomy: The Proper Uses of Coercion and Constraints in a Liberal Society*, New York: Free Press, 1996.

CHAPTER ONE: CHOICE'S ECHO

1. Wilmut, I., Schnieke, A. E., McWhir, J., Kind, A. J., Campbell, K. H. S., Viable Offspring Derived from Fetal and Adult Mammalian Cells, *Nature* 1997; 385:810–813.

2. de Saint Exupery, Antoine, *Le Petit Prince*, Paris: Gallimard, 1946, *The Courrier International* edition is dated March 12, 1997.

3. President's Commission for the Study of Ethical Problems in Medicine and Biomedical and Behavioral Research, *Splicing Life: The Social and Ethical Issues of Genetic Engineering with Human Beings*, Washington, DC: U.S. Gov. Printing Office, n. 5, 1982, p. 9.

4. *Report of the Human Embryo Research Panel*, Bethesda, MD: National Institutes of Health, Sept. 27, 1994. *And see* Annas, G. J., Caplan, A., Elias, S. The Politics of Human Embryo Research: Avoiding Ethical Gridlock, *N. Engl. J. Med.* 1996; 334:1329–1332.

5. Lederberg, J., Experimental Genetics and Human Evolution, *Am. Nat.* 1966; 100:519–531.

6. Watson, J. D., Moving Toward the Clonal Man, *Atlantic Monthly*, May 1971, 50–53.

7. Ramsey, Paul, *Fabricated Man: The Ethics of Genetic Control*, New Haven, Conn.: Yale U. Press, 1970.

8. Fletcher, Joseph, *The Ethics of Genetic Control: Ending Reproductive Roulette,* New York: Prometheus Press, 1988.

9. *Genetic Engineering: Evolution of a Technological Issue, Report to the Subcommittee on Science, Research and Development of the Committee on Science and Astronautics of the U.S. House of Representatives,* 92d Cong., 2d Sess., Science Policy Research Division, Library of Congress, Washington, DC: U.S. Gov. Printing Office, 1972.

10. Rorvik, David, *In His Image: The Cloning of a Man,* Philadelphia: J.P. Lippincott, 1978.

11. *Developments in Cell Biology and Genetics, Cloning,* Hearing before the Subcommittee on Health and the Environment of the Committee on Interstate and Foreign Commerce of the U.S. House of Representatives, 95th Cong., 2d Sess., May 31, 1978.

12. *See, e.g.,* Chomsky, Noam, *Language and Problems of Knowledge,* Cambridge, MA: MIT Press, 1988 ("It is quite possible—overwhelmingly probable one might guess—that we will always learn more about human life and human personality from novels than from scientific psychology") quoted by Horgan, John, *The End of Science,* New York: Broadway Books, 1996, pp. 152–153.

13. Elias, S., Annas, G. J., Social Policy Considerations in Noncoital Reproduction, *JAMA* 1986; 255:62–66.

14. Levin, Ira, *The Boys from Brazil,* New York: Dell, 1976.

15. Weldon, Fay, *The Cloning of Joanna May,* New York: Penguin, 1989, p. 121.

16. When I raised this issue at Senate hearings on cloning on March 12, 1997, Senator Thomas Harkin (D–Iowa) reacted quite negatively, suggesting that use of Frankenstein imagery was an attempt to scare the public, and that regardless, "cloning will be done." The testimony is available at http://www-busph.bu.edu/Depts/HealthLaw/.

17. Relman, A. S., The New Medical-Industrial Complex, *N. Engl. J. Med.* 1980; 303:963–970.

18. Reinhardt, U., Reforming the Health Care System, *Am. J. Law Med.* 1993; 19:21–36.

19. Lewontin, R. C., Confusion Over Cloning, *New York Review of Books,* Oct. 23, 1997, 20–23.

20. Robertson, John, *Children of Choice: Freedom and the New Reproductive Technologies,* Princeton, NJ: Princeton U. Press, 1994, p. 169.

21. Callahan, D., Responding to the NBAC, *Hastings Cent. Rep.,* Sept. 1997, 19.

22. Elias, Sherman, Annas, George J., *Reproductive Genetics and the Law,* St. Louis: Mosby-Yearbook, 1987.

23. Baram, M. S., Social Control of Science and Technology, *Science* 1971; 172:535–539.

24. Ethics Committee, American Fertility Society, Ethical Considerations of Assisted Reproductive Technologies, *Fertil. Steril.* 1994; 62:1S-124S.

25. New York State Task Force on Life and the Law, *Assisted Reproductive Technologies: Analysis and Recommendations for Public Policy,* New York: New York State Task Force on Life and the Law, 1998. *See also* Kass, L.R., The Wisdom of Repugnance, *New Republic,* June 2, 1997, 17–26.

26. Shnieke, A. E., Kind, A. J., Ritchie, W. A., et.al., Human Factor IX Transgenic Sheep Produced by Transfer of Nuclei from Transfected Fetal Fibroblasts, *Science* 1997; 278:2130–2133. *And see* Holtz, R. L., Scientists add Human Gene to Three Cloned Lambs, *Los Angeles Times,* Dec. 19, 1997, A1.

27. Kolata, G., Creator of Cloned Sheep Says he will try to Repeat Process, *New York Times,* Feb. 2, 1998, A7.

28. See *supra* note 16.

29. *See generally*, Cross, F. B., Paradoxical Perils of the Precautionary Principle, *Wash. & Lee L. Rev.* 1996; 53:851–925. For arguments against a ban *see* Kolata, Gina, *Clone: The Road to Dolly and the Path Ahead*, New York: Murrow, 1998, Tribe, L. H., Second Thought on Cloning, *New York Times*, Dec. 5, 1997, A39, Pence, Gregory, *Who's Afraid of Human Cloning?*, London: Rowman & Littlefield, 1997, and Silver, L. M., *Remaking Eden: Cloning and Beyond in a Brave New World*, New York: Avon Books, 1997.

30. *Cloning Human Beings: Report and Recommendation of the National Bioethics Advisory Commission*, Rockville, MD, June 1997.

31. Shapiro, H. T., Ethical and Policy Issues of Human Cloning, *Science* 1997; 277:195–196.

32. Knox, R. A., A Chicagoan Plans to Offer Cloning of Humans, *Boston Globe*, Jan. 7, 1998, A3; Kolata, G., Physicist on Stage with Plan for a Clinic to Clone Humans, *New York Times*, Jan. 8, 1998, A22.

33. 1997 CA S.B. 1344 (enacted Oct. 6, 1997).

34. Jonas, Hans, *Philosophical Essays: From Ancient Creed to Technological Man*, Prentice-Hall, Englewood-Cliffs, NJ, 1974, pp. 162–163.

35. Foucault, Michel, *The Order of Things: An Archaeology of the Human Sciences*, New York: Vintage, 1994.

CHAPTER TWO: WOMEN AND CHILDREN FIRST

1. Simpson, A. W. B., *Cannibalism and the Common Law*, Chicago: Chicago U. Press, 1984, p. 97. This chapter is adapted from Annas, G. J., Women and Children First. *N. Engl. J. Med.* 1995; 333: 1647-1651.

2. Kipling, Rudyard, *Complete Verse: Definitive Edition*, New York: Doubleday, 1940, p. 432.

3. Krauthammer, C., The Inevitability of Rationed Care, *Washington Post,* Sept. 22, 1995, A19.

4. Wertz, R. W., Wertz, D. C., *Lying-In: A History of Childbirth in America*, New York: Free Press, 1977.

5. Goodman, E., Lower Speed Limit on Highway to Drive-Thru Deliveries, *The Boston Globe*, July 9, 1995, 63.

6. Epidemiology Office of the Centers for Disease Control and Prevention. Trends in Length of Stay for Hospital Deliveries—United States, 1970–1992, *MMWR* 1995; 44:335–337.

7. Wilkie, D., Delivery Hospitals Know Where Mom Can Have All Comforts of Home, *San Diego Union Tribune*, June 26, 1995, A3.

8. Rovner, J., USA Divides over Early Discharge of Mothers, *Lancet* 1995; 346: 171–172.

9. Nordheimer, J., New Mothers Gain 2nd Day of Care, *New York Times,* June 29, 1995, B1.

10. Ch. 138, Laws of New Jersey, 1995.

11. 1995 N.C.S.B. 345, Sec. 58-3-170.

12. Declercq, E., Simmes, D., The Politics of "Drive-Through Deliveries": Putting Early Postpartum Discharge on the Legislative Agenda, *Milbank Q.* 1997; 75:175–202.

13. *Shaw v. Delta Airlines,* 463 U.S. 85 (1983); *New York Blue Cross Plans v. Travelers Insurance Co.*, 514 U.S. 645 (1995).

14. Arnold, L., N.J. Leads 'Drive Thru Delivery' Fight, *Ashbury Park Press*, Sept. 13, 1995, A3.

15. Bye-bye Baby, *American Medical News*, Aug. 7, 1995, 13.

16. 42 U.S.C. sec. 300gg-4 (West Supp. 1997).

17. Maier, T., 2-Day Maternity Stays Promised, *Newsday*, June 22, 1995, 6.

18. Hagigh, J., TGH Lets Mothers Stay Put, *St. Petersburg Times*, Aug. 29, 1995, 1A.

19. Liu, L. L., Clemens, C. J., Shay, D. K., Davis, R. L., Novack, A. H., The Safety of Newborn Early Discharge: The Washington State Experience, *JAMA* 1997; 287:293–298 (early discharge associated with an increased risk of readmission for jaundice, dehydration, and sepsis); and Edmonson, M. B., Stoddard, J. J., Owens, L. M., Hospital Readmission With Feeding-Related Problems After Early Postpartum Discharge of Normal Newborns, *JAMA* 1997; 278:299–307 (early discharge following an uncomplicated postpartum hospital stay appears to have little or no independent effect on the risk of rehospitalization).

20. Braveman, P., Kessel, W., Egerter, S., Richmond, J., Early Discharge and Evidence-based Practice: Good Science and Good Judgment, *JAMA* 1997; 278:334–336.

21. 42 U.S.C.A. 1395dd (1987), amended by 41 U.S.C.A. 1395dd (1991).

22. *Burditt v. U.S. Dept. of Health and Human Services*, 934 F.2d 1362 (5th Cir. 1991).

CHAPTER THREE: EXIT, VOICE, AND CHOICE

1. This chapter is adapted from Annas, G. J., Patients' Rights in Managed Care: Exit, Voice, and Choice, *N. Engl. J. Med.* 1997; 337:210-215; Hirschman's book is Hirschman, Albert O., *Exit, Voice, and Loyalty: Responses to Decline in Firms, Organizations, and States*, Cambridge, MA: Harvard U. Press, 1970.

2. Rodwin, M. A., Consumer Protection and Managed Care: Issues, Reform Proposals, and Trade-offs, *Houston Law Rev.* 1996; 32:1321–1381.

3. Bodenheimer, T., The HMO Backlash—Righteous or Reactionary? *N. Engl. J. Med.* 1996; 335:1601–1604.

4. *Grijalva v. Shalala*, 946 F.Supp. 747 (D.C. Arizona 1996).

5. 42 U.S.C. §§ 1395 mm.

6. HHS argued that it was doing all it was statutorily required to do by urging its private contractors to adopt continuous quality improvement procedures, and that the HMOs involved were "merely private providers who contract with the government to provide medical care to Medicare beneficiaries." HHS further argued that the government was not responsible for wrongful acts by private HMO contractors, so the due process requirements of the U.S. Constitution did not apply. This argument was based almost exclusively on *O'Bannon v. Town Court Nursing Home*, 447 U.S. 773 (1980), in which the Court decided that a nursing home's decision to transfer its Medicare and Medicaid patients to another facility was a private act. The transfer was necessitated by the government's decision to decertify the nursing home for Medicaid and Medicare patients. The Court concluded that since the transfer itself involved no action on the part of the government, the residents had no constitutional right to a hearing before the transfer. Judge Marquez, however, found that this case was not determinative in the *Grijalva* case, because HHS "had delegated the entire responsibility for its mandated . . . health care duties" to the HMOs. The judge cited a case involving certified home health care agencies, which are private entities, in which the court concluded, "It is patently unreasonable to presume that Congress would permit a state to disclaim federal responsibilities by contracting away its obligations to a private entity." *Catanzano v. Dowling*, 60 F.3d 113 (2d Cir. 1995).

7. Angell, M., Fixing Medicare, *N. Engl. J. Med.* 1997; 337:192–195. *And see* Morgan, R. O., Virnig, B. A., DeVito, C. A., Persily, N. A., The Medicare–HMO Revolving Door: The Healthy go in and the Sick go Out, *N. Engl. J. Med.* 1997; 337:169–175.

8. *Mathews v. Eldridge*, 424 U.S. 319 (1976).

9. *Goldberg v. Kelly*, 397 U.S. 254 (1970).

10. Breyer, S. G., Goldberg v. Kelly: Administrative Law and the New Property, (In) Rosenkranz, E. Joshua, Schwartz, Bernard, eds., *Reason and Passion: Justice Brennan's Enduring Influence*, New York: W.W. Norton, 1997, p. 256.

11. AAHP Urges Respect for Appeals Rights, Additional Safeguards in Medicare HMOs, *BNA's Health Law Reporter*, Nov. 7, 1996, 1631.

12. HCFA Official Says 'Gag' Clauses in Risk Contract HMOs May Violate Law, *BNA's Managed Care Reporter*, Dec. 11, 1996, 1159.

13. *Grijalva v. Shalala*, Civ. 93–711, March 3, 1997, U.S. Dist. Ct. Arizona (Marquez, J.).

14. Department of Health and Human Services, Health Care Financing Administration, Establishment of an Expedited Review Process for Beneficiaries Enrolled in Health Maintenance Organizations, Competitive Medical Plans, and Health Care Prepayment Plans, *Federal Register*, April 30, 1997; 62:23368–23376.

15. *Shea v. Eisenstein*, 107 F.3d 625 (8 Cir. 1997).

16. Chase, M., Knowing When You Need the Expertise of a Specialist, *Wall Street Journal*, April 14, 1997, B1.

17. Kinney, E. D., Procedural Protections for Patients in Capitated Health Plans, *Am. J. Law Med.* 1996; 22:301–330.

18. Annas, George J., *The Rights of Patients*, 2d ed., Carbondale, IL: Southern Illinois U. Press, 1989.

19. Hiltzik, M. A., Olmos, D. R., Kaiser-Justice System's Fairness Questioned, *Los Angeles Times*, Aug. 30, 1995, A1.

20. *Engalla v. Permanente Medical Group*, 938 P.2d 903 (Cal. 1997).

21. Annas, G. J., Healey, J., The Patient Rights Advocate: Redefining the Doctor–Patient Relationship in the Hospital Setting, *Vanderbilt L. Rev.* 1974; 27:243–269.

22. Mariner, W. K., State Regulation of Managed Care and the Employee Retirement Income Security Act, *N. Engl. J. Med.* 1996; 335:1986–1990.

23. Annas, G. J., A National Bill of Patients' Rights, *N. Engl. J. Med.* 1998; 338:695–699; Furrow, B. R., Managed Care Organizations and Patient Injury: Rethinking Liability, *Georgia Law Rev.* 1997; 31:419–509.

CHAPTER FOUR: METAPHORS, MEDICINE, AND THE MARKET

1. This chapter is adapted from Annas, G. J., Reforming the Debate on Health Care Reform by Replacing our Metaphors, *N. Engl. J. Med.* 1995; 332:744–747.

2. Lakoff, George, Johnson, Mark, *Metaphors We Live By*, Chicago: Chicago U. Press, 1980.

3. Barnes, Julian, *The History of the World in 10 ½ Chapters*, New York: Vintage, 1990, p. 137.

4. Childress, James, *Who Should Decide? Paternalism in Health Care*, New York: Oxford U. Press, 1982, p. 7; Sontag, Susan, *Illness as Metaphor and AIDS and Its Metaphors*, New York: Doubleday, 1990.

5. Fussell, Paul, *The Great War and Modern Memory*, New York: Oxford U. Press, 1975.

6. Keegan, John, *A History of Warfare*, New York: Vintage Books, 1994, pp. 56–57.

7. Beisecker, A. E., Beisecker, T. D., Using Metaphors to Characterize Doctor–Patient Relationships: Paternalism versus Consumerism, *Health Commun.* 1993; 5:41–58; *See also*, Rodwin, M. A., Strains in the Fiduciary Metaphor: Divided Loyalties and Obligations in a Changing Care System, *Am. J. Law Med.* 1995; 21:241–257.

8. Eckholm, E., While Congress Remains Silent, Health Care Transforms Itself, *New York Times*, Dec. 18, 1994, 1, 34 (quoting Uwe Reinhardt).

9. Relman, A. S., Shattack Lecture: The Health Care Industry: Where is it Taking Us? *N. Engl. J. Med.* 1991; 325:854–859; Relman, A. S., What Market Values Are Doing to Medicine, *Atlantic Monthly*, March 1992, 99–106; *See also*, Pellegrino, E. D., Words Can Hurt You: Some Reflections on the Metaphors of Managed Care, *J. Am. Board Fam. Pract.* 1994; 7:505–510.

10. Frankford, David M., The Normative Constitution of Professional Power, *J. Health Polit. Policy Law* 1997; 22:185–221.

11. McNamara, Robert, *In Retrospect*, New York: Random House, 1996, p. 238.

12. Flower, J., Pride and Prejudice, *Healthcare Forum J.* March 1996; 26,31.

13. Eichenwald, K., A Health Care Giant's Secret Payments Taint a Texas Deal, *New York Times*, March 29, 1997, 25, 17.

14. Hasan, M. M., Let's End the Non Profit Charade, *N. Engl. J. Med.* 1996; 334:1055–1057.

15. Bill and Hill, Auditions for "Americas' Funniest Health Videos," *Boston Globe*, March 27, 1994, 70. The most popular Harry and Louise ads centered on choice. In one, for example, Louise responds to an announcer saying that the government "may force us to pick from a few health plans designed by government bureaucrats" by saying, "having choices we don't like is no choice at all." Robin Toner, Harry and Louise were Right, Sort of, *New York Times*, Nov. 24, 1996, E1.

16. Horwitz, W. A., Characteristics of Environmental Ethics: Environmental Activists' Accounts, *Ethics Behav.* 1994; 4:345–367.

17. Thomas, Lewis, *The Lives of a Cell*, New York: Viking, 1974.

18. Potter, Van Rensselaer, *Bioethics: Bridge to the Future*, Englewood Cliffs, NJ: Prentice-Hall, 1971. Ecologists can also use the military metaphor themselves as Aldo Leopold did in his description of Bur Oaks:

> Bur Oaks were the shock troops sent by the invading forest to storm the prairie; fire is what they had to fight. Each April, before the new grasses had covered the prairie with unburnable greenery, fires ran at will over the land, sparing only such old oaks as had grown bark too thick to scorch. Most of these groves of scattered veterans, known to the pioneers as 'oak openings,' consisted of bur oaks. Engineers did not discover insulation; they copied it from these old soldiers of the prairie war. Botanists can read the story of that war for twenty thousand years. The record consists partly of pollen grains embedded in peats, partly of relic plants interned in the rear of the battle, and there forgotten. The records show that the forest front at times retreated almost to Lake Superior; at times it advanced far to the south. At one period it advanced so far southward that spruce and other 'rear guard' species grew to and beyond the southern border of Wisconsin; spruce pollen appears at a certain level in all peat bogs of the region. But the average battle line between prairie and forest was about where it is now, and the net outcome of the battle was a draw.

Leopold, Aldo, *A Sand County Almanac*, New York: Oxford U. Press, 1949, p. 27.

19. Sessions, George, ed., *Deep Ecology for the Twenty-First Century*, Boston: Shambhala, 1995.

20. Gaylin, W., Faulty Diagnosis: Why Clinton's Health-Care Plan Won't Cure What Ails Us, *Harper's* Oct. 1993; 57–62. *See also* Callahan, D., *False Hopes*, New York: Simon & Shuster, 1998.

21. Editorial, Population Health Looking Upstream, *Lancet* 1994; 343–429, 430.

22. McKinlay, J. B., *A Case for Refocusing Upstream: The Political Economy of Illness*, Proceedings of American Heart Association Conferences on Applying Behavioral Science to Cardiovascular Risk, Seattle: American Health Association, 1974.

23. Dubos, Renee, *Mirage of Health,* New York: Harper, 1959, p. 233.

24. Friedman, E., An Ethic for All of Us, *Healthcare Forum J.* March 1991; 11–12.

25. There are, of course, other possible metaphors, such as the sports metaphor and the religion metaphor, but none that offer the possibilities of the ecology metaphor. Of course, other fields, including the military and religion, themselves make use of the medical metaphor. *See* Harley, David N., Medical Metaphors in English Moral Theology, 1560–1660, *J. Hist. Med. Allied Sci.* 1993; 48:396–435; *and* Annas, G. J., The Phoenix Heart: What We Have to Lose, *Hastings Cent. Rep.* June 1985; 15(3):15–16.

26. Havel, V., The New Measure of Man, *New York Times,* July 8, 1994, A27. Havel himself wondered whether emphasis on the environment might itself be a product of "anthropocentrism," saying, "It implies that whatever is not human is just something that envelops man—surroundings that are inferior to him and that he should tend and develop in his own image." Havel, V., Rio and the New Millennium, *New York Times,* June 3, 1992, A1.

CHAPTER FIVE: CANCER, PROGNOSIS, AND CHOICE

1. This chapter is adapted from Annas, G. J., Informed Consent, Cancer, and Truth in Prognosis, *N. Engl. J. Med.,* 1994; 330:223–225.

2. Tuchman, Barbara W., *A Distant Mirror: The Calamitous 14th Century,* New York: Ballantine Books, 1978, p. 53.

3. President's Commission for the Study of Ethical Problems in Medicine and Biomedical and Behavioral Research, Making Health Care Decisions, *The Ethical and Legal Implications of Informed Consent in the Patient–Practitioner Relationship*, vol. 2, appendices, Washington, DC: U.S. Gov. Printing Office, 1982, pp. 245–246.

4. *Arato v. Avedon,* 5 Cal. 4th 1172, 23 Cal. Rptr.2d 131, 858 P.2d 598 (1993).

5. *Arato v. Avedon,* 13 Cal. App. 4th 1325, 11 Cal. Rptr.2d 169 (1992).

6. *Cobbs v. Grant,* 8 Cal.3d 229, 104 Cal. Rptr. 505, 502 P.2d 1 (1972).

7. *Truman v. Thomas,* 27 Cal.3d 285, 165 Cal. Rptr. 308, 611 P.2d 902 (1980).

8. *Moore v. Regents of University of California,* 51 Cal.3d 120, 271 Cal. Rptr. 146, 793 P.2d 479 (1990).

9. Capron, A. M., Duty, Truth, and Whole Human Beings, *Hastings Cent. Rep.* 1993; 23(4):13–14.

10. Annas, George J., *The Rights of Patients,* 2d ed., Carbondale, IL: Southern Illinois U. Press, 1989.

11. Tuchman, *supra* note 2.

12. Cassel, C. K., Meier, D. E., Morals and Moralism in the Debate over Euthanasia and Assisted Suicide, *N. Engl. J. Med.* 1990; 323:750–752; and Katz, Jay, *The Silent World of Doctor and Patient*, New York: Free Press, 1984.

13. Katz, J., Physician-Patient Encounters "On a Darkling Plain," *W. N. Engl. Law Rev.* 1987; 9:207–226.

14. *Supra,* note 1.

CHAPTER SIX: CULTURE, ECONOMICS, AND CHOICE

1. Ballard, J. G., *Empire of the Sun,* New York: Simon & Shuster, 1984.

2. This chapter is adapted from Annas, G. J., Miller, F. H., The Empire of Death: How Culture and Economics Affect Informed Consent in the U.S., the U.K. and Japan, *Am. J. Law Med.* 1994; 20:357–394, which should be consulted for much more extensive documentation.

3. Payer, Lynn, *Medicine and Culture*, New York: Henry Holt, 1988.

4. Chiara, S., Hirohito, 124th Emperor of Japan, Is Dead at 87, *New York Times,* Jan. 7, 1989, 1.

5. Fay, J., The Mouse and the Elephant: Can Primary Care Save the U.S. Health System?, *Lancet* Sept. 5, 1992; 340:594.

6. *Pratt v. Davis*, 118 Ill. App. 161, 166 (1905), *aff'd*, 244 Ill. 30, 79 N.E. 562 (1906).

7. President's Commission for the Study of Ethical Problems in Medicine and Biomedical and Behavioral Research, *Making Health Care Decisions,* Washington, DC: Presidents' Commission, 1982, pp. 2–3.

8. 8 Cal. 3d 229, 502 P.2d 1 (1972).

9. *Arato v. Avedon*, 5 Cal. 4th 1172, 23 Cal. Rptr. 2d 131, 858 P.2d 598 (1993).

10. Lubitz, J. D., Riley, G. P., Trends in Medicare Payments in the Last Year of Life, *N. Engl. J. Med.* 1993; 320:1092.

11. Relman, A., The New Medical-Industrial Complex, *N. Engl. J. Med.* 1980; 303:963, 966.

12. *Sidaway v. Bethlem Royal Hospital Governors*, 1 AC 871 (1985), 2 WLR 480 (1985), 1 All ER 643 (1985).

13. Meyers, David W., *The Human Body and the Law*, 2d ed., Chicago: Aldine, 1990, p. 131.

14. [1988] QB 481, 3 WLR 649 (1987), 2 All ER 888, CA. (failed sterilization procedure where alternative forms of contraception were not disclosed) *See also* Grubb, A., Contraceptive Advice and Doctors—A Law Unto Themselves?, *Camb. L.J.* 1988; 47:12.

15. Giesen, D., Hayes, J., The Patient's Right to Know—A Comparative View, *Anglo Am. L. Rev.* 1992; 21:101–146.

16. Boston, Sarah, Louw, Jill, *Disorderly Breasts,* London: Camden Press, 1987, pp. 31–32.

17. Heneghan, C., Medicine and the Law: Consent to Medical Treatment, *Lancet* 1991; 337:421 [emphasis added].

18. Kerrigan, D. D., Thevasagayam, R. S., Woods, T. O., McWelch, I., Thomas, W. E., Shorthouse, A. J., Dennison, A. R., Who's Afraid of Informed Consent?, *Br. Med. J.* 1993; 306:298.

19. Hattori, H., Salzberg, S., Kiang, W., Fujimiya, T., Tejima, Y., Furono, J., The Patient's Right to Information in Japan—Legal Rules and Doctor's Opinions, *Sci. Med.* 1991; 32:1007, 1009.

20. Nagoya District Court Judgment, 1325 Hanji 103 (May 29, 1989). My description of this case is taken entirely from Higuchi, Norio, The Patient's Right to Know of a Cancer Diagnosis: A Comparison of Japanese Paternalism and American Self-Determination, *Washburn L.J.,* 1992; 31:455, 458–461.

21. Higuchi, *supra* note 20, p. 462.

22. Kimura, R., In Japan, Parents Participate but Doctors Decide, *Hastings Cent. Rep.* Aug. 16, 1986; 22, 23.

23. Salzberg, S. M., Japan's New Mental Health Law: More Light Shed on Dark Places?, *Int. J. Law Psychiatr.* 1991; 14:137, 153.

24. Tandia, N., Patient's Rights in Japan, *Lancet* 1991; 337:242– 243.

25. Brown, K., Death and Access: Ethics in Cross-Cultural Health Care, (In) Friedman, E., ed., *Choices and Conflict: Explorations in Health Care Ethics,* Chicago: Am. Hosp. Ass'n., 1992, p. 85; *see also* Hoshino, K., Legal Status of Brain Death in Japan, *Bioethics* 1993; 7:234.

26. Miller, F. H., Denial of Care and Informed Consent in English and American Law, *Am. J. Law Med.* 1992; 18:37, 56–57; *and see* Miller, F. H., Competition Law and Anticompetitive Physician Behavior, *Mod. Law Rev.* 1992; 55:453, 455–463.

27. *See, e.g.* Benedict, Ruth, *The Chrysanthemum and the Sword*, Boston: Houghton-Mifflin, 1946; *and* Doi, Takeo, *The Anatomy of Dependence*, Tokyo: Kondansha International, 1971. Takeo Doi is unimpressed by individualism in America. As he observes about American conformity, "even in a society in which individuals stand out, the appearance of real individuals is strangely absent." Doi, Takeo, *The Anatomy of Self*, Tokyo: Kodansha International, 1985, p. 57.

28. Quoted in Klein, Rudolf, *The Politics of the NHS*, 2d ed., London: Longman, 1983, pp. 67–68.

29. Miyaji, N. T., The Power of Compassion: Truth-Telling Among American Doctors in the Care of Dying Patients, *Soc. Sci. Med.* 1993; 36:249.

30. Callahan, D., Living Within Limits: The Future of Health Care, *Trends Health Care Law Ethics* 1992; 7(3):15, 16.

31. Illich, Ivan, *Medical Nemesis*, New York: Pantheon Books, 1975, p. 122.

32. Kamura, R., Anencephalic Organ Donation: A Japanese Case, *J. Med. Philos.* 1989; 14:97, 100; (Kimura cites the Japanese text of Namihira, Emiko, *Culture of Illness and Death*, Tokyo: Shinzansha, 1990, to support his conclusions.)

33. Millenson, Michael L., *Demanding Medical Excellence: Doctors and Accountability in the Information Age*, Chicago: Chicago U. Press, 1997.

34. Wennberg, J., AHCPR and the Strategy for Health Care Reform, *Health Affairs* Winter 1992; 67:68.

CHAPTER SEVEN: TREATING THE UNTREATABLE

1. This chapter is adapted from Annas, G. J., Asking the Courts to Set the Standard of Emergency Care: The Case of Baby K, *N. Engl. J. Med.* 1994; 330:1542–1545.

2. Ingelfinger, F. J., Legal Hegemony in Medicine, *N. Engl. J. Med.* 1975; 293: 825–826.

3. Medical Task Force on Anencephaly, The Infant with Anencephaly, *N. Engl. J. Med.* 1990; 322:669–674.

4. Emergency Medical Treatment and Active Labor Act, P.L. 99–272, 42 U.S.C. sec. 1395dd (1985) (renamed in 1989).

5. *In the Matter of Baby K*, 832 F.Supp. 1022 (E.D. Va. 1993).

6. Rehabilitation Act of 1973, P.L. 93–112, 29 U.S.C. sec. 701–796i (1973); expanded by the Americans with Disabilities Act, P.L. 101–336, 42 U.S.C. sec. 12101–12213 (1990).

7. In the Matter of Baby K, 16 F.3d 590 (4th Cir. 1994).

8. Paris, J. J., Schreiber, M. D., Stratter, M., Arensman, R., Siegler, M., Beyond Autonomy—Physicians' Refusal to use Life-Prolonging Extracorporeal Membrane Oxygenation, *N. Engl. J. Med.* 1993; 329:354–357.

9. DiSalvo, C. R., Worshipping at the Alter of Technique: Manic Aggressive Medicine and Law, *Villanova L. Rev.* 1995; 40:1365–1393.

10. Annas, George J., Elias, Sherman, *Reproductive Genetics and the Law,* St. Louis: Mosby-Yearbook, 1987, pp. 182–185.

11. *United States v. University Hospital, State University of New York at Stony Brook,* 729 F.2d 144 (2d Cir. 1984); Office of Human Development Services, Dept. Health and Human Services, Child Abuse and Neglect Prevention and Treatment Program; Final Rule. *Fed. Reg.* April 15, 1985; 50:14878–14901 (45 CFR 1340).

12. Krushe, Helga, Singer, Peter, *Should the Baby Live?* New York: Oxford U. Press, 1985; Office of the Secretary, Dept. Health and Human Services, Nondiscrimination on the Basis of Handicap Relating to Health Care for Handicapped Infants; Proposed Rules. *Fed. Reg.* July 5, 1983; 48: 30845–30852.

13. Annas, George J., *Judging Medicine,* Clifton, NJ: Humana Press, 1988, pp. 132–146, 158–163.

14. *Parham v. J.L. and J.R.*, 442 U.S. 584 (1979).

15. *Youngberg v. Romeo*, 457 U.S. 307 (1982).

16. Miles, S. H., Informed Demand for Non-beneficial Medical Treatment, *N. Engl. J. Med.* 1991; 325:512–515; *In re Wanglie*, No. PX91-288 (Prob. Ct., Hennepin Co., Minn., June 28, 1991).

17. Schneiderman, L. J., Manning, S., The Baby K Case: A Search for the Elusive Standard of Medical Care, *Cambridge Q. Healthcare Ethics* 1997; 6:9–18.

CHAPTER EIGHT: OUTLAWED CHOICES

1. This chapter is adapted from Annas, G. J., Reefer Madness: The Federal Response to California's Medical Marijuana Law, *N. Engl. J. Med.* 1997; 337:435–439.

2. Sidney, S., Beck, J. E., Tekawa, I. S., Queensberry, C. P., Friedman, G. D., Marijuana Use and Mortality, *Am. J. Public Health* 1997; 87:585–590.

3. White House Briefing News Conference, *Federal News Service*, Dec. 30, 1996.

4. Kassirer, J. P., Federal Foolishness and Marijuana, *N. Engl. J. Med.* 1997; 336:366–367.

5. Cal. Code Sec. 11362.5 (1996).

6. *United States v. Rutherford*, 442 U.S. 544 (1979).

7. Treatment Use of an Investigational New Drug, 21 C.F.R. §312.34 (1988).

8. Annas, G. J., Faith (Healing), Hope and Charity at the FDA: The Politics of AIDS Drug Trials, *Villanova Law Rev.* 1989; 34:771–797.

9. Grinspoon, Lester, Bakalar, James, *Marijuana: The Forbidden Medicine* (revised and expanded ed.), New Haven, CT: Yale U. Press, 1997.

10. Gould, S. J., It Worked Like a Charm, *The Times*, May 4, 1993. Gould originally wrote of his experiences with marijuana at the request of Grinspoon, Lester, *supra* note 9, pp. 39–40.

11. Golden, T., Medical Use of Marijuana to Stay Illegal in Arizona, *New York Times*, April 17, 1997, A14.

12. *Conant v. McCaffrey*, 172 F.R.D. 681 (D. N. Cal. 1997).

13. *Rust v. Sullivan*, 500 U.S. 173 (1991).

14. Annas, G. J., Restricting Doctor–Patient Conversation in Federally Funded Clinics, *N. Engl. J. Med.* 1991; 325:362–364.

15. Golden, T., Federal Judge Supports California Doctors on Marijuana Issue, *New York Times*, April 12, 1997, 7.

16. Stapleton, S., Medical Pot: Feds, Talk is OK, Just Don't Recommend It, *American Medical News,* March 17, 1997, 1.

17. *Morei v. U.S.*, 127 F.2d. 827 (6th Cir. 1942).

18. *State v. Gladstone*, 474 P.2d. 274 (Wash. 1970).

19. *In the Matter of Marijuana Rescheduling Petition*, U.S. Dept. of Justice, DEA, Docket No. 86-22, Sept. 6, 1988 (Young, J.)

20. Doblin, R. E., Kleiman, M. A. R., Marijuana as Anti-Emetic Medicine: A Survey of Oncologists' Experience and Attitudes, *J. Clin. Oncol.* 1991; 9:1314–1319.

21. Leary, W. E., U.S. Panel Urges Study of Medical Marijuana, *New York Times*,

Feb. 21, 1997, A27. The group repeated these recommendations in a detailed report to the NIH Director entitled "Workshop on the Medical Utility of Marijuana" on Aug. 8, 1997 (*see* http://www.nih.gov/news/medmarijuana/MedicalMarijuana.htm).

22. *See* Grinspoon, *supra* note 9, p. 43.

23. Goodman, E., Clear Thinking in the Medical Marijuana Debate, *The Boston Globe*, Feb. 2, 1997, C7.

24. Wren, C. S., Phantom Numbers Haunt the War on Drugs, *New York Times*, April 20, 1997, 4E.

CHAPTER NINE: GENETIC PROPHECY AND GENETIC PRIVACY

1. This chapter is based principally on Annas, G. J., Privacy Rules for DNA Databanks: Protecting Coded "Future Diaries," *JAMA* 1993; 270:2346–2350; and Annas, G. J., When Should Preventive Treatment be Paid for by Health Insurance?, *N. Engl. J. Med.* 1994; 331:1027–1030.

2. Annas, George J., Elias, Sherman, eds., *Gene Mapping: Using Law and Ethics as Guides*, New York: Oxford U. Press, 1992; Privacy Commissioner of Canada, *Genetic Testing and Privacy*, Ottawa: Privacy Commissioner of Canada, 1992; deGorgey, A., The Advent of DNA Databanks: Implications for Informational Privacy, *Am. J. Law Med.* 1990; 16:381–398; Shapiro, Weinberg, DNA Data Banking; The Dangerous Erosion of Privacy, *Cleveland State Law Rev.* 1990; 38:455; Nobles, K., Birthright or Life Sentence: Controlling the Threat of Genetic Testing, *Cal. Law Rev.* 1992; 65:2081–2119.

3. *Domestic and International Data Protection Issues*, Hearings before the Subcommittee on Government Information, Justice, and Agriculture, U.S. House of Representatives, 102 Cong., 1st Sess., 1991.

4. Council of State Governments, *Advances in Genetic Information: A Guide for State Policy Makers*, Council of State Gov., Lexington, KY, 1992.

5. Proctor, Robert, *Racial Hygiene: Medicine Under the Nazis*, Cambridge, MA: Harvard U. Press, 1987.

6. *Designing Genetic Information Policy: The Need for an Independent Policy Review of the Ethical, Legal, and Social Implications of the Human Genome Project*, 16th Report of the Committee on Government Operations, U.S. House of Representatives, 102 Cong., 2d Sess., April 2, 1992.

7. *Whalen v. Roe*, 429 U.S. 589, 607 (1977) (Brennan J., concurring).

8. Annas, George J., *The Rights of Patients*, 2d ed., Carbondale, IL: Southern Illinois U. Press, 1989, pp. 160–195.

9. Annas, G. J., The Supreme Court, Liberty, and Abortion, *N. Engl. J. Med.* 1992; 327:651–654.

10. *Olmstead v. United States*, 277 U.S. 438, 478 (1928) (Brandeis, J., dissenting); *Estate of Berthiaume v. Pratt*, 365 A.2d 792, 793 (Me. 1976); *Horne v. Patton*, 291 Ala. 701, 287 So. 2d 824 (1973).

11. Westin, Alan, *Privacy and Freedom*, New York: Atheneum, 1967, p. 7.

12. Miller, A., Personal Privacy in the Computer Age, 67 *Mich. Law Rev.* 1968; 1091, 1107.

13. Solzhenitsyn, Alexander, *Cancer Ward*, New York: Farrar, Strauss & Giroux, 1969.

14. Bennett, C. J., *Regulating Privacy: Data Protection and Public Policy in Europe and the United States*, Ithaca, NY: Cornell U. Press, 1992.

15. Juengst, E. T., Priorities in Professional Ethics and Social Policy for Human Genetics, *JAMA* 1991; 266:1835–1836.

16. Council on Ethical and Judicial Affairs, American Medical Association, Use of Genetic Testing by Employers, *JAMA* 1991; 266:1827–1830.

17. Caskey, C. T., Molecular Medicine: A Spinoff From the Helix, *JAMA* 1993; 269:1986–1992.

18. *Katskee v. Blue Cross/Blue Shield of Nebraska*, 245 Neb. 808, 515 N.W.2d 645 (1994).

19. All quotations are from Transcript of Deposition of Henry T. Lynch, M.D. (Dec. 3, 1991).

20. *Witcraft v. Sundstrand Health*, 420 N.W.2d 785, 788 (Iowa 1988).

21. *Silverstein v. Metropolitan Life Ins. Co.*, 254 N.Y.81, 171 N.E. 914 (1930).

22. Biesecker, B. B., Boehnke, M., Calzone, K., Markel, D. S., Garber, J. E., Collins, F. S., Weber, B. L., Genetic Counseling for Families with Inherited Susceptibility to Breast and ovarian Cancer, *JAMA* 1993; 269:1970–1974.

23. King, M. C., Rowell, S., Love, S. M., Inherited Breast and Ovarian Cancer: What are the Risks? What are the Choices? *JAMA* 1993; 269:1975–1980.

24. Eddy, D. M., What Care is Essential? What Services are Basic? *JAMA* 1991; 265:782–788.

25. Hadorn, D. C., Setting Health Care Priorities in Oregon: Cost-Effectiveness Meets the Rule of Rescue, *JAMA* 1991; 265:2218–2225.

26. Ferguson, J. H., Dubinsky, M., Kirsch, P. J., Court-Ordered Reimbursement for Unproven Medical Technology: Circumventing Technology Assessment, *JAMA* 1993; 269:2116–2121; Peters, W. P., Rogers, M. C., Variation in Approval by Insurance Companies of Coverage for Autologous Bone Marrow Transplantation for Breast Cancer, *N. Engl. J. Med.* 1994; 330:473–477.

27. Callahan, D., Medical Futility, Medical Necessity: The Problem-Without-a-Name, *Hastings Cent. Rep.* July 1991; 21(4):30–35.

28. Payer, Lynn, *Disease-Mongers*, New York: John Wiley, 1992.

29. Siebert, C., The DNA We've Been Dealt, *New York Times Magazine*, Sept. 17, 1995, 50.

30. Robert Proctor, *The Cancer Wars*, New York: Basic Books, 1995, p. 239.

31. Smith, T., Genes and Ethics, *Br. Med. J.* 1995; 311:574.

32. Harris Poll #34, May 29, 1995.

33. Annas, George J., Glantz, Leonard, Roche, Patricia, *The Genetic Privacy Act and Commentary*, Boston, MA: Boston U. School of Public Health, 1995 (available at http://www-busph.bu.edu/Depts/HealthLaw/).

34. Nelkin, Dorothy, Lindee, M. S., *The DNA Mystique: The Gene as a Cultural Icon*, New York: W.H. Freeman, 1995, p. 2.

CHAPTER TEN: CHOOSING A (HEALTHY) PRESIDENT

1. Woodward, Bob, *The Choice*, New York: Simon and Shuster, 1996.

2. This chapter is based on Annas, G. J., The Health of the President and Presidential Candidates: The Public's Right to Know, *N. Engl. J. Med.* 1995; 333:945–948.

3. Altman, L. K., Doctors Say Dole is in 'Excellent' Health, *New York Times*, July 22, 1995; 9; Berke R. L., Dole, 72 Today, Issues Findings that his Condition is Excellent, *New York Times*, July 22, 1995.

4. Bloom, M., Should the Health of Presidential Candidates be a Campaign Issue? *Med. World News*, Feb. 9, 1976, 34–99.

5. Altman, L. K., Clinton, Citing Privacy Issues, Tells Little About His Health, *New*

York Times, Oct. 10, 1992, 1; Clinton Promises Medical Details, *Washington Post,* Oct. 11, 1992, A35.

6. Annas, George J., *The Rights of Patients,* Carbondale IL: Southern Illinois U. Press, 1989.

7. Post, Jerrold M., Robins, Robert S., *When Illness Strikes the Leader,* New Haven: Yale U. Press, 1993; Crispell, Kenneth Robert, Gomez, Carlos F., *Hidden Illness in the White House,* Durham: Duke U. Press, 1988; Ferrell, Robert H., *Ill-advised: Presidential Health and Public Trust,* Columbia: Missouri U. Press, 1992.

8. *Idem,* Ferrell.

9. Reagan, Ronald, *An American Life,* New York: Simon & Shuster, 1990. On Reagan's 1997 state of health see Altman, L. K., A President Fades into a World Apart, *New York Times,* Oct. 5, 1997, A1.

10. Tsongas, P., The Cancer Freed Me. It Freed Me. *New York Times,* May 6, 1992, A29.

11. Knox, R. A., Tsongas Responds: Acknowledges Cancer, Urges Full Disclosure by Candidates, *Boston Globe,* Dec. 1, 1992, 1.

12. Altman, L. K., Tsongas's Health: Privacy and the Public's Rights, *New York Times,* Jan. 17, 1993, 26.

13. Abrams, Herbert L., *'The President has Been Shot': Confusion, Disability, and the Twenty-fifth Amendment in the Aftermath of the Attempted Assassination of Ronald Reagan,* New York: W.W. Norton, 1992.

14. Brown, W. F., Cinquegrana A. R., The Realities of Presidential Succession: 'The Emperor has no Clones,' *Georgetown Law J.* 1987; 75:1389–1453.

15. Longaker, R. P., Presidential Continuity: the Twenty-fifth Amendment, *UCLA Law Rev.* 1966; 13:532–563.

16. Gilbert, Robert E., *The Mortal Presidency: Illness and Anguish in the White House,* New York: Basic Books, 1992. *See also,* Gilbert, R. S., The Political Effects of Presidential Illness: The Case of Lyndon B. Johnson, *Polit. Psych.* 1995; 16:761–776.

17. Greenberg, D. S., Political Pains, *Nature* 1993; 361:125.

18. Curran, W. J., Presidential Inability to Function: The Medicolegal Issues, *N. Engl. J. Med.* 1986; 314:300–301.

19. Toole, James F., et. al., *Disability in U.S. Presidents: Report, Recommendations and Commentaries by the Working Group,* Winston-Salem, NC: Bowman Gray Scientific Press, 1997. I was invited to join the group for their final meeting in December 1996, and concurred in the final report.

20. Post and Robins, *supra* note 7.

21. Abrams, *supra* note 13.

22. Ferrell, *supra* note 7.

23. Hruban, R. H, VanderRiet, P., Erozan, Y. S., Sidransky, D., Brief Report: Molecular Biology and Early Detection of Carcinoma of the Bladder—The Case of Hubert H. Humphrey, *N. Engl. J. Med.* 1994; 330:1276–1278.

24. Cramer, R. B., *What It Takes: The Way to the White House,* New York: Random House, 1992.

25. As Dole Counts Calories, Gramm Weighs, *New York Times,* Aug. 1, 1995, A10.

26. Annas, George J., Elias, Sherman, eds., *Gene Mapping: Using Law and Ethics as Guides,* New York: Oxford U. Press, 1992; Annas, G. J., Editorial: Genetic Prophecy and Genetic Privacy: Can We Prevent the Dream from Becoming a Nightmare? *Am. J. Public Health* 1995; 85:1196–1197.

27. Bloom, *supra* note 4.

28. Editorial, Will Anyone Believe?, *Wall Street Journal*, Sept. 16, 1996, A18.

29. In 1997 the U.S. Supreme Court ruled that states could not constitutionally require candidates for public office to subject themselves to a drug test for illicit drugs, although the Court specifically kept for another day the question of whether candidates could be required to undergo "a medical examination designed to provide certification of a candidate's general health." *Chandler v. Miller*, 117 S. Ct. 1295 (1997).

30. Altman, L. K., Clinton, in Detailed Interview, Calls His Health 'Very Good', *New York Times*, Oct. 14, 1996, A1, A12.

31. Dowd, M., Murder of an Anatomy, *New York Times*, Oct. 18, 1997, A25. The president's attitude toward his own privacy may have made cases like Paula Jones and Monica Lewinsky inevitable.

CHAPTER ELEVEN: A WOMAN'S CHOICE AT WORK

1. This chapter is adapted from Annas, G. J., Fetal Protection and Employment Discrimination: The Johnson Controls Case, *N. Engl. J. Med.* 1991; 325:740.

2. Barta, C., Engendered Power: Women's Voting Pattern Has Implications Beyond Re-election of President Clinton, *Dallas Morning News*, Nov. 30, 1996, 1C.

3. *Muller v. Oregon*, 208 U.S. 412 (1908); Becker, M.E., From *Muller v. Oregon* to Fetal Vulnerability Policies, *U. Chicago L. Rev.* 1986; 53:1219.

4. Fuchs, V. R., Sex Differences in Economic Well-Being, *Science* 1986; 232:459. 1996 data is that women earn 75 cents to a man's dollar. *Statistical Abstract of the United States*, U.S. Dept. Commerce, Washington, DC, 1996, p. 426; and Lewin, T., Wage Differences between Men and Women Widens, *New York Times*, Sept. 15, 1997, 1.

5. Pregnancy Discrimination Act of 1978, 92 Stat. 2076, 42 U.S.C. sec 2000e(k).

6. *International Union v. Johnson Controls*, 886 F.2d 871 (7th Cir. 1989) (en banc).

7. *International Union v. Johnson Controls*, 680 F. Supp. 309 (E.D. Wis. 1988).

8. *International Union v. Johnson Controls*, 499 U.S. 187 (1991).

9. *Fesel v. Masonic Home of Delaware*, 447 F. Supp. 1346 (D.Del. 1978).

10. *Buckus v. Baptist Medical Center*, 510 F. Supp. 1191 (E.D.Ark. 1981).

11. Sex in the Delivery Room: Is the Nurse a Boy or Girl? (In) Annas, G. J., *Judging Medicine*, Clifton, NJ: Humana Press, 1988, pp. 53–56.

12. *Security National Bank v. Chloride Industrial Battery*, 602 F. Supp. 294 (D. Kan. 1985).

13. Becker, M. E., Can Employers Exclude Women to Protect Children?, *JAMA* 1990; 264:2113–2117.

14. McKenna, E. P., What's Ahead for Working Men and Women, *New York Times*, Aug. 31, 1997, E9 (McKenna is the author of *When Work Doesn't Work Anymore*).

15. American College of Obstetrics and Gynecology Committee on Ethics, *Patient Choice: Maternal-Fetal Conflict*, Committee Opinion No. 55, Washington, DC: ACOG, 1987.

CHAPTER TWELVE: A SOLDIER'S CHOICE

1. This chapter is adapted from Annas, G. J., Changing the Consent Rules for Desert Storm, *N. Engl. J. Med.* 1992; 326:770–773.

2. Clausewitz, Karl von, *On War*, 1831; Washington, DC: Infantry Journal Press, 1950, p. 32.

3. Trials of War Criminals before the Nuremberg Military Tribunals, Tribunal I, Case I, The Military Case: *United States of America v. Karl Brandt et al.*, vol. 2, Washington,

DC: US Gov. Print Office, 1950, p. 183; *and see* Annas, G. J., Mengele's Birthmark: The Nuremberg Code in United States Courts, *J. Contemp. Health Law Policy* 1992; 7:17–45. The full text of the Nuremberg Code appears in chapter 14, note 8.

4. 21 U.S.C. sec. 355(i); 1991.

5. Informed Consent for Human Drugs and Biologics; Determination That Informed Consent Is Not Feasible, *Fed. Reg.* 1990; 55:52813–52817.

6. 21 C.F.R. sec. 50.23(d).

7. *Doe v. Sullivan*, 756 F. Supp. 12 (D.D.C. 1991).

8. *Doe v. Sullivan*, 938 F.2d 1370 (D.C. Cir. 1991).

9. Currie, D. P., *The Constitution in the Supreme Court: The Second Century, 1888–1986*, Chicago: Chicago U. Press, 1990, pp. 280–307.

10. Keefer, J. R., Huest, C. G., Dunn, M. A., Pyridostigmine Used as a Nerve Agent Pretreatment Under Wartime Conditions, *JAMA* 1991; 266:693–695.

11. Schuchardt, E. J., Walking a Thin Line: Distinguishing Between Research and Medical Practice During Operation Desert Storm, *Columbia J. Law Soc. Prob.* 1992; 26:77–115; ("it is reasonable to conclude that the Pentagon did not conduct 'research' on the soldiers in the Gulf." p. 105); Waivers for Military use of Investigational Agents, (Pharmacy ethics), *Am. J. Hosp. Pharm.* 1991; 48:1525–1529; Treating the Troops (Symposium), *Hastings Cent. Rep.* March 1991; 21(2):20–29.

12. *Treatment of Chemical Agent Casualties and Conventional Military Chemical Injuries*; FM 8-285, NAVMED P-5041, AFM 160-11, Washington, DC: Headquarters Depts. of the Army, the Navy, and the Air Force; Feb. 1990, pp. 2–15 to 2–19. Of course this argument assumes that "pretreatment" can be equated with treatment—and this is problematic, as discussed in chapter 9.

13. Epstein, K., Sloat, B., Objection to Gulf War Vaccine Was Overridden, *Cleveland Plain Dealer*, Dec. 21, 1997, 16A.

14. This instruction, however, apparently did not always make its way to the war zone. In one survey of 150 Gulf War Veterans, for example, of the 17 who reported getting the botulinum toxoid, 15 were told they could not refuse it. Committee on Veteran's Affairs, U.S. Senate, Staff Report, *Is Military Research Hazardous to Veterans' Health? Lessons Spanning Half a Century*, Washington, DC: U.S. Gov. Printing Office, Dec. 8, 1994.

15. Shenon, P., Panel Urges that Pentagon Lose Gulf Inquiry Authority: Cites Loss of Credibility on Chemical Arms, *New York Times*, Sept. 6, 1997, 11; Shenon, P., New Evidence on Nerve Gas in Gulf War Spurs Inquiry, *New York Times*, July 25, 1997, A13.

16. Haley, R. W., Kurt, T. L., Self-Reported Exposure to Neurotoxic Chemical Combinations in the Gulf War, *JAMA* 1997; 277:231–237; U.S. Senate Staff Report, *supra* note 13 p. 11; and Koplovitz, I., Harris, L. W., Anderson, D. R., Lennox, W. J., Steward, J. R., Reduction by Pyridostigmine Pretreatment of the Efficacy of Atropine and 2-PAM Treatment of Sarin and VX Poisoning in Rodents, *Fundam. Appl. Toxicol.* 1992; 18:102–106.

17. *Idem*, and Haley, R. W., Letter to the Editor, *JAMA* 1997; 278:386–387 (and sources cited therein).

18. *Idem, and see* Hearings before U.S. House of Representatives, Subcommittee on Human Resources and Intergovernmental Affairs, Committee on Government Reform and Oversight, April 24, 1997, and Waldman, A., Credibility Gulf: The Military's Battle over whether to Protect Its Image or Its Troops, *Washington Monthly*, Dec. 1996, p. 28.

19. Johnson, W. H., Civil Rights of Military Personnel Regarding Medical Care and Experimental Procedures, *Science* 1953; 117:212–215. [GCM 125224].

20. *United States v. Stanley*, 483 U.S. 669 (1987).

21. For current DoD biological warfare research proposals *see* Dept. of Army, Joint

Program Office for Biological Defense, *Final Vaccine Acquisition Program: Draft Programmatic Environmental Assessment*, JVA, Fort Detrich, MD, June 1997.

22. *Supra* note 10.

23. Quoted in editorial, The Harassment of Female Troops, *New York Times*, Sept. 13, 1997, p. 24.

24. Food and Drug Administration, Public Health Service, Dept. Health and Human Services, Accessibility to New Drugs for Use in Military and Civilian Exigencies When Traditional Human Efficacy Studies Are Not Feasible, Request for Comments, *Fed Reg.* July 31, 1997; 62:40 996 et. seq. The three major reasons DoD presents to retain the current waiver rule all confuse and conflate research with treatment:

1. When the President commits U.S. military forces to a combat, peacekeeping, or humanitarian deployment, the U.S. Government has a duty to take all reasonable precautions to bring about a successful completion of the mission and a safe return of the deployed forces.

2. The Government's duty to take all reasonable precautions to preserve the fighting force must include recognition of the startling proliferation of chemical and biological weapons among potential adversaries and terrorist organizations and an obligation to implement the best possible medical countermeasures.

3. Implementation of the best possible medical countermeasures may require the standardized treatment use of an investigational new drug or vaccine for all personnel at risk in a military combat exigency, including those personnel who, for whatever reason or no reason at all, would prefer an alternate treatment of no treatment. *Idem*, p. 4100.

It is also worth noting that even though it continues to support the rule, the DoD apparently does not follow it. In Bosnia, for example, "nearly 4,000 soldiers were told during military briefings that the vaccine, called TBE, was 'already known to be very safe and extremely effective,'" although it was a research vaccine designed to protect against tick-borne encephalitis and not approved by the FDA. Sloat, B., Epstein, K., Army Misled Troops who got Vaccine in Bosnia, *Cleveland Plain Dealer*, Jan. 25, 1998, 1A.

CHAPTER THIRTEEN: OUR MOST IMPORTANT PRODUCT

1. Shortly after this document was made public the Library of Congress put together the following suggested reading list for those interested in reviewing PP2020's past experiments:

Annas, George J., *Shelley's Brain* (play), 1988.

Committee to Evaluate the Artificial Heart Program, Institute of Medicine, *The Artificial Heart: Prototypes, Policies and Patients*, Washington, DC: National Academy Press, 1991.

Lawrence, R. J., David the 'Bubble Boy' and the Boundaries of the Human, *JAMA* 1985; 253:74–76.

Moravec, Hans, *Mind Children: The Future of Robot and Human Intelligence*, Cambridge, MA: Harvard U. Press, 1988.

Najarian, J. S., Overview of in vivo Xenotransplantation Studies: Prospects for the Future, *Transplant. Proc.* 1992; 24:733–737.

Pommer, R. W., Van DeKamp, Donaldson v., Cryonics, Assisted Suicide, and the Challenges of Medical Science, *J. Contemp. Health L. Policy* 1993; 9:589.

President's Commission for the Study of Ethical Problems in Medicine, *Splicing Life: The Social and Ethical Issues of Genetic Engineering with Human Beings*, Washington, DC: HHS, 1982.

Regis, Ed, *Great Mambo Chicken and the TransHuman Condition*, Reading, MA: Addison-Wesley, 1990.

Remington, C. L., An Experimental Study of Man's Genetic Relationship to Great Apes by Means of Interspecific Hybridization, (In) Katz, Jay, ed., *Experimentation with Human Beings*, New York: Russell Sage, 1972, pp. 461–464.

Sargent, Pamela, ed., *Bio-Futures: Science Fiction Stories about Biological Metamorphosis*, New York: Vintage Books, 1976.

Smith II, George P., *Medical-Legal Aspects of Cryonics: Prospects for Immortality*, Port Washington, NY: Associated Faculty Press, 1983.

Symposium, 1984 and Beyond, *Am. Med. News*, Jan. 26, 1979, Impact Section, 1–13.

Thomas, Gordon, *Journey into Madness: The True Story of Secret CIA Mind Control and Medical Abuse*, New York: Bantam Books, 1989.

CHAPTER FOURTEEN: PLAGUED BY DREAMS

1. This chapter is adapted from Annas, G. J., Questing for Grails: Duplicity, Betrayal and Self-Deception in Postmodern Medical Research, *J. Contemp. Health Law Policy* 1996; 12:297–324. On "holy grail" rhetoric *see* Swazey, J. P., Those Who Forget Their History: Lessons for the Human Genome Quest, (In) Annas, George J. & Elias, Sherman, eds., *Gene Mapping: Using Law and Ethics as Guides,* New York: Oxford U. Press, 1992, pp. 46–48.

2. *Tennyson's Poetry*, Hill, Robert W., editor, New York: W. W. Norton, 1971, p. 354, n. 7.

3. The most articulate (and most often quoted) statement of this principle is by Hans Jonas, and it deserves quotation here: Jonas understood that some of his suggested protections for human subjects might lead to slower medical progress, but nonetheless accepted this as a reasonable price to pay for the maintenance of important human values:

> Let us not forget that progress is an optional goal, not an unconditional commitment, and that its tempo in particular, compulsive as it may become, has nothing sacred about it. Let us also remember that a slower progress in the conquest of disease would not threaten society, grievous as it is to those who have to deplore that their particular disease be not yet conquered, but that society would indeed be threatened by the erosion of those moral values whose loss, possibly caused by too ruthless a pursuit of scientific progress, would make its most dazzling triumphs not worth having.

Jonas, H., Philosophical Reflections on Human Experimentation, (In) Ethical Aspects of Experimentation with Human Subjects, *Daedalus* 1969; 98:219, 245.

4. Hutcheon, Linda, *The Politics of Postmodernism*, London: Routledge, 1989, p. 15.

5. Lifton, Robert Jay, *The Nazi Doctors: Medical Killing and the Psychology of Genocide*, New York: Basic Books, 1986, p. 418. Lifton also discusses the "healing-killing paradox" in which Nazi physicians kill for the sake of the health of the state, the "German biotic community." He goes on to explain, "Since the healing-killing paradox epitomized the overall function of the Nazi regime, there was some truth in the Nazi image of Auschwitz as the moral equivalent of war. War is the only accepted institution . . . in which there is a parallel healing-killing paradox. One has to kill the enemy in order to preserve—to 'heal'—one's people, one's military unit, oneself." *Idem*, p. 431.

6. Fromm, Erich, *Afterward to 1984*, New York: New American Library, 1961, p. 263.

7. Annas, George J., Grodin, Michael, eds., *The Nazi Doctors and the Nuremberg Code: Human Rights in Human Experimentation*, New York: Oxford U. Press, 1992.

8. The Nuremberg Code:

1. The voluntary consent of the human subject is absolutely essential. This means that the person involved should have legal capacity to give consent; should be so situated as to be able to exercise free power of choice, without the intervention of any element of force, fraud, deceit, duress, overreaching, or other ulterior form of constraint or coercion; and should have sufficient knowledge and comprehension of the elements of the subject matter involved as to enable him to make an understanding and enlightened decision. This latter element requires that before the acceptance of an affirmative decision by the experimental subject there should be made known to him the nature, duration, and purpose of the experiment; the method and means by which it is to be conducted; all inconveniences and hazards reasonably to be expected; and the effects upon his health or person which may possibly come from his participation the experiment.

   The duty and responsibility for ascertaining the quality of the consent rests upon each individual who initiates, directs or engages in the experiment. It is a personal duty and responsibility which may not be delegated to another with impunity.
2. The experiment should be such as to yield fruitful results for the good of society, unprocurable by other methods or means of study, and not random and unnecessary in nature.
3. The experiment should be so designed and based on the results of animal experimentation and a knowledge of natural history of the disease or other problem under study that the anticipated results will justify the performance of the experiment.
4. The experiment should be so conducted as to avoid all unnecessary physical and mental suffering and injury.
5. No experiment should be conducted where there is an *a priori* reason to believe that death or disabling injury will occur; except, perhaps, in those experiments where the experimental physicians also serve as subjects.
6. The degree of risk to be taken should never exceed that determined by the humanitarian importance of the problem to be solved by the experiment.
7. Proper preparations should be made and adequate facilities provided to protect the experimental subject against even remote possibilities of injury, disability, or death.
8. The experiment should be conducted only by scientifically qualified persons. The highest degree of skill and care should be required through all stages of the experiment of those who conduct or engage in the experiment.
9. During the course of the experiment the human subject should be at liberty to bring the experiment to an end if he has reached the physical or mental state where continuation of the experiment seems to him to be impossible.
10. During the course of the experiment the scientist in charge must be prepared to terminate the experiment at any stage, if he has probable cause to believe, in the exercise of the good faith, superior skill, and careful judgment required of him, that a continuation of the experiment is likely to result in injury, disability, or death to the experimental subject.

And see Shuster, E., Fifty Years Later: The Significance of the Nuremberg Code, *N. Engl. J. Med.* 1997; 337:1436–1440, and Shuster, E., The Nuremberg Code: Hippocratic Ethics and Human Rights, *Lancet* 1998; 351:974–77.

9. Quoted in Refshauge, W., The Place for International Standards in Conducting Research for Humans, *Bull. World Health Organ* 55:133–135 (Supp. 1977). The full text of four versions of the Declaration of Helsinki appear in the Appendix to *Nazi Doctors and Nuremberg Code, supra* note 7.

10. *American Nuclear Guinea Pigs: Three Decades of Radiation Experiments on U.S. Citizens*, A Staff Report for the Subcommittee on Energy and Power of the Committee on Energy and Commerce, U.S. House of Representatives, Oct. 1986. A similar response

greeted a later report of the Staff of the Committee on Veterans' Affairs, *Is Military Research Hazardous to Veterans' Health? Lessons Spanning Half a Century*, Committee on Veterans' Affairs, U.S. Senate, 103d Cong., 2d Sess., Dec. 8, 1994.

11. Welsome, E., The Plutonium Experiment, *Albuquerque Tribune*, 1993 (reprint of a series of articles originally published Nov. 15–17, 1993).

12. Welsome, E., McPherson, K., DOE Chief Mum on Names, *Albuquerque Tribune*, Dec. 7, 1993, reprinted in *Id*, p. 47.

13. Advisory Committee on Human Radiation Experiments, *Final Report*, U.S. Gov. Printing Office, Washington, DC, (061-000-00849-7) Oct. 1995. The President not only accepted the report in a White House ceremony on Oct. 3, 1995, he also signed an executive order creating a National Bioethics Advisory Commission to advise the government on matters on research with human beings, as well as other bioethical issues. Executive Order, Protection of Human Research Subjects and Creation of National Bioethics Advisory Commission, Oct. 3, 1995.

14. Luessenhop, A. J., Gallimore, J. C., Sweet, W. H., Struxness, E. G., Robinson, J., The Toxicity in Man of Hexavalent Uranium Following Intravenous Administration, *Am. J. Roentgenol.* 1958; 79:83–100. There were 11 subjects altogether. *See Final Report Id.*, pp. 262–269.

15. Quoted in MacPherson, K., Radiation Tests in Past Decades Broke Ethics Rules, *Sacramento Bee*, Jan. 23, 1995, A5, and *Final Report, supra* note 14, p. 144.

16. The justification for treating human beings like rats was the same as one of the major justifications used by the Nazi doctors at Nuremberg: It was wartime (albeit a cold war) and "extreme circumstances demand extreme action." In addition, these subjects were "already condemned to death" and thus were not harmed by the experiments. Grodin, M. A., Historical Origins of the Nuremberg Code, (In) *The Nazi Doctors and the Nuremberg Code, supra* note 7, p. 132.

17. Saenger, E. L., Silberstein, E. B., Aron, B., Horowitz, H., Kereiakes, J. G., Bahr, G. K., Perry, H., Friedman, B. I., Whole Body and Partial Body Radiotherapy of Advanced Cancer, *Am. J. Roentgenol. Rad. Ther. Nuclear Med.* 1973; 117:670–685; *See also Final Report, supra* note 14, pp. 385–406. The principal investigator, Eugene L. Saenger of the University of Cincinnati, wrote his first (and last) description of the study in the medical literature (yearly reports had been provided to the US Defense Atomic Support Agency).

18. *Final Report, supra* note 13, p. 387.

19. Nor should it be believed, given the other types of studies that were conducted on these subjects (*e.g.*, the effect of whole body radiation on their cognitive ability, done for the Defense Atomic Support Agency, Louis Gottschalk, A., Kunkel, R., Wohl, T. H., Saenger, E. L., Winget, C. N., Total and Half Body Irradiation: Effect on Cognitive and Emotional Processes, *Arch. Gen. Psychiat.* 1969; 31:574–580. The literature that Saenger himself cites in his 1973 article indicates that whole body radiation is useless for cancers that involve localized tumors (Medinger, F. G., Craver, L. F., Total Body Irradiation with Review of. Cases, *Am. J. Roentgenol. Rad. Ther. Nuclear Med.* 1942; 48:651–671. "Except for transient relief of pain in a few cases, the results in these generalized carcinoma cases were discouraging. The reason for this is quickly apparent. Carcinomas are much more radio resistant than the lymphomatoid tumors, and by total body irradiation the dose cannot be nearly large enough to alter these tumors appreciably [without killing the patient]" p. 668).

20. *Final Report, supra* note 13, p. 405.

21. *In re Cincinnati Radiation Litigation*, 874 F. Supp. 796 (1995) (Beckwith, J.) It is heartening that the judge relied heavily on the Nuremberg Code as a basic human rights document in reaching her decision and was not swayed by the doublethink in the 1973 article.

22. Sontag, Susan, *Illness as Metaphor and AIDS and its Metaphors,* New York: Farrar, Straus & Giroux, 1989, p. 126.

23. Foucault, Michel, *The History of Sexuality* (Robert Hurley trans., 1990) New York: Pantheon, p. 138.

24. Grodin, *supra* note 16.

25. Ingelfinger, F. J., Informed (but Uneducated) Consent, *N. Engl. J. Med.* 1972; 287:465, 466.

26. Sontag, S., *supra* note 22, pp. 182–183. The use of the military metaphor in medicine is discussed at more length in chapter 4.

27. President's Commission for the Study of Ethical Problems in Medicine and Biomedical and Behavioral Research, *Protecting Human Subjects*, Washington, DC: U.S. Gov. Printing Office, 1981, p. 65.

28. Furman, W. L., Pratt, C. B., Rivera, G. K., Mortality in Pediatric Phase I Clinical Trials, *J. Natl. Cancer Inst.* 1989; 81:1193–1194 (a review of 31 phase I clinical trials in children involving 577 "patients" found "34 objective responses (11 complete and 23 partial) to 27 phase I agents, yielding an overall response rate of 5.9%. . . .The duration of the 11 complete responses ranged from 12 to 300 days, with a median of 60 days.")

29. Ackerman, T. F., The Ethics of Phase I Pediatric Oncology Trials, *IRB* Jan. 1995; 17:1–5.

30. Kodish, E., Stocking, C., Ratain, M. J., Kohrman, A., Siegler, M., Ethical Issues in Phase I Oncology Research: A Comparison of Investigators and Institutional Review Board Chairpersons, *J. Clin. Oncol.* 1992; 10:1810–1812; *and see* Lipsett, M. B., On the Nature and Ethics of Phase I Clinical Trials of Cancer Chemotherapies, *JAMA* 1982; 248:941–942.

31. Quoted in Bonfield, T., Heimlich Uses Malaria in Research on AIDS, *Cincinnati Enquirer*, Nov. 7, 1994. This "treatment" was also used in an episode of *Chicago Hope. See* Annas, G. J., Sex, Violence and Bioethics: Watching ER and Chicago Hope, *Hastings Cent. Rep.*, Sept. 1995; 25:40–43.

32. Anderson, F., What's the Rush?, *Hum. Gene Ther.* 1990; 1:109–110.

33. Annas, G. J., Baby Fae: The Anything Goes School of Human Experimentation, *Hastings Cent. Rep.* Feb. 1985; 15:15–17.

34. A more complete rationale for this protection of terminally ill persons is set forth in Annas, G. J., The Changing Landscape of Human Experimentation: Nuremberg, Helsinki and Beyond, *Health Matrix J. Law Med.* 1992; 2:119–140. *See also* Lipsett, *supra* note 30.

35. Katz, J., Human Experimentation and Human Rights, *St. Louis U. Law J.* 1993; 38:7; *and see* King, Nancy, Experimental Treatment: Oxymoron or Aspiration?, *Hastings Cent. Rep.*, July 1995; 6–15; *and* Capron, A., Informed Consent in Catastrophic Disease Research, *U. Penn. L. Rev.* 1974; 123:340.

36. Annas, G. J., Densberger, J., Competence to Refuse Medical Treatment: Autonomy vs. Paternalism, *Toledo L. Rev.* 1984; 15:561, 578.

37. This seems to be especially true in AIDS research. *See, e.g.*, Annas, G. J., Faith (Healing) Hope and Charity at the FDA: The Politics of AIDS Drug Trials, *Villanova L. Rev.* 1989; 34:771 (and examples described therein).

38. O'Reilly, B., Drug Makers under Attack, *Fortune*, July 29, 1991, 48.

39. Werth, Barry, *The Billion Dollar Molecule*, New York: Simon & Shuster, 1994, p. 355.

40. *See, e.g.*, Farr, L. E., Sweet, W. H., Locksley, H. B., Robertson, J. S., Neutron Capture Therapy of Cliomas Using Boron, *Trans. Am. Neuro. Assoc.* 1954; 110–113 and Sweet, W. H., Soloway, A. H., Brownell, G. L., Boron-Slow Neutron Capture Therapy of

Gliomas, *Acta Radiol. Ther.* 1963; 1:114–121; *See also*, Allen, S., Radiation Experiments Coming Back to Haunt Researches, *Boston Globe*, May 29, 1995, 27–28.

41. Quoted in Flam, F., Atomic Medicine's Second Chance: Brain Cancer Case Revives Boron Radiation Therapy Method Using Nuclear Reactor, *Washington Post, Health Magazine*, Dec. 13, 1994, 9. A parallel example involves the use of genetic experiments for glioblastoma. *See* Thompson, L., Should Dying Patients Receive Untested Genetic Methods?, *Science* 1993; 259:452.

42. Lawler, Andrew, Brookhaven Prepares for Boron Trials, *Science* 1995; 267:956.

43. Quoted in Warren, James, Positive Side of Nuclear Science: Energy Officials find Themselves Playing in Life and Death Dramas, *Chicago Tribune*, April 23, 1995, 2.

44. At least one critic, former head of the DOE's Office of Energy Research, has noted that calls to experiment with this procedure have been around for years, and have been led by what he calls the "reactor mafia" that "have to find some way to keep the reactors going." Lane, E., A Treatment Before its Time: O'Leary Fights Lab for Experimental Therapy, *Newsday*, Sept. 4, 1994, A7.

45. *Idem.* Nor should it surprise us that even before her death, when Ms. Magnus suffered her first setback, the medical director at Brookhaven announced: "'None of us view this as a failure in any sense.'" Arguing that what was going on was research, not treatment, he continued by noting that "the initial goals of the research are to show that treatment is safe and has no unintended side effects. 'Hopefully we get some information as to the effectiveness' as well." Lane, E., Pioneer Patient Hospitalized, Setback for Woman in Neutron Therapy, *Newsday*, May 3, 1995, A26.

46. *Final Report, supra* note 13, p. 713.

47. *Idem*, p. 853.

48. *See, e.g.*, Fox, Renee, Swazey, Judith, *The Courage to Fail*, Chicago: Chicago U. Press, 1974.

49. *Proposed Regulations Governing Research on Terminally Ill Patients:*

1. For the purpose of these regulations a "terminally ill patient" is one whose death is reasonably expected to occur within six months even if currently accepted and available medical treatment is used.
2. In addition to all other legal and ethical requirements for the approval of a research protocol by national and local scientific and ethical review boards (including IRBs), research in which terminally ill patients participate as research subjects shall be approved only if the review board specifically finds that:
   a. The research, if it carries any risk, has the intent and *reasonable probability* (based on scientific data) of improving the health or well-being of the subject, or of significantly increasing the subject's length of life without significantly decreasing its quality.
   b. There is no *a priori* reason to believe that the research intervention will significantly decrease the subject's quality of life because of suffering, pain, or indignity attributable to the research.
   c. Written informed consent will be required of all research participants over the age of 16 in research involving any risk, and such consent may be solicited only by a physician acting as a *patient rights advocate* who is appointed by the review committee, is independent of the researcher, and whose duty it is to fully and objectively inform the potential subject of all reasonably foreseeable risks and benefits inherent in the research protocol. The patient rights advocate will also be empowered to monitor the actual research itself.

3. The vote on and basis for each of the findings in subpart 2 shall be set forth in writing by the review board and be available to all potential subjects and the public.

4. All research protocols (including the financial arrangements between the sponsor and the researcher) involving terminally ill subject shall be available to the public, and the meetings of the scientific and ethical review boards on these protocols shall be open to the public. Annas, *supra* note 34, p. 138.

50. This suggestion has been made many times in the past, and the primary objections to it have not been philosophical but practical. In major cancer centers, for example, virtually every patient has been referred for "new" or experimental protocols because conventional therapy has failed. Their primary care physician may be from another city or state. Who is to be their physician, with only their best interests in mind? Simply appointing someone at the cancer research hospital may not be sufficient, since it can be assumed that this person will share the general research/science ideology of the institution itself. But the logistics can be mastered if the goal is taken to be one of high priority—and in this setting, there can be no higher priority than protection of the patient's welfare. One approach, for example, is to use retired or semi-retired physicians as patient advocates whose only job is to look out for the patient's welfare. *See also Final Report, supra* note 13, pp. 140–141.

51. It is not just the use of these magic words "nothing to lose" that would trigger the disqualification (since both researchers and subjects would quickly learn not to use them) but an objective evaluation of the experiment and the researchers and/or subject's evaluation of it that will indicate whether they are deluding themselves in pursuing it. The example of inducing malaria to treat AIDS, for example, necessarily requires both a researcher who thinks the patient has nothing to lose and a patient–subject who agrees with this assessment. *See supra* note 39 and accompanying text.

52. *Cf., Moore v. Regents of the University of California*, 793 P.2d 479, 271 Cal. Rptr. 146 (1990), discussed in Annas, George J., *Standard of Care: The Law of American Bioethics*, New York: Oxford U. Press, 1993, pp. 167–180.

53. *See, e.g., Final Report of the Tuskegee Syphilis Study Ad Hoc Advisory Panel*, Washington, DC: U.S. Dept. of Health Education and Welfare, 1973, pp. 23–24; and Katz in *Final Report, supra* note 13, pp. 855–856.

CHAPTER FIFTEEN: AIDS AND TB CHOICES

1. This chapter is adapted from Annas, G. J., Control of Tuberculosis: The Law and the Public's Health, *N. Engl. J. Med.* 1993; 328:585–588, and Annas, G. J., Detention of HIV-Positive Haitians at Guantánamo: Human Rights and Medical Care, *N. Engl. J. Med.* 1993; 329:589–592.

2. Klein, B. S., *Strategic Discourse and its Alternatives*, New York: Center on Violence and Human Survival, John Jay College of Criminal Justice, CUNY, 1992 (monograph).

3. *Haitian Centers Council v. Sale*, 823 F.Supp. 1028 (E.D.N.Y. 1993).

4. *Estelle v. Gamble*, 429 U.S. 97 (1976).

5. 823 F. Supp. 1028, supra note 3.

6. Friedman, T. L., U.S. to Release 158 Haitian Detainees, *New York Times*, June 10, 1993, A12.

7. Personal communication with Dr. Marie Pierre-Louis of the Haitian Centers Council (Aug. 5, 1997): A number of these refugees still have a precarious legal status according

to Betty Williams, chair of the Quaker Friends HIV Residence. About half have received asylum. Shortly after my first account of the conditions at Guantánamo was published in 1993, Paul Farmer replied that I had underestimated the lack of treatment there. See Farmer, Paul, *The Uses of Haiti*, Monroe, ME: Common Courage Press, 1994, p. 295. Since I had no first-hand knowledge, but relied on court documents, he may well be correct, and I offer no excuses for U.S. actions regarding the HIV-positive refugees.

8. Dubos, Renee, Dubos, Jean, *The White Plague: Tuberculosis, Man, and Society*, Boston: Little, Brown, 1952.

9. Bloom, B. R., Murray, C. J. L., Tuberculosis: Commentary on a Reemergent Killer, *Science* 1992; 257:1055–1064; *see also*, WHO Global Surveillance Monitoring Project, Assessment of Worldwide Tuberculosis Control, *Lancet* 1997; 350:624–629.

10. *Jacobson v. Massachusetts*, 197 U.S. 11 (1904).

11. *Whalen v. Roe*, 429 U.S. 589 (1977).

12. *O'Connor v. Donaldson*, 422 U.S. 563 (1975).

13. *Addington v. Texas*, 441 U.S. 418 (1979).

14. *Greene v. Edwards*, 263 S.E.2d 661 (W.Va. 1980).

15. Bloom, *supra* note 9. Although universal directly observed therapy is widely promoted, it is in fact not extensively used worldwide. It has also been estimated that, if mandatory directly observed therapy discourages 6% of initial TB patients from seeking care, it will be less effective than self-administered therapy. Heymann, S. J., Sell, R., Brewer, T. F., The Influence of Program Acceptability on the Effectiveness of Public Health Policy: A Study of Directly Observed Therapy for Tuberculosis, *Am. J. Public Health* 1998; 88: 442–445.

16. Bayer, R., Healton, C., Controlling AIDS in Cuba: The Logic of Quarantine, *N. Engl. J. Med.* 1989; 320:1022–1024; *and see* Burr, C., Assessing Cuba's Approach to Contain AIDS and HIV, *Lancet* 1997; 350:647 ("based on the statistics [Cuba's AIDS policy] is the most successful AIDS program in the world." Nonetheless, the current "boom in sex tourism" has turned past success into a "desperate situation.")

17. Bayer, R., End the Quarantine at Guantánamo, *Washington Post*, Jan. 12, 1993, A17.

18. Grodin, M. A., Annas, G. J., Glantz, L. H., Medicine and Human Rights: A Proposal for International Action, *Hastings Cent. Rep.* 1993; 23(4):4–12; and Mann, J. M., We are all Berliners: Notes from the Ninth International Conference on AIDS, *Am. J. Public Health* 1993; 83:10–11.

CHAPTER SIXTEEN: TOBACCO CHOICES

1. This chapter is adapted from Annas, G. J., Health Warnings, Smoking, and Cancer—The *Cipollone* Case, *N. Engl. J. Med.* 1992; 327: 1604–1607.

2. Office of Smoking and Health, *Reducing the Health Consequences of Smoking: 25 Years of Progress*, A Report of the Surgeon General. Washington, DC: DHHS Pub. No. (CDC) 89-8411., U.S. Dept. HHS, 1989.

3. U.S. Dept. Health and Human Services, Public Health Service, *Healthy People 2000: National Health Promotion and Disease Objectives*, Washington, DC: DHHS Pub. No. (PHS) 91-50213., U.S. Dept. HHS, 1991.

4. Greenhouse, L., Court Opens Way for Damage Suits over Cigarettes, *New York Times*, June 25, 1992, 1, B10.

5. *Cipollone v. Liggett Group*, 505 U.S. 504 (1992).

6. *Cipollone v. Liggett Group*, 789 F.2d 181 (3rd Cir. 1986), *cert. den.*, 479 U.S. 1043 (1987).

7. *Cipollone v. Liggett Group*, 893 F.2d 541 (3rd Cir., 1990).

8. Pub. L. 91-222, Stat. 87, as amended, 15 U.S.C. Sec. 1331-40.

9. *Haines v. Liggett Group*, 140 F.R.D. 681 (D.N.J. 1992).

10. Slade, J., A Retreat in the Tobacco War, *JAMA* 1992; 268:524–526.

CHAPTER SEVENTEEN: COWBOYS AND CAMELS

1. This chapter is adapted from Annas, G. J., Cowboys, Camels and the First Amendment—The FDA's Restrictions on Tobacco Advertising, *N. Engl. J. Med.* 1996; 335:1779–1783.

2. Food and Drug Administration, Dept. Health and Human Services, Regulations Restricting the Sale and Distribution of Cigarettes and Smokeless Tobacco to Protect Children and Adolescents, *Fed. Reg.* 1996; 61:44396–44618.

3. Gore speech: 'America is Strong. Bill Clinton's Leadership Paying Off.' *New York Times*, Aug. 29, 1996, B12.

4. White House, Press Briefing by Secretary of HHS Donna Shalala, FDA Commissioner David Kessler and Assistant Secretary Phil Lee. White House, Office of Press Secretary, Aug. 23, 1996.

5. Trends in Smoking Initiation Among Adolescents And Young Adults—United States, 1980–1989, *MMWR* 1995; 44:521–524.

6. Kessler, D. A., Witt, A. M., Barnett, P. S., Zeller, M. R., Natanblut, S. L., Wilkenfeld, J. P., Lorraine C. C., Thompson L. J., Schultz W. B., The Food and Drug Administration's Regulation of Tobacco Products, *N. Engl. J. Med.* 1996; 335:988–994.

7. *Central Hudson Gas & Electric Corp. v. Public Service Commission of New York*, 447 U.S. 557 (1980).

8. *Posadas de Puerto Rico Associates v. Tourism Company of Puerto Rico*, 478 U.S. 328 (1986).

9. *44 Liquormart, Inc. v. Rhode Island*, 517 U.S. 484 (1996).

10. *44 Liquor Mart, Inc. v. Racine*, 829 F. Supp. 543 (R.I. 1993).

11. *44 Liquor Mart, Inc. v. Rhode Island*, 39 F.3d 5 (1st Cir. 1994).

12. Committee on Preventing Nicotine Addiction in Children and Youths, Institute of Medicine, *Growing Up Tobacco Free*, Washington, DC: National Academy Press, 1994, p. 131.

13. Glantz, L., Regulating Tobacco Advertising: The FDA Regulations and the First Amendment, *Am. J. Public Health* 1997; 87:446–451.

14. Parker-Pope, T., Tough Tobacco-ad Rules Light Creative Fire. *Wall Street Journal*, Oct. 9, 1996, B1.

15. Brownlee, L., How Agency Teams Might Cope with U.S. Ad Restraints. *Wall Street Journal*, Oct. 9, 1996, B1.

16. *Supra* note 11.

17. U.S. Surgeon General's Report, *Preventing Tobacco Use Among Young People*, Washington, DC: U.S. Gov. Printing Office, 1994, p. 195.

18. Elliott, S., Joe Camel, A Giant in Tobacco Marketing, Is Dead at 23, *New York Times*, July 11, 1997, C1.

19. Ono, Y., Ingersoll, B., RJR Retires Joe Camel, Adds Sexy Smokers, *Wall Street Journal*, July 11, 1997, B1. *And see* Ono, Y., Tobacco Ads Seek Glamour Without Camels, Cowboys. *Wall Street Journal*, Feb. 20, 1998, B1.

20. Kessler, D. A., The Tobacco Settlement, *N. Engl. J. Med.* 1997; 337:1082–1083.

CHAPTER EIGHTEEN: SMOKING WITH THE DEVIL

1. The pre-settlement portions of this chapter are based on Annas, G. J., Tobacco Litigation as Cancer Prevention: Dealing With the Devil, *N. Engl. J. Med.* 1997; 336:304–308.

2. Grisham, John, *The Runaway Jury*, New York: Doubleday, 1996.

3. Todd, J. S., Rennie, D., McAfee, R. E., Bristow, L. R., Painter, J. T., Reardon, T. R., Johnson, D. H., Corlin, R. F., Coble, Y. D., Dicky, N. W. The Brown and Williamson Documents: Where do We go from Here? *JAMA* 1995; 274:256–258.

4. Hilts, Philip J., *Smoke Screen: The Truth Behind the Tobacco Industry Cover-Up*, Reading, MA: Addison-Wesley, 1996, p. 195.

5. Daynard, R. A., Kelder, G. E., Waiting to Exhale, *Boston Globe*, Feb. 11, 1996, E1.

6. Kluger, Richard, *Ashes to Ashes: America's Hundred-Year Cigarette War, the Public Health, and the Unabashed Triumph of Philip Morris*, New York: Knopf, 1996.

7. Kelder, G. E., Daynard, R. A., Tobacco Litigation as a Public Health and Cancer Control Strategy, 1996; 51:57–62; Glantz, S. A., Slade, J., Bero, L. A., Hanaher, P., Barnes, D. E., *The Cigarette Papers*, Berkeley: California U. Press 1996.

8. *Castano v. American Tobacco Co.*, 160 F.R.D. 544 (1995).

9. *Castano v. American Tobacco Co.*, 84 F.3d 734 (1996). *And see* generally on *Castano*, Pringle, Peter, *Cornered: Big Tobacco at the Bar of Justice*, New York: Henry Holt, 1998.

10. Reske, H. J., Tobacco Suit: Round II: Plaintiffs' Lawyers Pledge to File Class Actions in all 50 States, *ABA J.* July 1996; 18.

11. MacLachlan, C., Now Spotlight is on States in Tobacco War, *National Law Journal*, June 3, 1996, A1.

12. AG: Tobacco Papers are 'Astounding,' *National Law Journal*, Oct. 21, 1996, A5. Humphrey's lawsuit discovered and made public more tobacco documents than all the other sources put together. *See, e.g.,* Hwang, S. L., A Vast Trove of Tobacco Documents Opens Up, *Wall Street Journal*, April 23, 1998, B1.

13. *Supra* note 11.

14. Hwang, S. L., Geyelin, M., Freedman, A. M., Jury's Tobacco Verdict Suggests Tough Times Ahead for the Industry, *Wall Street Journal*, Aug. 12, 1996, A1.

15. Geyelin, M., Is Tobacco Trial a 'Must Win' for Industry?, *Wall Street Journal*, Aug. 21, 1996, B1.

16. Hwang, S. L., Will Liggett Deal Split Big and Small Rivals?, *Wall Street Journal*, March 14, 1996, B1.

17. Feder, B. J., Liggett's Tobacco Settlement in Danger of Coming Undone, *New York Times*, Sept. 7, 1996, 38.

18. Geyelin, M., States Greet Plan to Settle Tobacco Suits With Skepticism, But Leave Door Open, *Wall Street Journal*, Aug. 29, 1996, B14; Geyelin, M., Plan to Settle Tobacco Cases Draws Fire, *Wall Street Journal*, Aug. 27, 1996, A3.

19. Stolberg, S., Struggle Ensues for a Deal on Tobacco Curbs, *Los Angles Times*, Sept. 1, 1996, A1.

20. Kluger, R., A Peace Plan for the Cigarette Wars: Dance With the Devil, *New York Times Magazine*, April 7, 1996, p. 28.

21. Sugarman, S. D., Smoking Guns (book review), *Science* 1996; 273:744–745.

22. Feder, B. J., Keeping Cool in a Roomful of Smoke at RJR Nabisco, *New York Times*, July 28, 1996, F1.

23. Hwang, S. L., RJR's Profit Rose 4% in Third Period; Stock Price Frustrates Chief Executive, *Wall Street Journal*, Oct. 22, 1996, B12.

24. Broder, J. M., Cigarette makers in a $368 Billion Accord to Curb Lawsuits and Curtail Marketing, *New York Times*, June 21, 1997, A1.

25. Remarks by the President on Tobacco Settlement Review, White House Press Release, Sept. 17, 1997. *And see* Broder, J. M., Cigarette Makers Criticize Clinton Policy, *New York Times*, Sept. 18, 1997, A30.

26. Kessler, D. A., The Tobacco Settlement, *N. Engl. J. Med.* 1997; 337:1082–1083.

27. Koop, C. E., Kessler, D. A., Lundberg, G. D., Jama 1998; 279: 550–553. *And see* Goldstone, S. F., Don't Let the Tobacco Deal Go Up in Smoke, *Wall Street Journal*, Feb. 20, 1998, A18.

28. Weinstein, H., U.S. Judge Rejects Pa. Tobacco Suit, *Boston Globe*, Oct. 18, 1997, A3.

29. Cummings, J., Taylor, J., Democrats Target 'Smokin' Newt as Parties Jockey for Position in Tobacco Fight, Elections, *Wall Street Journal*, April 23, 1998, A20.

30. Ward, J., Tobacco Settlement: Companies Revolt, *Louisville Courier-Journal*, April 9, 1998, 9A.

CHAPTER NINETEEN: THE KEVORKIAN SYNDROME

1. This chapter is adapted from Annas, G. J., Physician-Assisted Suicide: Michigan's Temporary Solution, *N. Engl. J. Med.* 1993; 328:1573–1576.

2. Thomas, L., Dying as Failure, *Ann. Am. Acad. Pol. Soc. Sci.* 1980; 447:1–4.

3. Cassel, C. K., Meier, D. E., Morals and Moralism in the Debate over Euthanasia and Assisted Suicide, *N. Engl. J. Med.* 1990; 323:750–752; Solomon, M. Z., O'Donnell, L., Jennings, B., Guilfoy, V., Wolf, S., Nolan, K., Jackson, R., Koch-Weser, D., Donnelly, S., Decisions Near the End of Life: Professional Views on Life-Sustaining Treatment, *Am. J. Public Health* 1993; 83:14–22.

4. Kevorkian, Jack, *Prescription: Medicide*, Buffalo, NY: Promethens Books, 1991.

5. *People v. Roberts*, 211 Mich. 187, 178 N.W. 690 (1920).

6. *People v. Campbell*, 335 N.W.2d 27 (Mich. App. 1983).

7. A review of the trial transcript leads me to believe that the judge simply did not believe Frank Roberts' assertion that his wife asked for the poison in her drink. Nonetheless, the Michigan Supreme Court ruled in 1994 that *Roberts* is no longer good law, *People v. Kevorkian*, 447 Mich. 436, 527 N.W. 2d 714 (1994).

8. Lawyer Puts Kevorkian Cases at 'Nearly 100,' *New York Times*, Aug. 14, 1997, A21.

9. Annas, G. J., Killing Machines, *Hastings Cent. Rep.* 1991; 21(2):33–35.

10. Annas, George J., *Standard of Care: The Law of American Bioethics*, New York: Oxford U. Press, 1993, p. 243.

11. On the status of the law of assisted suicide in Michigan at this time *see People v. Kevorkian, supra* note 7.

12. Mich. Compiled Laws, sec. 752.1027 (Public Act 3 of 1993).

13. Kamisar, Y., Are Laws Against Assisted Suicide Constitutional?, *Hastings Cent. Rep.* 1993; 23(3):32–41.

14. Quill, T. E., Death and Dignity—A Case of Individualized Decision Making, *N. Engl. J. Med.* 1991; 324:691–694; and Quill, Timothy E., *Death and Dignity: Making Choices and Taking Charge*, New York: W.W. Norton, 1993.

15. Board of Registration in Medicine, *Prescribing Practice Policy and Guidelines*, Boston: Commonwealth of Massachusetts, Aug. 1, 1989.

16. Gianelli, D., Dr. Kevorkian Takes Case to Mich. Society, *Am. Med. News,* Oct, 5, 1992, 37.

17. Council on Ethical and Judicial Affairs, American Medical Association, Decisions Near the End of Life, *JAMA* 1992; 267:2229–2233.

18. It's Over, Debbie, *JAMA* 1988; 259:272.

19. Foderaro, L. W., New York will not Discipline Doctor for his Role in Suicide, *New York Times*, Aug. 17, 1991, 25.

20. Lifton, Robert J., *The Nazi Doctors: Medical Killing and the Psychology of Genocide*, New York: Basic Books, 1986.

21. Editorial: Doctors and Death Row, *Lancet* 1993; 341:209–210. In 1997 I filed an amicus brief on behalf of a group of bioethicists that urged a California court to take medical ethics seriously and enjoin California physicians from participating in executions. The brief is posted on the Health Law Department Website: http://www-busph.bu.edu/Depts/HealthLaw/.

22. Van Der Maas, P. J, Van Delden, J. J. M., Pijnenborg, L., Looman, C. W., Euthanasia and Other Medical Decisions Concerning the End of Life, *Lancet* 1991; 338:669–674.

23. Smith, G. P., All's Well That Ends Well: Toward a Policy of Assisted Rational Suicide or Merely Enlightened Self-Determination? *U. Cal. Davis Law Rev.* 1989; 22:275–419.

CHAPTER TWENTY: OREGON'S BLOODLESS CHOICE

1. This chapter is adapted from Annas, G. J., Death by Prescription: The Oregon Initiative, *N. Engl. J. Med.* 1994; 331:1240–1243.

2. Nuland, Sherwin B., *How We Die*, New York: Alfred A. Knopf, 1994, p. 288.

3. Capron, A. M., Euthanasia in the Netherlands: American Observations, *Hastings Cent. Rep.* 1992; 22(2):30–32.

4. Carson, R., Washington's I-119, *Hastings Cent. Rep.* 1992; 22(2): 7–9.

5. Humphry, Derek, *Dying With Dignity: Understanding Euthanasia*, Seacacas, NJ: Carol, 1992.

6. *Compassion in Dying v. Washington*, 850 F. Supp. 1454 (D.C. Wash. 1994).

7. Skelly, F. J., California Protects Doctors Who Prescribe for Pain, *Am. Med. News*, Sept. 12, 1994, 19. *Management of Cancer Pain Guideline Panel, Management of Cancer Pain*, US DHHS, Agency for Health Care Policy and Research, AHCPR Pub. No. 94-0592, Washington, DC, 1994, pp. 16–19.

8. Gianelli, D. M., Oregon Votes Face 'RX-only' Suicide Initiative, *Am. Med. News*, Sept. 12, 1994, 1, 34.

9. Humphry, *supra* note 5.

10. Worsnop, R. L., Oregon Residents to Vote Again on 'Right to Die' Law, *San Diego Union Tribune*, Sept. 22, 1997, A-1.

11. Callahan, Daniel, *The Troubled Dream of Life: Living With Morality*, New York: Simon and Shuster, 1993.

12. Quoted in Gianelli, *supra* note 8.

13. 21 CFR 1306.04.

14. Annas, G. J., Killing With Kindness: Why the FDA Need Not Certify Drugs used for Execution as Safe and Effective, *Am. J. Public Health* 1985; 75:1096–1099.

15. *Bouvia v. Superior Court*, 179 Cal. App. 3d 1127, 225 Cal. Rptr. 297 (1986).

16. Hoover, E., Patients Find Roadblocks to Suicide, *Oregonian*, Feb. 19, 1998, 1.

17. Booth, W., Oregon Suicide is Called First Under Law Legalizing Doctor Role, *Washington Post*, March 26, 1998, A7. *And see* Stolberg, S. G., Guide Covers Territory Law Does Not Explore, *New York Times*, April 21, 1998, C4.

18. The New York State Task Force on Life and the Law, *When Death is Sought:*

Assisted Suicide and Euthanasia in the Medical Context, New York: New York State Task Force on Life and the Law, 1994.

19. Yankelovich, D., What Polls Say—and What They Mean, *New York Times*, Sept. 17, 1994, 23; *and see* Cohen, J. S., Fihn, S. D., Boyko, E. J., Jonsen, A. R., Wood, R. W., Attitudes Toward Assisted Suicide and Euthanasia among Physicians in Washington State, *N. Engl. J. Med.* 1994; 331:89–94.

CHAPTER TWENTY-ONE: THE BELL TOLLS

1. This chapter is adapted from Annas, G. J., The Promised End—Constitutional Aspects of Physician-Assisted Suicide, *N. Engl. J. Med.* 1996; 335:683–687 and Annas, G. J., The Bell Tolls for a Constitutional Right to Assisted Suicide, *N. Engl. J. Med.* 1997; 337:1098–1103. I also filed an amicus brief on behalf of a group of Bioethics Professors when these cases went before the U.S. Supreme Court. The brief, which was co-authored with Leonard Glantz and Wendy Mariner, argued that neither the right to refuse treatment nor abortion provided a constitutional precedent supporting a right to physician assistance in suicide. The full text of the brief is available at http://www-busph.edu/Depts/HealthLaw.

2. *Compassion in Dying v. Washington*, 79 F.3d 790 (9th Cir. 1996).

3. *Quill v. Vacco*, 80 F.3d 716 (2d Cir. 1996).

4. *See, e.g.*, Humphrey, Derek, *Final Exit*, Eugene, OR: Hemlock Society, 1991.

5. Quill, T., Death and Dignity: A Case of Individualized Decision Making, *N. Engl. J. Med.* 1991; 324:691–694.

6. *Planned Parenthood v. Casey*, 505 U.S. 833 (1992).

7. *Cruzan v. Director, Missouri Dept. of Health*, 497 U.S. 261 (1990).

8. *Matter of Eichner*, 52 N.Y. 2d 363 (1981).

9. *Compassion in Dying v. Washington*, 49 F.3d (9th Cir. 1995).

10. *See* Kreimer, S., Does Pro-Choice Mean Pro-Kevorkian? An Essay on *Roe, Casey* and the Right to Die, *Am. U.L. Rev.* 1995; 44:803; and Wolf, S., Physician-Assisted Suicide, Abortion, and Treatment Refusal: Using Gender to Analyze the Difference, (In) Weir, Robert, ed., *Physician-Assisted Suicide*, Bloomington: Indiana U. Press, 1997.

11. Sontag, Susan, *AIDS and Its Metaphors*, New York: Doubleday, 1988.

12. Preston, T., Mero, R., Observations Concerning Terminally Ill Patients Who Choose Suicide, *J. Pharm. Care Pain Symptom Control* 1996; 4:183–192.

13. Annas, G. J., Death by Prescription—The Oregon Initiative, *N. Engl. J. Med.* 1994; 331:1240–1243.

14. Kamisar, Y., Against Assisted Suicide—Even a Very Limited Form, *U. Detroit Mercy Law Rev.*, 1995; 72:735–769.

15. *Lee v. Oregon*, 891 F. Supp. 1429 (D. Or. 1995), and see *supra* note 13.

16. Wolf, S. M., Holding the Line on Euthanasia, *Hastings Cent. Rep.* 1989; 19(1): Supp. 13–15.

17. *U.S. v. Rutherford*, 442 U.S. 544 (1979).

18. *Washington v. Glucksberg*, 117 S.Ct. 2302 (1997).

19. *Vacco v. Quill*, 117 S.Ct. 2293 (1997).

20. *Krischer v. McIver*, 697 So.2d 97 (Fla.1997).

21. *When Death is Sought: Assisted Suicide and Euthanasia in the Medical Context*, New York: State Task Force on Life and the Law, 1994; and *Supplement to the Report*, April 1997.

22. As discussed in chapter 19, the Michigan State Task Force met for less than two years.

23. New York Task Force on Life and the Law; *Supplement to the Report*, April 1997;

citing Hart, H. L., Honore, T., *Causation and the Law*, 2d ed., Oxford: Oxford University Press, 1985.

24. Foley, K. M., Controversies in Cancer Pain: Medical Perspectives, *Cancer* 1989; 63:2257–2265.

25. *Idem and* Wilson, W. C., Smedira, M. G., Fink, C., Ordering and administering of Sedatives and Analgesics During the Withholding and Withdrawal of Life Support from Critically Ill Patients, *JAMA* 1992; 267:949–953.

26. My colleagues and I made this point in some detail in a footnote in the brief of the Bioethics Professors in these cases:

It should be noted that no case has ever held that a physician who prescribes drugs a patient later uses to commit suicide is guilty of assisting suicide. No physician has ever been charged with such an offense. It is surprising that the Ninth Circuit Court of Appeals could simultaneously find that the doctors in Washington run a "severe risk of prosecution," 79 F. 3d at 795, and that there is "no reported American case of criminal punishment being meted out to a doctor for helping a patient hasten his own death." 79 F.3d at 811. In its footnote 54, it describes two cases where physicians were charged with directly administering lethal injections to patients. While the court refers to these as assisted suicide cases, they were in fact homicide cases. Both physicians were acquitted.

It is unlikely that the mere prescription of drugs for a patient constitutes assisted suicide. The named plaintiff in the Second Circuit Court of Appeals case, Dr. Timothy Quill, admitted in an article published in a prestigious medical journal that he had prescribed a lethal dose of sleeping pills for a patient so she could decide at some future time whether or not to commit suicide with these pills. Timothy Quill, Death and Dignity: A Case of Individualized Decision Making, *New Eng. J. Med.* 1991; 434:691. Based on this admission, a Grand Jury investigated the case and refused to indict. Furthermore, the New York Board for Professional Medical Conduct conducted an investigation to determine if Dr. Quill should be disciplined for his actions. The panel found Dr. Quill acted lawfully and appropriately. It noted that he could not determine with certainty what use the patient might make of the drugs he prescribed. Even if Dr. Quill prescribed the drugs believing they might be used by the patient to commit suicide, he did not participate in the taking of her life. The panel did not wish to interfere with the good medical practice of physicians who prescribe drugs to relieve a terminally patient's anxiety, insomnia or pain because the physician suspects the patient may later use the medication to terminate his or her life. *See*, John Alesandro, Comment, Physician Assisted Suicide and New York Law, 57 *Alb. L. Rev.* 1994; 57:820, 823 n. 19 and 21 (1994). Thus, in the only case ever investigated that resembles the activities the plaintiffs claim are illegal in New York, the authorities ruled that the actions were lawful.

It must be kept in mind that the activity in question is the *prescription* of drugs by physicians. Once the prescription is written the patient must decide whether to fill it, and then must decide whether to use the drugs for the lawful purpose for which a prescription is written, such as relief of insomnia, or to take these drugs to commit suicide. These decisions all occur over a lengthy period of time. Thus there is a long and tenuous chain of events between the writing of the prescription and its use for suicidal purposes.

This is quite different from prosecuted assisted suicide cases, where there is a close link between the assistance and the act of suicide. In one case a defendant helped her sister to commit suicide by attaching a vacuum cleaner hose to the end of an exhaust pipe of a car, gave her sister the other end of the hose, said good-bye and closed the garage door as she left. In another case a husband helped his cancer ridden wife commit suicide by preparing an overdose of sedatives, sitting with her while she ate it, and helping her put a plastic bag over her head. Catherine Shaffer, Note, Criminal Liability for Assisting Suicide, *Colum. L. Rev.* 1996; 86:348, 366, n. 77, 79. In these cases, and others cited in the article, the "assistance" that was found to be unlawful was much more direct than writing prescriptions, much closer in time to the commission of the suicide, and led directly to the suicide. At least three of the six patient-petitioners in these two appeals were not suicidal at the time they signed their declarations, but rather wanted exemptions from the drug laws so that they could have their physicians write them prescriptions for lethal drugs that they *might* use at some time in the future to commit suicide *if* their suffering became intolerable. 79 F.3d 794–5; 80 F.3d 720–21.

It is notable, given the relief sought in this case by the plaintiffs, that no court has actually concluded that writing a prescription constitutes assisting suicide. Perhaps the federal courts should have remanded the issue to the state courts for a definitive interpretation of the statutes in question. Both statutes are written in general terms and neither explicitly forbids physicians from writing prescriptions for their patients. Furthermore, it may have been possible for the federal courts to have interpreted the statutes in a way that would have made it unnecessary for them to decide the constitutional question. *Communications Workers of America v. Beck,* 487 U.S. 735, 762 (1988).

Interestingly, the Ninth Circuit opinion states "we are doubtful that deaths resulting from terminally ill patients taking medication prescribed by their doctors should be classified as 'suicide'." This is likely to be correct, and if it is correct then there is no need to resolve whether there is a constitutional right to assistance. If writing a prescription for drugs a patient may or may not use at some unspecified future time to commit suicide does not constitute assisted suicide under state law, then physicians may prescribe such drugs for their terminally ill patients without any constitutional determination by a federal court.

27. Joranson, D. E., Gilson, A. M., Improving Pain Management Through Policy Making and Education for Medical Regulators; *J. Law, Med. Ethics* 1996; 24:344–347; Johnson, S. H., Disciplinary Actions and Pain Relief: Analysis of the Pain Relief Act, *J. Law Med. Ethics,* 1996; 24:319–327.

28. Committee on Care at the End of Life, Institute of Medicine, *Approaching Death: Improving Care at the End of Life,* Washington, DC: National Academy Press, 1997.

29. *See supra* note 22.

30. The SUPPORT Investigators, A Controlled Trial to Improve Care for Seriously Ill Hospitalized Patients: The Study to Understand Prognoses and Preferences for Outcomes and Treatments (SUPPORT), *JAMA* 1995; 274:1591–1598.

31. Annas, G. J., How We Lie, *Hastings Cent. Rep.,* Nov. 1995; S12–14.

Chapter Twenty-Two: Toward a Globalization of Human Rights and Medical Ethics

1. Annas, George J., Grodin, Michael A., eds., *The Nazi Doctors and the Nuremberg Code: Human Rights in Human Experimentation,* New York: Oxford U. Press, 1992; and *Trials of War Criminals Before the Nuremberg Military Tribunal Under Control Council 10,* vols. 1 and 2, Washington, DC: Superintendent of Documents, U.S. Government Printing Office, 1950; Military Tribunal, Case 1, *United States v. Karl Brandt,* et al. Oct. 1946–April 1949.

2. Proctor, Robert, *Racial Hygiene: Medicine Under the Nazis,* Cambridge, MA: Harvard U. Press, 1987; Lifton, J. R., *The Nazi Doctors: Medical Killing and the Psychology of Genocide,* New York: Basic Books, 1986.

3. Katz, J., Human Experimentation and Human Rights, *Saint Louis U. Law J.* 1993; 38(1):7–54.

4. The Nuremberg Code is reprinted in chapter 14, note 8.

5. Routley, T. C., Aims and Objects of the World Medical Association, *World Med. Assoc. Bull.* 1949; 1(1):18–19.

6. Editorial, *World Med. Assoc. Bull.,* 1949; 1:3–14.

7. Grodin, M. A., Annas, G. J., Glantz, L. H., Medicine and Human Rights: A Proposal for International Action, *Hastings Cent. Rep.* 1993; 23(4):8–12.

8. Working Party, British Medical Association, *Medicine Betrayed: The Participation of Doctors in Human Rights Abuses,* London: Zed Books, 1992.

9. Teylor, Telford, *The Anatomy of the Nuremberg Trials,* New York: Knopf, 1992; Cherif Bassiouni, M., *Crimes Against Humanity in International Criminal Law,* Dordrecht: Martinus Nijhoff, 1992.

10. Mann, J., Gruskin, S., Grodin, M., Annas, G. J., *Health and Human Rights: A Reader,* New York: Routledge, 1998.

11. In 1994 the first effective intervention to reduce the perinatal transmission of HIV to newborns was developed in AIDS Clinical Trials Group (ACTG) Study 076. In that trial, use of zidovudine administered orally to HIV-positive pregnant women as early as the second trimester of pregnancy, intravenously during labor, and orally to their newborns for 6 weeks reduced the incidence of HIV infection by two-thirds (from about 25% to about 8%). Six months after the Public Health Service stopped the study it recommended the ACTG 076 regime as the standard of care in the U.S. In June 1994 the World Health Organization convened a meeting in Geneva at which it was concluded (in an unpublished report) that the 076 regime was not feasible in the developing world. At least 16 randomized clinical trials (15 using placebos as controls) were subsequently approved for conduct in developing countries, primarily in Africa, involving more than 17,000 pregnant women. Nine of these studies, mostly comparing shorter courses of zidovudine, vitamin A, or HIV immunoglobulin to placebo, are funded by CDC or NIH. Most of the public discussion about these trials has centered on the use of placebos. The question of placebo is a central one in determining *how* a study should be conducted. But the more important issue these trials raise is the question of *whether* they should be done at all. *See* Annas, G. J., Grodin, M., Human Rights and Maternal-Fetal HIV Transmission Prevention Trials in Africa, *Am. J. Public Health* 1998; 88:560–563.

12. Varmus, H., Satcher, D., Ethical Complexities of Conducting Research in Developing Countries. *N. Engl. J. Med.* 1997; 337:1003–1005.

13. Grosskurth, H., Mosha, F., Todd, J, Mwijarubi, Impact of Improved Treatment of Sexually Transmitted Diseases on HIV Infection in Rural Tanzania: Randomized Controlled Trial. *Lancet* 1995; 346:530–536; Robbins, J. B., Towne, D. W., Gotschlich, E. C., Schneerson, R. 'Love's Labours Lost': Failure to Implement Mass Vaccination Against Group A Meningoccal Meningitis in Sub-Saharan Africa. *Lancet* 1997; 350:880–882.

14. Grodin, M. A., Annas, G. J., Legacies of Nuremberg: Medical Ethics and Human Rights, *JAMA* 1996; 276:1682–1683.

15. Taylor, T., Opening Statement in the "Justice Case," *Trials of War Criminals before the Nuremberg Military Tribunals under Control Council Law No. 10,* vol. III, Washington, DC: U.S. Gov. Printing Office, 1951, p. 30.

16. Fuller, L., Positivism and Fidelity to Law—A Response to Professor Hart, *Harvard L. Rev.* 1958; 71:138–180.

17. Up to date information on Global Lawyers and Physicians is available on the Internet at http://www-busph.bu.edu/Depts/HealthLaw/.

18. Schlesinger, Arthur M., Jr., *The Disuniting of America: Reflections on a Multicultural Society.* New York: W.W. Norton, 1992.

INDEX

Some Choice
Law, Medicine, and the Market

The chant of choice, choice, choice, derived from the market, now dominates American medicine just as its companion, liberty, dominates American law. But the choices celebrated by law and medicine are becoming more and more trivial. Choice rhetoric increasingly camouflages critical personal and public policy issues at stake in contemporary debates in American medicine ranging from health care reform to research to end-of-life care. In *Some Choice,* America's leading commentator on health law and bioethics, George J. Annas, demonstrates that in contemporary medicine there is seldom a meaningful choice to be made by the patient; the important choices have been made by others. The illusion of choice perversely fosters complacency and prevents us from dealing with critical issues of life and death.

Professor Annas uses the cases of human cloning, drive-through deliveries, emergency medicine, genetic privacy, human experimentation, tobacco control, and physician-assisted suicide, among others, to suggest ways in which we can break through our vapid and superficial *"some choice"* public discourse on life and death issues and begin to engage in a public dialogue that enriches our lives and society rather than commodifies and cheapens them. The author's goal is to help open a deep and democratic dialogue on health and human rights that transcends slogans and chants, and can lead to local, national, and international cooperation to define, protect, and promote both health and human rights.